Indian and Chinese Immigrant Communities

ANTHEM-ISEAS INDIA-CHINA STUDIES

Anthem-ISEAS India-China Studies seeks to promote the field of Sino-Indian studies. This area of research includes ancient and contemporary interaction/dialogue between India and China, the comparative analysis of Indian and Chinese societies, and Indian and Chinese perceptions of and writings about each other. The series is a collaboration between Anthem Press and the Nalanda-Sriwijaya Centre at the Institute of Southeast Asian Studies, Singapore.

The Institute of Southeast Asian Studies (ISEAS) was established as an autonomous organization in 1968. It is a regional centre dedicated to the study of socio-political, security and economic trends and developments in Southeast Asia and its wider geostrategic and economic environment. The Institute's research programmes are the Regional Economic Studies (RES, including ASEAN and APEC), Regional Strategic and Political Studies (RSPS), and Regional Social and Cultural Studies (RSCS).

ISEAS Publishing, an established academic press, has issued more than 2,000 books and journals. It is the largest scholarly publisher of research about Southeast Asia from within the region. ISEAS Publishing works with many other academic and trade publishers and distributors to disseminate important research and analyses from and about Southeast Asia to the rest of the world.

Indian and Chinese Immigrant Communities

Comparative Perspectives

Edited by
Jayati Bhattacharya
and Coonoor Kripalani

Institute of Southeast Asian Studies, Singapore | ANTHEM PRESS INDIA

Anthem Press India
An imprint of Wimbledon Publishing Company India Private Limited (WPCIPL)
WPCIPL is a subsidiary of Wimbledon Publishing Company Limited (UK)

This edition first published in India 2015
by ANTHEM PRESS INDIA
www.anthempress.co.in

A copublication with
ISEAS Publishing
Institute of Southeast Asian Studies
30 Heng Mui Keng Terrace
Pasir Panjang
Singapore 119614
publish@iseas.edu.sg
bookshop.iseas.edu.sg

First published in hardback in UK and USA 2015
by ANTHEM PRESS *www.anthempress.com*
and ISEAS Publishing

ISBN-13: 978 93 80601 79 3 (Pbk)
ISBN-10: 93 80601 79 4 (Pbk)

Cover image: Toa55/Shutterstock.com

Exclusive distribution in South Asia by Anthem Press India
and in Southeast Asia by ISEAS Publishing

This title is also available as an ebook.

Digitally Printed at Replika Press Pvt. Ltd

CONTENTS

FOREWORD

From victims of "a new system of slavery" to valued non-residents, from sojourning abroad to eventual settlement and political integration, the images of generations of Indians and Chinese moving out of their homes flash across the pages of this volume of essays. Whether the boatloads of poor coming out of British India and the independent India inherited by the nationalists, or those contracted out of Imperial China and escaping a China in chaos or at war, the rich variety of peoples described here make words like migrant and diaspora quite inadequate to encompass them. Thus the authors of the essays in this volume are not content to find labels for these people, or pin down the correct terminology to describe what they have been through, but have dug deeply into a wide range of sources to explain the experiences that shaped the communities they established far away from home.

Indian and Chinese merchants have been trading abroad for centuries. Where the labour classes were concerned, however, it was the Indians who got onto official records first. By the early nineteenth century, the British who controlled the Indian economy also had a global trading and plantation empire to fill with hard-working labour. They institutionalized a system of contracts so that their enterprises could be assured of a dependable supply. In China, on the other hand, the Qing emperor pretended that good Chinese stay at home to look after their parents and tend their tax-producing fields. Those who traded outside the country or sought work and adventure overseas without explicit permission were outlaws or traitors hiding in foreign lands. In their desire to seek work outside China, they had to depend on their kinfolk or put themselves at the mercy of unscrupulous recruiters. Until the end of the second half of the century, no mandarin wanted to know about the working conditions of the Chinese communities in East and Southeast Asian ports and in the new lands across the Pacific Ocean. Few cared that thousands of their Chinese subjects were joining the Indians to do the work that African slaves were no longer available to do. Also, unlike the Indians, who were largely sent to the British tropical empire, the Chinese often had to confront more draconian discrimination policies in North America, Oceania, as well as in French, Dutch and Spanish-speaking territories.

As long as the British were still administering India, Indian labour was supplied along an officially approved trajectory of supply and growth. Independent India took time to review its policies towards non-resident Indians and gradually devised new contract systems to serve labour destinations close by, notably in the Middle East. In contrast, the successive governments of republican China after 1911 found political value in the overseas communities. In turn, the Chinese abroad often responded to political slogans with patriotic zeal. Both the Republic of China and the People's Republic of China maintained large offices in the country's major cities to manage the family and locality bonds that official policies went out of the way to strengthen. The contrast between Indian and Chinese official attitudes towards their respective communities is striking. This volume provides a fascinating account of the consequences of differing official policies on communities around the world.

Although this book is not the first to compare the two diasporic groups, this is the most probing and extensive set of studies available. Each of the essays advances our understanding of an aspect of the migratory process that characterized the formation of overseas communities. The editors and authors are to be congratulated on their enterprise and careful scholarship. The introduction, in particular, captures the spirit of inquiry with great clarity. I am struck, however, by the use of several words throughout the volume that mark some of the most interesting aspects of the Indian and Chinese story. I am particularly drawn to four of them that highlight important features of their joint experiences: *connecting*, *faith*, *spaces* and *reshaping*.

To connect has always been a challenge for people who leave the safety of their native lands, even when they come from the same country. Connecting different diasporic peoples is even more demanding. Where Indian and Chinese communities sometimes meet, mainly in parts of the former British Empire, the phenomenon deserves close attention. Whether this occurred in British Malaya, the West Indies or in the new nations that replaced former colonies, the encounters provide fine examples of culture – or even civilization – contact. These essays illustrate and describe them insightfully.

Faith in its many manifestations, not least among those who lack high literacy, is probably the most essential need among people who have left their native homes. What is particularly elevating, however, are examples of religious transference that the various Indian and Chinese communities have practiced with success. This is particularly meaningful as each designed their own places of worship and, as closely as possible, modelled them on those at home. But there were also those who went beyond that and adopted other faiths, most significantly those who converted to various branches of Christianity and were willing to cross ethnic boundaries. Although only small minorities, these converts connected with one another creatively through their common new faiths.

The word "spaces" adds another dimension to social connection and the practice of multiple faiths. It illuminates the migrants' capacity to bridge the distances between them and their original homes. More than that, it demonstrates their capacity to put the spaces made available to them to new and profitable use. For example, these opportunities allowed them to claim fresh spaces in order to savour unexpected freedoms, reaching out from the confines of their native villages and the dark alleys of their urban ghettos, and perhaps also from their sense of tradition itself. In their new homes, the act of venturing beyond Chinatowns and Little Indias marks but only the first steps to a more fulfilling future. This could be followed by a dramatic leap into the realm of modern technological skills, to mastering foreign languages and ultimately to immersion in new intellectual spheres. There are abundant examples of both communities producing a wide range of talented people who have entered into workspaces that were unimaginable not that long ago.

As for reshaping, this refers to the ongoing process that began with the earliest community formations more than a century ago. In several of the essays, we are given vivid pictures of how the communities conducted their activities in order to survive and grow. The ways in which Indian and Chinese community leaders shaped and reshaped their compatriots to fit their changing environments are inspiring, even if they do not always succeed very well. The varied and mixed efforts to reshape the human materials that come to them encourages me to think that this is a fruitful area for even closer research. It is not enough only to examine what has been done before. What these essays suggest is that distinctive methods could be devised to monitor the new social shapes that are emerging today. This volume has made a good running start.

Wang Gungwu
National University of Singapore
10 May 2012

ACKNOWLEDGEMENTS

For bringing together so many scholars to participate in the 2010 workshop "Indian and Chinese Migrant Communities: Comparative Perspectives," jointly organized by the Nalanda-Sriwijaya Centre at the Institute of Southeast Asian Studies (ISEAS), Singapore, and the Hong Kong Institute for the Humanities and Social Sciences (incorporating the Centre of Asian Studies), University of Hong Kong, our thanks go to Professor Wong Siu-lun, former director of the Institute of the Humanities and Social Sciences (incorporating the Centre of Asian Studies), University of Hong Kong, and Associate Professor (then head) Tansen Sen of the Nalanda-Sriwijaya Centre (NSC), Singapore. Professor Sen has also provided us with constant support and guidance throughout the process of editing and publication. We are grateful to him for his useful suggestions and advice.

We gratefully acknowledge the unstinting support of Ambassador K. Kesavapany, former director of ISEAS, Singapore, as well as and Dr Geoffrey Wade, former visiting senior research fellow at the Nalanda-Sriwijaya Centre, Singapore, whose assistance and guidance through the workshop as well as editorial inputs were invaluable.

For carrying on the baton, to see this manuscript through publication, our thanks go to the director of ISEAS, Mr Tan Chin Tiong, the deputy director of ISEAS, Dr Ooi Kee Beng, and the head of NSC, Dr Derek Heng. Special thanks to Mr Tej P. S. Sood, publisher, Anthem Press, and editors Mr Brian Stone, Ms Miranda Kitchener and Ms Camille Seldon for their patience and support through the editorial process and through publication of this important collection of essays.

We would like to specially thank Professor Wang Gungwu of the National University of Singapore (NUS) for so kindly writing the Foreword for this volume. Professor Wang Gungwu is chairman of the Board of Trustees, ISEAS, chairman of the East Asian Institute and chairman of the Lee Kuan Yew School of Public Policy, NUS. His invaluable research and insights through innumerable published articles and books over the many years of his remarkable career have greatly contributed to studies of the Chinese diaspora and inspired many a scholar to do further research in this field.

We are also indebted to Teresa Tsai, assistant registrar, and Ms Terrie Ip, senior secretary, both of the HKIHSS, University of Hong Kong, and Mrs Y. L. Lee, head and administration and executive secretary, ISEAS, and Joyce Zaide, Lucy Liu, Angela Oon, Betty Tan and all colleagues and friends at ISEAS for their behind-the-scenes support in the organization of the workshop and production of this volume.

To all our contributors – both senior scholars whose baseline research over the years has given us the framework to understand the process of migration and settlement, and younger scholars whose work explores fresh perspectives and dynamic ways of studying and viewing these processes – we extend our deep appreciation. It is their work and scholarship that makes this volume a great contribution to research in the field of diaspora studies.

We would like to dedicate this book to all the travelers, sojourners and migrants who left their homelands, by force or by choice, to settle in new lands, thereby enriching the life and culture of their new homelands, and creating new hybrids of social, economic and cultural patterns. To them we owe the greatest debt of gratitude.

Jayati Bhattacharya
Coonoor Kripalani

INTRODUCTION

Jayati Bhattacharya and Coonoor Kripalani

Migrations and transnational interactions carry with them numerous tales of differences and dilemmas, conflicts and coercion, encounters and integration. The traditional boundaries of language, culture and ethnicity are challenged and negotiated to yield newer forms of identity and consciousness, which thrive with their own sense of uniqueness and integrity. The increasing mobility of large-scale flows of capital, goods and people brings to the fore the complexities of transnational players on the regional, national and international levels. The "post-colonial deconstruction of residual Eurocentric epistemologies," as argued by some scholars, also brings in the question whether the "post-Westphalian" era "marks the end of the nation-state."[1] The complexities of spatial identities that then arise need to be addressed in multidisciplinary paradigms. Recent works in the humanities and social sciences have highlighted the importance of researching these interactions in various forms and over diverse geographical spaces. While a number of researches have been published on individual diasporas, there are few examples which incorporate a comparative approach among the diasporas in terms of lived spaces, economic networks, cultural interactions or religious synergies. This volume deals with two of the largest diasporas in the world: overseas Chinese, reportedly forty million–strong worldwide, and overseas Indians, who are said to number a little over half that at approximately twenty-two million.[2]

Though diverse geopolitical spaces have been addressed in this volume, the main focus has been the Southeast Asian region, as can be seen from the larger number of articles in that section. This region constitutes a veritable "contact zone" for the two communities, with centuries of interaction providing a fertile ground for a comparative framework and opportunities to explore the relationship between India and China through their respective diasporas. This regional focus also emphasizes how the notions of migration, diaspora and cultural contact have constituted the core of the Southeast Asian identity.[3] The papers that appear in this volume were first presented at "Indian and Chinese Migrant Communities: Comparative Perspectives," a workshop jointly organized by the Nalanda-Sriwijaya Centre at the Institute of Southeast Asian Studies (ISEAS), Singapore, and the Hong Kong Institute for the Humanities and Social Sciences (incorporating the Centre of Asian Studies), University of Hong Kong, in January 2010. The theme of the workshop had a precedent in the forum convened by the Centre of Asian Studies and the Consulate General of India in Hong Kong in 2000,[4] which gave rise to the volume *Chinese and Indian Diasporas: Comparative Perspectives*, edited by Wong Siu-lun.[5] It was said to be the first of its kind "to suggest ways for scholars and the business community to benefit from a mutual engagement of ideas,"[6] and provided a platform on which scholars and members of the entrepreneurial communities from both diasporas could interact. However, the workshop at ISEAS in Singapore was somewhat different. While trying to address and reflect upon the methodological approaches to a comparative study, it brought to attention many of the sociocultural, economic and religious spaces that were created by the transnational communities in different geographies, and the resonances of transition and accommodation that were then experienced in different spheres of activity.

The papers presented in this volume question who forms the diaspora: Are settlers of several generations – their cultural habits, foods and dress notwithstanding – considered diaspora, or only those who still have a connection with the homeland? Are migrant workers part of a diaspora, or are they akin to the indentured labour of previous centuries? Do they have the right to choose to stay on in the countries that they built, and acquire other nationalities, as did many indentured labourers in South Africa, Malaya, the West Indies and so on? While some of the papers study the historical antecedents, many of the issues discussed hold relevance for the present age. A landmark case on this issue was contested in 2011 and won in the Hong Kong Courts by Ms Evangeline Banao Vallejos, a Filipino domestic worker, whose bid for permanent residency in Hong Kong had been denied by the immigration authorities.[7] Vallejos is a contract worker, whose stay was limited by her contract.[8] There are significant numbers of contract workers like her of Chinese and Indian origin, who will no doubt be impacted by the outcome of her case. Another pertinent question pertains to transmigrations and dual or multiple nationalities, and which diasporas these persons fall under, if any. The researches at hand reveal many of the same push-and-pull factors that led to earlier migrations of Indians and Chinese, and often to the same destinations. The imperial enterprise channelled the flow of human movement in similar directions and also kept them away from each other administratively for purposes of effective colonial governance. In this volume we explore the intersections of these two diasporas and the interactions between them.

Presented here are contributions from a number of eminent scholars, whose work on Chinese and Indian diasporic communities has provided the essential groundwork for younger scholars to develop further research. The papers that deal with only one community are juxtaposed against papers that deal with the other, to provide the comparative element that this volume offers and point out the gaps in scholarly literature where the alternative perspective is lacking.

The volume is divided into four sections. While the first section provides us historical background, it also gives us a glimpse of the complex methodological issues regarding the comparative analyses of two diverse communities, and different ways the question of nationality has been dealt with by the respective nation-states. The other three sections have been categorized in terms of geographical spaces across the globe and deal with various aspects like religion, business, colonial administration, law and regulations, culture and identity. While the focus of the comparative analysis has been the Southeast Asian region for the two communities since ancient times, there are also researches on Indian communities in China and Chinese communities in India, as well as diverse perspectives on both these communities across the globe.

The first section begins with a paper by Sugata Bose on the historical precedents, and a paper by Tan Chee-Beng on the theoretical underpinnings to the discussion of migrations and growth of overseas communities.

Sugata Bose's paper sets the tone by telling the story of forced Indian migrations to far-flung parts of the British Empire and its multifaceted impact on the global economy, akin to Chinese labour migrations to work the tin mines in Malaya. He chronicles the movement of Indian labour in the nineteenth and twentieth centuries, and how these people became settlers. The slave trade and its successor, indentured labour, fuelled trade and the global economy. Once slavery was abolished, "the doors to freedom" were opened by trafficking indentured labour to plantations not only in Ceylon, Malaya, Burma, Mauritius, Natal, Reunion and East Africa, but also to British Guiana, the British West Indies, the French Caribbean, Dutch Guiana and Fiji. He shows how the coolie trade was linked with the opium trade in the early nineteenth century and how Indian intermediary capitalists – Gujarati merchants and the Chettiars – played a role in both. These early migrations sowed the seeds for later interracial disharmony. The socioeconomic ramifications of this trade were varied – Bose contends caste-based oppression left an indelible mark on subaltern and Dalit narratives, while at the same time, the need to keep food supplies available to this vast and dispersed labour force "spurred the opening of the rice frontiers of the Irrawaddy Delta in Lower Burma, the Chao Phraya Delta in Thailand and the Mekong Delta in Southern Vietnam." While the slave trade spawned a global economy, it also spawned numerous ideologies against it. The most powerful objectors to slavery came from the Islamic world. Thus, global migrations mobilized interactions in the transnational space that were little acknowledged, but played a significant role in determining intercommunity exchanges.

The emotional contextualization of homelands is addressed in the three papers that follow by Amrith, Tan and Suryadinata, which seek to define ethnicity and national identity. Tan Chee-Beng draws a distinction between diasporic people versus ethnic groups of people, who may define subcultures within societies of specific linguistic and ethnic identities. The diaspora for him are people who maintain a "diasporic consciousness" through identification with the "homeland of emigration." He suggests common cultural processes and points out gaps in the literature where further research and enquiry are needed. For example, he raises the idea of remigration and multiple homelands among migrants, which may strengthen one identity over another, and suggests that transnational identities and transnational connections are influenced by the role of kinship and religion.

On the question of nationality, two contributions, one from Leo Suryadinata and the other from Sunil Amrith, discuss this vexed issue from the Indonesian and Malayan perspectives. Apart from the emotional considerations of homeland, Leo Suryadinata discusses the issue of nationality of Chinese migrants, setting out the history and issues of Chinese nationality and dual citizenship. He discusses the Nationality Law for Chinese under the Qing dynasty and the complexities it created for Chinese migrants in the Nanyang region, particularly in Indonesia. While there is no comparable study for Indian migrants in this volume, this theme mirrors an ongoing demand for dual nationality by Indians overseas with strong emotional links to the homeland. India, like China, embraces its diaspora, apart from cultural and political considerations, for its contributions to economic development and for the foreign exchange it remits. So the question of dual nationality as quid pro quo is open to negotiation. It is hoped that this gap in scholarship on the issue of nationality will be filled by future research.

The issues of citizenship in Malaya are discussed by Sunil Amrith, whose paper echoes Sugata Bose's chapter, of how the patterns of migration were set by colonial histories. Comparisons between Indian and Chinese labour were made by the imperial authorities and by the mid-1930s, the Malay Peninsula was seen as "the dividing line between the Indian and Chinese Seas, and the Indian and Chinese races; consequently, in the Straits Settlements, the Indians and Chinese are found meeting on Malayan ground."[9] These "meetings" are explored by Amrith, by connecting the diasporic histories of these two communities – Indian labour being controlled by the imperial (British) state, while the Chinese labour migrations were seen as having been freer and more voluntary. Consequently, they had greater access to entrepreneurism and the rags-to-riches stories are more prevalent among the Chinese communities of Malaya. But by the 1940s, both communities were subject to the prevalent intellectual and political ideologies which saw the humiliation of their people through the ill treatment of their migrant workers, and exhorted the latter to reform and shed their traditional mores, frequently in each other's print media – the Chinese spoke of the Indians' problems in their newspapers and vice versa. Both communities began to negotiate the notion of Malayan citizenship, their homeland ties notwithstanding.

In Southeast Asia we see a meeting ground of both the Chinese and Indian diasporic communities through the centuries, both in the economic and the cultural spheres. The economic sphere is described in the second section by Hamashita, Gomez and Bhattacharya, whose papers address different perspectives of financial networks and business activities in different spaces in different periods of time. These studies give us a comparative look at networks, remittances and business aspirations as the two communities interact in their common diasporic spaces. The paper by Hamashita Takeshi, which describes the traditional networks used by the two immigrant communities to send remittances home, compares the system of *hundi* run by the moneylending Chettiar community with that of the Chinese moneylenders. In both cases, these informal remittance agencies came to be institutionalized, providing emigrants with the same sorts of services: recruitment, loans for passages, bookings of passages and commercial transactions. Hamashita's work provides revealing insights into the procedures of these remittances, which circulated capital in the region to be ploughed into enterprises such as property development in Amoy, telephone companies, rubber factories, sugar mills, alcohol plants and so on. The Chettiar moneylenders did not confine their profession to Indian immigrants alone, but counted among their clients Europeans, Chinese, Indian labourers, hawkers and peddlers, as well as Malay royalty and peasants – their work being recognized by the British authorities. In both cases, remittances were recycled for commercial payments and used as investment capital, becoming in the Chinese case a vital element in China's international financial ties.

The evolution of Chinese business networks is discussed in the next paper in this section by Terence Gomez, who challenges the arguments of earlier scholars who viewed the success of Chinese business enterprises in Southeast Asia as uniquely due to network and kinship ties. While he concedes that this may have been the case with the first generation of Chinese migrants, it is no longer so in Malaysia. The older small enterprises run by Chinese families have been overshadowed by big corporations and Bumiputera-backed SMEs. The successful Chinese enterprises, he contends, are those which have partnered with Bumiputera Malays, but most others choose to stay under the radar and do not go public, thus hindering their size and growth.

Jayati Bhattacharya's paper, which follows, connects the thread of Chinese business activity, but in a completely different scenario. Both Bhattacharya's and Gauri Krishnan's paper, which follows later in this section, shed light on the socioeconomic interaction between the diasporic Indian and Chinese communities in Singapore. Bhattacharya's research shows how Chinese merchants have come to dominate the gold jewellery business in Little India, selling traditionally designed Indian-style jewellery to a new clientele: migrant workers. This particular example shows how the two communities share common spaces and learn about each other's culture. Bhattacharya's research describes transnational circulation and the consumption of commodities, while adding to the discourse on patterns of consumption and business. It also reflects on the changing market operations in the urban spaces of a dominant Indian enclave in Singapore.

The interactions of Indians and Chinese in Southeast Asia are not only varied, complex and manifested on multiple levels, but also facilitate distinct identity formations. The paper by Renaud Egreteau provides an informative examination of Indian and Chinese migrations to Burma (now Myanmar). As in the case of Malaya, the Indians migrated within the British Empire while the Chinese migrated as "foreigners." As a result of the privileges accorded to the Indian population, the Burmese population became hostile and used derogatory words to refer to them. The Chinese population, owing to their ethnic characteristics, have been able to integrate more freely, and there is a continuous inflow of ethnic Chinese migrants from neighbouring provinces such as Yunnan. The impact of both communities is visible on various aspects of the Burmese landscape, particularly through their architecture – for example, the temples, mosques, clan associations, etc., built by these communities.

Gauri Krishnan discusses the practice of Thaipusam, a festival to celebrate devotion to Murukan, a Hindu deity. This practice in Singapore can be seen in a continuum of the influence of popular worship in India on Brahmanical practices. These practices gave rise to the creation of rural deities, which were incorporated into mainstream Hinduism.[10] In the diaspora, too, new deities are created that serve particular groups, as Vineeta Sinha's research shows.[11] Krishnan's empirical research shows both Indian and Chinese devotees observe this festival, a practice which again reflects the evolving inclusiveness of religious practices. She provides several instances of non-Hindus participating in the processions and ritual practices in Singapore and Malaysia. It is a testament to these countries' political tolerance towards a variety of cultures and faiths that these processions and rituals are accorded special provisions to continue. While this event has become one for "an audience of others,"[12] Krishnan is of the view that it has led to interfaith and inter-communal participation, and remains one of the many contributions of the Indian ethnic minority to the cultures of their adopted homelands, making the practice of Thaipusam uniquely Singaporean and creating a space for cultural interaction. Krishnan also acknowledges the administration, catering to a pluralist and syncretic society, both regulating yet facilitating the practice of the festival.

Similarly, in defining identity, Jayani Bonnerjee's paper investigates shared transnational spaces of religion and community, through the examples of Kolkata and Singapore, and thus elucidates some of the practices discussed in Krishnan's paper. Based on the specific examples of Kali temples in the Chinatowns of Kolkata and the Mariamman Temple in Singapore's Chinatown, she builds on Sinha's idea[13] that religious encounters are partly located in the role of nation-state and the multiracial paradigm. Bonnerjee's paper is related to both Krishnan's and Zhang's contributions in some aspects, but is distinct from both in terms of her search for alternate cosmopolitanism in the "diaspora space,"[14] with a focus on religion as space for interaction. Bonnerjee explains that the factors behind the creation and maintenance of these shared religious spaces are located in the politics of community identities.

Finally in this section, Stephanie Chung Po-yin's paper discusses the Muslim practice of *waqf* and the Chinese practice of *sinchew*, both a type of trust to ensure the aftercare of deceased persons. These practices clashed with the British rule against perpetuities, a law that prevented material holdings beyond 21 years of an individual's death. Chung's research into landmark legal cases of the late nineteenth century show a lack of sensitivity and understanding of Muslim and Chinese customs on the part of the colonial administration in Malaya (Penang), which seemingly favoured the *waqf* over the Chinese *sinchew*. In keeping with their divide-and-rule policy, after the 1867 riots in Penang, the British dismantled multi-ethnic power bases, instead creating racially segregated administrative units. By the twentieth century, the British authorities came to understand the customary laws of these communities and made certain concessions.

Among the papers looking at Indians in China and Chinese in India, Madhavi Thampi's research informs of the pull of China for Indian migration in the late nineteenth century. The first groups of Indian migrants went as policemen and soldiers safeguarding the opium interests of the British, participating in the China Coast wars and benefiting from the unequal treaties, thereby earning opprobrium of the local population in the treaty ports. Their working conditions were poor, and they became ideal candidates for recruitment in the struggle for freedom from the British. In 1927, they sided with the Chinese, refusing to fire upon Chinese workers. But many of them joined the INA (Indian National Army), and came to be seen as collaborators of China's enemies – first of the British and then of the Japanese, as Thampi points out. In the wake of the troops who spearheaded the opening of China to the British went the Indian merchants who partnered with the British in the opium trade, and their histories warrant separate studies. A number of them were prominent Parsi families, whose descendants continue to live in Hong Kong. Thampi brings to light the perceptions of this unconventional migrant community and the similarity of their conditions to those of the transported labour migrants.

They form one of the important means of transcribing mutual perceptions in India–China relations during the colonial period, a time when the earlier interactions between the two civilizations were disrupted by colonial interventions giving rise to mistrust and misconceptions.

Jia Haitao's paper juxtaposes a study of Indian migrants in China at present with Thampi's historic account. It is a valuable account, but with research still at a preliminary stage, it provides a starting point for further work in this field. Jia describes a vibrant Indian community – multinational executives, entrepreneurs and students (of medicine) – residing in the midst of "kind-hearted and friendly Chinese" in various cities in Guangdong province. Jia attributes the success of Indian entrepreneurs to happy Sino-Indian marriages and to opportunities afforded by progressive PRC economic policies. Sino-Indian political relations, he feels, have little impact on this community, and believes its presence bodes well for Sino-Indian relations. Jia ascribes very high qualities to the Indians in China: smart, sociable, international, English speaking, well educated, dynamic and interacting well with the Chinese. There is also a group of labourers (such as workers in restaurants, etc.) and others whom Jia describes as illegal – visa overstayers and people without proper papers. This profile that emerges from a small sample survey by Jia – in contrast to the soldiers and policemen of Thampi's research – can be read as an indicator that the current Chinese economy is attractive to dynamic Indian entrepreneurs. This is also reflective of the voluntary mobility of human capital in the present environment of globally circulated labour and capital, quite in contrast to the involuntary postings of the regiments under the British administration described by Thampi.

The other side of the story – that is, the issue of cultural identity of migrant Chinese to India – is taken up in the work of Zhang Xing. The issue of cultural identity is a central one for all migrants, and the experience Zhang describes of the Chinese in India speaks to all migrant communities. She presents the position of Chinese in India by the mid-twentieth century and explains the ambiguity a number of these migrants feel – are they Indian-Chinese or Chinese-Indian? Following the deportation of a number of Chinese in 1962 – a scarring experience for most – many ended up in Canada and China. Zhang's interviews with these transmigrants tell of their nostalgia for India and their continued identification as Chinese-Indians. Touchingly, those who returned to China, observe Indian festivals such as Diwali, and plan get-togethers with other Chinese from India, where they eat Indian food and listen to Indian music. The psychological and cultural implications on the Chinese of this process of relocation in various parts of the globe, including those who relocated to China as victims of political tensions, have been little studied, and Zhang's account gives these aspects due attention.

Zhang's descriptions are fleshed out by the personal account of Kwai-Yun Li, which appears last, in the postscript to this volume. It lends life to the accounts in Zhang's paper, as well as graphically shows the confusion of the Chinese community of India at the outbreak of the 1962 border war. Should they be communist or nationalist sympathizers? Or should they be followers of the Dalai Lama? Should they go to Chinese schools – if so, which ones? The nationalist or the Mainland-supported ones? Through this personal narrative, the reader gets a feel of the interactions between the host community and the Chinese immigrants.

In the last section on the Indian and Chinese diasporas across the globe, we have two papers that look at both diasporas across the globe. The paper by Coonoor Kripalani compares popular Hindi films that depict diaspora populations living in the West with Chinese films of a similar nature. The former category shows the Indian diaspora as mainly affluent, generally with a hankering for the home country, and keen to maintain their Indian-ness. To do so they uphold time-worn rituals, respect family elders and encourage marriages within their own communities. Subtle pressures are brought to bear on young women to uphold the patriarchal mores of traditional Indian society. In contrast, the Chinese films show the hardships that drove the first generation of migrants to seek a new life in the New World. This Chinese diaspora does not hanker for a return to the motherland, though it clashes with the second generation in terms of the maintenance of traditional social mores and identity. These auto-ethnographic Chinese films are then further compared to films made by the Indian diaspora, which are similar to the Chinese films in their depiction of the push-and-pull factors of migration, intergenerational conflict, as well as interactions with the host community. In both cases there is a sense of freedom outside the strictures of their respective homelands, yet there is the aim to protect ethnic and cultural identities, which are deemed superior to those of the host country.

While Laavanya Kathiravelu's paper examines low-wage NRIs (non-resident Indians), generally contract workers who work overseas for fixed periods and remit money home, her thesis is applicable to all migrant contract workers around the globe, including Chinese labour. Given that contract workers are tied to their employers and sponsors, Kathiravelu considers this system of migrant contract workers to be a perpetuation of the slave/indentured-labour trade. While she does not present figures for the financial contributions of Indian contract workers versus other Indians, it is assumed that theirs are quite substantial. These workers, she argues, have a low status, and are undervalued by their own government as well as that of the receiving nation. Kathiravelu argues that this group of migrants are not netted in the beneficial financial instruments and other enticements offered by the Indian government to its sons and daughters overseas, and instead are subject to gross exploitation by their recruiters and employers. Looking at their situation in the UAE, Kathiravelu suggests regulation of recruiters, and calls for a greater respect of these workers by the officials representing India overseas. She suggests that sending governments need to exert more political pressure to protect unskilled migrant workers, and argues for the transnationalization of rights debates for the free movement of marginalized peoples.

The papers presented in this volume aim at locating group relations and constructs of new identities created in the transnational spaces of interaction between the Indian and the Chinese communities in different geographies. These researches work on different premises from the unified representations of culture and economy; they work on different paradigms in the construction of identity through adoption and adaptation, convergence and conflict, revealing several untold stories in the process. A number of ideas and hypotheses presented here are important starting points for further research in transnational remigrations among the Indian and Chinese diasporas, and further explorations into cultural, religious and economic spaces of these two diasporic communities beyond Asia. Connections between diasporic histories, comparative studies of present-day Chinese and Indian labour migrations, the question of dual nationalities in relation to their respective government's diaspora policies and the implications on raising revenue through financial remittances, are all potential themes for further research. Having discussed the home remittance system of the two communities in the previous two centuries, a comparative look at the contemporary remittance systems would be a useful contribution to the literature. The preliminary study in this volume on the Indian diaspora in China provides a springboard for further in-depth analysis on this important community. Having looked at diaspora in film, another area of potential research is exploring visual and performance art exchanges as vehicles of influence that impact social and political landscapes, and effect the transfer of ideas. We hope the arresting glimpses of lesser-known stories in this volume create interest and greater opportunities to inform and inspire further scholarship in the study of comparative diasporas.

Notes

1 Andrea Riemenschnitter and Deborah L. Madsen in their "Introduction" to their edited volume, *Diasporic Histories: Cultural Archives of Chinese Transnationalism* (Hong Kong: Hong Kong University Press, 2009), p. 1.
2 Ministry of Overseas Indian Affairs, "Population of Non-resident Indians (NRIs): Country-Wise." http://moia.gov.in/writereaddata/pdf/NRISPIOS-Data(15-06-12)new.pdf. 10 June 2014.
3 J. Clammer, *Diaspora and Identity: The Sociology of Culture in Southeast Asia* (Selangor Darul Ehsan: Pelanduk Publications, 2002).
4 The forum convened by the Centre of Asian Studies, University of Hong Kong, along with the Consulate General of India in Hong Kong on 25 February 2000 was entitled "The Indian and Chinese Diasporas: Comparative Perspectives."
5 Wong Siu-lun, ed. *Chinese and Indian Diasporas: Comparative Perspectives* (Centre of Asian Studies: University of Hong Kong, 2004).
6 Wong Siu-lun, ed. *Chinese and Indian Diasporas*, p. v.
7 "Hong Kong Split over Maid's Landmark Bid for PR," *Straits Times*, Tuesday, 9 August 2011, p. A15.
8 In September 2011, Ms Vallejos won the case to be allowed to apply for permanent residency in Hong Kong. Quashed by a higher court, it remains to be seen if this will discourage such applications in the future, or will impact policy in other labour-importing countries. http://asiancorrespondent.com/66202/hong-kong-filipina-maid-wins-historic-residency-case. 7 November 2011.
9 R. Mukerjee quoted by Sunil Amrith in Chapter 2 of this volume, p. 14.
10 See for comparison, Sree Padma, *Vicissitudes of the Goddess: Reconstructions of the Gramadevata in India's Religious Traditions* (New York: Oxford University Press, 2013).
11 Vineeta Sinha, *A New God in the Diaspora? Muneeswaran Worship in Contemporary Singapore* (Singapore: Singapore University Press and the Nordic Institute of Asian Studies, 2005).
12 As Sunil Amrith mentions in Chapter 2 of this volume, p. 18.
13 Vineeta Sinha, "'Mixing' and 'Matching': The Shape of Everyday Hindu Religiosity in Singapore," *Asian Journal of Social Science* 37 (2009): 83–106.
14 Avtar Brah, *Cartographies of Diaspora: Contesting Identities* (London: Routledge, 1996).

Section I

HISTORICAL ANTECEDENTS AND THE QUESTION OF NATIONALITY

Chapter 1

BLACKBIRDERS REFITTED? THE JOURNEYS OF CAPITALISTS AND LABOURERS IN THE INDIAN OCEAN, 1830s–1930s[1]

Sugata Bose

"One thing Zachary did know about the *Ibis*," Amitav Ghosh writes in his novel *Sea of Poppies*, "was that she had been built to serve as a 'blackbirder,' for transporting slaves. [...] As with many another slave-ship, the schooner's new owner had acquired her with an eye to fitting her for a different trade: the export of opium." It is not until the *Ibis* reaches the river Hooghly that Zachary Reid, the son of a Maryland freedwoman, encounters Ben Burnham, the ship's new owner. Burnham informs young Zachary that the *Ibis* will not carry opium on its first voyage as the Chinese are having difficulty understanding the benefits of free trade. Instead, the vessel will do just the kind of work she was intended for. "D'ya mean to use her as a slaver, sir? But have not your English laws outlawed that trade?" a startled Zachary asks. Burnham replies that those who would stop at nothing to halt the march of human freedom have indeed outlawed the trade. "Well sir," Zachary demurs, "if slavery is freedom then I'm glad I don't have to make a meal of it. Whips and chains are not much to my taste." But Burnham reassures him; the *Ibis* will carry not slaves, but coolies. "Have you not heard it said that when God closes one door he opens another? When the doors of freedom were closed to the African, the Lord opened them to a tribe that was yet more needful of it – the Asiatick."[2]

Burnham's "doors of freedom" would remain open to African and Asiatic alike long after the formal abolition of slavery and the slave trade in various colonial territories. The stuff of self-congratulatory anniversaries and observances of expiation – the cleansing of collective guilt – the dates of declaratory promises of freedom for enslaved peoples hold little substantive meaning for historians. Slavery's long afterlife and the forms of servitude that took its place demand, however, the finest forensic skills that practitioners of comparative and connective history can bring to bear on the subject. Speaking the language of slavery after denuding it of its multiple meanings or neglecting its varied temporal and spatial contexts might make it easier for Indian Ocean historians to find a niche in the US academic marketplace. But steering such an easy course in the way we write the history of enslaved and subjugated peoples carries enormous costs in both intellectual and ethical terms. It is a route not worth taking. The answer is not a retreat into Indian Ocean exceptionalism, but an attentiveness to both connections and disconnections in a global history.

Economy

Let me begin with a consideration of a form of servile labour that is generally seen to have replaced slave labour in the plantation complex worldwide during the course of the nineteenth century. The abolition of slavery gave rise to insistent demands for Indian indentured labour from the 1830s onwards. The pernicious recruitment patterns, the horrors of the sea voyage and the dismal working and living conditions on the plantations led some historians to believe that indenture and its associated forms of labour were no better than "a new system of slavery." Aspects of this view have been effectively called into question. The depiction of women migrants, for example, as a "sorry sisterhood" of "single broken creatures" has been shown by Marina Carter to be "simply a parody of the colonial discourse" on the social ills afflicting Indian society. Yet, there seem to be no reasonable grounds for accepting the claim emanating from the opposite end of the spectrum that Indian indentured labour migration was more akin to the movement of free white labour to the dominions than the journey of African slaves to the New World. Mortality rates on oceanic journeys were much higher for indentured Indian labourers than free white labour but lower compared to those for African slaves. The prospect of real freedom following the term of the indenture contract was also severely constrained. The "crux of the indenture issue" lay in the ability of the planters to execute a "strategy of threatening the livelihoods of the ex-indentured market gardeners and hawkers, and organizing a new migrant stream to diminish the bargaining power of the existing plantation workforce."[3]

As in the case of the movement of Indian capital, a question arises as to the continuing significance of the Indian Ocean interregional arena at a time when migrant Indian labour travelled as far as the Atlantic and the Pacific. Within the Indian Ocean arena the approximate figures for streams of colonially regulated Indian labour exports in the century spanning the 1830s to the 1930s were as follows: Ceylon, 2,321,000; Malaya, 1,911,000; Burma, 1,164,000; Mauritius, 455,000; Natal, 153,000; Reunion, 75,000; and East Africa, 39,500. The corresponding figures of Indian labour movements to the Atlantic and Pacific worlds were: British Guiana, 239,000; Trinidad, 150,000; Jamaica, 39,000; other British West Indies, 11,000; French Caribbean, 79,000; Dutch Guiana, 35,000; and Fiji, 61,000. There was a circular quality to Indian labour flows, especially in the Indian Ocean arena. Mauritius, for example, received some 455,000 Indian indentured labourers between 1834 and the end of indenture early in the twentieth century, of whom as many as 157,000 returned to India. There were undoubtedly certain analogies, if not global uniformities, of forms of labour in the plantation complex worldwide. Yet not only did much larger numbers of Indian labourers migrate and circulate in the Indian Ocean arena, but the movements of Indian indentured workers in this zone displayed patterns of family and kin group recruitment that were different from those who went to the Atlantic or the Pacific. In this respect indentured labour on the sugar plantations of Mauritius has been shown to resemble what has been called *sardari* (overseers-led) or *kangani* (sponsored) migration based on pre-capitalist forms of loyalty and reciprocity that coexisted with the capitalist contract.[4]

The coolie trade was inextricably linked with the opium trade in the early nineteenth century and Indian intermediary capitalists had a role to play in both. From the 1810s China tea replaced Indian textiles as the most profitable item in the East India Company's trade. Without control over Indian territories the company would not have been able to survive for half a century after the loss of its Indian trading monopoly. The company met its requirement of remittances to the metropolis through the forced cultivation of indigo and financed its China tea trade by establishing a government monopoly over opium cultivation in India. Massive illegal sales of Indian opium in China made it unnecessary for the company to bring in silver to finance their purchase of tea. The opium monopoly provided about 15 per cent of the income of the company state, and accounted for nearly 30 per cent of the value of India's foreign trade until the mid-1850s. In the Eastern Indian Ocean the Chettiar capitalists from Tamilnadu began their operation in the 1820s by selling cotton piece goods from the Coromandel Coast. But the real breakthrough for Tamil capital in the Straits came with a waft of fragrant smoke and a whiff of notoriety, albeit not as sordid as the Gujarati involvement in the slave trade of East Africa. In the middle decades of the nineteenth century the Chettiars worked hand in glove with branches of various European exchange banks in financing the opium trade from India. By the turn of the twentieth century, however, the financial opportunities came from the rapid expansion of rubber plantations and tin mines to meet the rising demand from the industrial West.

Between 1820 and 1870 Gujarati merchants from the west coast of India had made their fortunes in the Western Indian Ocean through mostly dubious means. They were the chief financiers of the extensive slaving operations of the Imam of Muscat. By the mid-nineteenth century they had turned to more legitimate forms of trade as well. In 1860 Lt. Col. C. P. Rigby found between five and six thousand Indian residents in the Zanzibar territories and the number was "annually increasing." They included Hindu Bhatias from Kutch and Jamnagar as well as Muslim Khojas and Bohras from Kutch, Surat and Bombay. They were "gradually acquiring all the wealth and property of the island." "The Banians [Bhatias] never bring their families or females from India," Rigby wrote, "and always look forward to a return to their own country after having acquired a competence, but the Khojas and Bohras bring their wives and children, and become permanent settlers."[5] In 1873 Bartle Frere, a former governor of Bombay, was sent out to Zanzibar to finally stamp out the trade in slaves. The 1873 anti-slavery mission must not lead us into any naive assumptions about British altruism. Frere had intricate financial ties with the shipping magnate William Mackinnon, one of the prime movers behind the British colonial empire in East Africa, whose British India Steam Navigation Company had received immense official favours while Frere was governor of Bombay in the 1860s. While Frere could not "acquit any portion of the Indian community of indirect connection with the slave trade," he found "the more respectable Indian houses in Zanzibar" keen to see a final end to it. They realized that its continuation hampered all other trade and postponed "the full development of the unrivalled commercial capabilities of the coast."[6] As the slave trade died out in the last decades of the nineteenth century, cloves emerged as the most valuable item of international trade in Zanzibar.[7]

Indigo and opium were commodities of critical importance in the global economy of the first half of the nineteenth century and had key connections with the forms of servile labour that rose to prominence from the 1830s onwards. At one level indentured and "apprentice" labour and to a lesser degree convict or penal labour may be seen to have filled the breach in the plantation sector left by formal abolitions of slave trades and slavery. Yet there was something else of immense significance for the nineteenth-century world economy going on in the agrarian hinterlands of the Indian Ocean interregional arena. "The first half of the nineteenth century," Christopher Bayly argues, "was a critical period of the formation, by hammer blows from the outside, of the Indian peasantry." Having risen to a position of dominance by riding the wave of a relatively vibrant eighteenth-century economy, the British resorted to a form of conquistador imperialism, which contributed in no uncertain way to the economic stagnation of the early nineteenth century. As Bayly puts it in his major work *Rulers, Townsmen and Bazaars*, "Earlier despotisms were tempered by a political culture which insisted that rulers should offer service and great expenditures in return for high revenue demand," but "the British acknowledged few such restraints." The crisis of legitimacy of the early colonial state was, therefore, "a moral as much as an economic one."[8]

What was fashioned in the first half of the nineteenth century was a settled and sedentarized peasantry, which during its latter half produced primary products for a capitalist world market. The colonial state held wandering peoples without fixed addresses in deep suspicion. The mobility that characterized eighteenth-century rural society was replaced in the nineteenth with the immobility and stern discipline of agricultural commodity production. Indian rural society also became more hierarchically defined in the nineteenth century than it had been in the eighteenth. The intensification of caste-based oppression has left indelible marks on Dalit and other subaltern narratives of identity in much the same way as the history and memory of race-based slavery have shaped African and African American discourses.

In my own earlier work on the peasantry under colonial rule I advanced an argument about the need to consider peasant history as one of the more important branches of labour history. While noting variations and advancing a typology of agrarian social structures, I underscored the importance of conceptualizing peasant labour in relation to colonial capital. The social organization of production in much of agrarian Asia rested on a labour process utilizing the unremunerated and grossly under-remunerated work of family labour. Expanded commodity production for the capitalist world market was achieved efficiently and cheaply without resort to the formal commodification of labour. The refusal to be reduced to a commodity was itself a success of resistance by peasant labour determined to retain access to a combination of production-based and trade-based entitlement to consumption and subsistence. From the late nineteenth century onwards the surplus produced by peasant labour was extracted largely through the economic circuits of debt at the end of the production cycle. But this had to be tempered by the sharing of responsibility for the subsistence and minimal needs of peasant labour through adequate provision of credit by the owners of land and capital at the beginning of the production cycle. It was the lines of credit that tied together the domains of land, labour and capital, and geared agrarian society to undertake production that sustained colonial commerce. Over the long term, agrarian society "peasantized" during the early nineteenth century may be seen to have fought a drawn-out rearguard action contesting and warding off the tentative forces of "depeasantization" since the late nineteenth century. The human and social costs of the contradictions between capital and labour can be gauged by the direction of change in otherwise resilient social structures – the downward spiral of pauperization, the slower but significant shift in favour of demesne lords and a richer peasantry, and the subtle change in gender and generational roles to the disadvantage of women and children. The development of colonial capital resting heavily on peasant family labour resulted in the intensification of unpaid and underpaid women's and children's labour. Peasant labour clung on to the basic means of production – land – but became increasingly dependent on merchant and usury capital. In its more extreme manifestations the predicament of smallholding peasants caught in an unending cycle of debt attracted comparisons with the condition of slavery.[9]

Production relations based on settled peasant labour and migrant indentured or quasi-indentured labour were bound in a dialectical relationship. It may have been possible until the mid-nineteenth century to advance a simple demographic typology in the Eastern Indian Ocean of densely and sparsely populated zones. The rise of plantations and mines dramatically unsettled that dichotomy. They drew their labour from the old-settled thickly populated agrarian regions, which found an extended lease of life through this escape hatch of migration. Large contingents of Tamil labour, for instance, moved to the tea plantations of Ceylon and the rubber plantations of Malaya, just as Chinese migrant labourers were sent to work in the tin mines of the peninsula. But the new concentrations of population also needed new sources of food, which the old rice bowls of Bengal, Tamil Nadu, Java and Northern Vietnam were in no position to supply. This spurred the opening of the rice frontiers of the Irrawaddy Delta in Lower Burma, the Chao Phraya Delta in Thailand and the Mekong Delta in Southern Vietnam, largely financed by overseas Chinese and Indian capitalists. The triad of old agrarian zones, new plantations and mines, and newer rice frontiers linked by specialized flows of labour and capital remained in place from the mid-nineteenth century until the crisis of the depression decade arrested or reversed most of these flows.[10]

If these two strands of peasant labour and migrant labour dominated primary production in the Indian Ocean arena tied to a global capitalist economy during the hundred years from the 1830s to the 1920s, what was the significance of a labour process based on slavery after the formal abolitions? Was slavery a marginal issue restricted to the domestic, so-called "unproductive" sphere with a gender balance skewed heavily towards a preponderance of female slaves? Not quite. In the labour-scarce economies of the Eastern Indian Ocean slave raiding and slave labour were integrally connected to production well into the nineteenth century. James Francis Warren's work several decades ago on the Sulu zone trained the spotlight on these slaving operations, even though he was careful to distinguish the fate and prospects of mobility of "owned persons" in the

Eastern Indian Ocean from that of slaves in the Atlantic world.[11] The global economy of the late nineteenth century created new conditions of possibility for slave labour in certain productive economic sectors of the Western Indian Ocean. Slavery in Arab lands received a fresh impetus from the rise of an export-oriented pearl industry and date plantations in the late nineteenth century. A significant proportion of the labour force in these sectors were slaves from East Africa and the Makran Coast of Baluchistan, even though there was a drift in the direction of debt peonage from slavery in the first three decades of the twentieth century.

Ideology

Arabs and Muslims held slaves in the Western Indian Ocean from medieval until modern times. Islam had little to do with it.[12] The decade of the 1870s, which marked the high-water mark of the slave trade from East Africa, also witnessed the most powerful Muslim denunciations of the institution of slavery. The notion of Islamic slavery falls roughly in the same category as Islamic terrorism, advanced by those with either a colossal ignorance of Muslim intellectual history or a scarcely disguised bigotry towards Islam.

The concept of the *abd* or slave to Allah and to Allah alone supplies one of the most potent grounds for rejecting slavery to any mere mortal. Historians of early Islam concede that slavery was well entrenched as a social institution in pre-Islamic Arabia and that the Prophet in a pragmatic vein took ameliorative measures in the expectation of its early demise. The Quranic verses on the subject have been open to rival interpretations by both Muslims and non-Muslims, but what is of relevance here is the existence of a vibrant strand of Muslim thought through the centuries that was profoundly antithetical to human slavery. Islamic law developed its own conservative rigidities, but there is no reason to accept the legists and theologians as more representative of Islamic ethics than a wide array of philosophers, poets and intellectuals. In fact, the narrow focus on Islamic law is highly constricting and leaves out of consideration a vast mass of ethical literature that is part of the Islamic ecumene in the Indian Ocean interregional arena. If the domain of normative theory on the subject of slavery was marked by lively contestation, the actual history of Muslims produced in the medieval period a class of Mamluks or aristocratic slaves, which was decidedly not a contradiction in terms within the spatial limits of the Indian Ocean. Throughout the medieval and early modern periods the upward mobility of slaves, including the *sidis* from Africa, was relatively unhindered and they were often members of ruling elites. The Mughal emperor Akbar announced in 1582 the release of "all the imperial slaves" since it was "beyond the realm of justice and good conduct" to benefit from "force."[13] In doing so, he was following the path of reason illuminated by a tradition of Islamic ethical discourse on legitimacy and good governance.

This is not to say that there were no opposing points of view on the subject of slavery then or in the late nineteenth century, when a galaxy of Muslim "modernist" intellectuals reinvigorated Islamic ethics. Ayesha Jalal in her book *Partisans of Allah: Jihad in South Asia* has reclaimed modernist Muslim thought "from the dismissive stigma of apologia."[14] Towering Muslim intellectuals including Sayyid Ahmad Khan, Nawab

Abdul Latif Khan, Maulana Karamat Ali, Syed Ameer Ali, Mirza Ghulam Ahmad, Maulvi Chiragh Ali and Maulana Shibli Numani together pioneered a monumental intellectual project that recovered "the expansive dimensions of jihad as an ethical ideal rather than as perpetual warfare against infidels."[15] Most of these intellectuals also argued with reason and passion against slavery, a subject on which there was vigorous debate. There was a reason why the arguments by Sayyid Ahmad Khan, Syed Ameer Ali and Maulvi Chiragh Ali against slavery initially appeared in their biographies of the Prophet. They were responding in the immediate instance to evangelical diatribes, in particular William Muir's egregious four-volume *Life of Mahomet*, published between 1856 and 1861 portraying the Prophet of Islam as a patron of polygamy, divorce and slavery. As Ayesha Jalal has shown, both Sayyid Ahmad Khan and Chiragh Ali argued that it was "the secularization of Islamic law, and not Islam's religious teachings"[16] that stood in the way of Muslims embracing modernity. Far from being secularists, the modernist Muslim intellectuals were firmly grounded in the Islamic intellectual tradition, "even while redefining the debate in the light of rational modern thinking."[17] That dynamic tradition continued into the post-colonial era as exemplified by the intellectual battles fought in Pakistan by Ghulam Ahmad Parvez against Maulana Mawdudi on the questions of jihad as well as slavery.[18]

Slavery in the Indian Ocean arena was never enmeshed with race in the way it was in the Atlantic world. It was linked to identities of caste and class and has become part of the narratives of these identities. But tying slavery to religion requires recourse to some tortured logic. When the story of Bilal is narrated through "Bhar do Jholi," the subcontinent's most famous *quawwali* in praise of the Prophet Muhammad, it is not being put to any instrumental use, but rather is serving as an uplifting invocation of an equality transcending racial barriers. The message is quite simple: the day that Bilal did not give the call of azan, the sun just did not rise. Yet Islam's egalitarian and emancipatory appeal cannot be expected in and of itself to break the chains of slavery, an issue that must be treated squarely as a problem of resistance rather than as a problem of religion.

Eavesdropping on the backstage discourse of subordinated groups such as slaves and Dalits rather than simply observing their public performance of deference reveals the near bankruptcy of theories of hegemony and false consciousness. On this question James C. Scott's inversion of an important aspect of Gramsci's analysis of hegemony is compelling. Contrary to Gramsci's formulation, a reading of hidden transcripts suggests that subordinate classes are "less constrained at the level of thought and ideology" and "more constrained at the level of political action and struggle." Scott's theoretical work on "ideological insubordination" argues that the "infrapolitics" of resistance by subordinates against dominant elites is "very much of a material struggle in which both sides are continually probing for weaknesses and exploiting small advantages." I would make a stronger claim that the large contradictions within structures of the global political economy and international war crises are of critical importance, often enabling that "conquest of inevitability" of succumbing to power, which allows the hidden transcripts of cultural dissent and negation to make their dramatic entry onto the public stage.[19] The international war of 1861 to 1865 steeled the determination of many who might have wavered before to be slaves no more. The crisis of the depression emboldened peasants to rebel throughout the Indian Ocean interregional arena, snapping the bonds of debt and servitude.

The errors of decision during the economically decisive decade of the 1930s had grave social and political implications. The depression quickened the pace of anti-colonial nationalisms in Asia, but at the same time exacerbated a welter of class, caste, racial and religious conflicts. On 22 December 1930, the most spectacular of all the depression rebellions broke out in Lower Burma. It was led by Saya San, a charismatic monk, who portrayed himself as both "the *Setkya-min* (the avenging king of Burman legend) and the *Buddha Yaza* (the divinely sent creator of a Buddhist utopia)."[20] The Saya San rebellion undoubtedly had a staunchly anti-colonial character and was directed against British rule. The main unifying issue was the highly regressive and inflexible capitation tax that was due to the colonial government at the end of the calendar year. But Indian moneylenders had begun foreclosing on mortgages, sparking a massive alienation of agricultural land. So the movement, with its strong Buddhist millenarian overtones, was also directed against the migrant moneylenders from the land of the Buddha, who were seen as the immediate quill drivers of colonial oppression. The promised millennium without colonial taxes would also be free of debts owed to the Chettiars.

Back in the land of the Buddha the new apostle of non-violence, Mahatma Gandhi, launched his civil disobedience movement with a clear set of five economic demands: the abolition of the salt tax, the reduction of the land revenue demand by half, protection for the Indian textile industry, reservation of coastal shipping for Indians, and an alteration in the rupee–pound exchange rate to stimulate Indian exports. The agitation did not wholly remain non-violent, with agrarian jacquerie and revolutionary terrorism common occurrences in several parts of India. India and the United States were two very different types of "slave country." As Nico Slate has shown in his recent book *Colored Cosmopolitanism*, connections were forged between South Asian and African American discourses on freedom and slavery from the mid-nineteenth century onwards. In India the colour line separating the colonizer and the colonized inspired narratives of colonial slavery and aspirations of freedom that animated the anti-colonial movement. But there was also a second narrative authored by the downtrodden castes within Indian and, in particular, Hindu society that drew analogies between race-based and caste-based forms of servitude.[21]

"We live in a world in which slavery has not been eradicated," Adam Rothman says in the concluding sentence of his book *Slave Country*, "and if we are not vigilant, may again flourish under a new dispensation of global inequality."[22] The grim and grotesque history of Atlantic slavery and racial discrimination in the Americas is unlikely to be repeated. The hefty price in suffering paid by Africans and African Americans has by now elicited a degree of moral revulsion and a body of international human rights law that has expanded the definition of slavery to encompass a wide range of humiliations and human indignities. Islamic law, compiled and codified under colonial auspices, has remained relatively hidebound. But the richness of Islamic ethics ought not to be judged by the poverty of Islamic law. Islam, quite as much as Buddhism, remains a rich ideological resource for resistance against gross injustices when material conditions bring effective undermining of institutions of servitude within the realm of possibility. Modernist Muslim thought in the Indian Ocean arena made important contributions to the discourse on rights. "The time is now arrived," Syed Ameer Ali wrote in 1891, "when humanity at large should raise its voice against the practice of servitude, in whatever shape or under whatever denomination it may be disguised." He urged Muslims to proclaim "in explicit terms that slavery is reprobated by their faith and discountenanced by their code."[23] What Syed Ameer Ali wrote in prose, his contemporary – the beacon of individual freedom, Muhammad Iqpal – put in poetry:

> Ghulami main na kaam ati hain shamsheerain, na tadbiren
> Jo ho zauq-yaqin paida to kat jati hain zanjeeren.
>
> [In slavery, neither swords nor designs are of use,
> But if there is certainty of faith, chains are broken.][24]

Notes

1 This chapter draws on my earlier work on both Indian Ocean history and the agrarian history of Asia.
2 Amitav Ghosh, *Sea of Poppies* (New Delhi: Penguin Viking, 2008), pp. 11, 78–9.
3 Marina Carter, *Servants, Sirdars and Settlers: Indians in Mauritius, 1834–1874* (Delhi: Oxford University Press, 1995), pp. 2, 298. See also Hugh Tinker, *A New System of Slavery: The Export of Indian Labor Overseas, 1830–1920* (London: Oxford University Press, 1974); Ralph Shlomowitz, "Mortality of Indian Labour on Ocean Voyages, 1843–1917," *Studies in History* 6, no. 1 (January 1990): 35–65.
4 See Sugata Bose, *A Hundred Horizons: The Indian Ocean in the Age of Global Empire* (Cambridge, MA: Harvard University Press, 2006), pp. 76–7.
5 Lt Col. C. P. Rigby, Bombay Army, Her Majesty's consul and British agent at Zanzibar, "Report on the Zanzibar Dominions," 1 July 1860. Reprinted in Mrs Charles E. B. Russell, ed., *General Rigby, Zanzibar and the Slave Trade* (London: George Allen & Unwin, 1935), p. 329.
6 Bartle Frere to Earl Granville, May 31, 1873, cited in Haraprasad Chattopadhyay, *Indians in Africa: A Socio-Economic Study*. (Calcutta: Bookland, 1970), p. 389.
7 For a more detailed discussion, see Bose, *A Hundred Horizons*, pp. 100–102.
8 C. A. Bayly, *Rulers, Townsmen and Bazaars: North Indian Society in the Age of British Expansion, 1770–1870* (Cambridge: Cambridge University Press, 1983), p. 468.
9 Sugata Bose, *Peasant Labour and Colonial Capital* (Cambridge: Cambridge University Press, 1993).
10 C. J. Baker, "Economic Reorganization and the Slump in South and Southeast Asia," *Comparative Studies in Society and History* 23, no. 3 (July 1981): 325–49.
11 James Francis Warren, *The Sulu Zone: 1768–1898: The Dynamics of External Trade, Slavery, and Ethnicity in the Transformation of a Southeast Asian Maritime State* (Singapore: NUS Press, 1981, 2007).
12 Syed Ameer Ali, *The Spirit of Islam* (Lahore: Islamic Book Service, 1989; original publication date, 1891), pp. 258–67.
13 Cited in Amartya Sen, *The Argumentative Indian* (New York: Picador, 2005), p. 291.
14 Ayesha Jalal, *Partisans of Allah: Jihad in South Asia* (Cambridge, MA: Harvard University Press, 2008), p. 116.
15 Jalal, *Partisans of Allah*, p. 309.
16 Jalal, *Partisans of Allah*, p. 309.
17 Jalal, *Partisans of Allah*, p. 150.
18 Jalal, *Partisans of Allah*, chs 4 and 6.

19 James C. Scott, *Domination and the Arts of Resistance: Hidden Transcripts* (New Haven: Yale University Press, 1990), p. 184.
20 James C. Scott, *The Moral Economy of the Peasant: Rebellion and Subsistence in Southeast Asia* (New Haven, CT: Yale University Press, 1976), p. 149.
21 Nico Slate, *Colored Cosmopolitanism: The Shared Struggle for Freedom in the United States and India* (Cambridge, MA: Harvard University Press, 2012).
22 Adam Rothman, *Slave Country: American Expansion and the Origins of the Deep South* (Cambridge, MA: Harvard University Press, 2005), p. 224.
23 Ali, *The Spirit of Islam*, p. 267.
24 Muhammad Iqbal, *Kulliyat-i-Iqbal* (Lahore: Muhammad Bashir, n.d.), p. 319. Translation from Jalal, *Partisans of Allah*, p. 231.

References

Ali, Syed Ameer. *The Spirit of Islam*. Lahore: Islamic Book Service, 1989, original publication date, 1891.

Baker, C. J. "Economic Reorganization and the Slump in South and Southeast Asia." *Comparative Studies in Society and History* 23, no. 3 (July 1981): 325–49.

Bayly, C. A. *Rulers, Townsmen and Bazaars: North Indian Society in the Age of British Expansion, 1770–1870*. Cambridge: Cambridge University Press, 1983.

Bose, Sugata. *A Hundred Horizons: The Indian Ocean in the Age of Global Empire*. Cambridge, MA: Harvard University Press, 2006.

______. *Peasant Labour and Colonial Capital*. Cambridge: Cambridge University Press, 1993.

Carter, Marina. *Servants, Sirdars and Settlers: Indians in Mauritius, 1834–1874*. Delhi: Oxford University Press, 1995.

Chattopadhyay, Haraprasad. *Indians in Africa: A Socio-Economic Study*. Calcutta: Bookland, 1970.

Ghosh, Amitav. *Sea of Poppies*. New Delhi: Penguin Viking, 2008.

Jalal, Ayesha. *Partisans of Allah: Jihad in South Asia*. Cambridge, MA: Harvard University Press, 2008.

Rothman, Adam. *Slave Country: American Expansion and the Origins of the Deep South*. Cambridge, MA: Harvard University Press, 2005.

Scott, James C. *Domination and the Arts of Resistance: Hidden Transcripts*. New Haven, CT: Yale University Press, 1990.

Shlomowitz, Ralph. "Mortality of Indian Labour on Ocean Voyages, 1843–1917." *Studies in History* 6, no. 1 (January 1990): 35–65.

Slate, Nico. *Colored Cosmopolitanism: The Shared Struggle for Freedom in the United States and India*. Cambridge, MA: Harvard University Press, 2012.

Tinker, Hugh. *A New System of Slavery: The Export of Indian Labor Overseas, 1830–1920*. London: Oxford University Press, 1974.

Warren, James Francis. *The Sulu Zone: 1768–1898: The Dynamics of External Trade, Slavery, and Ethnicity in the Transformation of a Southeast Asian Maritime State*. Singapore: NUS Press, 1981, 2007.

Chapter 2

CONNECTING DIASPORA HISTORIES: INDIANS AND CHINESE IN COLONIAL MALAYA

Sunil S. Amrith

Writing from his base in South Africa in 1905, Mahatma Gandhi commented on the position of Indian and Chinese migration to Singapore. "Singapore can be said to be as near to the Chinese as it is to us. [...] Despite this," Gandhi lamented, "our people there cannot hold their own against the Chinese." Chinese were wealthier than Indians in Singapore, and – Gandhi was at pains to point out – "some even own motor cars." Gandhi then provided the readers of *Indian Opinion* with comparative statistics, showing that the number of Chinese arrivals in Singapore was nearly ten times greater than the number of Indian arrivals. These statistics led Gandhi to observe that "this shows how much is yet to be achieved by our people in the matter of emigration to, and settling in, foreign territories." "It is a shame," Gandhi concluded, "that we cannot keep abreast of the Chinese."[1]

More than anywhere else in the world, the Straits Settlements and Malaya provided a meeting ground for the Indian and Chinese diasporas in Asia. Overall, more Chinese journeyed to Malaya than to any single destination in the world between 1840 and 1940: around eleven million in all. Malaya, similarly, attracted more Indian emigrants (around four million) than any other territories except Burma and Ceylon. This chapter examines that Indian labour diaspora in Malaya, paying particular attention to the comparisons that were made – at the time and subsequently – with their Chinese counterparts.

The starting point for the chapter is my recent research on Tamil diasporas in Southeast Asia. In the course of this work, I have confronted constantly the problem of comparison with the concurrent history of Chinese migration: a comparison that is not merely analytically interesting, but one that suffuses the historical record. British colonial officials and Indian and Chinese intellectuals made constant comparisons at the time between Indian and Chinese migration. From this arose debates about "free" migration and its restraint, new mechanisms for the government of human mobility, and new ways of thinking about migration, settlement and the prospect of citizenship.

By the 1930s, these conflicts had come to shape the very way in which migration was conceived of, regulated and restricted in this mobile region of the world that sat astride the Eastern Indian Ocean and the South China Sea. Writing in the mid-1930s, the Bengali economist and population theorist Radhakamal Mukherjee wrote that the Malay Peninsula was "the dividing line between the Indian and Chinese Seas, and the Indian and Chinese races; consequently, in the Straits Settlements, the Indians and Chinese are found meeting on Malayan ground."[2] An exploration of the nature of those "meetings" forms the substance of this paper.

Comparisons and Connections

From the 1880s, there was a steep change in the magnitude and the character of both Tamil and Chinese migration to Malaya.[3] The annual number of arrivals in Malaya from Nagapattinam and Madras grew from approximately 20,000 each year by the late 1880s to an average of 50,000 annually in the early 1900s and over 100,000 arrivals a year by 1911. In this same period, the number of Chinese arrivals exceeded 100,000 each year. Both Tamil and Chinese patterns of migration were circular in nature; though arrivals exceeded departure every year from 1880 until 1930, the number of people leaving Malaya for India and China each year was nevertheless very significant. In terms of the resident population, there were around 30,000 Indians in Malaya in 1870, concentrated in and around Penang, 75,000 by 1891, 120,000 by 1901 and 275,000 by 1911. By 1911, the resident Chinese population of Malaya was 916,000.[4]

Indian and Chinese migration to the frontiers of Southeast Asia arose from a shared set of economic and political conditions.[5] Yet most observers at the time, and since, have emphasized the contrasts between Indian and Chinese migration. Colonial officials thought Tamils in Malaya were "not nearly so capable of taking care of themselves as are the Chinese clans."[6] "There is a vast difference," one Indian journalist in Malaya wrote, "between the methods by which the Chinese and Indian labour reaches Malaya. [...] The Chinese labour movement is free and voluntary."[7] Undoubtedly the sharpest contrast between the two experiences is that Indian migration from the 1870s took place under the close control of the colonial state. Indian labourers travelled on British ships. Colonial magistrates oversaw their journeys. They worked on European-owned plantations. Most Chinese migrant labour, by contrast, was destined for work in Chinese-owned enterprises. Chinese migration was much more autonomous of the colonial state, which is not to say that it was any less exploitative of labourers.

This "freedom" enjoyed by Chinese labour was double-edged. Colonial authorities saw that it involved also the "freedom" to exploit labour in an unrestrained fashion. As a result, the British colonial state attempted to extend the kind of control and surveillance they exercised over Indian migration to Malaya to cover the Chinese. In 1877, British authorities established the Chinese Protectorate. They were convinced that direct state involvement in the organization of migration was essential to restrict the abuse that could take place undetected within indigenous social institutions. The Protectorate was charged with responsibility for the welfare of Chinese migrants in Malaya, and with bringing under official surveillance and control the Chinese "secret societies" that were increasingly alarming to the state on account of their autonomy. In contrast with the government of Indian migrants to Malaya, however, the Protectorate almost invariably worked through Chinese intermediaries: the elite businessmen of the towns, who retained control over labour in the hinterland through a dense web of associations, above all through dialect and surname associations.[8]

By the 1880s, the Tamil and Chinese "immigrant races" in Malaya were governed under parallel sets of rules and institutions, which nevertheless evolved through interaction with each other. Observers at the time were probably right to see Tamil and Chinese communities of labour in Malaya as two very different kinds of long-distance societies. Chinese migrants to Malaya maintained transnational connections mainly outside the state, through the development of a range of diasporic social and economic institutions. Tamil migrants had little option but to engage with the state, on both sides of the Bay of Bengal. This process of engagement, however, opened new possibilities for their emergence as political subjects; subjects who could make claims and in whose name claims could be made.[9]

Chinese and Indian migrants filled different niches in the Malayan economy. The urban economy of the port cities drew in both Chinese and Indian labour, but in the Malayan hinterland, Indian labour went largely to the rubber plantations, whereas Chinese labour worked in tin mining. At the same time, the economic opportunities open to Chinese labourers in Malaya were wider. There were plenty of "rags to riches" stories of impoverished Chinese labourers who succeeded as merchants, virtually none in the case of Indian labourers. Colonial (and Indian) observers put this down to the Indian migrants' lack of initiative. A more convincing explanation lies in the fact that Indian migrants were much more closely tied to the world of plantation production, which was designed to prevent social mobility. As Kaoru Sugihara has argued, the Chinese system of recruitment through lodging houses allowed for greater social and geographical mobility than the *kangany* system,[10] since "the sense of 'trust' was apparently transferable from the broker to the lodging house, and then from the lodging house to the employer or foreman."[11]

In their brotherhoods (*kongsi*), the Chinese had a denser web of social institutions than Indian labourers in Southeast Asia. The British allowed Chinese society significantly more scope for self-government than they allowed Indian migrants. This was, in part, due to direct British control over India – their long experience of governing, categorizing and controlling Indian labour, which they felt they understood. The world of the Chinese overseas, by contrast, was less easily understood by British officials, who lacked the linguistic and cultural knowledge to intervene as they might have liked, and was ruled, rather, through Chinese intermediaries. Chinese social institutions allowed for a much closer set of links between urban Chinese merchants and labourers in the hinterland than in the case of the Indian communities, where a large gulf remained between plantation labour and the small world of urban intellectuals and merchants. In part, this may be explained by the longer history of Chinese labour migration and agricultural settlement in Southeast Asia.

Nevertheless, similarities between Indian and Chinese migration to Southeast Asia are equally notable. Indian and Chinese patterns of migration to Southeast Asia were both circular: Indians and Chinese alike were "sojourners" in Southeast Asia. Both streams of migration changed over time, from being overwhelmingly male to a gradual turn towards family migration and the migration of women in the twentieth century.

Despite the greater involvement of the colonial state in recruiting Indian labour, it is clear that informal social networks – based on kinship and locality – were significant at every stage of the migration process in the case of both Indian and Chinese labour. Debt played a central role in the journeys of most Chinese and Tamil workers to Southeast Asia, and the varieties of indebtedness bear many similarities. Finally, the fact that most Indian migration was under colonial control did not wholly prevent a steady and continuing stream of "illegal" migration from South India under the control of Indian shipping merchants and recruiters, more akin to the patterns of Chinese migration.

Already by the late nineteenth century, the sharper contrasts between Tamil and Chinese migration often broke down before the eyes of colonial administrators. Even as the colonial state aimed to control definitively every aspect of Tamil migration to Malaya, evidence emerged that "free" Tamil migration, under the control of Indian shipping merchants and labour recruiters, continued to flourish. The most common strategy employed by labour recruiters and migrants was to set sail for Southeast Asia from the French port of Karikal – an enclave, along with Pondicherry, that remained in French hands despite the defeat of French imperial ambitions in South Asia.[12]

Alongside evidence that "free" Tamil migration continued to evade colonial control, there was another sort of anxiety that linked discussions of Tamil with Chinese labourers in Malaya: anxiety surrounding the use of indentured labour. Spurred by pressure from Indian and Chinese nationalists and social reformers, and from humanitarian campaigners in Britain, the early twentieth century saw many official commissions of inquiry investigating the condition of indentured labourers in Malaya and throughout the British Empire. The Malayan investigation highlighted the appalling conditions that Tamil and Chinese indentured labourers faced, suggesting that the legal and political institution of indenture transcended, in its oppressions, the specific pathways by which Tamil and Chinese workers found themselves under its power.[13]

Indian and Chinese experiences of migration to Southeast Asia did not simply bear similarities. There were significant connections between them. In Malaya in particular, Indians and Chinese laboured under a shared legal regime that cast them as temporary "immigrant races" and differentiated them from the "indigenous" Malays. On the fringes of plantation lands, and above all in urban areas, Indian and Chinese cultural worlds came into contact, collision and interaction. Recognizing themselves (and each other) as diasporas, Indian and Chinese political and cultural leaders learned from one another, even as they competed to claim that their respective communities were suitably modern and fit for citizenship.

The Politics of Citizenship

The early years of the twentieth century saw the proliferation of a much wider range of claims on, and claims to speak for (literally, to represent), both Tamil and Chinese migrant workers in Malaya. Indian and Chinese journalists, social reformers and government officials – together with locally based Indian and Chinese intellectuals in Malaya and the Straits Settlements – turned their attention to the conditions of Indian and Chinese workers in Malaya (and throughout the world). In elaborating a critique of the system of indentured labour, these debates over the "coolie" turned on competing definitions of freedom: the freedom to move, the freedom of contract, and more abstract notions of human agency and dignity.

For Chinese and Indian political figures and social reformers, the inability to protect their countrymen abroad became a sign of national weakness and shame. For both Indian and Chinese elites, part of the problem was the problem of association. At a time when "free" Asian migrants began to experience legal discrimination in – and exclusion from – the settler colonies and the United States, the problem of the "coolie" seemed to brand all Indians and Chinese with the stigma of bondage and humiliation.[14] Addressing the imperial legislative council in 1912, the Indian liberal leader Gopal Krishna Gokhale spoke of the "vast and terrible amount of suffering" caused by the system of indentured labour, the "personal violence" and "bitterness" that continued to be reported from all the regions of Indian settlement in the British Empire. Beyond suffering, however, "disgrace" in the eyes of the world was the greatest concern of the Indian elites who condemned indentured labour. Indentured labour, Gokhale declared in 1912, was "degrading from a national point of view," for "wherever the system exists, there the Indian are only known as coolies, no matter what their position might be."[15]

The particular consciousness among Indian and Chinese elites of living as a diaspora in the Nanyang emerged concurrently with more expansive conceptions of a worldwide Indian and Chinese diaspora, and in the light of growing anxieties surrounding the place of India and China within the developing international system of nations.

The end of indentured labour migration to Malaya (the last contracts of indentured expired in 1913–14) gave a new cast to debates about "free circulation" and "free migration," and increasingly contested definitions of citizenship. On the one hand, there emerged a notion that the rights of migrants rested on their political and familial links with a distant homeland: they could make claims for protection or redress as "Indians overseas" or as "Chinese overseas." Conversely, at the same time there was emerging an increasingly exclusive notion of *local* citizenship, based on the idea that the Malay people were indigenous to Malaya, in sharp contrast with the "immigrant" Indians and Chinese.[16] For many, these new assertions of citizenship rested on a revival or even a rediscovery of the political and intellectual connections that linked the diasporas in Southeast Asia to their Indian or Chinese "homelands." The 1920s and 1930s saw an intensification of the traffic in ideas and inspirations, in both directions.

By the end of the 1920s, for instance, eminent political figures from India began to visit Malaya, deepening the connection between the two coasts of the Bay of Bengal. In 1929, the leading Tamil social reformer and anti-caste activist "Periyar" E. V. Ramasamy – founder of the Self-Respect Movement in Madras – toured Malaya, visiting towns and plantations and preaching his message of social and religious reform to large audiences.[17] Ramasamy took directly to the plantations his specifically South Indian message of marriage reform, combined with an attack on "superstition." A resolution passed during his visit declared support for the remarriage of widows, and "request[ed] the Tamil community to adopt it." He called for Tamils in Malaya to "sink their differences of caste, and of the place whence they came" and "to love their mother tongue." Finally, he decried the "old and uncivilized practice of beating drums, tom-toms and the like for deaths, funerals and other ceremonies," calling on Tamils in Malaya to reform their religious processions "in accord with the times and the country (in which they are living)."[18]

As is well known, from the work of Professor Wang Gungwu and many others, a strikingly similar process of "Sinification" was well underway at the same time.[19] The 1920s saw diverse experiments in Chinese education, and an assertion of pride in China's republican experiment alongside the continued vitality of more regional and local forms of identification by migrants with their home regions. Many of the themes of Tamil reform movements found an echo in debates within the Chinese community: marriage reform, the reform of popular religion, and repeated exhortations towards more respectable forms of behaviour and comportment in public. In this sense, we can even argue that the reform movements were connected in a direct way: each took the other as a point of comparison, and indeed as the audience for its own performance.

By the 1930s, as the public sphere of print and performance widened its reach, Chinese and Tamil reformers even began to write in each other's publications. I shall cite just one example of several. In a leading Tamil reformist publication, *Reform!*, which contained articles in both Tamil and English, there appeared in 1936 an article by one P. L. Wong, in which the Chinese poor were subject to the same reformist discourse as the publication used to describe the Tamils. The "poor Chinese," Wong wrote, were "blind to their superstition, which is gripping very tightly still. [...] If the other nationalities are not troubled by the evil spirits, why should the Chinese fear them; surely the Chinese will wake up one of these days!"[20] A particularly impassioned article in another Tamil reformist magazine argued for the suspension of "barbaric" religious rituals in public that would "only make us the laughing stock of our sister communities in this land."[21] Diasporic religious rituals, in the context of a cosmopolitan port city, were invariably performed for an audience of others.

The world of print was one important way in which reformist projects intersected and fed off one another. But they also worried about the physicality of the public sphere. There was an acute concern with audience. Virtually every public religious procession was depicted, in the media, as being watched by "thronged" observers.[22] Each public event was almost literally a performance of competing claims to civilization and modernity, and part of an ongoing struggle over the regulation and control of public space.

Sojourners to Citizens?

At the dawn of the 1930s, the global economic depression began to shatter the interconnected regional economy, and the position of Tamil and Chinese labour in Malaya became vulnerable.[23] As patterns of circular migration – sojourning – gave way to a raft of new immigration and emigration legislation in both sending and receiving countries, the question of citizenship, of where Indian and Chinese diasporas "belonged," became sharper, and began to carry practical consequences.

With the collapse in the price of rubber, the governments of Malaya and the Straits Settlements acted for the first time to restrict immigration. The restrictions initially applied primarily to Chinese immigrants, for the reason that they were "foreign"; Indian migrants, coming from within the British Empire, proved more difficult to exclude.[24] The Malayan government did, however, begin to differentiate between long-term and transient Indian residents of Malaya, and between "old" and "new" migrants from South India. With the suspension in the issue of fresh *kangany* licences in 1930, new standards of documentary proof came into effect, allowing only those Indians who could establish prior residence in Malaya to return for employment.[25] Many thousands of Tamil estate workers were repatriated to India upon the expiry of their contracts; others remained in Malaya, struggling to make a living by cultivating for subsistence on marginal lands, or drifting into the urban economy. For the first time since the 1870s, the number of people departing Malaya for India far exceeded the number of arrivals.[26] The reversals in patterns of migration were as significant in the case of the Chinese in Singapore and Malaya. While in 1929, the number of Chinese arriving in Singapore exceeded the number departing by over 100,000, by 1931, departures exceeded arrivals by 134,000 in 1931, 129,000 in 1932 and 58,000 in 1933.[27]

The other side of the attempt to restrict fresh migration, and to repatriate the "floating" or "surplus" workforce on the estates, were measures designed to stabilize the formation of a more settled Indian and Chinese population in Malaya. Crucially, women were exempted from the restrictions relating both to Chinese and to Tamil migration, leading to the large-scale migration of women to Malaya – many of them wives and daughters of male migrants who had been left behind. New regulations compelled planters to provide separate accommodation for married couples and families on the plantations. The depression both made evident, and in turn accelerated, a process that was already underway. We can see that the sex ratios among both Indians and Chinese – notoriously unbalanced in the early stages of mass migration – had already begun to improve in the 1920s. The number of locally born children increased steadily. Among the Tamil population in Malaya (excluding urban areas), there were some 17,000 local births in 1934 and over 23,000 in 1936.[28] Malayan labour officials were surprised to find that significant numbers of Tamil estate workers refused repatriation during the depression, preferring to cultivate for subsistence on small, marginal plots of land on the fringes of the rubber estates. The phenomenon of Chinese "squatters" cultivating for themselves was even more widespread. This phenomenon provoked an increasingly sharp tone on the part of Malay nationalists in the early 1930s. They insisted that Malaya was a Malay land, in which "foreign" Indians and Chinese could only ever be temporary labourers.[29]

To an increasing extent, however, Tamil and Chinese labourers in Malaya were confronted with the language of choice. Tamil intellectuals in Malaya's cities, many of whom sought to show the extent of their own loyalty and rootedness in Malaya, in their own quest for citizenship and recognition, admonished the mobile estate labourers for their rootlessness. As one Tamil journalist in Singapore wrote in 1937:

> So long as he considers himself to be a sojourner here, and allows only his carcass to move about here allowing his soul to cross the Indian waters and wait there anxiously for that blessed day when he can return, so long will he be looked upon with some suspicion and consequently never expect the status of a native or a domiciled citizen in this country.

Members of the Tamil community in Malaya, he argued, "must boldly choose one of the two alternatives – and consequently stand for the chances a sojourner might get, or be a full-fledged citizen."[30] Others, though, took a different view. Some Tamil journalists, for instance, began to assert a specifically diasporic claim to citizenship in Malaya: that is to say, they argued that diasporic connections with India (or China) strengthened, rather than undermined, the claims of Indians and Chinese in Malaya to local citizenship.[31]

Conclusion: Disconnections

In the unsettled conditions of the 1930s, when the fluctuations of markets were matched by a rapid reversal of legal restrictions on migration, Indian migration to Malaya was the first to cease. In 1938, the government of India quite abruptly banned all further labour migration to Malaya. Frustrated in their negotiations with the Malayan authorities over wages, the Indian authorities, supported by many Indian leaders in Malaya, decided to restrict all further labour migration to Malaya. The ban put an end to fresh migration to Malaya, but also interrupted a process of community formation that was underway. Malayan officials received several desperate petitions from Indians who wished to return to Malaya, after finding themselves "stuck" while on visits to India at the time the ban was passed.[32] The effects of the emigration ban on individuals, families and communities in Malaya were still being felt when the Second World War broke out, taking many more unawares.

Economic and legal transformations had come together in the 1930s to lend a more settled, less circulatory character to the Indian and Chinese diasporas in Southeast Asia. The Second World War completed that process of settlement and disconnected it with unforeseen brutality and violence.[33] The war gave rise to many "dramas of diasporic patriotism," as Sugata Bose has put it in writing about those Indians overseas who gave their lives to the cause of the Indian National Army. Bose's evocative phrase could well describe, too, the experience of thousands of Nanyang Chinese who lent their support to the anti-Japanese resistance. In the longer term, among the many social and political transformations it wrought, the war shattered patterns of inter-Asian migration that had flourished for close to seven decades. The end of the war gave new force to the struggle by both Indians and Chinese for Malayan citizenship on their own terms, not as "immigrants" but as settlers and citizens. One part of that struggle culminated in the Chinese-led Malayan communist insurrection in 1948, but it was also manifested in the development of a multiracial labour movement, with significant Tamil leadership, and in the rapid growth of the National Union of Plantation Workers in the 1940s and 1950s.

One of the characters in Amitav Ghosh's great novel of Indian migration to Southeast Asia, *The Glass Palace*, speaks these words, as war looms:

> Why should we expect that we're going to spend the rest of our lives here? There are people who have the luck to end their lives where they began them. But this is not something that is owed to us. On the contrary, we have to expect that a time will come when we'll have to move on again. Rather than be swept along by events, we should make plans and take control of our own fate.[34]

In making such "plans," in adapting when things went awry, in enduring suffering, in keeping their families together, Tamil and Chinese migrants, sojourners and settlers deployed all of the relationships, networks and knowledge they had developed while living transnational lives. These resources would come into play after the war, in the many struggles – both violent and non-violent – for citizenship and equality that would characterize Malaya's and Singapore's histories in the 1950s and beyond.

Viewed broadly,[35] the conditions that produced a sharper sense of Tamil and Chinese diasporic consciousness in 1930s Malaya were global ones, and they reshaped what it meant to belong to a diaspora right across the Indian Ocean and beyond. These include: the rise of controls over mobility, entry and exit; a sharper differentiation between insiders and outsiders in governing residence and employment; the rise of nationalisms that emphasized indigeneity as the basis for political rights and representation; and the entrenchment of global labour markets that functioned through ethnic differentiation. There is much potential, then, to write a connected as well as a comparative history of diasporas in this period, highlighting not only a convergence in the conditions and the painful choices faced by diasporas everywhere, but also the connections that emerged from the exchange of ideas about migration, citizenship and diaspora.

Notes

1 M. K. Gandhi, "The Chinese and the Indians in Singapore," *Indian Opinion*, 1 July 1905, in *Mahatma Gandhi on Indians Overseas*, compiled by the Purshotamdas Thakurdas Research Centre (Bombay: Purshotamdas Thakurdas Research Centre, 1970), 39.

2 Radhakamal Mukherjee, *Migrant Asia: A Problem in World Population* (Romc: Comitato Italiano per lo Studio dei Problemi della Popolazione, 1936), p. 109.

3 The classic histories of Indian migration to Malaya are K. S. Sandhu, *Indians in Malaya: Some Aspects of Their Immigration and Settlement (1786–1957)* (Cambridge: Cambridge University Press, 1969); and S. Arasaratnam, *Indians in Malaya and Singapore* (Oxford: Oxford University Press, 1970).

4 Figures compiled from successive censuses: J. R. Innes, *Report on the Census of the Straits Settlements Taken on the 1st March 1901* (Singapore: Government Printing Office, 1901); A. M. Pountney, *The Census of the Federated Malay States, 1911* (London: Darling, 1911); J. E. Nathan, *The Census of British Malaya, 1921* (London: Dunstable and Watford, 1921); C. A. Vlieland, *British Malaya: A Report on the 1931 Census and on Certain Problems of Vital Statistics* (London: Crown Agents for the Colonies, 1932). On the complexity of census definitions of "race," see Charles Hirschman, "The Meaning and Measurement of Ethnicity in Malaysia: An Analysis of Census Classifications," *Journal of Asian Studies* 46, no. 3 (1987): 552–82.

5 For a fuller discussion of this comparison, see Sunil S. Amrith, *Migration and Diaspora in Modern Asia* (Cambridge: Cambridge University Press, 2011), chapter 1.

6 Letter from F. H. Gottlieb, magistrate of Province Wellesley to lieutenant-governor of Penang, 16 November 1873: National Archives of India, New Delhi (hereafter NAI), Department of Revenue Agriculture and Commerce: Emigration Branch, proceedings 10–13 June 1874.

7 K. A. Neelakandha Aiyar, *Indian Problems in Malaya* (Kuala Lumpur: Indian Office, FMS, 1938), p. 14.

8 Carl A. Trocki, *Opium and Empire: Chinese Society in Colonial Singapore* (Ithaca, NY: Cornell University Press, 1990).

9 Sunil S. Amrith, "Indians Overseas? Governing Tamil Migration to Malaya, 1870–1941," *Past and Present* 208, no. 1 (August 2010): 208.

10 Mode of recruiting labour in South India through an overseer by the British colonial rulers in Malaya in the nineteenth century. In Tamil, *kangany* means an overseer or superior.

11 Kaoru Sugihara, "Patterns of Chinese Emigration to Southeast Asia, 1869–1939," in *Japan, China and the Growth of the Asian International Economy, 1850–1949*, ed. Kaoru Sugihara (Oxford: Oxford University Press, 2005), 260.
12 Amrith, "Indians Overseas?"
13 Federated Malay States, *Report of the Commission Appointed to Enquire into the Condition of Indentured Labour in the Federated Malay States*, submitted by C. W. C. Parr (Singapore: Government Printing Press, 1910).
14 Philip A. Kuhn, *Chinese among Others: Emigration in Modern Times* (Singapore: NUS Press, 2008).
15 John S. Hoyland, ed., *Gopal Krishna Gokhale: His Life and Speeches* (Calcutta: YMCA, 1933), pp. 176–7.
16 Amrith, "Indians Overseas?"
17 K. Veeramani, ed., *Malaysiavil Periyar* (Madras: Dravidar Kazhagam, 1989).
18 *Munnetram*, 16 January 1930. See also the account of the Indian Agent in Malaya, in NAI, Department of Education, Health and Lands (hereafter EH&L): Overseas Branch, proceedings 14–15 (B), February 1930.
19 Wang Gungwu, *The Chinese Overseas: From Earthbound China to the Quest for Autonomy* (Cambridge, MA: Harvard University Press, 1997); Kuhn, *Chinese among Others*.
20 P. L. Wong, "The Seventh Moon," *Reform!*, August 1936.
21 *Indo-Malayan Review: Journal of the Kinta Indian Association*, Ipoh, 1, no. 4 (July 1933).
22 See, for example, L. Elizabeth Lewis, "The Fire-Walking Hindus of Singapore," *National Geographic Magazine* 59, no. 4 (April 1931): 513–22.
23 The best account of the depression's effects on the region remains C. J. Baker, "Economic Reorganization and the Slump in South and Southeast Asia," *Comparative Studies in Society and History* 23, no. 1 (1981), 325–49; see also Amrith, *Migration and Diaspora*, chapters 1 and 3.
24 "Unemployment in Malaya: Restriction of Chinese Immigration" (1930), National Archives of the UK, Public Record Office, CO 273/566/2.
25 NAI, EH&L, file no. 206-2/32 – L & O: From K. A. Mukundan (agent in Malaya) to M. S. A. Hydari (deputy secretary to the Government of India, EH&L), 28 March 1934.
26 Memorandum presented by the agent of the Government of India in Malaya, to the Indian Immigration Committee of Malaya, Kuala Lumpur, 16 July 1930: NAI, EH&L: Overseas Branch, proceedings 76–162 (A), June 1931.
27 Bruno Lasker, *Asia on the Move: Population Pressure, Migration, and Resettlement in East Asia under the Influence of Want and War*, published by American Council, Institute of Pacific Relations (New York: Henry Holt, 1945), 78.
28 Federated Malay States, *Annual Report of the Labour Department, 1937* (Kuala Lumpur, Government Printer, 1937).
29 W. R. Roff, *The Origins of Malay Nationalism* (New Haven: Yale University Press, 1967); A. Milner, *The Invention of Politics in Colonial Malaya* (Cambridge: Cambridge University Press, 1995).
30 "Indians in Malaya," *Straits Times*, 1 June 1934.
31 "Malay Nāṭṭil Rājiya Urimaikaḷ," *Tamiḻ Nēcaṉ*, 20 April 1932; for a discussion of this source, see Sunil S. Amrith, "Tamil Diasporas across the Bay of Bengal," *American Historical Review* 115, no. 3 (2009).
32 Minutes of the Standing Emigration Committee, 13 February 1939: NAI, Department of Education, Health & Lands: Overseas Branch, 1938, file no. 44/38 – L & O; for further discussion, see Amrith, "Indians Overseas?"
33 There is a vast literature on the Second World War in Malaya, and constraints of space preclude a fuller discussion. See, among others, Christopher Bayly and Tim Harper, *Forgotten Armies: The Fall of British Asia, 1941–45* (London: Penguin, 2004); and Sugata Bose, *A Hundred Horizons: The Indian Ocean in an Age of Global Empire* (Cambridge, MA: Harvard University Press, 2006).
34 Amitav Ghosh, *The Glass Palace* (London: HarperCollins, 2000), p. 310.
35 This paragraph draws on the conclusion to Amrith, "Tamil Diasporas."

References

Aiyar, K. A. Neelakandha. *Indian Problems in Malaya.* Kuala Lumpur, Indian Office, FMS, 1938.

Amrith, Sunil S. "Indians Overseas? Governing Tamil Migration to Malaya, 1870–1941." *Past and Present* 208, no. 1 (August 2010): 231–61.

______. *Migration and Diaspora in Modern Asia.* Cambridge: Cambridge University Press, 2011.

______. "Tamil Diasporas across the Bay of Bengal." *American Historical Review* 115, no. 3 (2009): 547–72.

Arasaratnam, S. *Indians in Malaya and Singapore.* Oxford: Oxford University Press, 1970.

Baker, C. J. "Economic Reorganization and the Slump in South and Southeast Asia." *Comparative Studies in Society and History* 23, no. 1 (1981): 325–49.

Bayly, Christopher and Tim Harper. *Forgotten Armies: The Fall of British Asia, 1941–45.* London: Penguin, 2004.

Bose, Sugata. *A Hundred Horizons: The Indian Ocean in an Age of Global Empire.* Cambridge, MA: Harvard University Press, 2006.

Federated Malay States. *Report of the Commission Appointed to Enquire into the Condition of Indentured Labour in the Federated Malay States*, submitted by C. W. C. Parr. Singapore: Government Printing Press, 1910.

Federated Malay States. *Annual Report of the Labour Department, 1937.* Kuala Lumpur: Government Printer, 1937.

Gandhi, M. K. "The Chinese and the Indians in Singapore." *Indian Opinion*, 1 July 1905. In *Mahatma Gandhi on Indians Overseas*, compiled by the Purshotamdas Thakurdas Research Centre. Bombay: Purshotamdas Thakurdas Research Centre, 1970.

Ghosh, Amitav. *The Glass Palace.* London: HarperCollins, 2000.

Hirschman, Charles. "The Meaning and Measurement of Ethnicity in Malaysia: An Analysis of Census Classifications." *Journal of Asian Studies* 46, no. 3 (1987): 552–82.

Hoyland, John, ed. *Gopal Krishna Gokhale: His Life and Speeches.* Calcutta: YMCA, 1933.

Innes, J. R. *Report on the Census of the Straits Settlements Taken on the 1st March 1901.* Singapore: Government Printing Office, 1901.

Kuhn, Philip A. *Chinese among Others: Emigration in Modern Times.* Singapore: NUS Press, 2008.

Lasker, Bruno. *Asia on the Move: Population Pressure, Migration, and Resettlement in East Asia under the Influence of Want and War*, published by American Council, Institute of Pacific Relations. New York: Henry Holt, 1945.

Milner, Anthony. *The Invention of Politics in Colonial Malaya.* Cambridge: Cambridge University Press, 1995.

Mukherjee, Radhakamal. *Migrant Asia: A Problem in World Population.* Rome: Comitato Italiano per lo Studio dei Problemi della Popolazione, 1936.

Nathan, J. E. *The Census of British Malaya, 1921.* London: Dunstable and Watford, 1921.

Pountney, A. M. *The Census of the Federated Malay States, 1911.* London: Darling, 1911.

Roff, W. R. *The Origins of Malay Nationalism.* New Haven, CT: Yale University Press, 1967.

Sandhu, K. S. *Indians in Malaya: Some Aspects of Their Immigration and Settlement (1786–1957).* Cambridge: Cambridge University Press, 1969.

Sugihara, Kaoru. "Patterns of Chinese Emigration to Southeast Asia, 1869–1939." In *Japan, China and the Growth of the Asian International Economy, 1850–1949*, edited by Kaoru Sugihara, pp. 244–74. Oxford: Oxford University Press, 2005.

Trocki, Carl A. *Opium and Empire: Chinese Society in Colonial Singapore.* Ithaca, NY: Cornell University Press, 1990.

Veeramani, K., ed. *Malaysiavil Periyar.* Madras: Dravidar Kazhagam, 1989.

Vlieland, C. A. *British Malaya: A Report on the 1931 Census.* London: Crown Agents for the Colonies, 1932.

Wang, Gungwu. *The Chinese Overseas: From Earthbound China to the Quest for Autonomy.* Cambridge, MA: Harvard University Press, 1997.

Chapter 3

CHINESE AND INDIAN DIASPORA: SOME COMMON AND NOT-SO-COMMON CULTURAL PROCESSES

Tan Chee-Beng

Introduction

The historical and contemporary migrations of peoples from China and India are major movements of people that have changed the world significantly. Such migrations have shown similar and diverse processes. This paper will discuss some of these processes – namely, migration and remigration, localization, reproduction of traditions, and transnationalism and identity. An important process of transnationalism is the transnational connection between the diasporas and China and India respectively. And in these transnational connections, kinship and religion play important roles, further influencing the reproduction of traditions and identities.

Chinese in global distribution – and I am using the term here instead of diaspora (see below) – are more numerous than people of South Asian origins. But both the Chinese and Indians in global distribution form very significant populations that have a lot of impact worldwide as well as in China and South Asian countries. Both Chinese and Indian populations worldwide deserve serious comparative study, rather than just being studied separately. There is much to learn from such a study about migration, cultural life, economy and ethnicity.

Concept of Diaspora

The concept of diaspora has become popular in the humanities and social sciences since the 1990s. While some scholars still feel uncomfortable about using this term to refer to migrant settlers and their descendants in different parts of the world, the term has by now assumed quite a common usage. In the study of Chinese overseas, Wang Gungwu[1] and other ethnic Chinese scholars from Southeast Asia[2] have expressed reservations about the use of the term for Chinese overseas who have identified with their respective home countries rather than with China. The term evokes the image of the Jewish dispersal and their identification with their Jewish homeland even though, as pointed out by Robin Cohen,[3] *diaspora* in its original Greek usage was quite positive, being associated with expansion through trade, military conquest and settlement. Most scholars who use the term today to refer to migrant settlers generally do not mean to equate them with the Jewish diaspora. Over the years I have also found it, as have scholars from Europe and America, convenient to use the term Chinese diaspora to refer to Chinese worldwide. But can we give a more precise definition of "diaspora"? What exactly do these terms – Chinese diaspora and Indian diaspora – include or exclude?

We can begin the discussion by citing a comment by Robin Cohen:

> Clearly, it would be stretching the term to suggest that all groups who migrate internationally in search of work evolve into a diaspora. Where essentially, we are talking of individuals, family or small group migration for the purpose of settlement, a diasporic consciousness may not develop, particularly if the immigrants concerned both intend to assimilate and are readily accepted.[4]

The comment makes sense. Strictly, "diaspora" should refer only to migrants and their descendants who have a diaspora consciousness and still identify with their original homeland, what I have called the "homeland of emigration."[5] The diaspora identity that most scholars have theorized actually refers to this kind of diaspora rather than descendants of migrants who have become localized and identify with the local homeland of residence. However, when people talk of Chinese and Indian diasporas, it is often a convenient way of referring to all Chinese and Indians distributed all over the world irrespective of their local or diasporic consciousness. For theoretical discussion it is necessary to distinguish the diasporic population and the localized population that no longer has diasporic consciousness. In the case of the Chinese in global distribution, for instance, the term ethnic can be used to distinguish Chinese overseas from those in China, who need not be described as such.

I suggest we can use the term ethnic to distinguish that form from the diasporic – that is, the Chinese diaspora comprising Chinese who have diasporic consciousness and generally still identify with China, as in the case of the new Chinese migrants. The ethnic Chinese are those who have become rooted in the countries where they have chosen to live, and they differ from the diasporic Chinese in that they do not have diasporic consciousness anymore, even if they continue to have memory of migration and remigration. Most of these ethnic Chinese are what I have called CDN (Chinese of different nationalities). Similarly we can speak of Indian diaspora and ethnic Indian communities. Perhaps instead of using the term diaspora to cover both the diasporic and the ethnic, we can say, for instance, Chinese in global distribution and Indians in global distribution. While there are those who dislike distinguishing minorities as ethnic, migrants as minorities in a country do form distinct ethnic categories, and so one need not be sensitive about the term.

Diaspora is a convenient term for referring to people or settlements, as we have discussed. It is, however, worthwhile to note that some scholars define diaspora as "process." In one definition, diaspora is defined as "an ongoing and contested process of subject formation embedded in a set of cultural and social relations that are sustained simultaneously with the 'homeland' (real or imagined), place of residence, and compatriots or coethnics dispersed elsewhere."[6] We are already so short of a good term for people in global distribution, and so I prefer to treat diaspora as referring to the people in diaspora, while not neglecting the processes in diasporic formation.

Our next issue is: do Chinese and Indian diasporas form a single diaspora respectively? In both cases, who are Chinese and who are Indians is an issue that needs to be addressed. In the case of the Chinese, there are obviously people of different ancestral origin from China, such as Hokkien (Minnan people), Cantonese, Hakka, etc. At the same time, Chinese overseas as *huaren* (Chinese) has been closely associated with those of Han Chinese origin because of their history and number of migration. Today there are more and more people of "minority *minzu*" who have migrated overseas. In English these are also Chinese, being migrants from China, but they may form quite distinct diasporas from the Han-origin diaspora, which is also internally heterogeneous. Their common political identification with China may bring them together as fellow nationalists, but Uighur in significant number overseas really form a distinct diaspora, and we also need to take into consideration those separatists who do not wish to see themselves as belonging to China. Thus contemporary Chinese diasporas, and we are here concerned with those of diasporic consciousness, really comprise different diasporas other than the Han Chinese. Added to this complexity is the global distribution of Chinese of Taiwan origin, and there are also Chinese who have remigrated from different countries.

In the case of Indians, the term "Indians" is used outside India to refer to people from India, who may speak different languages and identify with different parts of India, or who identify with such ethnic categories as Tamil, Telegu, Punjabi, etc. And in countries like Malaysia and Singapore, "Indians" include people of South Asian origin, be they from India or Sri Lanka. While those in Malaysia and Singapore have generally identified with "Indians" as an ethnic group in relation to the Malays, Chinese and others, in other parts of the world some South Asian groups form distinct diasporas or perhaps subdiasporas because of political reasons. The Sikhs, for example, are a well-known diaspora that maintains close contact with the Sikh homeland.

While the diasporic and the ethnic can and need to be distinguished, we should also note that people can have multiple identifications and senses of belonging, and we should not impose exclusive boundaries between the diasporic and the ethnic. The old and new Chinese migrants may have political differences, but this does not necessarily hinder their interaction or even cooperation. At the same time a new Chinese migrant may identify his or her nationalism with China but he may see himself as also belonging to the local, such as being both Australian Chinese and Chinese of China. His local-born children may become ethnic Chinese Australian, for instance. This is true of the South Asians, too.

Localization and the Significance of Tradition

In the case of old migrants or descendants of migrants in diaspora, an important process following migration and settlement is adaptation and localization, by which I refer to that process of becoming local – culturally and in due time in identification, too. Localization of migrants and their descendants is thus an important and exciting aspect of study, especially for anthropologists. Migrants everywhere have to adapt to the local conditions, be it climate, social interaction or local ways of life. As I had learnt from my Hebei informants in Kota Kinabalu, Sabah, migrants who could not adjust to the local climate fell sick and some chose to return to their home countries.[7] It is thus no accident that historically white migrants mainly settled in North America, South Africa, Australia and New Zealand. Today, of course, migrants of different origins, whether Asians or Africans are migrating mainly to the richer industrialized countries in Europe, America and Australasia.

For anthropologists the most exciting kind of localization is cultural localization. From my experience of research among the ethnic Chinese, the Malay-speaking Babas[8] in particular, language and food are two cultural features to which ethnic Chinese everywhere have been quick to become localized. For migrants, among the first cultural encounter is the language of the local people, and so learning the local language is one of the first cultural adjustments. While Chinatowns in America and Europe provide a niche where some migrants never quite learn the local language, most migrants do. It is not difficult, especially if the migrants are few in number and especially if there is intermarriage with the local people. The migrant generation may not speak the local language so fluently, but their local-born children quickly learn to speak like the locals. We learn this from the experience of the Chinese Peranakans in Southeast Asia, and today we see that new migrants' local-born children in America speak English fluently, even to the extent of not being able to speak their parents' mother tongue. Not only ethnic Chinese speak the local language, their mother tongue is influenced by the dominant local language, too. Thus the Minnan languages (Hokkien) in Malaysia and the Philippines have Malay and Filipino influences respectively. CDN are thus linguistically very distinct from one another because of their diverse experiences of linguistic localization.

This is true of the ethnic Indians, too. In fact, early migration and intermarriage had also resulted in the formation of distinct localized Chinese and Indian communities, such as the Baba (Chinese origin) and the Chitty (South Indian origin) in Malacca. Like the Chinese overseas, Indians in global distribution experience linguistic and other cultural localizations, such as those in Fiji[9] and in Trinidad.[10] The Indo-Fijians, most of whom are descendants of indentured labourers, have adopted Fijian cultural elements in their daily life, including the consumption of kava and the incorporation of many Fijian words into Fiji Hindi.[11] While many ethnic Indians continue to practice specific Indian traditions, these may acquire new forms and meanings. Parminder Bhachu,[12] for instance, shows how South Asian women of Punjabi Sikh descent in Britain are active agents in generating new cultural forms, including aspects of wedding practices.

As for food, the ethnic Chinese not only inherited China-origin culinary heritage, they have also adopted local spices and food sources, acquired some local culinary knowledge and innovated their local Chinese cuisine, as anyone who has been to Penang can observe easily. This culinary interaction takes place in the local as well as in the global arena, giving rise to a special local Chinese cuisine. In food we see and get to taste the result of culinary localization and innovation, as well as the cultural impact of migrants on the local culinary scene. Similar processes can be found among Indian migrants and their descendants. The *foodscape*, to borrow a term from Appadurai's ethnoscape,[13] is thus an exciting area of research in our study of Chinese and Indians in global distribution. In fact ethnic restaurants and grocery stores can be important sites of research for understanding ethnicity, diasporas and homeland, and even local and transnational politics. Purnima Mankekar's article about Indian grocery stores in the San Francisco Bay Area, for example, is an excellent example of how research on Indian stores can highlight "the transnational circulation and consumption of commodities and discourses about India."[14]

I have selected language and food as examples. There are other overt cultural features which symbolize identities. While for the localized Chinese in Southeast Asia (such as in Burma or in Indonesia) wearing a sarong is an overt feature of local identity, for the Indians in Southeast Asia wearing a sarong is not perceived as localized since it is also common attire of the South Indians. The sari worn by Indian women is in fact an overt feature of Indian identity.

Migration and local adaptation of course result in many other cultural changes. The need for wives to help in business or even to register business enterprises under their names transformed the gender relations of early Chinese migrants, as shown by Wu and Wang[15] in their study of the Chinese in New Guinea. In the case of South Asian migration, caste stratification has been transformed after migration. In Malaysia, there is less caste consciousness among the younger generations. Nevertheless, it still has some influence on "matters of commensality and marriage."[16] By comparing the Indians in Malaysia and Trinidad, Ravindra K. Jain shows the disintegration of caste as a system of stratification, although it has become a cultural variable.[17] In the case of the Patidars in East Africa, they claimed a higher caste status by replacing their previous caste rules with Brahmanical customs like dowries, vegetarianism and the worship of Lord Krishna.[18] All these are aspects of adaptation and localization that we can study to contribute not only to Chinese and Indian studies but also to the understanding of gender, social stratification and other theoretical issues.

While there is localization and cultural transformation, there is also cultural continuity, and we need to study both. Because of the experience of the diasporas as minorities, cultural features seen as continuing and linking to the past have important roles in the cultural life and identities of the migrants and their descendants. This is obvious in the case of the Chinese and Indians in Southeast Asia. Chinese festivals like Chinese New Year and the Hungry Ghost Festival (*zhongyuan jie*) and the Indian celebrations of Thaipusam and Deepavali are obviously important to the cultural life of Chinese and Indians in Malaysia and Singapore and many other parts of the world. In fact, where there is high localization to the extent of Chinese and Indians losing their Chinese and Indian languages, as in the case of the Babas and the Chitty in Malacca, religious traditions play an even more significant role in the people's cultural life and expression of identity. Domestic worship of ancestors and Chinese deities is important on the occasions of all major Chinese festivals among the Babas in Malacca. While many Babas in Singapore today are Christians, Chinese festivals remain important for their cultural identification. In the case of the Malacca Chitty (who are really Indian Peranakans, just like the Malacca Babas are Chinese Peranakans), religion is so significant that they have many Hindu temples in their small geographical concentration in Gajah Berang in Malacca.[19]

Those who migrated from China after 1978 are a totally different kind of migrant. They comprise both highly educated people and ordinary farmers and workers seeking a better life overseas. Unlike migrants of earlier centuries, new migrants today share in common easy access to their kin and friends in China via the Internet. It is easier for them to maintain their Chinese languages and cultural life, even though their local-born children no doubt experience much more localization, as can be seen among the children of Chinese migrants in North America speaking English to the extent of not speaking their own mother tongue very much. The new Chinese migrants generally continue to identify with an economically powerful China, albeit many having also acquired new citizenship or permanent residency. They make up the diaspora in the true sense of the term. What about the case of the recent migrants from South Asia? A comparative study of new Chinese migrants and new South Asian migrants (if this category can be defined clearly) will help us understand more about the diasporas in relation to the countries of residence and their original homeland.

Migration, Ethnicity and Cultural Identity

Migrants not only adapt to new environments, but also form new perceptions of others and their own group belonging. In the case of migrants from South China to Southeast Asia, such as to a town or city in Malaysia or Indonesia, they came into contact not only with the indigenous people but also with Chinese others – namely, Hokkien, Hakka, Cantonese, Teochiu, Hainanese and others. While a Minnan person from Yongchun, for example, knows that he or she is a Yongchunren (that is, a Yongchun person), in Malaysia for instance, he not only identifies with fellow Yongchunrens but also with the other Minnan people called "Hokkien" in Southeast Asia, with whom he shares intelligible Minnan dialects. And the Hokkiens form group alignment in relation to the Cantonese, Hakka and Chinese from other provinces. In fact, the Hokkiens also distinguish themselves from migrants from other parts of Fujian with whom they do not share intelligible dialects, such as the Fuzhou people from East Fujian. Today in Malaysia, the Hokkiens, Cantonese and Chinese of other origins align themselves as *huaren* (ethnic Chinese) in relation to the Malays, Indians and others with whom they need to compete for resources and ethnic rights in the new nation-state. Both migration and state processes bring about new group alignment and ethnic consciousness.

Before migration from an ethnic homeland in China, people take for granted their belonging to a *ren* ("people" in Chinese) and do not articulate as an ethnic group in relation to another similarly organized group. Nicole Constable, who studied Hakka migrants in Hong Kong, found that her old informants had similar experiences, and an old man told her that it was not until his arrival in Hong Kong from his Hakka homeland in Meixian in Guangdong that he realized there were different kinds of Chinese.[20] Similar processes appear to have taken place among South Asian migrants, for we know that Indians of different origins in Malaysia and Singapore have identified themselves as "Indians."[21] "Those who do not think of themselves as Indians before migration become Indians in the diaspora," writes Peter van der Veer.[22] He writes about migratory experience and the strategy of having a more embracing form of identification. This embracing identification needs to be seen in specific national contexts, for even among the migrants from India there can be different diasporas based on religious and ethnic diversities.

Indeed, the nature and dynamics of group alignment depend on local politics and group diversities. In the contemporary United States, the relatively small population of Chinese has encouraged them to identify not just as Chinese Americans but also as "Asian Americans," so as to cooperate with Japanese, Koreans and other Asians in their political participation in mainstream American society. While "Asia" is merely a convenient label that the "West" has used to refer to the countries in the East, and while people in Asia do not really identify themselves as "Asians," in the United States today Asians as "Asian Americans" has become a convenient ethnic category. Anyway, migrants and their descendants in their ethnic articulation use history, tradition and common destiny to assert their identity.

While ethnicity is shaped by migration experience and state politics, the migrants' cultural identity is also very much influenced by localization. A result of localization is the formation of a particular kind of cultural identity of the migrants and their descendants. By this I refer to the cultural expression of a people's way of life. Obviously localization culturally transforms the migrants and their descendants, such that the ethnic Chinese and ethnic Indians are culturally different from similar people in China or India. Different ways and degrees of localization also culturally distinguish the ethnic Chinese or Indians among themselves, even within a country. Thus the localized Hokkiens in Penang, Kelantan and in different parts of Sarawak, all in Malaysia, are in some ways culturally distinct. This affects the perception of their cultural identities and even their ethnic consciousness as Chinese.

Remigration, especially of the ethnic Chinese or ethnic Indians who are already culturally localized in a particular country, produces multiple layers of cultural identity and ethnic identification as the remigrants experience a new process of localization. Jiemin Bao's study of Chinese Thai migrants in the United States is an interesting example, showing that the people of Chinese descent who have remigrated and settled in the United States identify as Thai Chinese, Thai, Chinese Americans and Asian Americans,[23] and they can remain culturally Chinese, Thai and American. This is an interesting case of migration, remigration, ethnicity and identity. We learn from the experience of the Chinese in Southeast Asia that once they have been highly localized, the acculturated features – such as the Chinese Indonesian speaking Bahasa Indonesia, or the Chinese Thai speaking Thai – do not just become insignificant after remigration to another country. In fact language and food are intimate cultural features and remigrants may continue to be attached to their formerly localized language and food. This is so also with the "returned overseas Chinese" (*guiqiao*) in China from Indonesia, as they continue to speak Bahasa Indonesia and regional languages from Indonesia, such as Javanese or Balinese, depending on which part of Indonesia they have remigrated from.[24]

There are some significant works, too, on the migration, remigration and transnational networks of the Indian diasporas. The remigration of Surinam Hindus to the Netherlands, for instance, is an interesting case for comparison with the remigration of the localized Chinese from Surinam to the Netherlands.[25] Equally interesting is the study of remigration to the original homeland. Vibha Puri Chandra, for example, describes the migration of the Patidar community to East Africa and its remigration to Gujarat, India. In East Africa the Patidars adopted a Brahmanical lifestyle and a new name, Patidar, to replace their former tribal name, Kanbi. They remigrated to India with accumulated wealth and the whole community was able to move up to a higher caste status.[26] Mark-Anthony Falzon's study of the Hindu Sindhis in Malta, London and Bombay (Mumbai), to give another example, provides an excellent account of the migration, remigration and Sindwork, which refers to a type of long-distance translocal commerce practiced by the Sindhis. The Sindhi migrants, called Sindworkis, were merchants from Hyderabad (in modern Pakistan) who, beginning in the nineteenth century, left their families behind in search of business opportunities all over the world. As a result of many migrations, today the Hindu Sindhis are dispersed "in well over a hundred countries."[27]

While ethnic alignment and identification is cultivated by local and global political processes, cultural identity is similarly influenced. As we have seen, localization is an important process that continuously influenced the production of cultural identity. Scholars like Stuart Hall have reminded us that identity is produced and is "always in process" and that its representation is necessarily *positioned.* Cultural identity is "a matter of 'becoming' as well as of 'being.'"[28] While scholars today generally reject seeing identity as essentialized in terms of sharing a common culture, in my view, the essentialized features, be they cultural traditions or historical constructions, are important to people articulating ethnicity and identity. In fact, essentialized components are always present in one's conception of identity in the form of "being." The comparative study of Chinese and Indians in global distribution will contribute to our understanding of identity formation and the politics of identity.

Transnational Networks

The nature and implication of transnational networks are important in the study of diasporas, and there is much to learn from a comparative study of Chinese and Indian diasporas and ethnic communities. There is the study in global networks and there is the study of transnational networks. While there have been transnational networks even in past migrations, transnational networking is much more convenient, frequent and intense in our contemporary world. Anthropologists have often cited Schiller, Basch and Blanc-Szanton[29] in their definition of transnationalism as "the processes by which immigrants build social fields that link together their country of origin and their country of settlement." How migrants affect the politics of their country of origin, for instance, is an important topic of study. In the study of Chinese and Indian diasporas, Chinese and Indians overseas do have an important impact on the political development in India and China. In fact migrants and their descendants have always had significant political influence in their homeland of emigration. This is obvious when one sees the roles of overseas Chinese in the 1911 Revolution of China or the roles of overseas Indians in the Indian independence movement. Today China has opened up economically but, compared to India, it is rather authoritarian in political suppression and the lack of the freedom of expression. What will be interesting to watch are the roles the Chinese in diasporas might play in promoting democratic reforms in China. We already know the significant roles played by the Taiwanese in America in contributing to democratic development in Taiwan.[30] Similarly, there are some works on the impact of the Indians in global distribution on the political and economic development in India.[31]

In this highly globalized world characterized by "an overwhelming sense of compression of our spatial and temporal worlds,"[32] no doubt brought about by technology and global capitalism, economic transnationalism is already taken for granted. Indeed it is increasingly common to see diasporic Chinese leaving their wives in America or in Australia to return to work in China, or conducting businesses in China out of their base in, for instance, the United States.[33] These diasporic Chinese and Indians contribute to both their site of diaspora and to their original homeland. The Chinese and Indians have significant presence in the Silicon Valley in the United States, while those who return to work in China or India contribute to technological development and business there, too. Comparative study of Chinese and Indian transnational migrants as well as the activities of Chinese and Indians in global capitalism will no doubt shed more light on migrants and modern capitalism as well as on economic transnationalism. One interesting topic to compare is the philanthropic contribution and the remittances sent from the diasporas to the ancestral homeland, as there are already some significant works on both the Chinese and the Indians with regards to these aspects.[34]

On the social side of transnationalism, two features, namely kinship and religion, which are not bounded by national boundaries, have been important in the transnational processes since early Chinese and Indian migration. Since the early migration, Chinese migrants had been able to maintain some links with their family members in China, some more than others. I have shown that as the local-born generations of ethnic Chinese do not have immediate kin in their ancestral homeland in China, religion plays an even more significant role in bridging the many Chinese overseas, especially via trips organized by Chinese clan and hometown associations, with *qiaoxiang* (emigrant regions) in China.[35] A clan ancestral tomb, for example, brings together Chinese of the same clan from within and without China. Similarly, the original temple in China honouring a deity attracts "pilgrimages" (*jinxiang*) from Chinese overseas, as in the case of the link between Phoenix Mountain Temple (Fengshan Si) in Nan'an, Fujian, and the many similar temples in Malaysia and Singapore. The patron deity honoured in these temples is Guangze Zunwang.

In terms of transnational kin networks between ethnic Chinese and China and ethnic Indians and India, there is one important difference. The establishment of the Peoples' Republic of China in 1949 cut off many Chinese overseas from China, and since then most Chinese had taken up local citizenship where available. It is only after 1978 that transnational kin networks were revived with much impact in the emigrant regions of China, contributing to the revival of lineages and the renovation or building of ancestral temples. In the case of South Asians and countries in South Asia, the transnational links have not been disrupted except for the period during the Second World War. To this day we find that there are Indians in Malaysia, Singapore and Hong Kong, for example, who continue to find spouses in their ancestral homeland in South Asia. While the new migrants today, whether Chinese or South Asians, are able to maintain close kin links with relatives in China and India respectively, ethnic "Indians" more than ethnic Chinese have been keeping continuous and, I suspect, closer kin ties with their original homeland.

The tradition of matchmaking by parents reinforces this kind of transnational network among the South Asians. Ka-Kin Cheuk's study of Sikhs in Hong Kong and Punjab shows the significance of transnational family connections not only between Hong Kong and India but also with other Sikhs worldwide.[36] The visits to the Punjabi homeland further provide opportunities for making contacts with Sikhs from different parts of the world. In fact, many Sikhs in Hong Kong buy land in India with the intention of retiring there. Religion also plays an important part in the Sikhs' transnational experience, as they not only participate in their local places of worship (*gurdwaras*) outside Punjab, they also identify with the Golden Temple in India. Like Muslims, Sikhs worldwide have a common sacred place of pilgrimage. In the case of South Asians practicing Hinduism, their religion plays an important role in their local social life wherever they are, but is there a similar kind of religious transnationalism between South Asians overseas and the temples in India, as in the case of ethnic Chinese and Chinese in diaspora? Comparative research is needed here.

Conclusion

Chinese and Indians form major populations in global distribution, and they make up the most important components of people seen as Asians. In fact, the presence of people of South Asian origin is so significant in the United Kingdom that the term "Asians" is usually associated with them, unlike in North America where the term is more associated with the Chinese, Japanese and Koreans. The growing importance of China and India in the world economy and politics in the twenty-first century makes their presence even more noticeable. Indeed, among the Chinese and Indian diasporas, in contrast to the ethnic Chinese and Indians, many still consider China and India as their homeland and country of identification. Nationalism thus transcends geographical boundaries and the people involved include those in the diasporas. These diasporic Chinese and Indians no doubt contribute to the economic and political development of China and India.

China and India as lands of Chinese and Indian civilization are culturally relevant to both diasporic and most ethnic Chinese and Indians. But they do not form a global Chinese or Indian "nation." Nevertheless, as I have discussed in the case of the Chinese overseas, there is an unbounded ethnicity that they can identify with when needed, such as when joining forces with other CDN against the discrimination of particular CDN or identifying with Chinese civilization. For lack of a suitable term, I have referred to this as "civilizational ethnicity."[37] While Chinese of different nationalities have their respective local identification, individuals can also identify as "Chinese" or "Huaren" in an unbounded way to identify with other Chinese of different ethnicity.[38] I am not happy with the term "civilizational ethnicity" for this kind of ethnic affinity. Perhaps a more specific alternative like "transnational Chinese ethnicity" or "transnational Sikh ethnicity" can be used to refer to this kind of unbounded ethnic identification.

As we read, new migrants continue to migrate from China and South Asia, and the diasporas are formed by continuous processes of migration and remigration. Diasporas are always in transition, as old migrants and their descendants identify with the land of their residence, a locality from where they spin their transnational networks. As old migrants and their offspring take root in a new land, new migrants arrive, while some of the old migrants may remigrate to other places in this globalized world, becoming diasporic all over again. Diasporas thus have become part of the modern time–space compressed world, and it is becoming increasingly common that people have multiple homelands as they remigrate. Homeland is then part of "an ongoing transnational network" and not "something simply left behind but [...] a place of attachment in a contrapuntal modernity."[39] At the same time, more and more people are having transnational families, with members spread over different parts of the world.

Acknowledgement: I thank Dr Jayati Bhattacharya for her comments on this paper, which helped me to improve my description of the Indian diasporas. I remain responsible for all the analyses.

Notes

1 Wang Gungwu, "A Single Chinese Diaspora?" in *Imaging the Chinese Diaspora: Two Australian Perspectives*, by Wang Gungwu and Annette Shun Wah (Canberra: Centre for the Study of the Chinese Southern Diaspora, Australian National University, 1999), pp. 1–17. Reprinted in Wang Gungwu, *Joining the Modern World: Inside and Outside China* (Singapore: Singapore University Press, 2000), pp. 37–70.

2 Tan Chee Beng, "Comments by Tan Chee Beng," in *Ethnic Chinese as Southeast Asians*, ed. Leo Suryadinata (Singapore: Institute of Southeast Asian Studies, 1997), pp. 25–32.

3 Robin Cohen, "Diasporas, the Nation-State, and Globalization," in *Global History and Migrations*, ed. Wang Gungwu (Boulder, CO: West View Press, 1997), p. 122.

4 Robin Cohen, *Global Diasporas: An Introduction* (London and New York: Routledge, 2008), p. 61.

5 Tan Chee-Beng, "Introduction: Chinese Overseas, Transnational Networks, and China," in *Chinese Transnational Networks*, ed. Tan Chee-Beng (London: Routledge, 2007), p. 7.

6 Rhacel Salazar Parreñas and Lok C. D. Siu, "Introduction: Asian Diasporas – New Conceptions, New Frameworks," in *Asian Diasporas: New Formations, New Conceptions*, ed. Rhacel S. Parreñas and Lok C. D. Siu (Stanford, CA: Stanford University Press, 2007), p. 1.

7 Tan Chee-Beng, "The Northern Chinese of Sabah, Malaysia: Origin and Some Sociocultural Aspects," *Asian Culture* (Singapore), no. 21 (1997): 19–37. The Chinese immigrants from Tianjin arrived in Sabah in 1913, but a number of people returned to China because they could not adjust to the hot climate.

8 The Babas in Malacca are Chinese who have become so localized that they generally speak a Malay creole (called Baba Malay) among themselves, and English is widely spoken, too. Specifically "Baba" refers to the men while the women are called "Nyonya," and the older women today generally still wear sarongs and the Indonesian-style *kebaya* blouse. The Malacca Babas also refer to themselves as "Peranakan"; that is, they are Chinese Peranakans, and they are comparable to the Chinese Peranakans in Indonesia. Historically, the Babas in Singapore originally came from Malacca, and so they were culturally similar to those in Malacca. However, "Penang Babas" were localized Chinese who spoke a localized Penang version of Hokkien, which has come to be known as Penang Hokkien. The educated among the Penang Babas were English speaking, too. Many of the descendants of these Baba families in Penang still see themselves as Babas. For a description of the Babas, see for example, Khoo Joo Ee, *The Straits Chinese: A Cultural History* (Amsterdam: Pepin Press, 1996); Jurgen Rudolph, *Reconstructing Identities: A Social History of the Babas in Singapore* (Aldershot, England: Ashgate, 1998); Tan Chee Beng, *The Baba of Melaka: Cultural and Identity of a Chinese Peranakan Community in Malaysia* (Petaling Jaya, Malaysia: Pelanduk, 1988); and Tan Chee-Beng, "Intermarriage and the Chinese Peranakan in Southeast Asia," in *Peranakan Chinese in a Globalizing Southeast Asia*, ed. Leo Suryadinata (Singapore: Chinese Heritage Centre, 2010), pp. 27–40.

9 See Brij V. Lal, "Indo-Fijians: Roots and Routes," in *The South Asian Diaspora: Transnational Networks and Changing Identities*, ed. Rajesh Rai and Peter Reeves (London, Routledge, 2009), pp. 89–107.

10 See Martin Baumann, "Becoming a Colour of the Rainbow: The Social Integration of Indian Hindus in Trinidad, Analysed along a Phase Model of Diaspora," in *South Asians in the Diaspora: Histories and Religious Traditions*, ed. Knut A. Jacobsen and P. Pratap Kumar (Leiden: Brill, 2004), pp. 77–96.

11 Carmen Voigt-Graf, "Transnationalism and the Indo-Fijian Diaspora: The Relationship of Indo-Fijians to India and Its People," in *Transnational Migrations: The Indian Diaspora*, ed. William Safran, Ajaya Kumar Sahoo and Brij V. Lal (London: Routledge, 2009), p. 107.

12 Parminder Bhachu, "New Cultural Forms and Transnational South Asian Women: Culture, Class, and Consumption among British South Asian Women in the Diaspora," in *Nation and Migration: The Politics of Space in the South Asian Diaspora*, ed. Peter van der Veer (Philadelphia: University of Pennsylvania Press, 1995), pp. 222–44.

13 Arjun Appadurai, *Modernity at Large: Cultural Dimensions of Globalization* (Minneapolis: University of Minnesota Press, 1996), pp. 48–85.

14 Purnima Mankekar, "'Indian Shopping': Indian Grocery Stores and Transnational Configurations of Belonging," in *The Cultural Politics of Food and Eating: A Reader*, ed. James L. Watson and Melissa L. Caldwell (Oxford: Blackwell Publishing, 2005), p. 210.

15 Wu Yanhe and Wang Weilan, "Haiwai huaren funü de shangye xingwei" [Commercial activities of overseas Chinese women], in *Dongnanya huaren shehui yanjiu* [The study of Chinese in Southeast Asia], vol. 2, ed. Li Yih-yuan and Guo Zhenyu (Taipei: Zhengzhong Shuju, 1985).

16 R. Rajoo, "Caste, Ethnicity, Class and National Unity: The Dilemma of the Indians," in *Malaysia: Ethnicity, Class and Development*, ed. S. Husin Ali (Kuala Lumpur: Persatuan Sains Sosial Malaysia, 1984), p. 215.

17 Ravindra K. Jain, "Race Relations, Ethnicity, Class and Culture: A Comparison of Indians in Trinidad and Malaysia," in *The Indian Diaspora: Dynamics of Migration*, ed. N. Jayaram (New Delhi: Sage, 2004), pp. 172–85.

18 Vibha Puri Chandra, "Remigration: Return of the Prodigals – An Analysis of the Impact of the Cycles of Migration and Remigration on the Caste Mobility," *International Migration Review* 31, no. 1 (1997): p. 163.

19 During my research on the Babas of Malacca in 1977, I visited this Chitty community a number of times. For studies on the Chitty, see for example, David J. Mearns, "Chitty Melaka: Hindus, 'Indians' or Marginal Indians?" *Contributions to Southeast Asian Ethnography*, no. 3 (1984): 72–83; and Samuel S. Dhoraisingam, *Peranakan Indians in Singapore and Melaka: Indian Babas and Nyonyas – Chitty Melaka* (Singapore: Institute of Southeast Asian Studies, 2006).

20 Nicole Constable, "History and the Construction of Hakka Identity," in *Ethnicity in Taiwan: Social, Historical, and Cultural Perspectives*, ed. Chen Chung-min, Chuang Ying-chang, and Huang Shu-min (Taipei: Institute of Ethnology, Academia Sinica, 1994), p. 78.

21 In Malaysia and Singapore, Indians are associated with South Indians, most of whom are Tamils. As R. Rajoo points out, the term Indian "came to be used widely among Indians only in recent decades as a result of political and administrative necessity." In these two countries, South Indians, North Indians and others such as Sri Lanka Tamils and Pakistanis are all classified as "Indians." See R. Rajoo, "Caste, Ethnicity, Class and National Unity: The Dilemma of the Indians," in *Malaysia: Ethnicity, Class and Development*, ed. S. Husin Ali (Kuala Lumpur: Persatuan Sains Sosial Malaysia, 1984), p. 213.

22 Peter Van der Veer, "Introduction: The Diasporic Imagination," in *Nation and Migration: The Politics of Space in the South Asian Diaspora*, ed. Peter van der Veer (Philadelphia: University of Pennsylvania Press, 1995), p. 7.

23 Jiemin Bao, "Chinese-Thai Transmigrants: Reworking Identities and Gender Relations in Thailand and the United States," *Amerasia* 25, no. 2 (1999): 95–115.

24 Cf. Michael R. Godley, "The Sojourner: Returned Overseas Chinese in the People's Republic of China," *Pacific Affairs* 62, no. 3 (1989): 330–50; and Tan Chee-Beng, "Reterritorization of a Balinese Chinese Community in Quanzhou, Fujian," *Modern Asian Studies* 44, no. 3 (2010): 547–66.

25 Corstiaan J. G. van der Burg, "The Hindu Diaspora in the Netherlands: Halfway between Local Structures and Global Ideologies," in *South Asians in the Diaspora: Histories and Religious Traditions*, ed. Knut A. Jacobsen and P. Pratap Kumar (Leiden: Brill, 2004), pp. 97–115. For a reference on the Surinam Chinese remigrating to the Netherlands, see Frank N. Pieke and Gregor Benton, "The Chinese in the Netherlands," in *The Chinese in Europe*, ed. Gregor Benton and Frank N. Pieke (London: Macmillan Press, 1998), pp. 134–5.

26 Vibha Puri Chandra, "Remigration: Return of the Prodigals – An Analysis of the Impact of the Cycles of Migration and Remigration on the Caste Mobility," *International Migration Review* 31, no. 1 (1997): 162–70.

27 Mark-Anthony Falzon, *Cosmopolitan Connections: The Sindhi Diaspora, 1860–2000* (Leiden: Brill, 2004), p. 6.

28 Stuart Hall, "Cultural Identity and Diaspora," in *Migration, Diaspora and Transnationalism*, ed. Steven Vertocec and Robin Cohen (Cheltenham and Northampton, MA: Edward Elgar, 1999), p. 302.

29 Nina Glick Schiller, Linda Basch and Cristina Blanc-Szanton, "Transnationalism: A New Analytical Framework for Understanding Migration," in *Towards a Transnational Perspective on Migration: Race, Class, Ethnicity, and Nationalism Reconsidered*, ed. Nina Glick Schiller, Linda Basch and Cristina Blanc-Szanton, Annals of the New York Academy of Sciences, vol. 645 (New York: New York Academy of Sciences, 1992), pp. 1–24.

30 Lien Pei-Te, "Transnational Homeland Concerns and Participation in US Politics: A Comparison among Immigrants from China, Taiwan, and Hong Kong," *Journal of Chinese Overseas* 2, no. 1 (2006): 56–78.

31 See for instance, Devesh Kapur, *Diaspora, Development, and Democracy: The Domestic Impact of International Migration from India* (Princeton, NJ: Princeton University Press, 2010); and Sumita Mukherjee, *Nationalism, Education and Migrant Identities: The England-Returned* (London: Routledge, 2010).

32 David Harvey, *The Condition of Post-Modernity: An Inquiry into the Origins of Cultural Change* (Oxford: Oxford University Press, 1989), p. 240.

33 Philip Yang, "Transnationalism as a New Mode of Immigrant Labor Market Incorporation: Preliminary Evidence from Chinese Transnational Migrants," *Journal of Chinese Overseas* 2, no. 2 (2006): 173–92.

34 See for example, Supriya Singh, Anuja Cabraal and Shanthi Robertson, "Remittances as a Medium of Relationship and Belonging," in *Migration, Belonging and the Nation State*, ed. Alperhan Babacan and Supriya Singh (Newcastle upon Tyne: Cambridge Scholars Publishing, 2010), pp. 85–103; Peter F. Geithner, Paula D. Johnson and Lincoln C. Chin, eds, *Diaspora Philanthropy and Equitable Development in China and India* (Cambridge, MA: Global Equity Initiative Asia Centre, Harvard University, 2004). On overseas Chinese remittances, Hamashita Takeshi, who writes mostly in Japanese, is a well-known authority.

35 Tan Chee-Beng, "The Shishan Ye People in Malaysia and the Ancestral Homeland in China," in *Chinese Transnational Networks*, ed. Tan Chee-Beng (London: Routledge, 2007), pp. 73–91.

36 Cheuk Ka-Kin, "Migration, Settlement, and Remigration: A Study of the Sikhs in Hong Kong," in *East Asia Forum – Mediation and Critique: Perspectives on East Asia* 11 (2008a): 47–81; Cheuk Ka-Kin, "Transnational Connections, Local Life, and Identity: A Study of the Sikhs in Hong Kong," MPhil thesis, Hong Kong: Chinese University of Hong Kong, 2008b.

37 Tan Chee-Beng, "Chinese in Southeast Asia and Identities in a Changing World Context," in *Chinese Populations in Contemporary Southeast Asian Societies: Identities, Interdependence and International Influence*, ed. M. Jocelyn Armstrong, R. Warwick Armstrong and Kent Mulliner (Richmond, Surrey: Curzon, 2001), pp. 210–36.

38 Tan Chee-Beng, "Chinese Identities in Malaysia," *Southeast Asian Journal of Social Science* 25, no. 2 (1997): p. 116.

39 James Clifford, *Routes: Travel and Translation in the Late Twentieth Century* (Cambridge: Harvard University Press, 1997), p. 256.

References

Appadurai, Arjun. *Modernity at Large: Cultural Dimensions of Globalization.* Minneapolis: University of Minnesota Press, 1996.

Bao, Jiemin. "Chinese-Thai Transmigrants: Reworking Identities and Gender Relations in Thailand and the United States." *Amerasia* 25, no. 2 (1999): 95–115.

Baumann, Martin. "Becoming a Colour of the Rainbow: The Social Integration of Indian Hindus in Trinidad, Analysed along a Phase Model of Diaspora." In *South Asians in the Diaspora: Histories and Religious Traditions*, edited by Knut A. Jacobsen and P. Pratap Kumar, pp. 77–96. Leiden: Brill, 2004.

Bhachu, Parminder. "New Cultural Forms and Transnational South Asian Women: Culture, Class, and Consumption among British South Asian Women in the Diaspora." In *Nation and Migration: The Politics of Space in the South Asian Diaspora*, edited by Peter van der Veer, pp. 222–44. Philadelphia: University of Pennsylvania Press, 1995.

Chandra, Vibha Puri. "Remigration: Return of the Prodigals – An Analysis of the Impact of the Cycles of Migration and Remigration on the Caste Mobility." *International Migration Review* 31, no. 1 (1997): 162–70.

Cheuk, Ka-Kin. "Migration, Settlement, and Remigration: A Study of the Sikhs in Hong Kong." *East Asia Forum – Mediation and Critique: Perspectives on East Asia* 11 (2008a): 47–81.

______. "Transnational Connections, Local Life, and Identity: A Study of the Sikhs in Hong Kong." M.Phil. thesis, Chinese University of Hong Kong, 2008b.

Clifford, James. *Routes: Travel and Translation in the Late Twentieth Century*. Cambridge, MA: Harvard University Press, 1997.

Cohen, Robin. "Diasporas, the Nation-State, and Globalization." In *Global History and Migrations*, edited by Wang Gungwu, pp. 117–43. Boulder, CO: Westview Press, 1997.

______. *Global Diaspora: An Introduction*. London and New York: Routledge, 2008.

Constable, Nicole. "History and the Construction of Hakka Identity." In *Ethnicity in Taiwan: Social, Historical, and Cultural Perspectives*, edited by Chen Chung-min, Chuang Ying-chang and Huang Shu-min, pp. 75–89. Taipei: Institute of Ethnology, Academia Sinica, 1994.

Dhoraisingam, Samuel S. *Peranakan Indians in Singapore and Melaka: Indian Babas and Nyonyas – Chitty Melaka*. Singapore: Institute of Southeast Asian Studies, 2006.

Falzon, Mark-Anthony. *Cosmopolitan Connections: The Sindhi Diaspora, 1860–2000*. Leiden: Brill, 2004.

Geithner, Peter F., Paula D. Johnson and Lincoln C. Chin, eds. *Diaspora Philanthropy and Equitable Development in China and India*. Cambridge, MA: Global Equity Initiative Asia Center, Harvard University, 2004.

Hall, Stuart. "Cultural Identity and Diaspora." In *Migration, Diaspora and Transnationalism*, edited by Steven Vertovec and Robin Cohen, pp. 222–320. Cheltenham, UK, and Northampton, MA: Edward Elgar, 1999.

Harvey, David. *The Condition of Post-Modernity: An Inquiry into the Origins of Cultural Change*. Oxford: Oxford University Press, 1989.

Jain, Ravindra K. "Race Relations, Ethnicity, Class and Culture: A Comparison of Indians in Trinidad and Malaysia." In *The Indian Diaspora: Dynamics of Migration*, edited by N. Jayaram, pp. 172–85. New Delhi: Sage, 2004.

Kapur, Devesh. *Diaspora, Development, and Democracy: The Domestic Impact of International Migration from India*. Princeton, NJ: Princeton University Press, 2010.

Khoo, Joo Ee. *The Straits Chinese: A Cultural History*. Amsterdam: Pepin Press, 1996.

Lal, Brij V. "Indo-Fijians: Roots and Routes." In *The South Asian Diaspora: Transnational Networks and Changing Identities*, edited by Rajesh Rai and Peter Reeves, pp. 89–107. London: Routledge, 2009.

Lien, Pei-Te. "Transnational Homeland Concerns and Participation in US Politics: A Comparison among Immigrants from China, Taiwan, and Hong Kong." *Journal of Chinese Overseas* 2, no. 1 (2006): 56–78.

Mankekar, Purnima. "'Indian Shopping': Indian Grocery Stores and Transnational Configurations of Belonging." In *The Cultural Politics of Food and Eating: A Reader*, edited by James L. Watson and Melissa L. Caldwell, pp. 197–214. Oxford: Blackwell, 2005.

Mearns, David J. "Chitty Melaka: Hindus, 'Indians' or Marginal Indians?" *Contributions to Southeast Asian Ethnography*, no. 3 (1984): 72–83.

______. *Shiva's Other Children: Religion and Social Identity amongst Overseas Indians*. Thousand Oaks, CA: Sage, 1995.

Mukherjee, Sumita. *Nationalism, Education and Migrant Identities: The England-Returned*. London: Routledge, 2010.

Parreñas, Rhacel Salazar and Lok C. D. Siu. "Introduction: Asian Diasporas – New Conceptions, New Frameworks." In *Asian Diasporas: New Formations, New Conceptions*, edited by Rhacel S. Parreñas and Lok C. D. Siu, pp. 1–27. Stanford, CA: Stanford University Press, 2007.

Pieke, Frank N. and Gregor Benton, "The Chinese in the Netherlands." In *The Chinese in Europe*, edited by Gregor Benton and Frank N. Pieke, pp. 125–67. London: Macmillan, 1998.

Rajoo, R. "Caste, Ethnicity, Class and National Unity: The Dilemma of the Indians." In *Malaysia: Ethnicity, Class and Development*, edited by S. Husin Ali, pp. 212–23. Kuala Lumpur: Persatuan Sains Sosial Malaysia, 1984.

Rudolph, Jurgen. *Reconstructing Identities: A Social History of the Babas in Singapore*. Aldershot: Ashgate, 1998.

Schiller, Nina Glick, Linda Basch and Cristina Blanc-Szanton. "Transnationalism: A New Analytical Framework for Understanding Migration." In *Towards a Transnational Perspective on Migration: Race, Class, Ethnicity, and Nationalism Reconsidered*, edited by Nina Glick Schiller, Linda Basch and Cristina Blanc-Szanton, pp. 1–24. Annals of the New York Academy of Sciences, vol. 645. New York: New York Academy of Sciences, 1992.

Singh, Supriya, Anuja Cabraal and Shanthi Robertson. "Remittances as a Medium of Relationship and Belonging." In *Migration, Belonging and the Nation State*, edited by Alperhan Babacan and Supriya Singh, pp. 85–103. Newcastle upon Tyne: Cambridge Scholars Publishing, 2010.

Tan, Chee Beng. "Chinese Identities in Malaysia." *Southeast Asian Journal of Social Science* 25, no. 2 (1997c): 103–16.

______. "Chinese in Southeast Asia and Identities in a Changing World Context." In *Chinese Populations in Contemporary Southeast Asian Societies: Identities, Interdependence and International Influence*, edited by M. Jocelyn Armstrong, R. Warwick Armstrong and Kent Mulliner, pp. 210–36. Richmond: Curzon, 2001.

______. "Comments by Tan Chee Beng." In *Ethnic Chinese as Southeast Asians*, edited by Leo Suryadinata, pp. 25–32. Singapore: Institute of Southeast Asian Studies, 1997a.

______. "Intermarriage and the Chinese Peranakan in Southeast Asia." In *Peranakan Chinese in a Globalizing Southeast Asia*, edited by Leo Suryadinata, pp. 27–40. Singapore: Chinese Heritage Centre, 2010.

______. "Introduction: Chinese Overseas, Transnational Networks, and China." In *Chinese Transnational Networks*, edited by Tan Chee-Beng, pp. 1–19. London: Routledge, 2007a.

______. *The Baba of Melaka: Culture and Identity of a Chinese Peranakan Community in Malaysia*. Petaling Jaya, Malaysia: Pelanduk, 1988.

______. "The Northern Chinese of Sabah, Malaysia: Origin and Some Sociocultural Aspects." *Asian Culture* (Singapore), no. 21 (1997b): 19–37.

______. "The Shishan Ye People in Malaysia and the Ancestral Homeland in China." In *Chinese Transnational Networks*, edited by Tan Chee-Beng, pp. 73–91. London: Routledge, 2007b.

Van Der Burg, Corstiaan J. G. "The Hindu Diaspora in the Netherlands: Halfway between Local Structures and Global Ideologies." In *South Asians in the Diaspora: Histories and Religious Traditions*, edited by Knut A. Jacobsen and P. Pratap Kumar, pp. 97–115. Leiden: Brill, 2004.

Van der Veer, Peter. "Introduction: The Diasporic Imagination." In *Nation and Migration: The Politics of Space in the South Asian Diaspora*, edited by Peter van der Veer, pp. 1–16. Philadelphia: University of Pennsylvania Press, 1995.

Voigt-Graf, Carmen. "Transnationalism and the Indo-Fijian Diaspora: The Relationship of Indo-Fijians to India and Its People." In *Transnational Migrations: The Indian Diaspora*, edited by William Safran, Ajaya Kumar Sahoo and Brij V. Lal, pp. 97–135. London: Routledge, 2009.

Wang, Gungwu. "A Single Chinese Diaspora?" In *Imaging the Chinese Diaspora: Two Australian Perspectives*, by Wang Gungwu and Annette Shun Wah, pp. 1–17. Canberra: Centre for the Study of the Chinese Southern Diaspora, Australian National University, 1999. Reprinted in Wang Gungwu, *Joining the Modern World: Inside and Outside China*, pp. 37–70. Singapore, Singapore University Press, World Scientific, 2000.

Wu, Yanhe and Wang Weilan. "Haiwai huaren funü de shangye xingwei" [Commercial activities of overseas Chinese women]. In *Dongnanya huaren shehui yanjiu* [The study of Chinese in Southeast Asia], vol. 2, edited by Li Yih-yuan and Guo Zhenyu, pp. 141–64. Taipei: Zhengzhong Shuju, 1985.

Yang, Philip. "Transnationalism as a New Mode of Immigrant Labor Market Incorporation: Preliminary Evidence from Chinese Transnational Migrants." *Journal of Chinese Overseas* 2, no. 2 (2006): 173–92.

Section II

THE MEETING GROUND: INDIANS AND CHINESE IN SOUTHEAST ASIA

Chapter 4

CHINA'S NATIONALITY LAWS AND THE CHINESE OVERSEAS

Leo Suryadinata

Introduction[1]

Nationality or citizenship is the product of the modern nation-state. It began in the West, where the first nation-states emerged. When Westerners came to Asia they brought with them this concept with some modifications. In response, Asian countries began to formulate their own nationality laws or citizenship laws in the twentieth century, especially after they gained political independence. China was one of the first in Asia to announce its nationality law in 1909. It is also clear that nationality/citizenship law is linked to foreign policy, or is meant to serve the "national interest" of a state as well as its domestic politics. This argument also applies to the case of China.

The history of nationality/citizenship law of China has not been long. The law began during the end of the Qing dynasty (1644–1911), about three years prior to its demise. It was first reissued in 1912 by the Republic of China (1912–49) under the Guomindang, and again in 1929 after the Guomindang reunited South and North China. When the People's Republic of China (PRC) came into existence in 1949, the old nationality law was still in use, until the 1955 Afro-Asian Conference in Bandung, when Zhou Enlai, then the prime minister of the PRC, offered the solution of dual nationality status for overseas Chinese between China and Southeast Asian countries. However, there was no PRC nationality law *proper* until September 1980.

Therefore when we talk about China's nationality law today, we are in fact referring to the 1980 nationality law. What are the differences between the 1980 nationality law and those prior to that? What are the contents of the 1980 law? Why was it promulgated and what has been the impact on the "Chinese overseas"? Has this law, which was issued over thirty years ago, been amended? Have there been any problems for China in implementing this law, and what have been the responses of the Afro-Asian states, especially the Southeast Asian states, where about 80 per cent of the Chinese overseas are residing? These are some of the issues that this paper attempts to address.

Prior to discussing the 1980 law, it is important to examine the earlier nationality laws issued by both the Qing dynasty and the Republican government.

The 1909 Law: Dual Nationality Status

China's first "nationality law" was issued in 1909 at a time when the Qing dynasty was facing tremendous difficulties, especially in dealing with the "overseas Chinese." It was argued that the law was a reaction to the Dutch government, which intended to declare the Chinese in the Dutch East Indies (Colonial Indonesia) Dutch subjects. Fearing tremendous pressure, many China-born migrant Chinese appealed to the Qing government to promulgate a nationality law which would enable them to remain as subjects under the protection of the Qing dynasty.

In fact, the Qing government had earlier realized the importance of the overseas Chinese. Prior to the appeal of the Chinese in the Dutch East Indies, it had already negotiated with the Dutch authorities on their rights in the Indies. Nevertheless, the pressure of the Chinese officials in colonial Indonesia hastened the process whereby the Qing nationality law came into being. In 1909 it promulgated the first nationality law, stipulating that all Chinese born in and outside China were "nationals" (subjects) of Imperial China.

Because of this law, the Dutch hurriedly issued the Nederlandsch Onderdaanschap (Dutch subject-ship law) the following year, making it mandatory for all Chinese born in the Dutch East Indies (mainly Peranakan)[2] to be classified as Dutch subjects. Therefore, both the Chinese and Dutch governments were claiming jurisdiction over the Chinese in the Dutch East Indies. Negotiations between China and the Netherlands, which had begun in 1908 but soon stalled, were resumed in 1910 in The Hague. The talk led to a consular treaty between the Netherlands and Imperial China in 1911, with China acknowledging that the Dutch East Indies–born Chinese in the Netherlands and its territories were subject to Dutch law. But they were free to choose either Chinese nationality or Dutch subject-ship if they left the Dutch territories. In return, the Dutch agreed to the establishment of a Chinese consulate in the Dutch East Indies, which would primarily serve as a commercial agency.

China had not abandoned its claim over the overseas Chinese, but merely agreed to the application of the Dutch law to the Peranakan Chinese when they were in the Indies for practical purposes. By then the Dutch East Indies–born Chinese were holding dual nationality. It should be noted that strictly speaking, subject-ship was not really citizenship, but a position with a lower status than citizenship or nationality. The Dutch East Indies–born Chinese were thus Dutch subjects, but not Dutch nationals. This was also the case with the Straits-born Chinese in Malaya and Singapore, who were British subjects but not British nationals. Nevertheless, to simplify the matter, when discussing Chinese nationality during the colonial period we often do not differentiate these two concepts. As in the case of the Peranakan Chinese in Java, the Straits-born Chinese held dual "nationality" (subject-ship) status.

However, the Qing dynasty did not have much time to implement the 1909 "nationality law" as it was overthrown during the 1911 revolution; nevertheless the law served as a basis for the subsequent nationality law in Republican China.

The 1929 Law: Still Dual Nationality Status

There is no doubt that the 1912 law and the 1929 law were both based on the 1909 law; the 1912 nationality law had been in force before the unification of North and South China. Many overseas Chinese hence held dual nationality, the case in point being the Indies-born Chinese. It was not a problem as long as the person concerned stayed within Dutch territory. But when he/she went to China, the person would automatically be subjected to Chinese law. A notable case concerned Oen Keng Hian, a Peranakan Chinese who committed an offence in Java and fled to China. Oen was arrested in China at the request of the Dutch government, who attempted to have him extradited to the Indies to be tried there under Dutch law, but the Chinese government rejected the request as Oen was a Chinese national according to Chinese law. China won the case and Oen could only be tried in the Chinese court in Shanghai.[3]

The 1929 law was the first Guomindang law after Chiang Kai-shek succeeded in unifying China. It used the *jus sanguinis* (birth or blood 血統主義) rather than *jus soli* (birth place 出生地主義) as the principle of Chinese nationality law. Under this nationality law, "no Chinese could divest himself of his nationality without first obtaining a certificate of denationalization from the Ministry of the Interior, and such a certificate was rarely gained."[4]

A number of factors contributed to the *jus sanguinis*–based nationality law. Guomindang China, like its predecessor, was aware of the value of the overseas Chinese. It intended to keep them culturally and politically loyal to China. Throughout Southeast Asia the Guomindang supported Chinese schools as part of Chinese education and encouraged Chinese nationalism. However, so long as Southeast Asian countries remained under colonial rule, where they could be portrayed as struggling against Western imperialism, they provided Chinese nationalism the opportunity to coexist with Southeast Asian nationalism. (The exception was Thailand, where there was a clash between Chinese nationalism and Thai nationalism.) Nevertheless, Chinese nationalism posed a challenge to Southeast Asian nationalism after independence.

The 1955 Afro-Asian Conference and After: Towards the Single Nationality Status

The PRC was established on 1 October 1949, but there was initially no PRC nationality law. In the absence of this new law, it seemed that the 1929 Guomindang law was still in use, although it was modified. The Fifth National People's Congress eventually adopted the PRC nationality law thirty-one years later, on 10 September 1980.

Why did the PRC only issue this law in 1980, not earlier? I have argued that the ASEAN countries (at that time only comprising six countries) had been sensitive to the ethnic Chinese issue and the Deng Xiaoping group appeared to have appreciated this more after Deng's Asian tour in 1978. The new PRC nationality law can be seen as a means to win the trust of ASEAN leaders, especially after the Sino-Vietnamese conflict in early 1979. Beijing, in its effort to break the perceived encirclement of the Soviet–Vietnamese alliance, wanted to woo the ASEAN states. It is thus not surprising that there was a promulgation of the nationality law of the PRC after Sino-Vietnamese relations deteriorated.

In fact, the principles used in the 1980 law were practiced by the PRC as early as 1955 when Premier Zhou Enlai introduced his "good neighbour" policy, which intended to solve the dual nationality problem. Aware of the suspicion of the new Southeast Asian governments, Zhou was willing to sign a dual nationality agreement with Southeast Asian countries which had sizeable Chinese communities. Once such an agreement was signed, local Chinese could only have one nationality. In other words, an ethnic Chinese was required to choose one nationality and renounce the other, but only Indonesia signed such a treaty. This was during the Cold War, when many non-communist and anti-communist Southeast Asian countries remained strongly suspicious of the PRC until the normalization of relations between Washington and Beijing took place in the early 1970s.

Nevertheless, it took another few years before Malaysia, the Philippines and Thailand established diplomatic ties with the PRC. It is important to note that in all communiqués, China required the signatory country to recognize a one-China policy – that the PRC was the only China and the signatory country would not establish diplomatic ties with Taiwan (Republic of China). In return, the PRC would recognize that Chinese overseas could only acquire a single nationality, as China did not recognize dual nationality (dual citizenship).[5] (Nevertheless, it is worth noting that all the communiqués have a clause that the acquisition of local citizenship should be based on one's own free will.)

In other words, Beijing renounced its judiciary power over the Chinese who chose foreign citizenship in order to show to the Southeast Asian governments that it would like to establish friendly relations with them. During that period, many Southeast Asian states were newly independent, and were at the stage of "nation building." They were suspicious of the PRC, which was not only different ideologically but also projected a revolutionary image. However, Chinese leaders such as Zhou Enlai considered the so-called "Chinese problem" a historical legacy to be resolved in order to promote good relations with local governments. It seemed that Zhou was sincere, and his government encouraged local Chinese to choose local citizenship and integrate themselves into local societies. The 1980 law thus perpetuated this policy of rejecting dual nationality.

The 1980 Law: Single Nationality Status and Its Challenges

The law consists of 18 articles. It reinforces the notion that the persons belonging to any nationalities of China have Chinese nationality. But those who settle abroad can no longer have Chinese nationality if they accept foreign nationality of their own free will.[6] In discussing the 1980 law, Johannes Chan forcefully argued that it "reaffirms the principles of the *jus sanguinis* and non-recognition of dual nationality." On denationalization, it adopts a more liberal approach: "While maintaining the general principle of no-denationalization without the government's consent, it allows, for the first time, automatic loss of Chinese nationality for those who have settled abroad and have acquired a foreign nationality of their own free will."[7] The promulgation of the 1980 nationality law only reaffirmed the existing national status of the Chinese in Southeast Asia. This has officially resolved the dual nationality problem between China and Southeast Asian countries with significant ethnic Chinese minorities.

However, with the end of the Cold War and the rise of China as an economic if not a political and military power, accompanied by the new wave of Chinese immigration to the West, "returned overseas Chinese" and some new migrants began to question the "old policy" of single nationality status. They thought that many Chinese in reality had dual nationality or multi-nationality. China should not be afraid of offending other countries and it should not introduce a single nationality policy. However, this view was overruled by Deng Xiaoping.[8]

Around 1994, there was again a discussion on Chinese nationality among these "returned overseas Chinese." Although they no longer directly made demands for dual nationality status, they urged the Beijing government to make it easy for foreign Chinese to become Chinese nationals again.[9] They also argued that the PRC nationality law had been issued at a specific time for Southeast Asia where the majority of Chinese overseas had been domiciled. However, to date, the situation had changed in that the centres of the ethnic Chinese were no longer concentrated in that region but had expanded to North America and Europe.[10] With the rise of a new "Overseas Chinese Centre" it was necessary for China to have a new policy towards the ethnic Chinese.

Interestingly, the ones to raise this issue were not Southeast Asians, but the Chinese in China. In 1999, during the National Overseas Chinese Affairs Working Committee Meeting held in Qingdao, Shandong Province, a Chinese leader from the Overseas Chinese Affairs Office under the State Council called for the dual citizenship status of Chinese overseas to be revived.

In the same year, during the second session of the 9th People's Political Consultative Conference (PPCC), Chen Duo, Ye Peiying[11] and 10 other committee members made a proposal (no. 2172) suggesting that "the dual nationality status of Chinese nationals should have not been abrogated."

In 2004, during the second session of the 10th PPCC, another proposal (no. 0222) was made to amend the part of the PRC's constitution relating to the citizenship law, so that Beijing "can selectively recognize the dual nationality status."[12] In response to such developments, Hong Kong TV channels and Internet websites hosted a debate on the issue of the Chinese dual citizenship status, which had been temporarily put aside without being completely resolved at the time. If dual nationality status is revived, what will its impact be on the ethnic Chinese in Southeast Asia in general and in Malaysia in particular? This is an interesting topic for discussion and study. First of all, let us look at the developments of Chinese nationality law from the Qing dynasty to Republican China in order to understand the current situation.

To the best of my knowledge it was never put forward officially in the People's Congress before 1999. It was only in 1999 that the proposal of re-examining the 1980 nationality law was raised in the People's Political Consultative Conference.

Why Dual Nationality?

Why did some of the overseas Chinese officials in China raise the issue at this time? This is related to the new wave of Chinese migrants, often known as *xin yimin*. In addition, it has something to do with the re-emergence of Chinese nationalism in China together with the rise of China as a new economic giant. Originally, the voices came from these *xin yimin* or the first generation Chinese migrants from Canada, New Zealand, the United States[13] and of course some Chinese leaders in Beijing.

Those who agreed with the dual national status for the Chinese overseas argued that there are benefits for both the PRC and the Chinese:[14]

1. It is beneficial to attract a large number of talent, technology, capital and experience; because those with dual nationality can enter and leave the country freely, they will bring more business, remittances and taxes.
2. With dual nationality, the Chinese overseas will be oriented towards China, to defend national interests; individuals from overseas can be invited back to be a member of the People's Congress as a Chinese citizen, to express their views and contribute to the development of China.
3. As Chinese nationals, they will foster and support the unification of China, rather than support Taiwan's independence.
4. It will be easy for China to manage these Chinese; if they commit crimes in China, they can be tried in accordance with Chinese law and thus not jeopardize the interests of China.
5. Many countries in the West (e.g., the United States, Canada and Australia) recognize dual nationality status.

In short, this group argues that dual nationality would bring both political and economic benefits to China and provide the Chinese overseas an emotional platform for their sentiment for the traditional motherland. If we examine the above argument, it is clear that it strongly reflects China's domestic point of view, and it represents the idea of new Chinese migrants to the West rather than old migrants in Southeast Asia. In addition, the benefits that the group mention may not necessarily be true; implementation may jeopardize Beijing's foreign policy interests. Below are the pitfalls of the above-mentioned arguments:

1. The first point assumes that the majority of the Chinese overseas with skills and capital want to obtain dual nationality (one of them being PRC nationality). In fact, many Chinese overseas may not be interested in having PRC nationality at all. The argument that dual nationality will give the overseas Chinese the freedom to move around in China is false. The "green card" (PR status) policy, which was implemented in 2004, will serve this purpose; one does not have to change his/her nationality status. Therefore, the argument that a dual nationality policy will bring more business, remittances and taxes is questionable.
2. This argument assumes that the majority of overseas Chinese are interested in participating in China's politics, which may not be the case at all.

3. The Chinese overseas are not a homogeneous group and they have different ideologies. Many are loyal to their adopted country. It is also a fact that Mainland China and Taiwan are still separated, and the Chinese overseas are also divided in their views. It is unrealistic to expect that the Chinese overseas will support only Beijing.
4. The Chinese nationality status for the "overseas Chinese" would enable the Chinese government to arrest and try nationals who have committed all sorts of crimes (including "political crimes") in China. It is also possible that the Chinese government would use the nationality issue as a foreign policy tool. But it may not be without problems (see the opposition argument below). To use the nationality issue to intervene in another country's domestic affairs would not be welcome by the country concerned.
5. Every country has a different historical background and China does not have to follow other countries if this is neither in the national interest of China nor in the group interest of the Chinese overseas. In fact, the United States began to review the dual nationality status of people from some countries after the 9/11 incident.

Opposition to Dual Nationality

However, those who disagree are from Southeast Asia, or "returned overseas Chinese" scholars from the Southeast Asian region. They maintain that dual nationality status would harm Chinese individuals, China and interstate relations. Their views are reflected in the following:[15]

1. It would jeopardize China's relations with friendly states; they would begin to suspect the motives of China in reintroducing dual nationality.
2. It would also create problems for the Chinese individuals concerned, with regard to their rights and obligations.
3. Citizens holding dual nationality who receive discriminatory treatment from one country will not be able to seek protection from the other country, as each of the two countries have equal rights.
4. The question of allegiance to two countries would put individuals in a very difficult position.
5. Also, the dual nationality status often gives rise to diplomatic problems and conflicts: for instance, when a Chinese who commits a crime escapes to the other country to avoid arrest. It may also create further diplomatic problems if he/she flees to a third country.

The opposition arguments also consider the points of view from both China and the Chinese overseas. Nevertheless, it appears that this reasoning is more convincing than that of the first group. In fact, many argue that since the PRC has been gaining benefits from practicing the single nationality policy, why should it be changed at this moment if it continues to serve the interest of the PRC? Furthermore, it is also in the interest of the majority of the Chinese in Southeast Asia and beyond.

Some scholars, including Prof. Wang Lingchi (Berkeley) and Prof. Zhou Nanjing (Peking University), argue that those overseas Chinese who want dual nationality are small in number. They are either new migrants or Chinese businessmen who would like to have their cake and eat it too. But they do not represent the majority of Chinese overseas. Their attitude and interests should not prevail at the expense of the majority interest.

The Response of the PRC to New Demand

The majority of Southeast Asian states do not recognize dual nationality status for their citizens, especially citizens of Chinese descent. They introduced a single nationality policy, whereby those Chinese who became nationals of one of these countries were required to give up their other citizenship (including PRC citizenship). It is in fact an offence to hold dual nationality. If China reintroduces dual nationality to these Chinese, it will not be welcome by either the ethnic Chinese or the countries concerned. The so-called indigenous population will have more excuses to discriminate against their fellow citizens of Chinese descent.

Nevertheless, not all Chinese in Southeast Asia are Southeast Asian nationals. There are still significant numbers of alien Chinese in Southeast Asia, and the majority are Chinese nationals not affected by the dual nationality status. They have single nationality status: either from the PRC, Taiwan or other countries.

However, in the era of globalization, due to more intensive interactions between Southeast Asia and China, increasing numbers of Chinese migrants have begun to enter and reside in Southeast Asia. Even if they receive permanent resident status, they are still alien Chinese, not Southeast Asian citizens, unless they have succeeded in being granted local citizenship. Therefore the majority do not have a "dual nationality" status.

The number of Chinese new migrants is much larger in the West and Australia/New Zealand than in Southeast Asia. A significant number have also become citizens of Western countries. Some of them may not be able to integrate themselves into local society and might feel alienated; they thus want to regain PRC citizenship. These individuals might form a small minority.

The problem of dual nationality is complex and for many ethnic Chinese who live in Southeast Asia it will only bring more problems for them. They will encounter more difficulties in the local setting. With regard to China too, it is unlikely to bring any benefits. The fear of the "China threat" and the "Fifth Column" will become stronger if China amends the nationality law and recognizes dual citizenship – a position it had abandoned after the Afro-Asian conference.

The PRC was aware of this and the status quo in fact has served the national interest of China well. Nevertheless, in order to address the problem of globalization, the Prime Minister's Office of China on 13 December 2003 endorsed the management regulation on permanent residence status in the PRC, which was jointly issued as Act no. 74 by the Ministry of Security and the Ministry of Foreign Affairs on 15 August 2004.[16] This act, known as China's green card policy, serves the purpose of those who want to stay and work in China for a long period of time.

The act consists of 29 articles, comprising regulations on conditions of applicants, the method of application, the period of stay and the approval and rejection of application, and the renewal and suspension of the green card. This act was aimed at those people who would be able to help promote China's social development, as well as to develop in the economic and technological fields. These people include high-level management personnel (at least deputy director of factory), leading academics (at least at associate professor level) and scientists, investors (investing at least US$500,000) and relatives of Chinese nationals (including spouses, children and parents) for the purpose of family union.

According to the act, applicants who fulfil the requirements can make an application after entering China for more than 30 days, and will be notified about the result within 6 months. Successful applicants will receive a green card, which is valid for 5 years (for children) and 10 years (for adults). The card is renewable and will only be suspended under four circumstances: the holder is considered to be a national security risk, they are expelled by the People's Court, they obtained the green card through illegal means, or if it is cancelled by the Security Department.

No recent information is available on the number of green card holders in China. In late 2004, it was reported that there were 23,000 foreigners living in China, of whom 3,000 were permanent residents.[17] Nevertheless, many Chinese complain online that it is difficult for them to obtain a Chinese green card as the requirements are so high.

China's Recent Practice with regard to Citizenship Law

It is quite clear that in recent years, China has observed the single citizenship principle towards Southeast Asia, as manifested in the May 1998 anti-Chinese riots in which Beijing displayed a constrained attitude. Beijing refused to intervene in the event, stating that those involved were Indonesian citizens. Nevertheless, the PRC appealed to the Indonesian authorities to protect the rights and safety of the Indonesians of Chinese descent.

In the case of American citizens of Chinese descent, the PRC attitude was slightly different. These American citizens and residents were arrested on China's soil and the PRC claimed that they were involved in "espionage" and "selling state secrets" to a foreign country. The cases in point are Li Shaomin, Gao Zhan, Wu Jianmin, Qing Guangguang and Teng Chunyan. They were arrested and detained by the Chinese authorities in early 2001 and only later were sentenced to 10 years imprisonment.

However, the US House of Representatives' resolution on US citizens/residents of Chinese ancestry detained in China, passed on 25 June 2001, not only "condemns and deplores the continued detention" of these people but also "calls for their immediate and unconditional release."[18] It condemned the PRC's violation of human rights and warned the PRC government that the continuing detention of American citizens and residents would hurt Sino-American relations and the PRC national interest.

Responding to American pressure, the PRC held trials of these detainees. Xin Hua News Agency reported that Li Shaomin was tried on 14 July 2001, found guilty of espionage for Taiwan and expelled from China before the scheduled visit by US secretary of state Colin Powell.[19] In fact, in addition to Li Shaomin, Gao Zhan and Qin Guangguang were also released. Later, when US president George W. Bush was scheduled for a summit with Chinese president Jiang Zemin in February 2002, more detainees were released.[20]

The American case shows that the PRC arrested these Chinese Americans not on the basis that they were formerly Chinese citizens but on the pretext of "espionage." Therefore, it had nothing to do with citizenship. The PRC still practiced the single citizenship principle and even in this "espionage" case, Beijing gave in under American pressure. One wonders what would have happened if the PRC citizenship law was based on the principle of dual citizenship. The problem might have been more complicated than the present case.

Conclusion

The citizenship issue is one of the major problems in China–Southeast Asia relations. In the past, both the Qing dynasty and the Guomindang government declared that all ethnic Chinese born in China or abroad were Chinese nationals (citizens). The colonial powers in Southeast Asia also recognized local-born Chinese as their subjects. This is the origin of the question of dual citizenship status of Chinese overseas. The PRC, established in 1949, has continued the old "overseas Chinese" policy, giving rise to suspicions on the part of Southeast Asian governments with regard to the real motives of Beijing.

Sensing the concern of the Southeast Asian governments, Beijing offered to sign a dual citizenship treaty with their countries to resolve the citizenship issue during the Afro-Asian conference in 1955. Only Indonesia signed the treaty. In 1980, China unilaterally issued the first PRC "nationality law," which recognizes only single citizenship. All Chinese abroad who voluntarily acquire foreign citizenship lose their Chinese citizenship automatically. The issue of citizenship for the ethnic Chinese is thus settled.

However, in the wake of the rise of China in a globalizing world, a small group of Chinese decision makers who are not specialists on "Chinese overseas" has begun to feel that China should follow the United States and Canada in introducing the "dual citizenship law." They may have been influenced by new Chinese migrants (*xin yimin*) in Western countries who would like to have the "best of both worlds." They seem to be unaware of the history of the dual citizenship law and the world situation, especially in Southeast Asia where approximately 75 per cent of the "overseas Chinese" live.

Nevertheless, the above "Chinese nationalist view" is not shared by older migrants or the local born. A leading Chinese American scholar, Prof. Ling-chi Wang, argues that "restoring the dual citizenship law will harm both China and Chinese abroad."[21] Those Chinese who live in Southeast Asia and know the situation well still favour the single citizenship law, as the so-called indigenous population still harbour suspicions against China and the ethnic Chinese. It is important to note that Beijing has not yet made a move to amend the constitution, as the present citizenship law is perceived as being still beneficial to China. Nevertheless, the possibility of adjustment and amendment is there, depending on who is in power. What has now been done is the promulgation of the green card policy, which meets the demand of both *huaren* (Chinese who hold foreign nationality, or Chinese who are non-PRC citizens) and non-Chinese. This policy, in fact, does not touch on the sensitive issue of political loyalty, nor does it affect China's relations with other countries.

Notes

1 I have written a number of articles or chapters of books on China's nationality laws and the Chinese overseas. They include *China and the ASEAN States: The Ethnic Chinese Dimension* (Singapore: Singapore University Press, 1985); "China's Citizenship Law and the Chinese in Southeast Asia," in *Law and the Chinese in Southeast Asia*, edited by M. Barry Hooker (Singapore: Institute of Southeast Asian Studies, 2002), pp. 169–202; "China's Nationality Laws, Dual Nationality Status and the Chinese in Southeast Asia," in *CHC Bulletin*, nos 7–8 (May/November 2006), pp. 4–10. This paper is based on the above articles with some new information. However, a slightly revised version of this paper was published in my book entitled *The Making of Southeast Asian Nations: State, Ethnicity, Indigenism and Citizenship* (Singapore: World Scientific, 2014), pp. 85–99. It should also be noted that for this publication, I originally intended to write a comparative study between China and India with Dr Kripa Sridharan, but due to unforeseen circumstances it ended up as a country study paper. I am sure that it would be extremely useful to conduct a comparative study as there are a lot of similarities and differences between these two major countries in Asia.

2 Refers to local-born and Indonesian/Malay-speaking Chinese.

3 For a discussion of Oen's case, see Leo Suryadinata, *Peranakan Chinese Politics in Java 1917–1942* (Singapore: Singapore University Press, 1980), pp. 26–7.

4 Johannes Chan, "Nationality," in *Human Rights in Hong Kong*, ed. Raymond Wacks (Hong Kong: Oxford University Press, 1992), p. 488.

5 For instance, this clause was inserted into the PRC–Malaysia joint communiqué. See *Peking Review* 17, no. 23 (June 1974): 8. It should be noted that if a Chinese was forced to become a foreigner, he or she would remain a Chinese national. The case in point is that of Vietnam in 1976 after reunification. But apart from Vietnam, it appears that ethnic Chinese have become Southeast Asian nationals of their own free will.

6 "The Nationality Law of the People's Republic of China," in *Selected Articles from Chinese Yearbook of International Law*, ed. Chinese Society of International Law (Beijing: China Translation and Publishing Corporation, 1983), pp. 267–8.

7 Chan, "Nationality," p. 489.

8 Leo Suryadinata, "China's Citizenship Law and the Chinese in Southeast Asia," in *Law and the Chinese in Southeast Asia*, ed. M. Barry Hooker (Singapore: Institute of Southeast Asian Studies, 2002), p. 178.

9 Mao Qixiong 毛起雄 and Lin Xiaodong 林曉東, *Zhongguo Qiaowu falu fagui gaishu* 中國僑務法律法規概述 [A brief introduction to the laws and regulations relating to Overseas Chinese Affairs] (Beijing: Zhongguo huaqiao chubanshe, 1994), pp. 328–40.

10 Mao and Lin, *Zhongguo Qiaowu*.

11 Chen Duo (陳鐸) is from the literary circle while Ye Peiying (葉佩英) is from the Overseas Chinese Affairs Office (僑辦 Qiaoban). See Zhou Nanjing 周南京, ed., *Jingwai huaren guoji wenti taolun ji* 境外華人國籍問題討論輯 [The citizenship problems of the Chinese overseas: A collection of documents and articles] (Hong Kong 香港: Hong Kong Press for Social Sciences, 2005), pp. 175–6.

12 For the documents, see Nanjing, *Jingwai huaren*, pp. 241–3.

13 Liang Yingming 梁英明, "Shuangchong guoji bufuhe haiwai huaren shengcun fazhan de changyuan liyi" 雙重國籍不符合海外華人生存發展的長遠利益 [Dual citizenship does not serve the long-term interest of overseas Chinese for their survival and development], published in Nanjing, *Jingwai huaren*, pp. 413–25.

14 For the arguments, see "Huaqiao huaren guoji wenti chuyi" 華僑華人國籍問題芻議 [On the problems of Overseas Chinese nationality], Zhongguo ribao wangzhan huanqiu cixun 中國日報網站環球諮詢. *China Daily*, 3 March 2006. http://www.chinadaily.com.cn/gb/doc/2005-06/08/content_4496424htm. 11 November 2014.

15 "Huaqiao huaren guoji wenti chuyi." As above.

16 "Waiguoren zai Zhongguo yongjiu juliu shenpi guanli banfa" 外國人在中國永久居留審批管理辦法 [Regulations regarding the management of foreigners to reside permanently in China] Sina.com, 20 August 2004. http://news.sina.com.cn/c/2004-08-20/10304086859.shtml. 11 November 2014.

17 Liu Guofu, "Jianlun weiguoren zai Zhongguo yongjiu juliu (zhongguo Luka) zhidu", 刘国福: "简论外国人在中国永久居留（中国绿卡）制度"(Critical Legal Thinking on Chinese Permanent Resident [Green Card] System Reform), 《河北法学》*Hebei Law Science*, vol. 26, no.3 (March 2008), pp.51–58. "Zhongguo luka zhidu menkan gao" 中國'綠卡'門檻高 [The green card requirements in China are high], Boxun.com 博訊. http://d.wanfangdata.com.cn/Periodical_qiaoy200501002.aspx. 1 September 2004.

18 For the resolution, see "Chinese Injustice," *New York Times*, 25 July 2001. http://www.nytimes.com/2001/07/25/opinion/chinese injustice.htm. 11 November 2014.

19 Charles Burress and Ryan Kim, "China Frees 3 Scholars; Release Comes in Advance of Powell Visit, but Others Remain in Custody," *San Francisco Chronicle*, Thursday, 26 July 2001.

20 John Pomfret, "China Easing Way for Bush Visit: Invitation to Taiwanese Officials among 'Good Faith' Efforts," *Washington Post*, Foreign Service, Friday, 25 January 2002, p. A21.

21 "Restoring Dual Citizenship Law Will Harm China and Chinese Abroad," published in Nanjing, *Jingwai huaren*, pp. 352–61.

References

Chan, Johannes. "Nationality." In *Human Rights in Hong Kong*, edited by Raymond Wacks, pp. 470–508. Hong Kong: Oxford University Press, 1992.

Liang Yingming 梁英明. "Shuangchong guoji bufuhe haiwai huaren shengcun fazhan de changyuan liyi" 双重国籍不符合海外华人生存发展的长远利益 [Dual citizenship does not serve the long-term interest of overseas Chinese for their survival and development]. In *Jingwai huaren guoji wenti taolun ji* 境外华人国籍问题讨论辑 [The citizenship problems of the Chinese overseas: A collection of documents and articles], edited by Zhou Nanjing 周南京, pp. 413–25. Hong Kong: Hong Kong Press for Social Sciences, 2005.

Mao Qixiong 毛起雄 and Lin Xiaodong 林晓东. *Zhongguo Qiaowu falu fagui gaishu* 中国侨务法律法规概述 [A brief introduction to the laws and regulations relating to Overseas Chinese Affairs]. Beijing: Zhongguo huaqiao chubanshe, 1994.

"The Nationality Law of the People's Republic of China." In *Selected Articles from Chinese Yearbook of International Law*, edited by Chinese Society of International Law, pp. 267–8. Beijing: China Translation and Publishing Corporation, 1983.

Suryadinata, Leo. *China and the ASEAN States: The Ethnic Chinese Dimension*. Singapore: Singapore University Press, 1985.

______. "China's Citizenship Law and the Chinese in Southeast Asia." In *Law and the Chinese in Southeast Asia*, edited by M. Barry Hooker, pp. 169–202. Singapore: Institute of Southeast Asian Studies, 2002.

______. "China's Nationality Laws, Dual Nationality Status and the Chinese in Southeast Asia." In *CHC Bulletin*, nos 7–8 (May/November 2006): 4–10.

______. *Peranakan Chinese Politics in Java 1917–1942*. Singapore: Singapore University Press, 1980.

Zhou Nanjing 周南京, ed. *Jingwai huaren guoji wenti taolun ji* 境外华人国籍问题讨论辑 [The citizenship problems of the Chinese overseas: A collection of documents and articles]. Hong Kong: Hong Kong Press for Social Sciences, 2005.

Chapter 5

A COMPARISON OF THE HOME REMITTANCE SYSTEMS OF INDIAN AND CHINESE MIGRANTS IN SOUTHEAST ASIA: NINETEENTH AND TWENTIETH CENTURIES

Hamashita Takeshi

Introduction: Migration and Remittance

There were many differences in the history and dynamics of emigration between South Asia, Southeast Asia and South China over the nineteenth and twentieth centuries. These differences had, in turn, a far-reaching impact on patterns of remittance transmission back to home villages of origin. While these remittances were earmarked by their senders as household expenses and investment capital, the present study reveals that the financial instruments in which these funds were actually used were conditioned by a wide range of locally specific environmental, infrastructural and politico-economic factors. To understand migration and its relationship with remittances, we need to consider thoroughly the environmental, infrastructural and politico-economic circumstances affecting migrants and their families. This chapter, however, will discuss the similarity in the procedures of home remittances between Indians and Chinese in Southeast Asia. As their business networks utilized informal financial markets, they quite commonly used their local, business and family ties for remittances. The relations between overseas and home towns, at the same time, were strengthened by exchanging money, achieving credit for each other.

Politically and economically speaking, Hong Kong and Singapore have a strong connection as former British colonies. In 1858, the British East India Company, its trade monopoly gone, lost control over the Straits Settlements of Penang, Singapore and Malacca, established as a crown colony in 1867. In the late nineteenth century rubber plantations and tin mines attracted many Indian and Chinese labourers to the Malay Peninsula. During this period, Singapore and Hong Kong became transit points for immigrants and their home remittances, as well as entrepôts for Western capital and settlement points for financial transactions.[1]

Hong Kong and Chinese Migration

Abolition of the slave trade in the 1830s exacerbated a labour shortage in the British Empire and led to the recruitment of Indians and Chinese to work on the sugar plantations of the West Indies and the new rubber and sugar plantations of Southeast Asia. From the mid-nineteenth century tens of thousands of Chinese migrated to the United States to work in mines and build railroads, and to Australia and Southeast Asia. The colony of Hong Kong became an entrepôt for Chinese emigrants bound for Southeast Asia, a stable source for the labour Western powers needed to develop their colonies (see Table 1).

Table 1: Chinese Immigrants to Singapore and Penang

Year	Immigrants to Singapore		Chinese leaving Singapore	Immigrants to Penang		Chinese leaving Penang	Labour contracts
	Total	Females		Total	Females		
1890	96,230	3,820	31,706	36,044	1,726	5,921	26,204
1891	93,843	4,710	32,245	49,066	2,416	383	17,538
1892	93,339	4,804	–	45,227	2,529	–	–
1893	144,558	6,387	–	68,251	3,868	–	38,326
1894	106,612	5,007	31,083	46,230	2,425	371	22,302
1895	150,157	6,997	–	60,559	3,653	–	–
1896	142,358	6,451	–	57,055	3,216	–	29,825
1897	90,828	5,247	24,150	41,124	3,224	2,333	17,268
1898	106,983	6,192	26,575	44,811	3,301	1,890	20,459
1899	117,794	5,514	31,903	51,299	2,594	2,764	22,233
1900	159,571	8,482	41,376	72,821	3,847	4,026	27,033
1901	157,657	11,822	39,512	66,411	4,128	4,594	22,408
1903	172,770	14,539	47,551	75,401	5,346	4,450	18,768
1904	163,079	10,163	41,717	39,215	4,156	1,260	17,045
1905	136,001	13,714	37,130	35,645	4,833	1,475	14,864
1906	–	–	–	–	–	–	18,675
1907	179,756	13,785	47,580	44,495	5,682	1,809	24,089
1908	121,639	11,147	31,813	29,387	4,295	2,296	13,604
1909	120,954	9,602	30,798	27,529	3,901	3,540	13,379
1910	173,423	14,121	42,898	37,955	5,333	867	23,935
1911	215,036	19,754	54,818	49,875	7,302	4,516	24,345
1912	203,124	21,779	48,520	44,284	6,384	4,236	13,600
1913	240,979	28,547	41,018	37,161	5,611	3,862	14,198
1914	124,032	13,096	13,118	41,988	2,714	3,345	2,648
1915	80,352	10,632	15,382	26,698	4,123	1,743	–

Source: Ta Chen, *Chinese Emigrations, with Special Reference to Labor Conditions* (Washington, DC: Government Printing Office, 1923), p. 84. Statistics for 1902 are missing.

Chinese immigration to Southeast Asia dates from the seventh and eighth centuries.[2] Economic, political and social reasons are cited for this egress, including the low productivity of the South China coastal region, political upheavals that brought waves of newcomers from North China, like the Hakka, and conflict between social classes and organizations (families and clans).[3]

Traditional studies of the overseas Chinese emphasize "push" factors like population pressure, the shortage of arable land and poverty. The interplay of "push" and "pull" factors in this outflow deserves attention, in such areas as comparison of the agricultural output in South China and in the areas where Chinese settled.

Adding the "pull" dimension would also bring research on immigration within the scope of colonialism. However, scholars of emigration and colonialism treat the Chinese as having permanently relocated and have not been interested in the networks created when a people move between regions and return to their home country.

Expansion of the Indian Merchant Community in Singapore

Among the commercial groups that began migrating to Singapore during the nineteenth century were the early petty traders who came to supply the needs of the local Indian community in Singapore. The most prominent among them were the South Indian Muslims. The Chuliahs, as they were called locally, were renowned retail traders with a long tradition of trading with Southeast Asia. Most of these came from the southern districts of Tamil Nadu, primarily Tanjore and Ramnad, where traders of the earlier period had also originated. Other South Indian traders included the Malabar Muslims or Moplahs, a community traditionally engaged in the retail trade in Indian provinces.

The Chettiars were another prominent commercial group from South India. The Nattukodai (Nattukottai) Chettiars, from the Ramnad and Pudukottai districts in southern Madras (now Tamil Nadu), had been migrating into the Straits Settlements since the early part of the nineteenth century and were primarily engaged in the moneylending business. In a period when economic enterprise was often hampered by the lack of modern banks and cooperatives, the Chettiars performed an invaluable function as a source of credit for small businessmen who needed capital but had no collateral to offer. Their clientele was not restricted to Indian traders but often included European proprietary planters and Chinese businessmen. As moneylenders, the Chettiars were to remain an institution in Singapore until the 1970s, when the growth of banks and financial institutions and changing aspirations among the newer generation finally dealt a severe blow to their traditional economic activity.

Towards the end of the nineteenth century, as Singapore continued to prosper and develop, more and more Indians came to the island in search of employment opportunities. There were still a significant number of labourers, but there were now some who came to take advantage of the trading opportunities in the thriving island economy, while others who had had the benefit of an English education in India came to find white-collar employment in the government, in municipal services and in various businesses. There were also a number who were in the railways and others who were schoolteachers.

At the end of the nineteenth century, the Indian community in Singapore stood at over sixteen thousand, constituting nearly 9 per cent of the population of Singapore. The community was essentially transient. The Indian immigrants in nineteenth-century Singapore were mainly labourers, with some traders, merchants and white-collar workers. Most of these immigrants, especially the labourers, were often indebted for passage money, and had come without their families. Most would remain in Singapore to work for one or two years before going back to India for a three- to six-month break to visit their families, after which they would return to Singapore again. The Indian community was thus predominantly male, and from 1871 to 1901 there was an average sex ratio of over four thousand males to one thousand females. It was not until the 1930s, that more and more Indian females began migrating into the island. The Indian community was also a heterogeneous one, compartmentalized by occupational, religious, educational and linguistic differences, as well as ethnic and sub-ethnic differences based on place of origin. The many groups which comprised the Indian community included Tamils, Malayalees, Telegus, Ceylonese, Gujaratis, Sikhs, Punjabis, Sindhis, Biharis and Bengalis.[4]

Nattukottai Chettiars in Malaya

Among the Indian commercial groups were the Chettiar, a Tamil caste of businessmen and financiers, with a long historic tradition in such activities. Chettiars must have moved into the Straits Settlements by the middle of the nineteenth century, through agencies if not through the main Chettiar houses. The subgroup of the Chettiar caste most important in migration to Malaya was the Nattukottai Chettiar. They are said to be the most distinct of the Chettiar groups and in modern times the most prosperous. Their business enterprises today consist predominantly of moneylending. In India they live in a few villages in the Ramnad district in the south of Tamil Nadu. They were the most enterprising of all trading castes of South India. They were the most mobile: from their village base they would willingly go out to any part of the world to further their business, always returning to the ancestral village. In a traditional Chettiar home, right down to the early decades of the twentieth century, all sons lived with the father even after marriage, but had to manage their own families separately. Sons at a young age were sent as agents of a relative to some distant place, overseas if necessary, with a certain sum of money. This was generally for a three-year period during which they received a salary as well as a percentage of the profits. At the end of the three-year term some other relative was sent to take over from them, and they returned home to render account to their employer.[5]

Among the Indian commercial groups, the Chettiars had the widest impact on the country, because of the nature and range of their activities. They came to Malaya primarily as moneylenders. Their moneylending activities brought them into contact with the economy of the country and, as in Burma, gave rise to a process of change affecting many classes of people. They provided credit to people of various groups – European entrepreneurs, Chinese speculators, Indian hawkers and peddlers, and Malay royalty and peasants. The government was aware of the function they were performing, and the chief secretary made favourable references to the Chettiars, defending them against criticism in the Federal Council in 1923. It was their relations with Malay peasants and smallholders that attracted the greatest attention in this period. From the early days, Chettiar firms opened branches in rural townships from where they could draw on a large clientele in search of credit.[6]

This circulation of Chettiar moneylenders played almost the same role as private remittance agents and Chinese moneylenders, who provided various services: recruited settlers, loaned passage money, booked passages, and also handled commercial transactions, which are explained below.

Home Remittances by Overseas Chinese

Overseas Chinese went abroad to earn money and send it home, not intending to settle permanently in a new land. The individual's wages were considered part of household income. They also remitted funds to agents for their passage.[7] Overwhelmingly from Fujian and Guangdong, the immigrants' funds helped to finance transactions across the South China–Southeast Asia trade zone.[8] In addition, some money was remitted for investment purposes.[9]

Remittances did not disappear into household expenditures. Recycled for commercial payments and investment capital, this money became a vital element in China's international financial ties. When Great Britain, France, the United States and Japan developed important interests in Southeast Asia, all of them utilized this financial network.

Chinese immigrants could get money back to China in five ways: (1) mail, (2) hand-carried, (3) private remittance agents, (4) remittance houses and (5) foreign banks.[10]

1. Mail

The Universal Postal Union was created in 1878, but the Chinese government did not sign the convention until 1917. Foreign countries set up branch post offices in China that handled international mail; however, few overseas Chinese used these services.[11]

2. Hand-Carried

Overseas Chinese personally brought back gold/silver, foreign drafts and local paper currency, or they entrusted funds to a returnee.

3. Private Remittance Agents

The agents provided various services: recruited labourers, loaned passage money, booked passage and also handled commercial transactions. They stayed in close contact with the immigrants, visiting each Chinese community every few months. The newcomers invariably dealt with an agent from the same home town in China in order to send money as well as personal letters. In areas not serviced by remittance houses, agents were the main conduits.

4. Remittance Houses

Chinese immigration to Southeast Asia reached significant proportions in the fifteenth century and steadily increased despite the Ming dynasty's ban on overseas settlement. Chinese merchants abroad sold rice, sugar, raw cotton, foodstuffs and handicrafts to China, and imported sundries, handicrafts and tea. In addition, the Siamese, Vietnamese and Burmese states made a profit on the tributary trade with China, a mercantile policy that helped to shape a trade zone between South China and Southeast Asia. In the seventeenth century the European powers moved into the region in search of certain Asian products. Thanks to this well-established commerce, Western merchants were able for the first time to buy highly prized goods like tea, silk, pepper and cotton with profits from the entrepôt trade.[12]

The remittance house, the principal instrument by which Chinese persons sent money home, was the financial linchpin of trade between South China and Southeast Asia. Called "silver remittance houses," "Guangdong and Fujian silver houses" and other names, remittance houses were a combination of post office and foreign exchange bank. Many also engaged in trade, financed trade deals, and dealt in gold and silver. This exchange/remittance network predated the arrival of foreign banks, which also competed for the business as a source of capital. Tian Yi Ju, one of the large remittance houses in the early twentieth century, was based in Amoy and had branches or agents in Manila, Saigon, Penang, Singapore, Medan, Batavia, Bandung, Semarang and Rangoon. With subunits throughout Fujian and Guangdong, including Quanzhou, Chaozhou, Dongan, Anxi, Jinmen and Huian, Tian Yi Ju handled most of the remittances sent by people from the province.

There were many remittance houses in Southeast Asia. Headquartered in Singapore, Bangkok, Malacca, Batavia or Manila, they had branches or agents in Hong Kong, Guangdong, Hainan and across Fujian. The approximately four million Chinese living in Southeast Asia in the early twentieth century sent about $57 million annually to their homeland.[13]

Remittance houses transferred money in several ways – cash, drafts and as commercial goods. A customer purchased a draft for a certain amount in Chinese dollars. Rather than immediately send the money, the houses waited until individual transactions amounted to a fairly large sum or until the exchange rate was favourable. In lieu of actual transfers, they also purchased goods for sale in China or bought gold and silver. Some transactions were Yuan-denominated, while others via Hong Kong were in Hong Kong dollars. The Hong Kong dollar was the settlement currency for so much of the commercial activity between China and Southeast Asia that, although typically the final destination of a remittance was a family in a rural village, in variegated forms the money was used for trade, finance capital and investment.[14] The huge volume of drafts through Hong Kong involved double conversions – first to Hong Kong dollars and then to Chinese dollars. Remittance houses also used the money to offset bills paid in Hong Kong for export/import transactions; some turned a profit on the price differential in gold and silver bullion between Singapore and Hong Kong. There was a synergistic interplay of trade and foreign exchange dealing.

5. Foreign Banks: Institutional Remittance Business

It was possible for the huge one-way flow of remittances by overseas Chinese to South China to affect exchange rates. Falls of exchange rates in Southeast Asia were prevented by offsetting the receipts of gold/silver and imports (i.e., liabilities to Shanghai and Hong Kong). This trade pattern solidified ties, through foreign banks, between the region and Japan, Europe and the United States. Great Britain's financial interests in Asia, anchored in Singapore and Hong Kong, depended on trends in the region – China, Southeast Asia and India. British colonial banks were vital cogs, extending the financial grid to Japan and Europe.

Shanghai's commercial ties increased the capital there and strengthened its connections between East Asia and Southeast Asia. Hong Kong, an important player in trade, increasingly became a financial entrepôt for account settlements and remittance transactions.[15]

From the mid-nineteenth century, when Hong Kong gained importance as a financial intermediary and Singapore emerged as a supplier of rubber and tin to European markets, foreign banks seriously entered the field. Chinese exchange banks also began operations in Southeast Asia during the same period.[16] These so-called modern banks enlarged and reshaped the channels originally formed by the remittance houses to create an Asian financial region around the Singapore–Hong Kong artery. Far from being supplanted by the banks, the remittance houses used the exchange rates set by the foreign banks (especially those of the Hongkong and Shanghai Bank) and entered new fields of business activity.

Foreign banks opened branches in commercial centres created by the overseas Chinese and overseas Indians. The Chartered Bank of India, Australia and China was strongest in India and the Malay Peninsula, the Hongkong and Shanghai Bank in Hong Kong and China, and Bank l'Indochine in Indochina (see Table 2). All three institutions had branches or agents in the main business hubs and trading ports of Southeast Asia. However, all of them were established by following historical trading and financial centres inherited from tributary trade networks and overseas Chinese and overseas Indian trade and remittance networks.

Home Remittance and Amoy: Land and Manufacturing Investment

The greatest category among remittance use was unquestionably investment. Generally, in home towns of overseas Chinese commercial or other businesses such as transport were either initiated by overseas Chinese or were being operated wholly or partly by them in some way.

Table 2: Foreign Bank Branches and Agents in Asia

	Chartered Bank	Hongkong and Shanghai Bank	Bank l'Indochine
1858	Calcutta, Bombay, Colombo, Shanghai		
59	Hongkong		
1861	Singapore, Rangoon		
63	Hankow, Batavia		
65		Hong Kong, Shanghai, Canton	
66	Yokohama	Yokohama, Saigon	
67		Calcutta	
68		Hankow, Tientsin	
69		Bombay	
1870		Kobe, Nagasaki	
72	Manila	Osaka	
75	Penang	Manila, San Francisco	Paris, Saigon
77	Surabaya	Singapore	Pondicherry
1880		New York	
81		Lyon	
83	Various		
84	Medan	Penang, Jakarta, Surabaya, Semarang	
85		Peking, Amoy, Foochow	Tonkin, Haiphong
87		Haiphong	Hanoi
88	Taiping, Kuala Lumpur	Bangkok	Noumea (New Caledonia)
89		Hamburg	
1891			Phnom Penh
92		Rangoon, Colombo	
94	Bangkok		Hong Kong
95	Kobe, Tientsin		
97			Bangkok
98			Shanghai
1900	Madras, Cebu		
02	New York		Hankow, Canton
03	Saigon		
04	Hamburg		Battambang
05			Singapore
06	Karachi		
07			Peking, Tientsin
08			Gipti
09	Klang, Phuket		
1910	Seremban, Amritsar		
11	Malacca, Delhi, Canton	Dalian, Harbin	Mengzi (in Yunnan)
12	Ipoh	Changchun, Qingdao	

Source: Compiled from Sir Compton Mackenzie, *Realms of Silver 1883–1972* (London: Routledge and K. Paul, 1954); Maurice Collis, *Wayfoong: The Hongkong and Shanghai Banking Corporation; A Study of East Asia's Transformation, Political, Financial and Economic, during the Last Hundred Years* (London: Faber, 1965); and Gonjo Yasuo, *Furansu Teikoku Shugi to Ajia* [French imperialism and Asia] (Tokyo University Press, 1985).

One of the very important positions occupied by overseas Chinese capital was in the land deals that were vigorously carried on for a number of years in Amoy – individually managed, through companies or the syndicate.

This syndicate was founded by overseas Chinese in the Philippines who from 1928 were affected by a slump and returned to China in a growing stream. However, China itself was not very secure and the overseas Chinese were forced to remain in Amoy. Some of them bought land on Amoy Island, built new houses and decided to live there. Once this trend began, many others followed the example and among them some wealthy overseas Chinese organized the syndicate and constructed the Great Southern New Village in South Putou. Funds of 200,000 yuan were invested in this.

More than ten modern Western-style houses were built both for rental and to attract returning overseas Chinese to rent or buy land in the New Village and build there. Apart from this, the Yinan Company and the Overseas Chinese Bank dealt in land. The total investment in individually managed land at one time reached as high as 7,000,000 yuan. Later on, with the gradual decline in land values and the slump in Amoy, most construction stagnated.

The Amoy Telephone Company, established by Lin Er-jia, was the first case of an overseas Fujian Chinese returning home and investing in a business. This company was founded in 1907, originally with only 40,000 yuan, but this was gradually increased to 1,000,000. Every year it suffered damage from war or banditry, with losses of about 2,000,000 yuan, but fortunately it benefitted from skilful management and was able to compensate for its losses. The enterprise was inherited by Huang Yiju and had a monthly income of over 10,000 yuan, making a committed dividend of 0.5 per cent, apart from outlays. The company established branches in Gulangyu, Hoshan, Haicang, Zhangzhou, Shima, Quanzhou and elsewhere, so that calls were possible to all towns in southern Fujian.

The first modern sugar mills managed by Chinese entrepreneurs themselves originated with the Huaxiang Company, established in southern Fujian in 1908 by an overseas Fujian Chinese, Guo Zhen-xiang, with 450,000 yuan in capital. To establish it, 2,500,000 cane seedlings were purchased from Java and the Philippines and cultivated in such areas as the Wangxue mudflats and Tianbian, in Longqi, and Shuitou in Tongan County. Sugar mills were installed in Shuitou and Hutou. Eighty tons of sugar cane per day were used at the Shuitou mill, although later on, for reasons that are not clear, production gradually declined.

Overseas Fujian businessmen who invested in areas of China other than Fujian are too numerous to list, but the more important among them are Hu Wen-hu's Yungantang, Chen Jia-geng's [Tan Kah-kee's] rubber factory and Huang Yi-ju's alcohol plant, which give a glimpse of the magnitude of the contribution of overseas Fujianese to the nation.

There were altogether four banks in Amoy which were established by purely overseas Chinese capital:

(a) The Zhongnan Bank, with paid-up capital of 7,500,000 yuan. The Amoy branch was opened in 1921.
(b) The Overseas Chinese Bank, registered in British territory, had a paid-up capital of 10,000 Straits dollars. The Amoy branch was established in 1932 (it had a predecessor of the same name).

(c) The Zhongxing Bank, registered in the United States, with paid-up capital of 5,700,000 pesos. The Amoy branch was established in 1927.
(d) The Amoy Commercial Bank, established in Amoy in 1930 and closed in 1935.

There are as yet no accurate statistics for the net proportion of overseas Chinese capital among remittances sent via Fujian private mail exchanges, either for direct or indirect investment. However, the fact that such mail exchanges found it necessary to set up numerous branches overseas and head offices in every area of Southeast Asia shows that these facilities were the most convenient for overseas Chinese investment.

It is true that expectations in Amoy commercial circles regarding overseas Fujianese investment were somewhat dashed by falling land values in 1934. From that year, most overseas Fujianese funds were sent for deposit in banks in Amoy and Hong Kong with a view to watching for investment opportunities. These funds were kept as current deposits, and from the business reports of one or two of the leading banks in Amoy we can surmise – in view of the yearly increase in the proportion of current and private deposits in those years – how much of this type of idle capital there was. A large amount of idle capital, viewed economically, is an unhealthy phenomenon and can relentlessly develop into a threat to financial stability. Of course if it is utilized, with proper inducements, it can prove very efficacious.

Part of the remittance to middle-class migrant households was invested in rural areas. The rural economy in Fujian had long been indigent and there was an intense desire for relief funds in all quarters – an ideal situation for usurers. A widespread means of increasing wealth in rural areas of southwest Fujian – apart from investing overseas savings in normal business fields – was lending money at interest.[17]

Trading and Use of Remittance in the Exchange Market

Hundi (Hawala) Transaction among Chettiars

The remittance business among Chettiars is described as *hundi* transactions. The Chettiars of Ceylon kept detailed records about their *hundi* transactions. One of the important reasons for this was that disputes and negotiations regarding formal financial markets and informal financial markets had been debated from legal aspects, so that they tried to follow colonial rules. Here, we will take a Ceylon moneylender as an example for better understanding of how *hundi* functioned in the external exchange market.[18]

Nakarattar commercial activities extended even beyond the Tamil mainland. By the end of the eighteenth century, they had gained control of pearl fisheries in the Ceylon Straits and the Gulf of Mannar, usurping this position from Muslim Maryakarar merchants who had previously been granted control of the fisheries by the Setupati (Raja) of Ramnad in the seventeenth century. Various factors seem to have been at play. For one thing, the Setupati's influence in granting fishery rights had become considerably eroded. As early as the eighteenth century, administrative rights over the fisheries were being strongly contested by the Dutch, by the Raja of Thanjavur and by the Nawab of the Carnatic. The various claims by these parties were apparently withdrawn only

Fig 1: Simple *Hundi* Exchange System

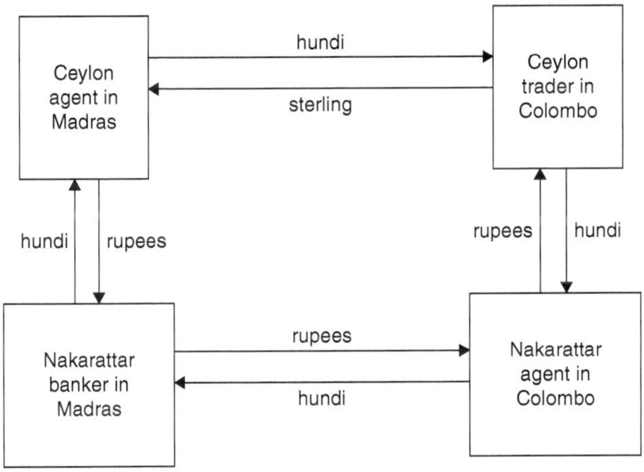

Source: Rudner David West, *Caste and Capitalism in Colonial India: The Nattukottai Chettiars* (Oakland: University of California Press, 1994), p. 59.

in return for a financial settlement from the Nakarattars. In addition, the Nakarattar takeover may reflect a close financial relationship that the Nakarattars built with the Setupati, who was, perhaps, their largest client zamindar. That is, Nakarattar merchants may have been in a position to influence the Setupati to exercise whatever powers he still retained over the Straits. In any case, the Nakarattars were ultimately able to exercise monopoly control over the fisheries until 1836, renting them out to Maravar and Paravar boating crews from Tuticorin.

From at least 1820, Nakarattars also dominated the major coastal trade in arrack and other coconut products from Ceylon to Madras, in rice and cloth from Madras to Ceylon and, arguably, in salt from Madras to Calcutta and rice from Calcutta to Madras and Ceylon. It is difficult to gauge the degree of their domination, but according to contemporary observers, they had cornered the Ceylon rice market, controlling all imports not only of Thanjavur rice but of Bengal rice as well.

The Nakarattars' position in the Ceylonese rice market allowed them to take advantage of a marked imbalance of trade strongly tilted in favour of rice exports from Madras to Ceylon. Ceylonese importers made up differences in the trade balance with British sterling, which was earned by trading in the European market with Ceylon cinnamon, spices, coconut products and increasingly coffee (until the coffee blight appeared in 1868). But Nakarattar agents in Colombo – holding a monopoly on the import of rice – were unwilling to accept sterling as payment unless there were exceptional sterling shortages in India. Accordingly, Ceylonese rice traders appointed their own agents in Madras to whom they sent their sterling bills for sale. They then sold rupee drafts through those agents to the Nakarattar bankers in Ceylon, who discounted (i.e., cashed) the *hundi* in rupees or rupee credit at a standardized discount rate. The Nakarattar bankers, in turn, sent the *hundis* to Madras where they could be redeemed at face value (see Figure 2).

British merchants and plantation owners in Ceylon met their rupee needs in a similar fashion. The Nakarattars "were thus in a position practically to hold the Colombo merchants [Ceylonese and British] to ransom, while the latter were at the same time dependent on the sterling exchange in India." Here, in the case of remittance by Chettiars, *hundi* was a method of transferring money, including private remittance.[19]

Remittance from Southeast Asia to South China

Though the main purpose of home remittances was to send money back to their home villages from Singapore or elsewhere, these funds inevitably had to pass through financial markets, formal and/or informal, before they arrived at their home town.

The remittance sum received by a private postal exchange in Southeast Asia and sent to an exchange in the home country (e.g. Amoy) generated a certain credit and liability relationship between the two areas. Unless this relationship was settled by some other means, for example by inclusion in commercial accounts or by the movement of gold or silver, it resulted in an outstanding debit balance. Remittances were sent either by direct bank draft or by postal exchanges; but, as the exchange received local currency, it had to be sent directly via the foreign exchange market by being exchanged to Chinese currency through banks. Since remittances traversed the exchange market, the market was strongly influenced by them and many complex reactions occurred through discrepancies in the process.

The simplest method of settling remittance transfers between Southeast Asia and Amoy postal exchanges was for the Southeast Asian exchange to have on its books a debit to the Amoy exchange, equal in amount to the remittance sent. If the Amoy exchange combined export/import business with its remittance business, and suitable stocks of Southeast Asian goods were commissioned by local traders for transport to Amoy, the amount of overseas Chinese remittances on the books was reduced. Thus, even if what was generated in the interim was an intangible transfer, it could have an effect equal in amount to a remittance draft sent from Amoy to Southeast Asia.

However, this was not the usual situation and often it did not go so simply. This is because the price of the goods was not necessarily the same as the amount of the remittances and the processes were not necessarily concurrent. If the settlement of remittance items in Southeast Asia did not proceed concurrently and were allowed to be used to earn interest, the Amoy end lost an amount equivalent to the interest. However, if a corresponding sum of interest was sent to the Amoy end and deposited, a financial adjustment would occur.

Another method enabling settlement was for the postal exchange at the Amoy end to jointly handle transfers to Southeast Asia, although there were not many exchanges of this kind.

If the exchange itself could not directly handle transfer business, it could balance credit and debit by transfer through banks. Banks carried out transfers in several forms. One was to sell overseas Chinese remittances accepted by Southeast Asian banks by means of Amoy remittance drafts, the bearer of the drafts taking them to the Amoy branch or agency of the Southeast Asian bank to receive payment; at the same time the

Amoy bank, with the directly sold Southeast Asian drafts as security, paid the money to the recipient. This relationship may be expressed by the following figure:

Fig 2: Remittance between Southeast Asia and Amoy

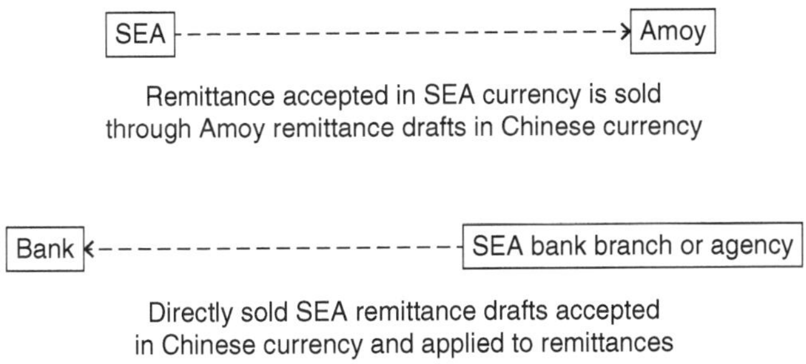

However, in Amoy itself there was not much demand for Southeast Asian remittance drafts, so remittance transfers were only settled through the foreign exchange market in Hong Kong and Shanghai, while at times it was also necessary to go through the Hong Kong and Shanghai market to obtain advantageous arbitrage. At the postal exchange end, in some cases, the remittance was not sent directly to Amoy but first sent to Hong Kong and then sold as a Hong Kong draft, to make the remittance more favourable. The foreign goods stocked in Fujian were largely imported from Hong Kong. As these goods were also paid for in Hong Kong dollars, the demand for Hong Kong drafts was greater than the supply. Thus the exchange rate was comparatively high and the postal exchange made a profit by utilizing the higher value of drafts. Banks handling remittances also disposed of foreign currency obtained in Southeast Asia, Shanghai or Hong Kong by the same method. They also immediately sold overseas remittances received in Amoy on the market, changing them to Hong Kong or Shanghai remittance drafts and exchanging them for Chinese currency in Amoy to pay recipients. Otherwise, if they were disadvantaged when acquiring foreign exchange from Southeast Asia sold in Hong Kong or Shanghai, they would incur an intangible loss.

Remittance drafts were not made directly from Amoy to Southeast Asia but, depending on circumstances, part of the Southeast Asian remittance drafts sold were applied to overseas remittances and the other part was simply a stop-gap, using transfers re-forwarded from Hong Kong and Shanghai. It was unavoidable that in the course of transfer procedures, remittance recipient areas in Fukien depended on transfers re-forwarded from Shanghai. But in the 1930s in the Quanzhou (Chuanchow) area, as the supply of Shanghai drafts was greater than the demand, the value of drafts fell, requiring an extra 5 yuan per 1,000 yuan. However, at the same time, the re-forwarding of remittances from Hong Kong and Shanghai reduced the tension in transfer drawing between Fujian and Southeast Asia and there were many respects in which the differences between the two were averaged out, without such effects as a fall in Southeast Asian remittance drafts through an excess in direct forwarding or, conversely, a rise in Fukienese drafts in Southeast Asia.[20] This credit was the accumulation of individual credit formed of remittee–recipient relations, which we can recognize as a function of the *gu* (share), which proved membership of the clan to which every migrant maintained his or her affiliation.

Hundi Transaction and Transfer of Credit among Nakarattars

Now we will turn to credit transactions among Chettiars to understand the internal function of *hundi*. The major Nakarattar financial instrument for all transactions was the *hundi*, a kind of bill of exchange or written order for payment that its drawers used much in the way that Americans use cheques drawn on their cheque accounts. In order to draw a *hundi*, a client had to open an account and maintain a correspondence relationship with a banker. Compared to Chinese remittance houses, *hundi* transactions included wider coverage from individual settlement to banking draft transaction. It involved almost all functions of the Chinese remittance business: (1) mail, (2) hand-carried, (3) private remittance agents, (4) remittance houses, and (5) foreign banks, as described above.

Hundis were sometimes used just to transfer funds from one location to another (a service employed primarily by Nakarattars among themselves), but they were more typically employed in financing trade transactions by Nakarattars and non-Nakarattars alike. Tun Wai estimates that, before 1930, perhaps 75 per cent of Nakarattar *hundis* in Burma were trade *hundis*.[21] In such cases, a paddy merchant, for example, bought a shipment of paddy at a local market in Burma with cash that he transferred to the seller by drawing a *hundi* on his account in a local Nakarattar banking office. The Nakarattar banker cashed the *hundi*, receiving a discounting fee of 1 to 3 per cent, and took custody of the railroad receipt for the paddy shipment, even though the transaction was not a loan and did not incur rates of interest charged on loans. The banker sent the *hundi* and the receipt to his firm's main office in Rangoon along with instructions to debit the merchant's account. If the banker had no office in Rangoon, he sent the *hundi* and receipt to another banker (perhaps, but not necessarily, an *adathi* [parent banker]) with whom he maintained an account. The first banker could thus rediscount the *hundi* with the second banker, who normally extended the service without charging a further discounting fee. In order to regain the railway receipt and take possession of his paddy from either banker, the merchant had to maintain a deposit account with the Rangoon banker in a satisfactory manner.

Origins of Shareholding

The idea of shareholdings in social activities plays a basic role as an organizing principle for units of social networks and social credit ties. Broadly extended, the idea of shareholding extends over a much wider sphere of social activities and, from this, we can hypothesize that Chinese social ties do not provide for unlimited credit, but rather a limited shareholding. So members within social networks can be recognized firstly as individuals, but also through the social ties formed on the basis of the amount of shares they hold in a particular interest.

By differentiating social ties from social networks conceptually, the two overlapping functions of shareholding will be clarified more definitely so that we can avoid having to employ an unrestricted idea of "networks."

Consequently, "share" does not always mean capital or fund. Of course, capital could be calculated as share, but sometimes the labour input could also be classified as a share. For example, some persons invested a certain amount of shares in terms of a certain amount of money. But besides this calculation of money input, labour and managerial talent could also be calculated as shares. So instead of investing money, some individuals contributed their managerial skills. At the same time, the tools or machines that some people provided or offered the company were also counted as shares. In the history of Chinese economic relations, the relationship between capital and labour traditionally was not vertical but rather horizontal, observed through dividing shares. Thus the relationship between capital and labour was very different from the Western pattern of capital-and-labour. Labourers recognized themselves as a sort of shareholder of an enterprise. This shows the peculiar characteristics of Chinese economic relations: labour and capital were mutually related by shares. So from this idea of shares, we can see characteristics of Chinese society as a network of shareholdings. Chinese society is thus rather strong in commercial activities rather than in intensive investment into industrial spheres. But in the historical context, particularly in the context of development of the economy, industry and commerce were separated very sharply and capital was recognized very differently.

The Religious Ritual of Moneylending

Hundi in Chettiar communities and "shares" in Chinese communities had an important role in credit making and credit keeping for many centuries in South Asia, Southeast Asia and South China. Both were revitalized through everyday social life such as religious activities through temples, clan associations and local associations. In the case of Indian communities in Singapore, the temple was never the only source of funds for the Chettiar moneylenders. They frequently borrowed from each other in times of need. This, however, was regulated in the temple. For example, interest rates for both long- and short-term loans were fixed in the temple once every month on the day of *karthigai* – an auspicious day honouring Murugan, a Hindu god.

The inter-Chettiar interest rate for a long-term loan is referred to as *Thavanai-vatti* and that for a short-term loan is called *Nadapu-vatti*. The former rate is nowadays fixed at a level slightly higher than the current prime rate in the formal banking sector; and compound interest is charged for the long-term loans. As for the latter, the level is slightly higher than the *Thavanai* rate, and since the loan is a short-term one, the rate is charged for the number of days borrowed. There is also a compound interest involved in this type of loan.

When credit is extended to other Chettiar moneylenders, the god Murugan is used as their divine witness. He is seen as the presiding chairman of every business and social meeting. He is also considered the supreme witness of every oral contract and economic transaction made among the Chettiars. Dishonesty and default of payment invokes religious sanctions through divine intervention, expressed in punishment through calamities and bad luck. Thus, religious surveillance and control over the social and economic life prevail and function to stabilize the entire Chettiar economy. Recalcitrant offenders are also barred from vital rituals like marriage and ostracized by the Chettiar community. Clearly, while the temple acts as a regular place of worship for all Hindus including the Chettiars in Singapore, it performs an additional social and economic role as both a community and a business centre.

In continuation of historical practices, daily religious devotions and worship are still performed on an individual basis in the place of residence (*kittangi*) before an image or before an altar in the Chettiar temple. No business activity is conducted without first completing morning prayers (*puja*) and no day is ended without the evening prayers. Furthermore, the first principal entry made into the accounts book is a statement of expenditure written off daily to their god. The small amount of, say, a few cents only further signifies the articulation of religion and economic activity. The overt emphasis placed on their religion cannot, therefore, be overlooked or ignored.[22]

Chinese temples and clan associations also played an important role in credit making and credit keeping functions. In Singapore, with its very large and diverse Chinese population, there were various such organizations, each serving a particular group based on dialect, surname or village/province of origin in China. Singapore Kwong-Wai-Siew Peck San Theng (廣惠肇碧山亭), for instance, was a temple-cum-burial organization formed in 1871 among migrants from Guangzhou, Huizhou and Zhaoqing in Guangdong Province.[23]

With regard to credit and finance, Chinese temples and other sociocultural associations not only acted as loan agencies, or housed such agencies, but also facilitated capital pooling activities in indirect ways. Meetings of rotating credit and capital pooling societies (*hui* and *kongsi*) were very often conducted on the premises of a temple or clan association. In some cases a commercial *kongsi* was actually synonymous with a temple or clan. An example was the Tan Kongsi of nineteenth-century Melaka, which was one and the same as the Tan Clan Association, headed by the renowned merchant Tan Tock Seng. Another was the Khoo Kongsi of Penang, also known as the Khoo Lineage Association. This *kongsi* belonged to one of the so-called "Big Five" mercantile families in nineteenth- and twentieth-century Penang. The Khoo Kongsi built its own temple, called the Leong San Tong, in 1851. Later, in the 1930s, it also established its own burial ground at Batu Gantong in Penang.[24]

Some so-called lineage organizations were actually multi-lineage contractual formations, as in the case of the Tan ancestral temple, also known as the Wee Hwee Kiong temple, in Semarang, Java. This temple was established in the early nineteenth century by Tan Tiang Tjhing (1770–1833) and his descendants. Members of his family occupied the highest administrative positions available to the Chinese in the port town during this period and held the opium revenue farm (to manage a monopoly opium-selling business by paying tax to government officials), perhaps the most lucrative of all business opportunities in nineteenth-century Java, up to the 1870s.[25] As they rose to become the most prominent merchants in Semarang, they built alliances with other powerful Tan lineages, such as those of Tan Goan Kong and Tan Tieng, to whom they were not related by blood. In the Wee Hwee Kiong temple, the centre point of the emerging multi-lineage organization, rituals were performed in honour of the deity Tan Seng Ong (陳聖王), who was consecrated as a putative common ancestor. Also known as Tan Guan Kong (陳元光) and Khay Tjiang Sing Ong (開漳聖王), Tan Seng Ong was a popular deity in South China whose surname made him an obvious choice for this role. God, temple and surname thus became the symbolic foundation for a commercial and financial alliance.[26]

Conclusion: Comparison between Chinese and Indian Ties: Joint Families

Strong joint family ties are apparent in the Chettiar system, which, as a discipline, covered whole swathes of social life of family and family members in the Hindu family system in Ceylon.

In resolving disputes between Chettiars doing business in the island, the Courts held that a business carried on jointly by them as members of a Hindu undivided family is presumed to be joint family business and not an ordinary commercial partnership. The legal position appears to be the same in India. Section 5 of the Indian Partnership Act no. 9 of 1932 enacted that the relation of partnership arises from contract and not from status and, in particular, members of a Hindu undivided family carrying on a family business are not partners in such business. The joint Hindu family system is a status which can only be acquired by birth or by adoption. However, it is important to note that, like an ordinary partnership, an undivided Hindu family as such has no legal persona as distinct and separate from that of its members.[27]

Once a joint Hindu family has been established, it follows, almost as a corollary in the case of families, that in addition to "jointness" of food and worship, and ownership of property, that within that family there is a narrower body called the "coparcenary" composed of those members who acquire by birth an interest in that property. This coparcenary usually consists of sons, grandsons and great grandsons, and the property that falls to them is ancestral property as distinct from self-acquired property.

The question, then, was whether property was coparcenary or self-acquired. On this question, Mulla says on page 256 of the 1936 edition of his *Principles of Hindu Law*:

> There is no presumption that a family, because it is joint, possesses joint property or any property [...]. To render property joint, the plaintiff must prove that it was purchased with joint family funds or that it was produced out of the joint family property or by joint labour. None of these alternatives is a matter of legal presumption.[28]

The reason for the extraneous loyalty of the Indian minority lay partly in the social morals and ethics of India. The Chinese, once cut off from China, were not expected to feed their families at home. Once planted into foreign soil, Chinese culture flourished but its individuals were not necessarily tethered to remote members of the family left in China. The Chinese raised enormous sums for the cause of the country but did not remit savings to China by regular money orders, to a very great extent. The Indian, to whatever religion he may have belonged, did not cease to remain a member of the large joint family. The duty to contribute for the maintenance of the family was enshrined in the social ethics of India. Thus, however dispersed the members may have been, they gravitated towards the central family by the principle of common property. The question of remittances sent by the Indians to their families in India has even now left a scar on Indo-Burmese relations.[29]

However, regardless of their motivation and necessities of remittance to their home towns, observations here on Indian and Chinese ways of remittance reveal that they were rather similar. Both of them included:

a) The use of local networks for their remittances rather than formal financial institutions such as banks and post office.
b) From the point of view of business institutions, remittances by both Indians and Chinese did involve some sort of company. Indian remittance firms – which include Chettiar banking – were rather strong forms of institutions.
c) The remittance business played an intermediary role between the local communities of migrants' home towns and the financial markets of East Asia and South Asia, with Singapore in between. Also, it intermediated local finance and international finance with a variety of devices to avoid increased risks by utilizing various networks with social ties such as clan ties and business ties with reliable credit on the one hand and by strengthening financial ties with banks to increase their profit through the remittance business on the other. In this respect, there were no big differences between overseas Indian and overseas Chinese remittance systems.
d) The use of other social ties, such as religion and worship, with Hindu temples providing the meeting place for Chettiar moneylenders in Singapore and the Chinese temple as a meeting point by local Chinese merchants.
e) Transfer of credit in one direction and receipt of money in the other direction compensated each other in both cases.

To sum up, Indians and Chinese identify their position in families through strong social units such as *hundi* and shareholdings, which also function as tools of negotiation for ties to connect with each other.

Notes

1 British Parliamentary Papers, *Statistical Abstract for the Several British Self-Governing Dominions, Colonies, Possessions, and Protectorates in Each Year from 1899 to 1913* (London, 1915), pp. 285–6; Hamashita Takeshi, "Geopolitics of Hong Kong Economy," in *Rethinking Hong Kong: New Paradigms, New Perspectives*, edited by Elizabeth Sinn, Wong Siu-lun and Chan Wing-hoi (Hong Kong: Centre of Asian Studies, University of Hong Kong, 2009), pp. 101–43.

2 W. L. Mathieson, *Great Britain and the Slave Trade* (London: Longmans, Green, 1929).

3 Li Changzhuan, *Zhongguo Zhiminshi* [China's colonization history] (Beijing: Commercial Press, 1936).

4 Sinnappah Arasaratnam, *Indians in Malaysia and Singapore* (Kuala Lumpur: Cambridge University Press, 1979), pp. 36–7.

5 Arasaratnam, *Indians in Malaysia and Singapore*, pp. 62–3.

6 Arasaratnam, *Indians in Malaysia and Singapore*, pp. 92–3.

7 The major foreign trading companies serving as agents for foreign steamship firms were (from Hongkong General Chamber of Commerce, *Annual Report 1901*, p. 97): David Sassoon, Sons & Co. (agents, Apcar Line of Steamers); H. A. Ritchie (superintendent, P&O SN Co.); Jardine, Matheson & Co. (general managers, Indo-China SN Co. Ltd); Butterfield & Swire (agents, Ocean SS Co., China Navigation Co., NEL Orient Line, Taikoo Sugar Refinery); Bradley & Co. (Agents, Shan Steamers); Melchers & Co. (Agents, Nordd, Lloyd, East Asiatic Co.).

8 Fukuda Shozo, *Kakyo keizairon* [Overseas Chinese economy] (Tokyo: Ganshodo, 1939), chapter 2.

9 Sarasin Viraphol, *Tribute and Profit: Sino-Siamese Trade, 1652–1853* (Cambridge, MA: Council on East Asian Studies, Harvard University, Harvard University Press, 1977).

10 Lin Jinzhi, *Jindai Huaqiao touzi guonei qiyeshi yanjiu* [A history of modern Chinese investment in domestic enterprises] (Fuzhou: Fujian People's Publisher, 1985).

11 "Xingma qiaohui yu minxinye" [Overseas Chinese remittances and private remittance agencies in Singapore and Malaysia] in *Xingma tongjian* [Encyclopedia of Singapore and Malaysia] (Singapore: World Publishing, n.d.), pp. 624–33.

12 China's modern postal system began in 1896 and operated through the Imperial Customs network.

13 Takeshi Hamashita, "Choko boeki shisutemu to kindai Ajia" [The tributary trade system and modern Asia], *Kokusai Seiji* [Journal of International Politics] 82 (May 1986).

14 Bank of Taiwan, *Nanyo ni okeru kakyo, fu kawase kankei* [Overseas Chinese in the South Seas: The foreign exchange business] (Taipei: Research Department of Bank of Taiwan, 1914).

15 Zheng Linkuan, *Fujian Huaqiao zhi huikuan* [Remittances by Overseas Chinese from Fujian], (Fuzhou: Office of Statistics, Secretariat 秘书處 of the Fujian Provincial Government), Chapter 5.

16 Many banks were established in Singapore in the early twentieth century: Guangyi Bank (Guangdong capital) in 1903, Sihaitong Bank (Chaozhou capital) in 1907 and Huaqiao Bank (Fujian capital) in 1912.

17 Zheng Linkuan, *Fujian Huaqiao zhi huikuan*, pp. 276–8.

18 W. S. Weerasooria, *The Nattukottai Chettiar Merchant Bankers in Ceylon* (Sri Jayewardenepura Kotte, Dehiwala, Sri Lanka: Tisara Prakasakayo, 1973).

19 Rudner David West, *Caste and Capitalism in Colonial India: The Nattukottai Chettiars* (Berkeley: University of California Press, 1994), pp. 58–9 and 69.

20 George Hicks, ed., *Overseas Chinese Remittances from Southeast Asia 1910–1940* (Singapore: Select Books, 1993), pp. 312–14.

21 U Tun Wai, *Burma's Currency and Credit* (Rangoon: University of Rangoon, Department of Economics), 1962.

22 Hans-Dieter Evers and Jayarani Pavadarayan, *Asceticism and Ecstasy: The Chettiars of Singapore* (Bielefeld: Sociology of Development Research Centre, Faculty of Sociology, University of Bielefeld, Germany), 1985, pp. 11–12.

23 Zeng Ling, "Bangqun fenshan" [Community group cemeteries], in *Yueyang zaijian jiayuan* [Reconstructing home overseas] (Nanchang: Jiangxi High School Publisher, 2003), pp. 60–98.

24 Franke Wolfgang and Chen Tieh Fan, eds, *Chinese Epigraphic Materials in Malaysia* (Kuala Lumpur: University of Malaya Press, 1985), pp. 765–6, 856–65.

25 Opium farms were monopoly concessions which the governments of all Southeast Asian colonies and Siam usually auctioned to the highest bidder for a specified period. The winning bidder gained the right to manufacture *chandu*, or smokeable opium from raw opium, as well as the right to retail *chandu* to the local population. Carl A. Trocki, *Opium, Empire and the Global Economy: A Study of the Asian Opium Trade, 1750–1950* (London: Routledge, 1999), pp. 137–55.

26 Kwee Hui Kian, "Money and Credit in Chinese Mercantile Operations in Colonial and Precolonial Southeast Asia," in *Credit and Debt in Indonesia, 860–1930*, edited by David Henley and Peter Boomgaard (Singapore: ISEAS, 2009); Wolfgang Franke and Chen Tieh Fan, eds, *Chinese Epigraphic Materials in Malaysia* (Kuala Lumpur: University of Malaya Press, 1982–85).

27 Weerasooria, *The Nattukottai Chettiar Merchant Bankers in Ceylon*, p. 111.
28 Weerasooria, *The Nattukottai Chettiar Merchant Bankers in Ceylon*, p. 115.
29 Sinnappah Arasaratnam, *Indians in Malaysia and Singapore*, pp. 25–6.

References

Arasaratnam, Sinnappah. *Indians in Malaysia and Singapore.* Kuala Lumpur: Oxford University Press, 1979.

Cheong, Yong Mun and V. V. Bhanoji Rao, eds. *Singapore–India Relations; A Primer.* Singapore: Singapore University Press, 1995.

Deshingkar, Giri. *Security and Science in China and India.* New Delhi: Samskriti, 2005.

Evers, Hans-Dieter and Pavadarayan, Jayarani. "Religious Fever and Economic Success: The Chettiars of Singapore." In *Indian Communities in Southeast Asia*, edited by K. S. Sandhu and A. Mani, pp. 847–65. Singapore: ISEAS, 1993.

Franke, Wolfgang and Chen Tiee Fan, eds. *Chinese Epigraphic Materials in Malaysia.* Kuala Lumpur: University of Malaya Press, 1982–85.

Gupta, Anirudha, ed. *Indians Abroad: Asia and Africa, Report of an International Seminar.* New Delhi: Orient Longman, 1971.

Hamashita, Takeshi. "Geopolitics of Hong Kong Economy." In *Rethinking Hong Kong: New Paradigms, New Perspectives*, edited by Elizabeth Sinn, Wong Siu-lun and Chan Wing-hui, pp. 101–43. Hong Kong: Centre of Asian Studies, University of Hong Kong, 2009.

Hamilton, G. G. "The Organizational Foundations of Western and Chinese Commerce: Historical and Comparative Analysis." Paper presented at the Conference on Business Groups and Economic Development in East Asia. Hong Kong: Centre of Asian Studies, University of Hong Kong, 1989.

Hicks, George, ed. *Overseas Chinese Remittance from Southeast Asia 1910–1940.* Singapore: Select Books, 1993.

Ito, Izumi. "1930 nendai kouhan no Yokohama chukagai to sono shuhen – chugokukei/indokei shoten no jyokyo wo chushin ni" [Yokohama Chinatown and its vicinity in the latter half of the 1930s – with a focus on Chinese and Indian shops]. *Journal of Yokohama Archives of History* (published by Yokohama Archives of History) 29, no. 3 (2011): 1–54.

Kian, Kwee Hui. "Money and Credit in Chinese Mercantile Operations in Colonial and Precolonial Southeast Asia." In *Credit and Debt in Indonesia, 860–1930: From Peonage to Pawnshop, from Kongsi to Cooperative*, edited by David Henley and Peter Boomgaard, pp. 124–42. Singapore: ISEAS, 2009.

King, Frank H. H., *The Hongkong Bank in Late Imperial China 1864–1902*, vol. 1. Cambridge: Cambridge University Press, 1987.

Mahajani, Usha. *The Role of Indian Minorities in Burma.* Bombay: Vora, 1960.

Nair, Gopinathan P. R. "Migration of Keralites to the Arab World." In *Kerala's Economy: Performance, Problems, Prospects*, edited by B. A. Prakash. New Delhi: Sage, 1994.

Prakash, B. A. "Gulf Migration and Its Economic Impact: The Kerala Experience." *Economic and Political Weekly*, 12 December 1998.

______. ed. *Kerala's Economy: Performance, Problems, Prospects*. New Delhi: Sage, 1994.

Ray Chaudhuri, Jayasri. *Migration and Remittances: Inter-urban and Rural–Urban Linkages*. New Delhi: Sage, 1993.

Rudner, David West. *Caste and Capitalism in Colonial India: The Nattukottai Chettiars*. Berkeley: University of California Press, 1994.

Schrader, Heiko. "The Socioeconomic Function of Moneylenders in Expanding Economies: The Case of Chettiars." *Saving and Development* 16, no. 1 (1992): 69–82.

Shigematsu, Shinji. *Kokusai Ido no Rekishi Shakaigaku* [Socio-history on International Migration]. Nagoya: Nagoya University Press, 1999.

Thampi, Madhavi, ed. *India and China*. New Delhi: Social Science Press, 2005.

Tinker, Hugh, *A New System of Slavery: The Export of Indian Labour Overseas, 1830–1920*. London: Oxford University Press, 1974.

Trocki, Carl A. *Opium, Empire and the Global Economy: A Study of the Asian Opium Trade 1750–1950*. London: Routledge, 1999.

Vaid, K. N. *The Overseas Indian Community in Hong Kong*. Hong Kong: Centre of Asian Studies, University of Hong Kong, 1972.

Wang, Bangwei and Tansen Sen, eds. *India and China: Interactions through Buddhism and Diplomacy: A Collection of Essays by Professor Prabodh Chandra Bagchi*. London: Anthem Press, 2011.

Weerasooria, W. S. *The Nattukottai Chettiar Merchant Bankers in Ceylon*. Sri Jayewardenepura Kotte: Tisara Prakasakayo, 1973.

White, Barbara-Sue. *Turbans and Traders: Hong Kong's Indian Communities*. Hong Kong: Oxford University Press, 1994.

Wong, Siu-Lun. *Emigrant Entrepreneurs: Shanghai Industrialists in Hong Kong*. New York: Oxford University Press, 1988.

Zeng Ling, "Fenshan zuzhi, shequn gongzu yu bangqun zhenghe: Shijiu shiji de Xinjiapo huaren shehui" [Burial grounds administration, common ancestry and bang associations: Singapore Chinese society in the nineteenth century] *Asian Culture* 24 (2000): 122–37.

Websites

http://www.icicibank.com/aboutus/history.page?. 14 October 2014.

http://www.mustafa.com.sg/frmAboutUs.aspx. 14 October 2014.

Chapter 6

IDENTITY, TRANSNATIONALISM AND CORPORATE DEVELOPMENT: CHINESE BUSINESS IN MALAYSIA

Edmund Terence Gomez

Introduction

At the tail end of the last century, as most studies on China hailed the dawn of a new economic superpower, other research highlighted the emergence of a tightly interlocked diaspora whose combined corporate power through business "networks" would enable both China and Chinese entrepreneurs to emerge as a global force. Meanwhile, a popular narrative about Chinese business has grown up in reciprocal interaction with transnational studies. According to its exponents, contemporary Chinese capitalism has distinctive characteristics that facilitate its growth. Chinese culture and value systems determine decision making among firms owned by Chinese, while intra-ethnic networks, based on trust and kinship ties, help reduce transaction costs and diminish risks.[1] These business networks are said to be tightly knit and embedded through interlocking ownership and interlocking directorships with strong dimensions of ethnicity and solidarity.

However, generational shifts have occurred which have had an important impact on decision making in business. In Southeast Asia, as a result of curbs on immigration introduced after the start of the Great Depression in the 1930s, obtaining citizenship has become increasingly difficult. The emergence of new identities among immigrants' descendants undermines claims that the Chinese act collectively to protect vested interests. When new generations take over, there is little evidence that they depend on Chinese networks and interlocking directorships to help develop their enterprise.[2] Even so, many studies argue that Chinese of the diaspora normatively practise business networking, involving interlocking ownership ties, and that as a result they are now (with the rise of China) emerging as a major force in an increasingly globalized economy.[3]

The key questions in this study are the following: To what extent does common ethnic identity and culture provide a basis for business alliances, local and global, involving interlocking directorships and stock ownership? How and when does group identity count?

This chapter will trace the creation and evolution of intra-ethnic corporate networks and organizational forms of business enterprise among Chinese-owned small- and medium-size enterprises (SMEs).[4] This study will also review the links between local SMEs and Taiwanese firms that have invested in Malaysia. By tracing how business ties and organizational forms have evolved across generations, and in national and transnational perspectives, this study will provide insights into identity change among migrants' descendants.

Business, Culture and Transnationalism

In the 1990s, the term transnationalism was adopted to describe the links between migrants in places of settlement and origin and among diasporic communities. Transnational studies also emerged at the height of the revival of mass emigration out of China, a reason why this country's "new migrants" feature centrally in them. The revival coincided with the propagation of the belief that Chinese business is distinguished by its networks, tightly knit and bound by solidarity, a theory that emerged (especially in books written by journalists) as a response to public discourses about the rise of China.[5] This argument has given rise to some misconceptions.

Ever since the late nineteenth century, the Chinese state has striven, with a brief interruption in the Mao years, to make emigrants and their descendants a tool of foreign policy and a source of funds and investment. Today, China protects the interests even of Chinese with foreign nationality, by treating them better than "common foreigners" and allowing them a "flexible form of citizenship."[6] The Mainland government has argued that the Chinese diaspora would gain much by investing in its burgeoning economy, an idea accepted by most business analysts and economists. In transnational studies, some scholars, building on China's state rhetoric, assumed that this tie was not just economic but based on values and allegiances. Much of this literature has focused on migrants, but its findings also have implications for their descendants. Importantly too, many of the theories about ethnic and national identity have been based on research in migrant-receiving countries, but their conceptual frameworks have been applied to minorities in countries that restrict access to citizenship. Yet studies on ethnic minorities in Southeast Asia formed by immigration over the last two centuries show that they identify largely with the country of their birth, not with China.[7]

The tripartite link between transnationalism, capital and identity is explained most clearly by Ong and Nonini in their *Ungrounded Empires: The Cultural Politics of Modern Chinese Transnationalism.* They argue that in the course of the transnational experience, Chinese migrants develop a "third culture," defined as a "modern Chinese transnationalism" that "provides alternative visions in late capitalism to Western modernity and generates new and distinctive social arrangements, cultural discourses, practices, and subjectivities." This culture includes the deployment of economic strategies such as the family firm and networks of social relations (or *guanxi*) as a means of accumulating capital.[8]

Theorizing such a tripartite linkage essentializes capitalism and intra-ethnic business networks. Redding and Hamilton[9] have been the most vocal proponents of the growing transnational impact of Chinese businesses and networks, though they do not write within the framework of transnational theory. Studies on ethnic enterprise, particularly the work of Light and Gold,[10] have taken the essentializing of Chinese-owned enterprises even further, while concepts such "Chinese commonwealth"[11] are the most extreme examples of the homogenizing of ethnic communities and culture.

The idea that diasporic Chinese have a strong collective identity that influences their business style and the development of their enterprises has given rise to a literature that is sometimes called the "culturalist perspective."[12] Its proponents argue that members of ethnic groups share patterns of values, behaviour and cognition that distinguish them from other such communities. Diasporic Chinese enterprise is, in essence, said to be characterized everywhere by the same "ethnic style"; that is, the family firm and intra-ethnic national and transnational social connections play a crucial role in capital formation and accumulation. These two modes of business and social organization are central to the "Confucian ethic," a perennial theme and key explanatory tool for analysts of Chinese enterprise who think culture matters in business decision making.

Few scholars would disagree that family and kinship ties are a key constituent of Chinese enterprise.[13] It is commonly accepted that kinship ties are an important consideration when hiring staff and obtaining funds in the initial stages of enterprise formation. At the point of its creation, a firm is usually under the control of its founder and his close relatives, who play a crucial role in setting its style of management. It should be added that this phenomenon is not uniquely Chinese.[14]

The argument about "networks" is more contentious. Redding, for example, maintains that Chinese networks in Taiwan and Hong Kong share commonalities that indicate "cultural predispositions."[15] Supporters of this view argue that Chinese enterprise is a form of "*guanxi* capitalism."[16] Networks are said to be a unique institutional feature of "Asian capitalism," one that distinguishes it from the Western notion of bureaucratization and efficiency.[17] This form of capitalism supposedly provides Chinese firms in Southeast Asia with major competitive advantages.[18]

Others go even further, and talk about "Chinese diaspora capitalism." Lever-Tracy and Tracy argue that this form of capitalism is based on personalized, long-term horizontal networks that bind together Chinese-owned family companies.[19] These networks are "embedded in relations of reciprocity" and rest on the principle of trust. This type of capitalism is said to predate "modern capitalism" and to attach less weight than other forms of capitalism to corporate expansion and maximizing profit.[20]

The main concern of critics of this perspective is not the idea of networks as such but the notion of "Chinese-ness," which in the critics' opinion plays only a minor role in determining how Chinese businesspeople make decisions and develop their enterprises.[21] In the critics' view, culturalist analyses misrepresent the basis for and extent of business ties among Chinese firms. Interlocking stock ownership ties involving large-scale firms have not been sustained,[22] while production networks do not form in a single dimension but primarily comprise chains of producers or subcontractors that operate at multiple levels and whose membership changes over time.[23] Co-ethnic cooperation for the benefit of the community, the basis on which such networks form according to those who adopt a culturalist analysis, fails to explain these ties.

The history of ethnic Chinese communities in Southeast Asia suggests that triadic-style definitions of transnationalism apply only to migrants.[24] However, the identity and national allegiance of some longer-settled members of the migrant cohort undergo a profound reconfiguration.[25] The Chinese communities in Southeast Asia provide interesting examples of the complexity of ethnic and national identity, its evolution over time, its reconfigurations in the context of political and economic change, and the erosion of migrant solidarity and cohesion.

It is important to explore the idea of national identity from the perspective of the descendants of immigrants, which may be more profound and robust than is often thought. An understanding of concepts such as "new" and "multiple" identities and the related idea of "cultural fluidity" would need to feature in the exploration.[26] These concepts highlight identity change across generations and focus attention on the need to challenge the notion that common ethnicity helps engender global flows of capital and information through international business networks and influences enterprise development.

Importantly too, this attribution of the dynamism of enterprises owned by ethnic minorities in Southeast Asia to intra-ethnic business networks reflects a poor understanding of the evolution of Chinese enterprise. Southeast Asian history indicates that in the early stages after the migration of the Chinese to the region, it was common sub-ethnicity – rather than common ethnicity – that had been a key factor in enabling Chinese to work together.[27] The main sub-ethnic Chinese communities, the Hokkien, Cantonese, Hakka, Teochew and Hainanese, have historically shown little inclination in going beyond their sub-ethnic community to act as one community in any country in Southeast Asia. The establishment and role of clan-based organizations were then important, and functioned effectively in bringing together sub-ethnic communities.

Sub-ethnic groups came to dominate particular economic sectors. The Hokkiens in Malaysia and Singapore had control of domestic banking, the Teochews in Thailand had a long history of domination of the rice trade industry, while the Hokchias in Indonesia had a long history of control over petty trade in rural areas on the island of Java. Sub-ethnic Chinese control of these sectors has now diminished significantly, and while many of these sub-ethnic clan-based organizations still exist, their importance has declined appreciably in Southeast Asia.[28] The decline of the importance of these ethnically based institutions is indicative of important identity transformations taking place among the descendants of migrants.

For this reason, the most dangerous aspect of this argument about the mode of operation and development of Chinese enterprise is what it suggests about the sense of national identity of members of this community in Asia. In multi-ethnic Southeast Asia, home to a large Chinese population, the nature of ethnic politics fostered by some government leaders has reinforced the idea among the indigenous communities that Chinese have little or no sense of loyalty to the "host country." These Chinese owe loyalty only to the "home country" – that is, the motherland of their forefathers who had migrated to the region. This idea of the doubtful loyalty of Chinese to the nation of their birth, while erroneous, is dangerous as well, for new generations of Chinese have emerged who have a deep sense of their national identity. In most of Southeast Asia, the issue of the Chinese's supposed questionable loyalty to the nation takes on added importance because of this community's influential presence in these economies.

Chinese Enterprise in Malaysia

The Chinese in the SME Sector

Chinese business history in Malaysia reveals a community that has always been fragmented, even when under siege through public policies.[29] Malaysian history indicates that family businesses were common among migrants during the colonial period, though the incorporation of this type of enterprise has little to do with Chinese culture. Family firms emerged because of the problems migrants faced in securing start-up capital and hiring labour. In a number of cases, partnerships were forged to deal with the problems encountered when starting a business. In the colonial period, while the Chinese had a history of intra-ethnic business cooperation, most of these partnerships have either fallen apart or evolved into family enterprises.[30]

In the immediate post-colonial period until 1970, since SMEs were predominantly Chinese owned, there was little government support for these enterprises. When affirmative action, through the New Economic Policy (NEP), was introduced in 1970, although the government voiced its intent to promote SMEs, the state's primary emphasis was on employing public enterprises, later called government-linked companies (GLCs), to venture into various sectors of the economy on behalf of the Bumiputeras.[31] The NEP stipulated that 30 per cent equity of all quoted firms be transferred to Bumiputeras, to ensure greater Malay corporate ownership of all sectors of the economy. Inevitably, SMEs owned by minority ethnic groups prefer to remain small for fear of expropriation of their companies when they relinquish a substantial portion of their equity to private individuals after publicly listing their enterprise.

Most SMEs are therefore also predisposed to functioning as family-based firms. In this environment, Chinese-owned companies have survived because they were aware that since the risks involved in investing were high, they had to be sure they had the capacity to turn a profit or secure adequate returns on their investments when they ventured into business.[32] Not all Chinese have managed to subsist profitably in this environment, while entrepreneurial businesspeople were reluctant to invest in research and development (R&D), preferring to remain small-sized firms operating merely as subcontractors.

For this reason too, in manufacturing, the government has not been able to foster entrepreneurial SMEs, in spite of the efforts by the Small and Medium Industries Development Corporation (SMIDEC) – now renamed the SME Corporation – formed in 1996 as a unit under the Ministry of International Trade and Industry (MITI), to involve small firms, particularly those owned by Bumiputeras, in the industrial sector through ties with multinational companies or GLCs.[33] SMEs, however, including those owned by the Chinese, have not been able to develop export capacity because they have not invested adequately in R&D.[34]

Another reason for their limited investment in R&D is that Chinese SMEs are reputedly reluctant to approach banks for loans for fear of the need to divulge information that they feel can be used against them through the NEP. As such, they prefer the option of internal financing and credit from suppliers to run their operations. The owners of small family firms tend to have a short-term mentality. Since these enterprises serve primarily as a source of income and employment, their children are discouraged from joining the enterprise.[35]

SMEs are also reluctant to divide up large orders, even if this entails keeping down production costs. In a situation where a firm is unable to perform a particular order, it is unlikely that the job will be channelled to another company, an indication that Chinese SMEs tend to prefer to go it alone.[36] The reason for this is that Malaysian corporate history has shown that in order for firms owned by minorities to survive, in view of the discrimination they face because of affirmative action, they have to compete in a manner which would also involve keeping information to themselves.

The common features of Chinese SMEs inevitably are that they seldom integrate with other firms, refrain from drawing attention to themselves, and prefer to establish numerous small firms to venture into an enterprise that offers hope of a quick profit.[37] These factors have impaired Malaysia's industrialization drive, in spite of the country's impressive record of economic growth, specifically in the manufacturing sector. Malaysia's reputation in manufacturing has, for these reasons, primarily been due to investments from foreign firms.

Among SMEs, most owners are not interested in passing on their businesses to their children and would prefer that they become professionals. Most descendants of the founders of SMEs resist joining the enterprise, which eventually has to close down or be sold off. This suggests that generational change has an important bearing on the manner of enterprise development; in particular, it threatens the survival of family firms. Some descendants try to recruit professional managers, because they are better educated or equipped to develop the enterprise or better able to work with non-Chinese. The development of inter-ethnic management and business ties leads eventually to major changes in ownership and control, a reflection of the companies' growing in organizational complexity. This evolutionary pattern, from family firm to professional management, is not yet evident among Chinese enterprises in Malaysia because most are still under the control of the founding or the second generation. In other words, they are still young firms.

Importantly too, during the 1990s, among smaller firms, including those that were being quoted on the local stock exchange, the Bursa Kuala Lumpur, there was growing evidence of inter-ethnic business ties. These links indicated a transition that reflected two things about implementation of the NEP: first, the creation of an independent Bumiputera middle class through affirmative action; second, among the new generation of Malaysians, there is greater openness to inter-ethnic cooperation in business for mutual benefit. Among middle-class Bumiputeras, it reflected a feeling of confidence and ability to hold their own in business, given the skills they have acquired through state support under the NEP.[38] A similar trend has been noted among new SMEs that are being incorporated, specifically those owned by professionals, particularly in the services, information communication technology (ICT) and manufacturing sectors.[39] The partners in these relationships appeared to be equally competent.

Networks and Intra-ethnic Foreign and Domestic Business Ties

The race riots of 1969 and the subsequent emphasis of the NEP on building Bumiputera enterprises meant that strict requirements were imposed on later economic policies regarding both foreign direct investment (FDI) promotion and FDI–SME linkages. Initially Malaysia treated SME development as a desirable but lower priority appendage to larger industrialization objectives, with both policies constrained by NEP requirements. For SMEs, Bumiputera preferences exerted a double impact, inhibiting the growth of local Chinese SMEs while discouraging some FDI that might provide linkage opportunities. Economic crises twice altered these priorities, resulting in a temporary suspension of some NEP mandates, but not until 2003 was SME promotion accorded a distinct priority status that drew greater attention and resources, including for the promotion of FDI–SME linkages.

In 1987, for example, following a severe recession, the government recognized the need to promote domestic private investment, particularly among Chinese, in the manufacturing sector. That year, the government amended legislation such as the *Industrial Coordination Act 1975* (ICA), which, when introduced in the 1970s, had stringent Bumiputera investment and employee quotas for enterprises in the manufacturing sector. The government also either suspended or relaxed some NEP requirements to promote investments. These policy moves, coupled with favourable external market conditions, resulted in a resurgence of export-oriented manufacturing, largely under the auspices of foreign, especially East Asian, capital, including from Taiwan.[40]

With FDI playing a crucial role in Malaysia's economy as well as its future development plans, the concept of linkages between FDI and SME promotion seemed both logical and inevitable. As SME promotion assumed more importance and FDI attraction gained greater urgency in periods of economic downturn, government agencies with portfolios involving FDI, such as the Malaysian Industrial Development Authority (MIDA) and SME Corp., began to explore more ways to encourage FDI–SME linkages that would benefit both FDI and SME policy goals. Malaysia's most successful model for developing targeted FDI–SME supplier links occurred in the state of Penang, which focused on using FDI to build an electronics and electrical (E&E) manufacturing sector. Penang's effort received praise for its targeted resources, efficient administration and promotion of competitive SMEs. Penang is also the only state in the Malaysian federation with an ethnic Chinese majority population.

Although the efforts of the Malaysian government to encourage FDI–SME linkages have favoured specific types of domestic firms, especially in line with affirmative action policies, foreign investors normally want to identify and choose their own local partners. Multinational firms do contact important government agencies such as MIDA and SME Corp. where they receive a list of companies in compatible areas of business. However, most multinational firms also conduct independent research before entering the market, often using feasibility studies from consultants to help identify supply chains that can be created with SMEs. Once established, multinational firms may seek other local SMEs to integrate in their supply chain, mainly in a continuing effort to maintain low production costs. Various business associations and chambers of commerce play a role in helping match multinational firms with local firms. Some organizations represent domestic firms, while others are created along regional and country lines, such as the American Chamber of Commerce, the EU–Malaysia Chamber of Commerce and Industry, and the Japan External Trade Organization (JETRO).

In the case of investments from Taiwan, in spite of the inflow of investments from this country, there is little evidence that these foreign firms cooperate closely with local Chinese, including those running manufacturing enterprises in Penang, one of Malaysia's most industrialized states and the only one where the Chinese are the majority population.[41] Taiwanese investors specialize in establishing SMEs in the electronic and electrical sectors. These firms "network" when they first enter the region by creating loose groupings of SMEs, brought together for the manufacture of special items.[42] These supply chains and subcontracting ties benefit all parties engaged in producing a particular merchandise. Taiwanese SMEs usually belong to several production networks led by different enterprises. These networks, operating at multiple levels and evolving constantly in response to changes in demand, seldom survive for long. Once Taiwanese firms settle down in Malaysia, they try to become more profitable by disbanding old networks and creating new ones. The competition within and between these networks contributes to their constant evolution. Even partners within a single enterprise tend to break away, form their own businesses and emerge as competitors.[43]

Many subcontractors evolve through a process of vertical integration into producers, because it is more cost-efficient to do so. Among Chinese-owned small firms that have acquired a reputation for a process of vertical integration is Proreka (M) Sdn Bhd, incorporated in 2000. A manufacturer and supplier of OEM (original equipment manufacturer) parts and components for car manufacturers, Proreka commenced business as a prototype builder and supplier of small plastic automotive parts. By 2007, Proreka had evolved into a firm specializing in the design of car components with total sales of RM50 million. Proreka presently has the capability to undertake automotive projects, from the design stage (including whole vehicle styling deliberations with prototype and model building) to the mass production of parts and components.[44]

This process of vertical integration indicates that these firms have little interest in remaining within the production networks. Even in the face of competition and takeovers, SMEs are loath to merge, however much it might be in their interests to do so, a further indication of limited co-ethnic cooperation. Importantly too, government officials as well as local firms point out that multinational companies from Europe and North America appear more willing to share and transfer technology, up to a point, than enterprises from East Asia, including Taiwan.[45]

Conclusion

While transnational theory argues that common ethnic identity inspires mutual trust and support among diasporic groups, where intra-ethnic networks do form, they are based on a firm's capacity to contribute to the production of particular merchandise. Among SMEs, business ties in the shape of production chains were created for mutual benefit but seldom lasted long or with little commitment on the part of members to help each other grow. They were situational and episodic, patterned to serve common business interests rather than to support the supposed welfare of the larger Chinese community. Common ethnic identity served as a basis for business ties, but only for as long as all participants benefitted: it was quietly binned as soon as it became more profitable or viable to develop other forms of business links.

There is little evidence of intra-Chinese business cooperation, even though the Malaysian government has an affirmative-action policy that favours the development of Bumiputera-owned firms. The list of directors and shareholders of the leading Chinese companies shows little evidence of interlocking stock ownership or interlocking directorships.[46] Shareholding patterns indicate that Chinese firms function independently of one another.

Although Chinese enterprises are predominantly family owned, in the case of SMEs, most descendants of migrants show little interest in maintaining these enterprises, and this form of ownership rarely outlasts the migrant generation. Where the new generation do take the firms over, business ties are becoming increasingly inter-ethnic. In 1998, a review of the twenty-eight new companies listed on the stock exchange indicated that 29 per cent of them were Chinese–Bumiputera partnerships, while only two firms were intra-ethnic Chinese partnerships.[47] The growing evidence of inter-ethnically owned firms, without state intervention, is a positive development because, from the 1970s until the late 1980s, such trans-ethnic relationships, where company ownership was on a rather equal basis, were seen to prevail primarily among an elite group.

There is more evidence of competition than of cooperation among Chinese firms, contradicting the widely held view that the dynamism of these enterprises is due to intra-ethnic business linkages. Competition rather than cooperation explains the growth of Chinese firms and their potential to emerge as a dynamic force, nationally and internationally. Even so, Chinese enterprises are seldom seen as innovative in terms of creating new brand products. Very few Chinese-owned Malaysian companies are associated with a brand product of international repute.

These conclusions call into question the existence of a distinct type of "Chinese capitalism" and "ethnic enterprise." This suggests that among the concepts more useful for understanding Chinese enterprise are entrepreneurship,[48] class resources,[49] firm development and organization,[50] and patronage.[51]

These conclusions also draw attention to the multifaceted and intricate interplay of ethnic and national identities in the lives of minorities. While transnational theorists adopt a perspective whereby ethnic commonalties are said to help bring about dynamic and global entrepreneurial communities, the mode of operation and development of Chinese enterprises provides a searching test of such theorizing. Identity formation in diaspora is far more complex than current studies suggest and they neglect change in identity and cultural practices among migrants' descendants. Where descendants do take over companies, the changes they make in business strategy, organizational structure and management style suggest they are more inclined than their forebears to link up with non-Chinese business interests in inter-ethnic partnerships. The partnerships noted among SMEs owned by middle-class professionals are a result chiefly of the narrowing and even erasure of the educational gap between Chinese and Bumiputeras. The Chinese in Malaysia may share an ethnic label, but they clearly lack the uniformity ascribed to them, an issue that questions many of the principles of transnational theory.

Notes

1 S. Gordon Redding, *The Spirit of Chinese Capitalism* (Berlin: De Gruyter, 1990); Richard Whitley, *Business Systems in East Asia: Firms, Markets and Societies* (London: Sage, 1992).

2 In the case of large-scale enterprises in Southeast Asia, see Edmund Terence Gomez, *Chinese Business in Malaysia: Accumulation, Ascendance, Accommodation* (Honolulu: University of Hawaii Press, 1999) and Christian Chua, *Chinese Big Business in Indonesia: The State of Capital* (London: Routledge, 2009).

3 See, for example, Constance Lever-Tracy, David Ip and Noel Tracy, *The Chinese Diaspora and Mainland China: An Emerging Economic Synergy* (New York: St Martin's Press, 1996); Henry W. C. Yeung and Kris Olds, eds, *Globalization of Chinese Business Firms* (Basingstoke: Macmillan, 2000).

4 For a study of large enterprises owned by Chinese in Malaysia, where the research drew similar conclusions, see Gomez 1999.

5 See, for example, Joel Kotkin, *Tribes* (New York: Random House, 1993); and Murray Weidenbaum and Samuel Hughes, *The Bamboo Network* (New York: The Free Press, 1996).

6 Aihwa Ong, *Flexible Citizenship: The Cultural Logics of Transnationality* (Durham, NC: Duke University Press, 1999).

7 Anthony Reid, ed., *Sojourners and Settlers: Histories of Southeast Asia and the Chinese* (St Leonards: Allen and Unwin, 1996); Leo Suryadinata, ed., *Southeast Asian Chinese: The Socio-cultural Dimension* (Singapore: Times Academic Press, 1995); Chan Kwok Bun and Claire Chiang, *Stepping Out: The Making of Chinese Entrepreneurs* (Singapore: Prentice Hall, 1994).

8 Aihwa Ong and Donald M. Nonini, eds, *Ungrounded Empires: The Cultural Politics of Modern Chinese Transnationalism* (London: Routledge, 1997), pp. 11 and 21.

9 Redding, *The Spirit of Chinese Capitalism*; Gary G. Hamilton, ed., *Asian Business Networks* (Berlin: W. de Gruyter, 1996).

10 Ivan Light and Steven J. Gold, *Ethnic Economies* (San Diego: Academic Press, 2000).

11 John Kao, "The Worldwide Web of Chinese Business," *Harvard Business Review*, March–April, 1993.

12 See, for example, Redding, *The Spirit of Chinese Capitalism*; Lever-Tracy, Ip and Tracy, *The Chinese Diaspora and Mainland China*; Yeung and Olds, *Globalization of Chinese Business Firms*; and Francis Fukuyama, *Trust: The Social Virtues and the Creation of Prosperity* (New York: Random House, 1995).

13 See, for example, Wong Siu-lun, "The Chinese Family Firm: A Model," *British Journal of Sociology* 36, no. 1 (1985); Redding, *The Spirit of Chinese Capitalism*; Whitley, *Business Systems in East Asia*; Manuel Castells, *The Information Age I: The Rise of the Network Society* (Oxford: Blackwell, 1993); Fukuyama, *Trust: The Social Virtues and the Creation of Prosperity* (New York: Random House, 1995); and Martin King Whyte, "The Chinese Family and Economic Development: Obstacle or Engine?" *Economic Development and Cultural Change* 45, no. 1 (1996).

14 Alfred D. Chandler Jr, *Strategy and Structure: Chapters in the History of the American Industrial Enterprise* (Cambridge: MIT Press, 1962); Edith T. Penrose, *The Theory of the Growth of the Firm* (Oxford: Basil Blackwell, 1980). Among European Union countries, between 75 and 90 per cent of all firms are said to be family enterprises. One in eight firms quoted on the London Stock Exchange is a family firm. According to an estimate by the magazine *Fortune* in 1993, nearly a third of the top 500 firms in the United States were family owned.

15 Redding, *The Spirit of Chinese Capitalism*.

16 See, for example, Hamilton, *Asian Business Networks*.

17 Whitley, *Business Systems in East Asia*; Nicole W. Biggart and Gary G. Hamilton, "On the Limits of a Firm-Based Theory to Explain Business Networks," in *The Economic Organization of East Asian Capitalism*, ed. Marco Orrù, Nicole Woolsey Biggart and Gary G. Hamilton (Thousand Oaks, CA: Sage, 1997), pp. 33–54.

18 Yeung and Olds, *Globalization of Chinese Business Firms*.

19 Lever-Tracy and Tracy, *The Chinese Diaspora and Mainland China*.

20 Lever-Tracy and Tracy, *The Chinese Diaspora and Mainland China*, p. 5.

21 See, for example, Gomez, *Chinese Business in Malaysia*; Edmund Terence Gomez and Michael H. H. Hsiao, eds, *Chinese Business in Southeast Asia: Contesting Cultural Explanations, Researching Entrepreneurship* (London: RoutledgeCurzon, 2004); David C. Schak, "Networks and Their Uses in Taiwanese Society," in *Chinese Business Networks: State, Economy and Culture*, ed. Chan Kwok Bun (Singapore: Prentice-Hall, 2000); Gregor Benton and Edmund Terence Gomez, *Chinatown and Transnationalism: Ethnic Chinese in Europe and Southeast Asia* (Canberra: Centre for the Study of the Chinese Southern Diaspora, 2000); Gregor Benton and Edmund Terence Gomez, *The Chinese in Britain, 1800–Present: Economy, Transnationalism, Identity* (Basingstoke: Palgrave-Macmillan, 2008).

22 See, for example, Gomez, *Chinese Business in Malaysia*; Chua, *Chinese Big Business in Indonesia.*

23 See Kung I-Chun, "Taiwanese Business in Southeast Asia," in *Chinese Business in Southeast Asia: Contesting Cultural Explanations, Researching Entrepreneurship*, ed. Edmund Terence Gomez and Hsin-Huang Michael Hsiao (London: Routledge, 2004).

24 Benton and Gomez, *Chinatown and Transnationalism*; Chan and Chiang, *Stepping Out: The Making of Chinese Entrepreneurs.*

25 See Gomez, *Chinese Business in Malaysia*; Chan and Chiang, *Stepping Out: The Making of Chinese Entrepreneurs*; Chua, *Chinese Big Business in Indonesia.*

26 See for example Stuart Hall, "New Ethnicities," in *"Race," Culture and Difference*, ed. J. Donald and A. Rattansi (London: Sage, 1992).

27 See G. William Skinner, *Chinese Society in Thailand: An Analytical History* (Ithaca, NY: Cornell University Press, 1957); Victor Purcell, *The Chinese in Southeast Asia* (London: Oxford University Press, 1965).

28 James V. Jesudason, "Chinese Business and Ethnic Equilibrium in Malaysia," *Development and Change* 28, no. 1 (1997); Benton and Gomez, *Chinatown and Transnationalism.*

29 See James V. Jesudason, *Ethnicity and the Economy: The State, Chinese Business and Multinationals in Malaysia* (Singapore: Oxford University Press, 1989); Hara Fujio, ed., *Formation and Restructuring of Business Groups in Malaysia* (Tokyo: Institute of Developing Economies, 1993); Peter Searle, *The Riddle of Malaysian Capitalism: Rent Seekers or Real Capitalists* (Honolulu: University of Hawaii Press); Gomez, *Chinese Business in Malaysia.*

30 See Hara, *Formation and Restructuring*; Chan and Chiang, *Stepping Out*; Lee K. H. and Chow M. S., *Bibliographical Dictionary of the Chinese in Malaysia* (Kuala Lumpur: Institute of Advanced Studies, University of Malaya, 1997); Gomez, 1999.

31 Literally translated, "Bumiputera" means "sons of the soil," an epithet used to refer to the members of the Malay community, although it includes the indigenous people of Sabah and Sarawak.

32 For a discussion on this matter, see Lee Kam Hing and Lee Poh Ping, "Malaysian Chinese Business: Who Survived the Crisis?" *Kyoto Review*, no. 3 (October 2003).

33 Interview with director of Chinese-owned SME Globetronics Bhd, which has strong ties with multinational companies. Interview on 7 July 2009.

34 Interview with Malaysian Industrial Development Authority (MIDA) officials on 2 July 2009.

35 Interview with SME Association representatives, 29 June 2009.

36 Interview with SME Association representatives, 29 June 2009. See Gomez, *Chinese Business in Malaysia*, for an in-depth discussion on similar limited intra-ethnic business cooperation among Chinese owners of large-scale enterprises.

37 Interview with SME Association representatives, 29 June 2009.

38 Edmund Terence Gomez, "Family Firms, Transnationalism, and Generational Change: Chinese Enterprise in Britain and Malaysia," *East Asia: An International Quarterly* 24, no. 2 (Summer 2007): 153–72.

39 Interview with SME Association representatives, 29 June 2009.

40 Edmund Terence Gomez and Jomo K. S., *Malaysia's Political Economy: Politics, Patronage and Profits* (Cambridge: Cambridge University Press, 1997).

41 See Kung, "Taiwanese Business in Southeast Asia"; and Chen Tian-Jy and Ku Ying-Hua, "Networking Strategies of Taiwanese Firms in Southeast Asia and China," in *Chinese Enterprise,*

Transnationalism, and Identity, ed. Edmund Terence Gomez and Hsin-Huang Michael Hsiao (London: Routledge, 2004).

42 Interview with Malaysian Industrial Development Authority (MIDA) officials on 2 July 2009. Interview with director of a Chinese-owned SME that has strong ties with multinational companies on 7 July 2009.

43 Chen and Ku, "Networking Strategies of Taiwanese Firms."

44 See Bank Negara Malaysia, *Small and Medium Enterprise (SME) Annual Report 2006*, Kuala Lumpur: BNM, 2007. This report provides examples of other Chinese SMEs that have adopted the practice of vertical integration to enhance innovation capacity.

45 Interview with director of Chinese-owned SME that has strong ties with multinational companies. Interview on 7 July 2009.

46 See Gomez, *Chinese Business in Malaysia*, 1999.

47 See *Malaysian Business*, 1 March 1999. For a further discussion on this issue, see Gomez, "Family Firms."

48 F. Barth, *The Role of the Entrepreneur in Social Change in Northern Norway* (Bergen: Norwegian University Press, 1967); Joseph A. Schumpeter, *Capitalism, Socialism and Democracy* (London: George Allen & Unwin, 1943).

49 Class resources such as educational qualifications, access to funds, and business experience have been useful in explaining why some Chinese have managed to develop their enterprises. See Ivan Light and Edna Bonacich, *Immigrant Entrepreneurs: Koreans in Los Angeles, 1965–1982* (Berkeley: University of California Press, 1988).

50 Chandler, *Strategy and Structure*; Alfred D. Chandler Jr., *The Visible Hand: The Managerial Revolution in American Business* (Cambridge: Harvard University Press, 1977); Penrose, *Growth of the Firm*; Oliver E. Williamson, *Markets and Hierarchies: Analysis and Antitrust Implications* (New York: Free Press, 1975); Michael Porter, *Competitive Strategy: Techniques for Analysing Industries and Competitors* (New York: Free Press, 1980); Michael Porter, *Competitive Advantage: Creating and Sustaining Superior Performance* (New York: Free Press, 1985).

51 Gomez and Jomo, *Malaysia's Political Economy*.

References

Barth, F. *The Role of the Entrepreneur in Social Change in Northern Norway*. Bergen: Norwegian University Press, 1967.

Benton, Gregor and Edmund Terence Gomez. *Chinatown and Transnationalism: Ethnic Chinese in Europe and Southeast Asia*. Canberra: Centre for the Study of the Chinese Southern Diaspora, 2000.

Benton, Gregor and Edmund Terence Gomez. *The Chinese in Britain, 1800–Present: Economy, Transnationalism, Identity*. Basingstoke: Palgrave-Macmillan, 2008.

Biggart, Nicole W. and Gary G. Hamilton. "On the Limits of a Firm-Based Theory to Explain Business Networks." In *The Economic Organization of East Asian Capitalism*, edited by Marco Orrù, Nicole Woolsey Biggart and Gary G. Hamilton, pp. 33–54. Thousand Oaks, CA: Sage, 1997.

Castells, Manuel. *The Information Age I: The Rise of the Network Society*. Oxford: Blackwell, 1993.

Chan Kwok Bun and Claire S. N. Chiang. *Stepping Out: The Making of Chinese Entrepreneurs*. Singapore: Simon & Schuster, 1994.

Chandler, Alfred D., Jr. *Strategy and Structure: Chapters in the History of the American Industrial Enterprise*. Cambridge: MIT Press, 1962.

———. *The Visible Hand: The Managerial Revolution in American Business*. Cambridge: Harvard University Press, 1977.

Chen Tian-Jy and Ku Ying-Hua. "Networking Strategies of Taiwanese Firms in Southeast Asia and China." In *Chinese Enterprise, Transnationalism, and Identity*, edited by Edmund Terence Gomez and Hsin-Huang Michael Hsiao, pp. 151–71. London: Routledge, 2004.

Fukuyama, Francis. *Trust: The Social Virtues and the Creation of Prosperity*. New York: Random House, 1995.

Gomez, Edmund Terence. *Chinese Business in Malaysia: Accumulation, Ascendance, Accommodation*. Honolulu: University of Hawaii Press, 1999.

______. "Family Firms, Transnationalism, and Generational Change: Chinese Enterprise in Britain and Malaysia." *East Asia: An International Quarterly* 24, no. 2 (Summer 2007): 153–72.

Gomez, Edmund Terence and Jomo K. S. *Malaysia's Political Economy: Politics, Patronage and Profits*. Cambridge: Cambridge University Press, 1997.

Gomez, Edmund Terence and Michael H. H. Hsiao, eds. *Chinese Business in Southeast Asia: Contesting Cultural Explanations, Researching Entrepreneurship*. London: RoutledgeCurzon, 2004.

Hamilton, Gary G., ed. *Asian Business Networks*. Berlin: W. de Gruyter, 1996.

Hara Fujio, ed. *Formation and Restructuring of Business Groups in Malaysia*. Tokyo: Institute of Developing Economies, 1993.

Jesudason, James V. *Ethnicity and the Economy: The State, Chinese Business and Multinationals in Malaysia*. Singapore: Oxford University Press, 1989.

Jesudason, James V. "Chinese Business and Ethnic Equilibrium in Malaysia." *Development and Change* 28, no. 1 (1997): pp. 119–41.

Kao, John. "The Worldwide Web of Chinese Business." *Harvard Business Review*, March–April 1993: pp. 24–36.

Kotkin, Joel. *Tribes*. New York: Random House, 1993.

Kung I-Chun. "Taiwanese Business in Southeast Asia." In *Chinese Business in Southeast Asia: Contesting Cultural Explanations, Researching Entrepreneurship*, edited by Edmund Terence Gomez and Hsin-Huang Michael Hsiao, pp. 146–65. London: Routledge, 2004.

Lee K. H. and Chow M. S. *Bibliographical Dictionary of the Chinese in Malaysia*. Kuala Lumpur: Institute of Advanced Studies, University of Malaya, 1997.

Lee Kam Hing and Lee Poh Ping. "Malaysian Chinese Business: Who Survived the Crisis?" *Kyoto Review*, no. 3 (October 2003): 7–8.

Lever-Tracy, Constance, David Ip and Noel Tracy. *The Chinese Diaspora and Mainland China: An Emerging Economic Synergy*. London: Macmillan, 1996.

Light, Ivan and Edna Bonacich. *Immigrant Entrepreneurs: Koreans in Los Angeles, 1965–1982*. Berkeley: University of California Press, 1988.

Light, Ivan and Steven J. Gold. *Ethnic Economies*. San Diego: Academic Press, 2000.

Miyoshi, Masao. "A Borderless World? From Colonialism to Transnationalism and the Decline of the Nation-State." *Critical Inquiry* 19 (Summer 1993): 726–51.

Ong, Aihwa. *Flexible Citizenship: The Cultural Logics of Transnationality*. Durham, NC: Duke University Press, 1999.

Ong, Aihwa and Donald M. Nonini, eds. *Ungrounded Empires: The Cultural Politics of Modern Chinese Transnationalism*. London: Routledge, 1994.

Penrose, E. T. *The Theory of the Growth of the Firm*. Oxford: Basil Blackwell, 1980.

Porter, Michael. *Competitive Advantage: Creating and Sustaining Superior Performance*. New York: Free Press, 1985.

______. *Competitive Strategy: Techniques for Analysing Industries and Competitors*. New York: Free Press, 1980.

Purcell, Victor. *The Chinese in Southeast Asia*. London: Oxford University Press, 1965.

Redding, S. Gordon. *The Spirit of Chinese Capitalism*. Berlin: De Gruyter, 1990.

Schak, David C. "Networks and Their Uses in Taiwanese Society." In *Chinese Business Networks: State, Economy and Culture*, edited by Chan Kwok Bun, pp. 112–28. Singapore: Prentice-Hall, 2000.

Schumpeter, Joseph A. *Capitalism, Socialism and Democracy*. London: George Allen & Unwin, 1943.

Searle, Peter. *The Riddle of Malaysian Capitalism: Rent-Seekers or Real Capitalists*. Honolulu: University of Hawai'i Press, 1999.

Skinner, G. William. *Chinese Society in Thailand: An Analytical History*. Ithaca, NY: Cornell University Press, 1957.

Vertovec, Steven. "Conceiving and Researching Transnationalism." *Ethnic and Racial Studies*, special issue, 22, no. 2 (March1999): 447–62.

Weidenbaum, Murray and Samuel Hughes. *The Bamboo Network*. New York: The Free Press, 1996.

Whitley, Richard. *Business Systems in East Asia: Firms, Markets and Societies*. London: Sage, 1992.

Whyte, Martin King. "The Chinese Family and Economic Development: Obstacle or Engine?" *Economic Development and Cultural Change* 45, no. 1 (1996): 1–30.

Williamson, Oliver E. *Markets and Hierarchies: Analysis and Antitrust Implications*. New York: Free Press, 1975.

Wong Siu-lun. "The Chinese Family Firm: A Model." *British Journal of Sociology* 36, no. 1 (1985): 58–72.

Yeung, Henry W. C. and Kris Olds, eds. *Globalization of Chinese Business Firms*. Basingstoke: Macmillan, 2000.

Chapter 7

BEYOND THE GLITTERATI: THE INDIAN AND CHINESE JEWELLERS OF LITTLE INDIA, SINGAPORE

Jayati Bhattacharya

Introduction

The extraordinary variations presented by the ethnic structures of Southeast Asia make an interesting and complex area of research. The historical legacies, local cultures and traditions contribute to distinguish the Asian cities from their Western counterparts, and each in turn with particularities of their own. In the larger background of the multicultural social setting in Singapore, a predominantly ethnic Indian population in the landscape of Little India presents a fascinating dimension of shared "community space"[1] as well as various aspects of "competing multiculturalisms"[2] in a rapidly growing Asian city. If diasporic[3] communities attempt to recreate a sociocultural version of their homeland in their memory and imagination,[4] no other setting could be more pertinent than the visual construct of Little India in Singapore. It presents to us all the elements of being Indian – saris, sweets, spices, flowers, deities, Indian provisions, utensils and gold ornaments! Though the area is dominated by migrants from South India as manifested by the Tamil lingua franca and most of the available consumer products in the area, it is also frequented by the migrants and expatriates from North India and other parts of the Indian subcontinent. There are also a few well-established North Indian businesses in the area, like the Mustafa Centre and Meena Gold Jewellery. The common grounds in products and preferences as well as in the sharing of community space have been comfortably worked out between businessmen and the general ethnic Indian clientele. They manage to fit in quite well in the negotiation of their demands and supplies of everyday culinary ingredients, provisions, necessities of religious obligations and festive decorations. However, the overall impact of the whiffs of Indian cuisine, incense sticks, flowers and garlands and the blaring Indian movie songs undoubtedly have a mesmerizing effect, transporting one to some place in India until one suddenly hears "ok, la!"[5] and is jolted back to the reality of an interactive shared space in Singapore.

The intra-ethnic complexities in the community space have been witness to different phases of transnational mobility, but the overall identification of the "lived space" with Indian ethnicity has remained – partly due to the neo-colonial legacy of the city-state's cultural and historical ethos and also to efforts by the government to promote tourism by preserving these cultural memories and architecture.[6] Over the past few decades, this community space has been increasingly shared by medium-level ethnic Chinese businessmen who operate in the area in the adapted framework of ethnic Indian[7] consumerism and necessities. The presence of a growing number of Chinese businessmen might be seen as an intervention in the conventional structure of "racialized urban zones" on the one hand, but more in synergy with the "multiculturalism" promoted by the government on the other. The gradual integration of business structures and negotiation of inter-ethnic forces in the traditional Indian enclave is unique and interesting, and also promotes the creation of multiple layers and determinants of culture and economic power in the "community space."

Small and mid-level Indian businessmen traditionally have had a locational advantage in Little India,[8] but years of multiracial coexistence have enabled the different communities to understand and appreciate each other better, so much so that Chinese businessmen have been trying their hands at the traditional monopoly of the Indians, and to a large extent have emerged immensely successful. The gold jewellery business is one such area of shared community space in terms of retail-based business within the historical enclave structure in the city-space. At the same time it involves a much larger investment than any other business in the locality, overwhelmingly based on people-to-people contact and daily transactions. In the larger context of commercial discourses and practices set up by Chinese business in Southeast Asia, there is also the possibility of participation in the traditional operational mechanisms, like that of *guanxi* (relationships/connectivity) and/or *xinyong* (credit) in the intra-ethnic transnational networks of production and distribution, though the framework for very small and medium-level gold jewellery business is quite different from the hegemonic Chinese capitalist overtures in Southeast Asia. Though it is difficult to acquire empirical evidence for this, it has been observed that the supply chain and manufacturing across the borders, especially from places in Malaysia to eventual distribution in the retail markets in Singapore and elsewhere in Southeast Asia, are more or less controlled by ethnic Chinese entrepreneurs.

The expanding jewellery business in the area of Little India, though glitteringly visible, is one of the least studied aspects of the area. Its uniqueness lies in the fascinatingly paradoxical display of typical Indian designs in the increasing number of Chinese jewellery shops in the area. The rising price of gold has not deterred the flourishing of the business, though traditional gold businessmen do not, perhaps, share a similar upbeat experience elsewhere in the city, as will be discussed later. The locational factor is one of the main components of its success. But why would an ethnic Chinese opt for such a business? How does he manage to attract his clients with Indian designs when there are Indian businessmen dealing with them? This paper tries to address these questions and trace the experiences of the gold business in the area, particularly over the last half-century and aims to contribute an added dimension to the changing identities of the shared "community space." The article is largely based on conversations and interviews with businessmen and others in the Serangoon Road area who have lived through different phases of social and economic transition in the city-state. The oral history recordings from the National Archives of Singapore, mostly in Tamil, have also contributed to the present narrative. They form an invaluable source of information in the absence of any substantial printed primary or secondary materials related to the subject.

Traditional Indian Goldsmiths and Jewellers

The early generations of ethnic Indian goldsmiths in Singapore belonged to a group of sojourners who had voluntarily opted to relocate themselves to Malaya with their hereditary profession. Gold has remained an essential part of the traditions and customs of the life of an Indian irrespective of economic or social categories of caste and class. India remains one of the highest consumers of gold in the world, only to be recently surpassed by an aggressive demand in China[9] and will, perhaps, continue to sustain this position while the traditional values, customs and the mindset of its people survive. Apart from an inclination for self-adornment in both men and women, almost all Indians regard the metal as an asset of high value and hoarding of gold comes quite naturally to them. Besides, traditionally, the possession, display and gifting of gold is directly related to social prestige and ranking. In fact, it was customary for the rich, upper-middle and even middle-class households to attach a goldsmith to their families to provide them with services on festive occasions, religious ceremonies and for various other purposes. Thus, a large number of Indian goldsmiths made their way to the island, where almost all passages of transnational migrants were catalysed by the hope of economic betterment. It is almost impossible to give statistical figures for the early goldsmiths in Singapore, but some early photographs from the Singapore National Archives, dating back to 1900, bear testimony to their presence and prevalence in the island nation.

According to a member of one of the rare surviving families of goldsmiths, present for three generations in Singapore, there were around five hundred Indian goldsmiths who made their living in Singapore in the early 1950s and 1960s.[10] Other sources have also suggested the number to be around three to five hundred.[11] About 80 per cent of them came from the Tanjore district in Tamil Nadu in South India.[12] Perhaps their coming to Singapore was prompted not so much by the lure of big money, but rather by a regular income, which was substantial by Indian standards considering the rates of exchange. A number of goldsmiths would be housed in a jewellery shop, each with a front desk, catering to their personal customers and also catering to the clients through the contacts of the shop owner. The ornaments were all "made to order" from the designs either offered by the goldsmith or as suggested by the customers. A goldsmith would sometimes go to his customer's house either to take the order or deliver the ornaments. Thus, the business thrived to a large extent on the interpersonal skills of the goldsmith and the quality of services that he offered to his clientele. There would be shops with a number of goldsmiths sitting in a row to cater to the customers, each of them working independently on their individual designs.[13]

Oral history recordings in the National Archives of Singapore also suggest that there were a number of goldsmiths situated in Buffalo Road, Kerabau Road, Upper Dickson Road, Serangoon Road and Kinta Road.[14] According to Subramaniyan Boopalan, a goldsmith who came to Singapore in 1947,[15] Thangoor Maka Shop was the biggest gold shop from 1948 to 1960 and employed about twenty-five people during those years.[16] Ani Mani Porchalai and Selvasegara are the other old shops that have survived to this day. In fact, Ani Mani Porchalai provided employment to many goldsmiths from India and also became an ideal training ground for many future jewellery businessmen. Another goldsmith by hereditary profession, Vadivelu Muthuipalahrichi, came to Singapore in 1953[17] and worked in a shop in Upper Dickson Road.[18] According to him, there were about forty goldsmiths in Upper Dickson Road and a number of them in Buffalo Road, each shop housing about six to eight goldsmiths. It should be mentioned that the number of goldsmiths during the 1950s and 1960s far outnumbered the number of jewellery businessmen in the area.

A goldsmith would, almost invariably, come to the region by himself, leaving his family behind, returning annually to them, or once in two years. His migration would be self-motivated and self-supported with no contractual obligations, in direct contrast to the "contract labourer" system that was prevalent across the Malay Peninsula,[19] or even those employed by firms under individual contracts. He lived a very simple life working at his front desk with simple tools to smelt the gold and make handcrafted designs. The tools needed in the workshop, according to one of the correspondents, were simple and comprised of hammer, drill, stove, a blowing pipe, nitric acid, sulphuric acid, salt and tamarind.[20] They would also have a catalogue for customers to choose their designs. A goldsmith was required to be good at drawing the designs, as according to Boopalan this was very important in the manufacture of gemstone-set jewellery.[21] This skill was, perhaps, also necessary to give shape to the designs in the imagination of his customers. The labour charges were, however, meagre and his main income depended on the salary given by the employer with whom he worked,[22] unless the goldsmith had a workshop of his own. He lived a simple life, mostly in the shophouse dormitories, trying to save and send home as much of his hard-earned money as he could. The income as compared to the labour that went into the craftsmanship did not appear to be as lucrative as it should have been, considering the number of goldsmiths that thronged the area, but conversion of that income into the Indian currency helped to make a difference at home.[23]

Besides creating handcrafted ornaments of different designs for sale, the goldsmiths participated in the social and religious customs of everyday life of the migrant settlers. In the traditional Indian system of social hierarchy, goldsmiths belonged to the Viswakarma group of the Shudras.[24] Two very important customs in a South Indian family involving customary participation of goldsmiths were the:

(a) *Karnapushanam*: ear-piercing ceremony for both young boys and girls, and
(b) *Poonurukau*: gold-melting ceremony in the groom's house before the wedding.

The goldsmith would charge fees for the service provided by him. In addition, he would also try to convince the client to buy the necessary gold ornaments for the respective ceremonies from his shop, as Muthukrishnan reveals, when talking about his hereditary trade.[25] Besides, other sources of clients could be the relatives and friends of the respective families invited for the ceremonies, who would generally make gifts of ornaments of gold bought from the same jewellery shop. Thus, one social ceremony would have different avenues of business potential both for the jewellery businessmen and the goldsmiths. Modern ways of living have brought changes to traditional practices, but many customs involving the use of gold have remained. It is this sentiment of prioritizing gold over other valuables (even diamonds to a certain extent, as the resale value and process for diamonds are not as smooth as in the case of gold) in matters of assets, gifts, dowry or even collateral that has kept the gold jewellery business in Little India not only sustainable but actually prosperous, irrespective of the rising gold prices. People may buy less gold because of the price rise and other factors, but they would certainly buy it as a first step towards building up their asset base. This has continued to be the traditional psyche of the people of South Asia in general. Indians are one of the largest consumers of gold in the world, accounting for about 20 per cent of the world demand.[26]

In Singapore, the goldsmiths also play an important role in the *ubayam* ceremony, which takes place on the very first day of the *Navaratri*. At this ceremony all the goldsmiths assemble at the Mariamman Temple to give the first offerings to the deity. This has continued as a unique customary practice in Singapore for many years now, their attendance being maintained in the temple records[27] as shown in Table 1 below. However, the numbers at present are more representative of the caste than those currently in the profession. As the number of goldsmiths dwindled over the years, participation in the

Table 1: Participation of Goldsmiths in the *Navaratri Ubayam* Ceremony

Year	No. of goldsmith participants
1974	158
1975	112
1981	76
1983	146
1992	102
1993	98
1994	91
1995	91
2002	74
2003	83
2004	78
2005	60
2006	60
2007	67
2008	67

Source: Pamphlets and records of the Mariamman Temple Committee for consecutive years from the personal collection of Mr M. Kuppusamy, former treasurer of the Mariamman Temple in Singapore. Mr Kuppusamy is duly acknowledged for sharing this information.

Navaratri celebrations has been taken over by people of other professions, but belonging to the same caste. The participants sometimes include persons from outside Singapore as well.

Changing Market Dynamics

The situation of the goldsmiths began to change in the 1980s, when many of those who had come in the early 1950s were looking forward to their retirement. Since most of them did not bring their families along, there was no question of succession in the business. Even the few families that came along to settle in Singapore did not make much of an impact on the hereditary family business model.[28] The children received better education and modernized along with the prosperity of Singapore. Quite naturally they opted for other professions that were more lucrative and would offer them a better economic status and standard of living.

The physical appearance of the area around Serangoon Road also went through an overhaul in the years immediately after Singapore's independence in 1965. The Urban Redevelopment Authority of Singapore was engaged in modernizing the area with the Housing Development Board's buildings and better infrastructure facilities, and the shop owners in the area were offered either a space in the new structure or a lump sum of money. Lack of foresight, inadequate future planning and, above all, the strong will to return to their native land drove most of them to opt for the financial gain at hand. The conversion into Indian currency made the choice all the more worthwhile, or so it seemed. One such jeweller, Dawood Maraikar & Sons, owned by a group of Indian Muslims hailing from Nagore, was one of the biggest jewellers in the 1960s. They employed a number of goldsmiths in their shops. One of the respondents feels that if he had not taken the choice of leaving his property in exchange for money, the gold jewellery business in Little India would have been different. Some jewellers of the older generation did survive, like the Ani Mani jewellers, which only very recently changed hands, though the name of the shop remains unchanged.

Thus the suppliers, businessmen and craftsmen began to retreat in the 1980s, but the demand from the ethnic Indian settlers remained – with certain modifications. The vacuum thus created was filled by ethnic Chinese businessmen, who emerged specifically as dealers in Indian designs. It is indeed interesting to see that such a specialized Indian craft would become a choice of livelihood and business option for ethnic Chinese who apparently seemed to be complete strangers to the language, customs, religion and ceremonies of the Indians. However, Chinese also have a fascination for gold, and Chinatowns usually have a number of jewellery shops. It can be argued that some of their experiences in working with the gem and jewellery merchants increased their interest in the trade, and they found an opportune moment to make inroads into the business landscape of Serangoon Road and establish their own businesses. One other view is that the Chinese pawnshops accumulated many of the Indian gold ornaments, which inspired their interest in the designs and the asset value of Indian gold jewellery.[29] Lam Kiang Ming, the present owner of Batu Pahat, was one of the earliest of the Chinese jewellery shop owners in Little India. Lam Seng Lai, uncle of Lam Kiang

Fig 1: Batu Pahat, one of the oldest Chinese shops selling Indian jewellery in Little India. © Jayati Bhattacharya

Ming, was originally the owner of a pawnshop and one of the first few Chinese diamond importers in Chinatown. He later was instrumental in the opening of Batu Pahat, and eventually his nephews imbibed his interest in the jewellery business.[30] At first they were few in number, but the gradual increase in the business potential encouraged a lot of salesmen in the older Chinese shops to start out on their own. Whatever might have been the factors for them to engage in this business, the Chinese businessmen had to acquire the skills of producing typical Indian ornaments, as well as the knowledge of Indian traditions and customs. They have also learned the linguistically different terms for typical ornaments and ceremonies. This is one of the unique manifestations of the influence and adaptation of a different culture in business initiatives and social interactions. However, it might be mentioned that the oldest surviving ethnic Chinese shop at present, Batu Pahat, started as early as in 1969[31] and was the training ground for many Chinese who worked in the shop and started out on their own in later years.

A number of factors facilitated the entry of Chinese into this business in a big way:

1. The retreat of goldsmiths in large numbers to India for retirement created the space for business opportunities for ethnic Chinese.
2. The introduction of machine-made ornaments replaced the handiwork of the craftsmen, thus minimizing the role of traditional Indian goldsmiths.

Fig 2: Ban Chong Pawnshop recently opened by Batu Pahat as an extension of their jewellery business, Little India. ©Jayati Bhattacharya

3. Fashion trends changed, generating an interest in ornaments that were smaller and lighter. Younger generations are hardly interested in the traditional jewellery, except on the occasion of marriage and a few other ceremonies. Neither did they have the patience to wait for several days for the ornaments to be made by hand. In the age of machines and mechanization, they were becoming accustomed to ready-made products, be it garments or jewellery.

The fashion trends of machine-made products have made it easier for the ethnic Chinese to handle typical Indian designs. They can simply order the jewellery from local factories either in Singapore or in the neighbourhood from Johor, or Kuala Lumpur, or even Penang in Malaysia. They can also buy from wholesale dealers who source the jewellery from various places in India, including Coimbatore, Pune or Mumbai. Thus, there are middlemen involved in sourcing the products. This remains true of the Indian jewellery businessmen as well, but marketing is mainly done on the basis of interpersonal relationships and word of mouth. Interestingly, there has been no tradition of visible advertisement campaigns, except for some jewellers advertising on the radio.[32] However, very recently, with the popularity of local newspapers like *tabla!* gaining ground, advertisements have been more profound, especially on occasions like *Akshay Tritiya*, when it is considered customary and auspicious for Indians to buy gold.[33]

Locational factors have been very important for the survival of this business for both Chinese and Indians in the trade. The maintenance of the shophouse architecture of Little India has influenced the sustained traditional visual aspects of the trade, which has also played a role as a major tourist attraction. In spite of the machine-made products, the designs still remain traditional and cater to a clientele who have a yearning for these designs. The changes in design trends and the increasing popularity among younger generations of white gold and diamonds, which are easily available in big shopping complexes all over the city, posed a challenge to the traditional jewellery shops in Little India in terms of retaining customers and winning potential consumers. They were left with a customer base made up of the elderly population, some traditional families and a handful of expatriates and tourists interested in typical Indian designs. However, the visibly flourishing business and ever-increasing shops in the vicinity today calls for an examination of the factors contributing to a significant increase in the demand for this kind of jewellery and its relation to the locational factors.

The most interesting aspect of the business was the emergence of a new customer base, which increased the potential for business by leaps and bounds and encouraged an increasing number of Chinese to start up showrooms in the area. The clientele was provided by the increasing number of work permit holders and contract workers, such as construction site workers, domestic helpers and dockyard workers, mainly from South Asia, where the tradition of possession of gold as a symbol of status and prosperity still persists. Work permit holders, who, in almost all cases, have either mortgaged their land or other assets to pay for the hefty agency fees to come to Singapore, invariably like to take back some mementos of yellow gold for family members or for increasing their personal asset base and personal security. The supply of cheap and temporary labour from the South Asian region has produced a new paradigm for the study of market dynamics of Singapore and other places in Southeast Asia. Thus, according to present statistics, there are approximately four hundred thousand such workers in Singapore, and even if half of them contributed to the possible client base for the jewellery shops, there is bound to be a huge business potential, and this rightly justifies the rapidly increasing number of jewellery shops in the area. The overwhelming presence in Little India, especially on Sundays, of work permit holders – who are otherwise regarded as invisible and ignored in the daily interactive spaces in Singapore – is a unique phenomenon.[34] Anyone who has visited the area on a Sunday can confirm the large numbers of prospective clients thronging the shops for *jhumkas* (typical Indian earrings), *thalis* (a special gold chain made for weddings, and which is worn by the bride, especially applicable to South Indian brides), gold chains, pendants, nose studs, bracelets and other varieties of traditional Indian ornaments.

The Shifting Paradigm of Business Operations

The increased participation of ethnic Chinese in the jewellery business has changed the business and structural paradigms. The set-up has been simplified by initial investments in the shops to stock up showrooms with machine-made jewellery. The complicated process of maintaining goldsmiths along with their machines and tools in the workplace

Fig 3: Chinese jewellers selling to Indian customers, Little India. © Jayati Bhattacharya

has given way to the appointment of only a few sales persons who are familiar with the culture and customs of Indians. Speaking Tamil is an added advantage. This kind of set-up also makes it easy to sell the business if necessary.

All the Chinese respondents were aware that the peak seasons of their businesses are the important Indian festivals like *Deepavali*, *Thaipusam*, *Navaratri* and *Akshay Tritiya*, when most Indians like to buy gold to celebrate. However, the complexities of caste-related issues could be a problem for them; the *thali* required during the marriage ceremony, for example, is different for each caste and may also have specific family designs. To cope with these and other custom-related issues, the Chinese shop owner would almost invariably hire Indian goldsmiths to work for them, as was done by Batu Pahat earlier.[35]

It is also interesting to observe how a jeweller runs his business. All the shops, as can be seen by any visitor, are fully stocked at all times of the year. According to some of my respondents, a businessman will buy back the quantity of gold that he sells that very day at the market price to restore the level of his stock. If the price increases the next day, he sells gold at the prevailing market price to make a profit. He will again replenish his stock that day at the current market price and will not take the risk of waiting for the prices to go down. Going by the trend of constantly rising prices of gold, the businessman always manages to make his investments profitable. In case of a fall in the market prices, he will buy more gold to increase his stock. He appears to be more than sure to cover the risks taken with more investments. Thus, business profitability is maintained in spite of the surging global price of gold. The business also remains unhampered by the rising prices due to the sentiments and traditions of the South Asian population. Buying of gold remains a customary habit, and only the quantity may differ if there are steep price rises. Thus, no businessman is at risk with the rise of prices. In fact, such a safe investment has led to a mushrooming of several competitors in the market.

Locational advantages and the distinctive market dynamics of the area have made the operations of the gold business in Little India an unparalleled phenomenon in the entire city-state. While some shop owners have complained of the reduction in the volume of business compared with a decade before, they would readily agree that it is still a profit-making area. This is so in spite of an extremely competitive sellers' market, with numerous shops mushrooming in the area. However, ethnic Chinese jewellery shops in other parts of the city like the Chinatown area have to cope with dwindling business, so much so that, in some cases, they might have to contemplate shutting down.[36] Reasons for this disparity in not-so-distant market areas are the diminishing lack of interest of the younger generation of Chinese in buying traditional yellow gold and the absence of the unique clientele base of the Little India area, where the traditional customs and sentiments of the Indian subcontinent have helped retain market success.

Success of the Chinese Goldsmiths

The Chinese gold businessmen have been immensely successful in the Serangoon Road area and have come to numerically dominate the trade and business in the area. Of the approximately sixty-two shops in the area, almost 80 per cent of them are ethnically Chinese, while the ethnic Indians comprise of about 20 per cent.[37] The community space has been readjusted and renegotiated by the various ethnic communities in the successive phases of Singapore's growth and progress. The gold business in Little India is one such manifestation of the shared business space and operations. The timing of the increasing Chinese interest in this kind of business has been somewhat opportune. However, there were several other factors besides the retreat of the old goldsmiths to India that accounted not only for survival of the Chinese businesses, but also their becoming increasingly successful and leaving the Indian businessmen behind.

Chinese businessmen tend to be capable of making larger investments and are financially more competitive than their Indian counterparts. Investments were made in buying large quantities of gold for mass production as well as installing machinery. The earlier practice of first buying gold (possibly from Chinese shops)[38] and giving it to the goldsmith to design into an ornament gave way to a preference for ready-made products directly accessible to customers, who had multiple choices. Thus, they successfully marketed the most cost-effective and the least time-consuming or labour-intensive jewellery. Boopalan points out that Indian goldsmiths needed three days to make a gold chain with a labour charge of $60. The Chinese, on the other hand, would use machines to finish the same work in two hours at a cost of $15, thus generating a huge difference in terms of money and time saved. Shop owners would obviously prefer the latter.[39] To the customer, this meant the ready availability of ornaments at a cheaper price, which was an obvious advantage, unless there was a need for special designs to be

Fig 4: Indian and Chinese gold shops in typically shop-house structures in Little India ©Jayati Bhattacharya

made. The Indian jewellers could not be as prompt in the switchover to the new mode, due both to the unavailability of adequate finance and their inability to quickly adapt to the mechanized makeover of their traditional artistic talent and business practices. It also meant that traditional goldsmiths would either have to lose their hereditary occupation or would have to diversify. However, there still existed some designs and products where the Chinese were unable to replace Indian craftsmanship.[40]

Chinese jewellers also offer competitive prices to customers and demonstrate better business acumen in attracting their clients. Many Chinese shop owners have either ethnic South Indians as partners or employees to manage the salesmanship at the front desk and everyday dealings with the customers, while they, the proprietors, remain in the background as either a major investor or taking care of structuring the business. To an outsider, the shop looks very Indian, as most of them have names written in Tamil and sales persons of that ethnicity, which helps the shop owner to attract Indian clientele.

There is a prevalent belief among general consumers that the Chinese shops sell purer gold. While adulterations could be the handiwork of any shop owner irrespective of his ethnicity, it is quite obvious that maintenance of exactly the same level of purity is much more difficult for the goldsmiths who work by hand with less sophisticated tools than it is for those who source it from more standardized machine-made products. In the face of problems regarding the gold standard, the government regularized it to be .916 (22k) and .999 (24k), which means that gold pieces should contain at least 91.6 per cent and 99.9 per cent of gold respectively. Some organizations in Singapore, like the Consumers Association of Singapore (CASE), the Singapore Assay Office (SAO) and the Singapore Jewellers Association (SJA), help directly or indirectly to maintain the gold standard. In fact, most of the sources for both Chinese and Indian shops – whether they are factories in Malaysia or wholesalers sourcing their jewellery from India – are the same at present, and the quality or purity of gold is little affected by the ethnicity of the owner. However, this confusion gave the Chinese shops a business advantage for some time.

The Present Scenario

It is interesting to note some of the characteristic features that have emerged in the gold business through the period of transition and the changing market dynamics. Different categories of business specialization have emerged, including Chinese, Indian or a partnership between the two. A joint partnership between the two ethnic groups in most cases brings together the financial backing of Chinese proprietors, with the front desk showcasing Indians to attract customers.

In the face of the increasing competition, each businessman has tried to specialize in certain ornaments or extend a value-added service to the customers. Batu Pahat is known for its *jhumkas*,[41] while Mukuthi Corner is renowned for its nose studs. There are others like Abhirami Jewellers who deal in precious stones and offer astrological consultations. Other shops also offer services such as nose and ear piercing for their customers. They also offer their clients no gold reduction if they resell the ornaments in the same shop in which they purchased them. Another prominent player is the gold jewellery section of the Mustafa Centre, which, with its huge display of diverse items, has brought new dynamics and bigger scales of operation in the gold trade in the area. However, apart from increasing the retail space and visibility of the gold business, the effect of this on the other Indian jewellery businessmen cannot be directly correlated.

In an interesting turn of events in recent years, there has been a re-emergence in interest and involvement of Indian gold jewellery businessmen in the local landscape of Singapore. These are ambitious players in the international gold market with ready availability of finances and other resources, representative of the increasing number of Indian transnational business entities that have made their presence felt in the world market, and in a remarkable way in Singapore. Already established as popular brand names, Malabar Gold & Diamonds and Joy Alukkas are examples of emerging competitors in the existing business interests in the area. Quite distinct from the local businessmen in the same vicinity, they have invested in big showrooms and professional manpower resources, and make a visible distinction from the local business models, whether Indian or Chinese. They have created additional attractions like selling watches made of precious gems and metals, or creating conveniences like online buying facilities for jewellery.[42] They have also been successful in using the popularity of film stars to promote their products, as was recently done for the inauguration of the Malabar Gold showroom, when the South Indian film star Suriya was brought in amid much fanfare in the latter half of 2013. Malabar Gold also claimed to open its largest showroom in Singapore among the 102 outlets worldwide.[43] Within a short span of time, the jewellery retailer opened its second showroom in Singapore, its 114th across the globe, and has also declared a target of 224 outlets by 2015 as a part of their 20th anniversary celebrations.[44] This certainly brings to light the ambitious and aggressive strategy and vision of the young business group, something that was not so common among the earlier generation of businessmen. The target clientele are almost the same – tourists, migrant workers, Indian residents and all those with a taste and penchant for Indian designs. The increasing number of tourists has successfully added to the clientele; however, the personal relationship between the seller and the consumer, which had been an interesting pivot of previous generations of gold jewellery business, is perhaps missing.

Almost all of the local gold shop owners in Little India are members of the Little India Shopkeepers Heritage Association (LISHA). An early attempt in 1977 by the Indian goldsmiths to form an association of their own, known as the Singapore Indians Vishvabirmma Association[45] eventually did not come to fruition. There are some Chinese gold businessmen in the area who are members of the Singapore Jewellers Association (SJA), but almost all of them are members of LISHA. Though LISHA is a comparatively recent institution, its members already benefit from the cultural activities and festive decorations organized by it to draw in the crowds. It might be mentioned in this context that in keeping with the tradition of other businessmen in the Serangoon Road area, there are hardly any Indian businessmen who have become members of the Singapore Indian Chamber of Commerce and Industry (SICCI), and as most of the respondents reveal, neither do they aim to be. This aloofness from what is considered the umbrella organization of Indian business interests in Singapore is noteworthy.

Conclusion

The Little India jewellery shops represent small and medium-level businesses that are completely localized within their geographical periphery and dependent on many factors unique to the area. General market trends might affect circumstantial factors like rising rent and property prices or gold price fluctuations, but the viability of the core business is completely dependent on traditions and sentiments of its exclusive group of clientele. However, the picture may well alter in the face of changing governmental policy and restrictions or reductions of the numbers of work permit holders. In such a situation, new equations of demand and supply would have to be worked out.

In Little India, one might also come across the contradictions of thriving and prosperous businesses on the one hand and, on the other, businesses changing hands or closing. Whether Chinese or Indian, both the communities face a common problem of succession. While Batu Pahat or Mukuthi Corner have managed to carry on successfully in their own ways (both of them have enjoyed three generations of business in the area), other big showroom owners like the Little India Jewellers, who have been in the business since the 1980s, have had to sell out recently to a pawnshop owner due to problems related to succession. The succeeding generations are professionals (doctors, etc.) and are uninterested in carrying on the father's trade.

A new trend that has emerged with the Chinese gold shops in the area is the opening up of pawnshops along with the gold shops. It is undoubtedly an interesting phenomenon to witness the revitalization of the traditional moneylending business in the age of modern-day banking and other institutional facilities. Talking about his new pawnshop, Ban Chong Pawnshop Pte Ltd, just beside their gold shop, Lam Kiang Ming of Batu Pahat reveals that the pawnshop serves as the poor man's bank, where he can get ready cash very fast, based on the collateral provided, which is redeemable within six months.[46] It is a kind of service provided to customers in need of immediate cash smoothly and efficiently without the hassle of complicated paper work, to tide over a temporary period of financial crisis. The increasing number of pawnshops in the area has also been facilitated by the recent relaxation of government regulations on the entry level for pawnshops. It might be recalled in this context that the once-thriving Chettiar moneylenders, the Indian counterpart of the "poor man's bank," are almost extinct in contemporary times.

The gold business in Little India has long existed in small and medium-level business entities and is likely to remain that way with little scope for innovation, diversification or expansion. Conversion to machine-made products has indeed increased the competitiveness and scope of profitability of products, but there has been no effort to pursue any kind of corporatization of these business concerns. Quality control has also been weak and there has been no standard customer service in operation. This business has also failed to look beyond the enclave of Little India or associate with the larger business bodies and the chambers of commerce. However, with new Indian international players in the market, there has been a change in the business model, and efforts at corporatization are noticeable. The new brands have also enabled the "local" business to make a connection to the "global." The new business entrants have been facilitated by increasing consumerism and globalization, but have also led to a remarkable decrease in personal relationships between sellers and consumers, one of the unique features of this business. Custom-made ornaments have given way to the mass production of ready-made jewellery. The only reflection of the big new showrooms can be seen in Mustafa Gold Mart, a part of the Mustafa Centre which has shared space with the other local businesses of the area for a few decades now. In view of the robust rise of global gold demand from both Indian and Chinese consumers, the effects of competition and collaboration between the multinational gold players and local business concerns are yet to emerge. In the larger context of the diverse historical trajectories of Asian transmigratory communities and their changing identities, there have been few attempts to compare the business communities of Chinese and Indian ethnicity and their shifting paradigms of business identity in their adopted homeland, whereas there have been studies of business networking within their respective communities.[47] It might be argued that the extent and influence of the Indian mercantile groups and their relationships with the state through history pales in comparison with the volume and influence of their Chinese counterparts in Southeast Asia, and in larger parts of Asia. The Indian mercantile groups have often been marginalized and the shifting paradigms of their social and economic networks have been ignored. In comparative perspective, this business in Little India in Singapore, in spite of all the limitations, constitutes an example of identity formation arising out of the interactive and cohesive forces at work between the two communities, and with direct connections to factors related to the emerging global labour market in the diaspora.

Notes

1 For detailed discussions on community space and the CMIO (Chinese, Malay, Indian and Others) factor, refer to Sharon Siddique and Nirmala PuruShotam, *Singapore's Little India: Past, Present and Future* (Singapore: ISEAS, 1982).

2 Robbie B. H. Goh, *Contours of Culture: Space and Social Difference in Singapore* (Hong Kong: Hong Kong University Press, 2005), p. 3. In his words, "Issues of city and state, nascent nationalisms, postcolonial heritages, competing multiculturalisms, the balance of emigration/immigration, are particularly nuanced when studying the postcolonial city, in ways which are not often or always evident in the major urban centres in America and Europe."

3 Though subject to endless debate and discussion, the term "diaspora" generally refers to a dispersed community who continue to survive and adapt along with transmission of the heritage of their homeland.

4 P. Reeves and R. Rai, "The Indian Context," in *The Encyclopedia of the Indian Diaspora*, ed. B. V. Lal, P. Reeves and R. Rai (Singapore: Editions Didier Millet, 2006), p. 18.

5 This is a typically Singlish colloquial address used by almost all Singaporeans.

6 Henderson and Chang, for example, have conducted studies on Little India as a heritage landscape and as a site of tourist attraction: Joan C. Henderson, "Managing Urban Ethnic Heritage: Little India in Singapore," *International Journal of Heritage Studies* 14, no. 4 (2008): 332–46; T. C. Chang, "Singapore's Little India: A Tourist Attraction as a Contested Landscape," *Urban Studies* 37, no. 2 (2000): 343–66.

7 Ethnic Chinese or ethnic Indian will henceforth be referred to solely as either Chinese or Indian.

8 For further details on Indian businesses in the Serangoon Road area, refer to Jayati Bhattacharya, *Beyond the Myth: Indian Business Communities in Singapore* (Singapore: ISEAS, 2011), pp. 54–61.

9 Laura Clarke and Yue Li, "China Overtakes India as Top Gold Consumer," *Wall Street Journal*, 18 February 2014. http://online.wsj.com/news/articles/SB10001424052702304675504579389261432501856. 25 May 2014.

10 A. Muthukrishnan, a second-generation member of a goldsmith family, in conversation with the author on 11 January 2010.

11 Vadivelu Muthuipalahrichi, Oral History Recordings, "Vanishing Trades," accession no. A001165, reel no. 3, 10 May 1990 (Tamil), *National Archives of Singapore*. Muthuipalahrichi gives a figure of more than three hundred goldsmiths, mostly in the Upper Dickson Road and Buffalo Road. Narayanasamy Kandasamy, Oral History Recordings, "Communities of Singapore," accession no. A001166, reel no. 5, 27 May 1990 (Tamil), *National Archives of Singapore*. Kandasamy talks of some people mentioning the presence of four to five hundred goldsmiths in the past.

12 Muthukrishnan, 11 January 2010.

13 Interview with Rajakumar Chandra, president of LISHA, on 24 December 2009. He spent his childhood in the area and was referring to the decade of the 1960s.

14 Subramaniyan Boopalan, Oral History Recordings, accession no. A001170/06, reel no. 4 (Tamil), *National Archives of Singapore*. Boopalan was a hereditary goldsmith by profession who came to Singapore following his father and uncle, and eventually operated a gold shop of his own.

15 Boopalan, Oral History Recordings, reel no. 1.

16 Boopalan, Oral History Recordings, reel no.5.

17 Muthuipalahrichi, Oral History Recordings, reel no. 1.

18 Muthuipalahrichi, Oral History Recordings, reel no. 3.

19 A significant amount of research has been done on the prevailing system of labour recruitment in the Malayan Peninsula that was popularly known as the *kangany* system of labour. For details, refer to Sinnappah Arasaratnam, *Indians in Malaya and Singapore* (Kuala Lumpur: Oxford University Press, 1979); K. S. Sandhu, *Indians in Malaya: Some Aspects of Their Immigration and Settlement (1786–1957)* (Cambridge: Cambridge University Press, 1969).

20 Muthuipalahrichi, Oral History Recordings, reel no. 1, 27 April, 1990.

21 Boopalan, Oral History Recordings, reel no.4.

22 Boopalan, who worked with his uncle when he first came to Singapore in the late 1940s, was working for a salary of $30. This was at the time of his apprenticeship when he was only helping other goldsmiths to make the jewellery. Reel no. 2.

23 Muthukrishnan, 11 January 2010.

24 The Viswakarma sect of goldsmiths wore the sacred thread, usually associated with the Brahmins in the caste hierarchy, on the day of the Avani Avitam, an auspicious day celebrated by the goldsmiths with offerings and prayers in the temple. This information was given to the author by Sathappan Meyyappan in Singapore.

25 Muthukrishnan, 11 January 2010.

26 Philippe Dozolme, "India to Remain the World's Largest Consumer of Gold in 2011." http://mining.about.com/od/MiningCommodities/a/India-To-Remain-The-Worlds-Largest-Consumer-Of-Gold-In-2011.htm. 14 February 2011. However, China has recently surpassed India in gold consumption, as mentioned earlier: Clarke and Li, "China Overtakes India."

27 Dozolme, "World's Largest Consumer of Gold." According to Dozolme, the practice is still carried on by the Viswakarma goldsmiths in the Mariamman Temple. This fact has also been corroborated by M. Kuppusamy, an accountant by profession but goldsmith by caste, who has been associated with the management of the Mariamman Temple for several years.

28 Dozolme, "World's Largest Consumer of Gold in 2011." Mr Muthukrishnan recalls about fifteen or twenty other children of goldsmiths' families had come to stay in Singapore almost contemporarily with his coming to the island, but none of them continue in the trade at present.

29 Interview with Rajakumar Chandra on 24 December 2009.

30 Lam Seng Lai, the uncle of Lam Kiang Ming and one of the original partners who started Batu Pahat talked about his shop and others in the 1960s in his conversation with the author on 10 November 2009.

31 Interview with Lam Kiang Ming, one of the present owners of Batu Pahat, on 10 November 2009.

32 Joel Ngau, owner of Great United Jewellers, one of the prominent Chinese jewellery shops in the Tekka Market area, in conversation with Nalina Gopal, assistant curator, Asian Civilizations Museum, Singapore, on 29 July 2009. I am indebted to Nalina for sharing this information with me.

33 A number of advertisements by different jewellery shops in *tabla!*, a weekly English publication by the Singapore Press Holdings on the Indian community, 25 April 2014.

34 Glimpses of appropriation of the space in Serangoon Road may be made from the article by Darren Soh, "The Paradox of Space and Its Appropriation by Migrant Labour in Singapore," *Inter-Asia Cultural Studies* 2, no. 1 (2001): 95–7.

35 Interview with Lam Kiang Ming. Boopalan also mentions his father working as a goldsmith in Batu Pahat. Boopalan, reel no. 1.

36 Muthukrishnan, 11 January 2010.

37 Interview with Rajakumar Chandra on 24 December 2009. He gauges this on the basis of LISHA membership of the jewellers.

38 Thambusamy Santhanam, Oral History Recordings, "Communities in Singapore," accession no. A001227, reel no. 6 (Tamil), 29 November 1990, *National Archives of Singapore.*

39 Boopalan, Oral History Recordings, reel no. 5.

40 Narayanasamy Kandasamy, Oral History Recordings, "Communities in Singapore," accession no. A001166, reel no. 6 (Tamil), 27 May 1990, *National Archives of Singapore.* Kandasamy talks of some intricate design jewellery like the *naga* designs or the *Yalpanamthaali* (a particularly complicated and time-consuming design of the *thali* for a specific caste), which takes about a week to complete, and is usually done by Indian goldsmiths.

41 Interview with Lam Kiang Ming on 10 November 2009.

42 Malabar Gold & Diamonds offer a variety choices on their website: http://www.shopmgd.com/gold-jewellery/women/earring.html. 22 May 2014.

43 Razy Shah, "Malabar Gold to Open Its First Outlet in Singapore," *Little India Directory*, 23 October 2013. http://littleindiadirectory.com/malabar-gold-and-diamonds-open-first-outlet-singapore. 22 May 2014.

44 "Malabar Gold & Diamonds Opens Second Outlet in Singapore," *Daily Tribune*, 20 April 2014. http://dt.bh/malabar-gold-diamonds-opens-second-outlet-in-singapore. 22 May 2014.

45 Letter from R. A. Murugaiyan, "Singapore Indians Vishvabirmma Association" to the Registrar of Societies, Ministry of Home Affairs, Singapore, personal collection of M. Kuppusamy. I am indebted to Mr Kuppusamy for sharing his personal files with me.

46 Interview with Lam Kiang Ming on 10 November 2009.

47 Medha Kudaisya and Ng Chin-keong in their book on Chinese and Indian business look at both communities from the perspective of business but focus on the historical precursors of their respective communities, and do not examine the different aspects of their interactions. See Medha Kudaisya and Ng Chin-keong, eds, *Chinese and Indian Business: Historical Antecedents*, Social Sciences in Asia, vol. 24 (Leiden, Boston: Brill, 2009).

References

Amrith, Sunil. *Migration and Diaspora in Modern Asia*. Cambridge: Cambridge University Press, 2011.

Arasaratnam, Sinnappah. *Indians in Malaya and Singapore* (Kuala Lumpur: Oxford University Press, 1979).

Bhattacharya, Jayati. *Beyond the Myth: Indian Business Communities in Singapore*. Singapore: Institute of Southeast Asian Studies, 2011.

Brah, A. *Cartographies of Diaspora: Contesting Identities*. London: Routledge, 1996.

Chang, T. C. "Singapore's Little India: A Tourist Attraction as a Contested Landscape." *Urban Studies* 37, no. 2 (2000): 343–66.

Evers, Hans-Dieter and Rudiger Korff. *Southeast Asian Urbanism: The Meaning of Power and Social Space*. Munster: Lit Verlag, 2000.

Goh, Robbie B. H. *Contours of Culture: Space and Social Difference in Singapore*. Hong Kong: Hong Kong University Press, 2005.

Gomez, Edmund Terence and Michael H. H. Hsiao, eds. *Chinese Business in Southeast Asia: Contesting Cultural Explanations, Researching Entrepreneurship*. London: RoutledgeCurzon, 2004.

Hamilton, Gary G., ed. *Asian Business Networks*. Berlin: W. de Gruyter, 1996.

Henderson, Joan C. "Managing Urban Ethnic Heritage: Little India in Singapore." *International Journal of Heritage Studies* 14, no. 4 (2008): 332–46.

Jomo, K. S. and Brian C. Folk, ed. *Ethnic Business: Chinese Capitalism in Southeast Asia*. RoutledgeCurzon Studies in the Growth Economies of Asia. London: RoutledgeCurzon, 2003.

Kudaisya, Medha and Chin-keong, Ng, eds. *Chinese and Indian Business, Historical Antecedents*, Social Sciences in Asia, vol. 24. Leiden, Boston: Brill, 2009.

Lal, B. V., P. Reeves and Rajesh Rai, eds. *The Encyclopedia of the Indian Diaspora*. Singapore: Editions Didier Millet, 2006.

Pal, Adesh and Tapas Chakrabarti, eds. *Theorizing and Critiquing Indian Diaspora*. Creative New Literatures Series, vol. 64. New Delhi: Creative Books, 2004.

Patterson, Rubin. "Transnationalism: Diaspora-Homeland Development." *Social Forces* 84, no. 4 (June 2006): 1891–1907.

PuruShotam, Nirmala Srirekam. *Negotiating Language, Constructing Race: Disciplining Difference in Singapore*. Berlin: Mouton de Gruyter, 1998.

Sandhu, K. S. *Indians in Malaya: Some Aspects of Their Immigration and Settlement (1786–1957)* (Cambridge: Cambridge University Press, 1969).

Siddique, Sharon and Nirmala PuruShotam. *Singapore's Little India, Past, Present and Future*. Singapore: Institute of Southeast Asian Studies, 1982.

Soh, Darren. "The Paradox of Space and Its Appropriation by Migrant Labour in Singapore." *Inter-Asia Cultural Studies* 2, no. 1 (2001): 95–7.

Vertovec, Steven. "Conceiving and Researching Transnationalism." *Ethnic and Racial Studies* 22, no. 2 (March 1999): 447–62.

Chapter 8

INDIAN AND CHINESE COMMUNITIES IN CONTEMPORARY BURMA: A COMPARATIVE ANALYSIS OF THEIR PRESENCE AND INFLUENCE

Renaud Egreteau[1]

Tayok lo sha, Kala lo suu, Bama lo ma phyon ne.
(Burmese proverb: Earn like a Chinese, save like an Indian, but don't spend like a Bamar.)

Introduction

Anyone wandering for the first time in Downtown Rangoon or in the streets of Mandalay would be struck by the visible Indian and Chinese influence – yet with a strong Burmanized[2] flavour – that these vibrant Burmese cities still boast today. Bearded South Asian–looking shopkeepers wearing *longyi* (sarongs), chewing betel or puffing *bidi*-type Burmese cigars (*cheroots*) under huge Bollywood movie posters, the abundance of Chinese signboards displayed in gold, or the numerous shops selling Yunnan-made televisions – all are common snapshots. The Indian cultural influence on Burma is certainly the more obvious to the outsider: a Theravada Buddhist legacy, a Burmese language and script derived from Pali and Sanskrit are indeed palpable heritages. But the Chinese cultural impact on the country is deeply rooted too. Ancient migrations poured southward, from Central and Southwest China down to the Irrawaddy basin. In fact, nothing reflects the cultural Sino-Indian node that is Burma better than the Burmese way of dressing: Indian *longyi* down below, Chinese Mao-style shirt on top.

But it was in the age of colonial empires that Burma became far more open to Indian and Chinese demographic, cultural and commercial thrusts than ever before. The British Raj (1826–1948) fostered massive migrations of Indian communities, and to a lesser extent Chinese settlers and seasonal workers, into the Burmese colonial province. Extensive academic research has been done over the past decades on this phenomenon.[3] However, the contemporary political difficulties of Burma call for a reassessment of the current situation of the Burmese Indian and Chinese communities. Six decades after independence from British rule, it is estimated that still one-tenth of the 55-million-strong Burmese population might have Indian or Chinese origins, however remote their linkages are to India or China's modern societies and cultures. This article compares the significance of these communities in post-1988 Burma. How visible is their presence today? What socioeconomic or political impact have they had and what networks have they kept and maintained? How far have their identities been "Burmanized" since the end of the colonial era? How are they perceived by the rest of the Burmese population?

Apart from dealing with a brief historical background, this paper innovatively seeks to underline and compare the difficulties they have been facing in a post-1988 Burmese society bruised by decades of political instability, xenophobic nationalism and underdevelopment. It is argued that the initial "colonial trauma" anchored strong "Indophobic" sentiments into the Burmese psyche, but that these age-old negative perceptions of Indian populations (or *Kala* in Burmese) are now either vanishing or, as is commonly perceived, taking shape in more localized anti-Muslim sentiments. Besides, recent and extensive overland migrations of Yunnanese communities in a post-1980s context appear to have bolstered new "Sinophobic" trends in the country. This was not witnessed before when old settled Fujianese or Cantonese migrants managed to integrate more easily in Burmese society. Yet the strong propensity of the Burmese to "Burmanize" their society has deeply impacted the evolution of the identity construction of these "Burmese Indians" and "Burmese Chinese" minorities. To conclude, this article considers the challenges of the rise of the Burmese Chinese/Indian middle class, reflecting on the past domination of Burma's economy by foreign forces, a lingering "Islamophobia," and the growing geopolitical interactions between China and India in and around Burma. These issues present a new configuration that may have strong implications for Burma's domestic and foreign policymaking as well as for the fate of its "foreign" communities.

A Colonial Backgrounder

The Diversity of Indian Migrations to British Burma (1826–1937)

Incorporated into the British Raj from 1826, Burma witnessed tremendous Indo-Burmese and intra-empire maritime links, boosting the colonial enterprise and severely impacting the Burmese landscape. From the mid-1800s, but with more intensity after the First World War, the trading networks, socio-educational spheres and security forces of the Burmese province became largely controlled by Indian community-based groups (and castes). Chettiars, Tamils, Bengalis, Gujaratis, Marwaris and Gurkhas steadily imprinted their domination on every sector of the Burmese colonized society. British-facilitated migrations and Indian fortune seekers thus considerably transformed the Burmese province.[4] Rangoon, Mandalay and the harbour cities of Moulmein, Akyab and Bassein became swiftly tinged with Indian influence.[5]

Mostly originating from the Madras and Bengal Presidencies, and extending to the Ganges plains (Orissa, Bihar and United Provinces), Punjab and the Muslim-dominated Sindh and Gujarat, Indian diasporic groups progressively settled in Burma's commercial centres, and also in rural areas where today a few pockets of Indian settlements are noticeable between the towns of Toungoo and Pegu, such as the district of Zeyawadi[6]

Fig 1: Sir Krishna Temple, Mandalay © Renaud Egreteau

and Kyauktaga in Central Burma. Coolies alongside rich moneylenders (the Chettiars above all),[7] rural labourers as well as domestic servants and *sepoys*, a rising middle class of civil agents, police officers and intellectual or health professions alike, all participated in the British overseas colonial enterprise in Burma. Furthermore, the Indian immigration created a new religious mosaic within a traditionally Buddhist-dominated Burmese society. The arrival of Sunni Bengalis, Shaivite Chettiars, Sikh Punjabis, Christian Telugu speakers, and even Shias and Ismailis from Western India, considerably transformed the region, with a new architecture mushrooming in many urban areas (mosques, Hindu *gopurams* and Sikh *gurdwaras* – see Figures 1, 4, 5 and 6).

Most of the Indian migrants came with their own families, faiths, cultural traditions, languages, casteist organizations and religious prohibitions, and hardly assimilated with the rest of the indigenous society – not even with other Christianized non-Bamar ethnic groups such as the Kachins, Karens or Chins. They also gradually became despised for their resistance to local assimilation. Specifically, the Muslim Indian communities (Bengalis, Sindhis and Gujaratis) faced rising hostility from local populations.[8] Before the Japanese invasion of Burma in 1942, there were about 1.1 million Indians in the 16-million-strong British province (1.017 million out of 14.7 million according to the 1931 Census).[9] In 1931, Rangoon counted around 212,000 Indians, 30,000 Chinese and

14,000 Europeans/Anglo-Indians among its 400,000 inhabitants,[10] while most of the Burmese commercial towns along the eastern Rangoon–Toungoo–Kalaw–Mandalay infrastructure corridor were also densely populated with Indian settlements.

Chinese Settlements and Networks in Colonial Burma

The Chinese in British Burma also grew as an important and wealthy community – more evidently than during the successive Burmese royal eras. Beyond ancient migrations from the north (from Southwest China) and pre-colonial Sino-Burmese interactions through extensive maritime commercial routes,[11] Chinese immigration to British Burma – mostly urban – was boosted after the first Anglo-Burmese War (1824–26). Chinese overseas merchants from British-controlled Penang took advantage of the British "pacification" of the Tennasserim coast to foster trading, mining (tin extraction) and fishing activities, especially from Mergui, Moulmein and then Rangoon and the Irrawaddy Delta after 1853.[12] As early as the 1820s, Konbaung local authorities had allowed Chinese settlers a burial ground in western Rangoon. Through cross-empire economic linkages, despite displaying more modest population proportions than the Indians, the Chinese had developed wide junk-trading networks between the Burmese, Malayan and Chinese eastern coasts, and used Burmese ports as valuable entrepôts throughout the nineteenth century. Commercial relations with the North Chinese neighbour were tentatively increased (Yunnan being in a far better geographical position than Assam or Siam from a Burma-centred perspective), but not to the extent it would reach decades later, when China's internal strife (the Panthay Rebellion of 1856–73, the collapse of the Qing empire in 1911–12) generated further migration. Thus, with localized exceptions along the China–Yunnan borders (with the Mandarin-speaking Kokang minority for instance), the Chinese overseas (more than overland) migrations mostly found their origins in the British Straits Settlements (Penang, Melaka, Singapore), as well as in various China ports in Fujian and Guangdong, including Hong Kong. According to Burmese scholar Mya Than, only a quarter of the total Sino-Burmese population in British Burma came from neighbouring Yunnan.[13]

The socio-ethnic diversity of the Chinese communities was reflected in Burma's urban landscape. Rangoon, Monywa, Mandalay or Moulmein's "Chinatowns" (or *Tayok-tan* in Burmese) visibly displayed the cultural and linguistic differences offered by ethnic Fujianese (traditionally *Letshe* or *In-gyi-she* – short jackets – as they used to be called by the Burmese in the nineteenth century) and ethnic Cantonese (*Leto* or *In-gyi-to* – long jackets).[14] From the nineteenth century Rangoon had a distinct Cantonese area (west of Sule Paya) and a Hokkien and Hakka district (western Strand Road) next to it, both organized around community-based clans and associations, as well as religious sites (temples, cemeteries and charity buildings).[15] Two noticeable Hokkien temples were built on Strand Road (Kheng Hock Keong or Qingfugong Temple, dedicated to Mazu, the sea goddess, ca. 1860s – Figure 2) and on Canal Street (today's Anawrahta Street; Long Shan Tang Temple – or Liao San Tao, ca. 1870s) both financed by Fujianese donors for Hokkien families. The Cantonese had earlier established another temple (Guan Yin Si, ca. 1820) on Dalhousie Street (today's Mahabandoola Street) dedicated to Guan Yin, the goddess of mercy.

Fig 2: Kheng Hock Keong (Qingfugong) Temple, Rangoon © Renaud Egreteau

Although few Yunnanese "refugees" fleeing the Panthay Rebellion had settled in Upper Burma in the second half of the nineteenth century, most of the Chinese migrants had followed European-led settlements from the coast towards the Burmese inland areas. They grew as an important community of traders, artisans, manufacturers and shopkeepers in Rangoon, Moulmein, Mergui, Pegu, up to Mandalay, with seasonal Chinese coolies brought in by the mining industry along the Tennasserim coast or in Mogok's gem centre. They took great care not to directly compete with Indian coolies and dockers in Rangoon's and Akyab's harbours while establishing teashops and restaurants in various Burmese towns, as well as rice mills in the Irrawaddy Delta. A Burmese–Chinese Chamber of Commerce was formerly set up in 1910.[16] However, they faced more difficulties in their travel and migration enterprises than the Indians as the latter's legal status during the British Raj enabled them to move far more freely throughout the empire than the Chinese, who were legally "foreigners" in imperial India. Competition nevertheless appeared among upper-class Chinese and Indian migrant communities, especially in the pawnbroker/moneylender sector. While Chinese pawnbrokers made significant forays throughout the nineteenth century, they were dramatically challenged by Indian Chettiar moneylenders and Marwari bankers, who from the 1920s dominated Burma's credit system.[17]

Before 1942, only 1.3 per cent (or 193,589 individuals) of Burma's population was of Chinese origin according to the 1931 census.[18] More integrated in Burmese society than did Indian settlers, they often took Burmese or ethnic wives and more commonly spoke

Burmese. Particularly in semirural areas, the line between ethnic Burmese and ethnic Chinese gradually blurred after one or two generations. Yet, in the urban centres, Chinese communities were not fully blended into the Burmese Buddhist environment – even in the case of the Chinese "Buddhists." Chinese customary laws and traditions continue to be observed in Burma, with funeral rites, ancestor worship or legal succession rights still distinguishing these communities from Burmese indigenous ones.[19]

Indigenous Burmese Perceptions of Indian and Chinese Immigrants, between Hostility and Resentment

As a consequence of the domination of Indians and Chinese in the colonial enterprise, a growing xenophobic resentment had been nurtured from the late nineteenth century. Burmese indigenous communities (mainly the Burmans) felt unfairly deprived by the economic, cultural and political domination of "alien" communities.

A Burmese Linguistic Approach

The Burmese traditional perceptions of these two important actors of the country's landscape differ slightly. Linguistics is very revealing of this Burmese psyche. Indeed, according to linguists, the Burmese language over the past two centuries has tended to portray the Indians in far more derogatory terms or idiomatic phrasings than the Chinese. In short, the Indians (and more and more specifically the Muslim communities) are for the Burmese the "black foreigners," whereas the Chinese are the "elder brothers" that have nonetheless to be accommodated.

Since the colonial period the Indian communities have traditionally been referred to in Burmese as *Kalas*, with clearly negative connotations. Today this Burmese word has actually deepened its restrictive meaning compared to a century ago. The Burmese language tended to label any person coming from the outside world (a "foreigner") as a *ku-la* – from *ku*, meaning "crossing maritime space," and *la*, meaning "to come."[20] Until the eighteenth century, most of the foreigners coming to Burma by sea were thus called *kula*, whether Arab merchants, Armenian traders, Tamil sailors or Portuguese mercenaries (although *feringhi/bayinghi* was common for the latter).[21] *Kula* also had connotations of believing in a different religion to Buddhism (Islam, Christianity, Hinduism, etc.). Thus, the Chinese/Mongols, the Siamese or the Arakanese (*Rakhine*) of Western Burma were not considered *kula*, contrary for instance to the Europeans (*kula phyu* or "white kula"). But with the advent of British rule and massive Indian immigration, the term *kula* merged with the similarly phonetic *kala*, which has another signification in Sanskrit (as well as in Hindustani or Urdu, spoken by most of the Indian minorities in British Burma): "black."[22] Progressively, as the Indians too used this term in their daily life, *kula* moved to *kala* (with a tone change) and designated from then on a black person of Indian origin (Figure 3).

In 1886, the Hobson-Jobson Anglo-Indian dictionary had already developed an entry on "kula, kla," or "Burmese name of a native of Continental India" (p. 495). With the colonial exploitation of Burma being mainly perceived as "managed" by Indians, the

Fig 3: Burmese Indian Girls with *thanaka* (a paste made from the bark of a tree and used as sunscreen and other cosmetic properties by Burmese women), Thanlyin (Southeast Rangoon) © Renaud Egreteau

appellation *kala* rapidly took on the same hostile meaning the word "nigger" had in the nineteenth-century Western world. The main targets of the vindictive Burmese society in the early twentieth century were primarily the rich Chettiars (moneylenders). *Chetti-kala* has been used ever since as a pejorative term in the Burmese language.[23] Gradually, derogatory attitudes and pejorative terms have thoroughly stigmatized the Burmese people of Indian – but more overtly Muslim[24] – origins, to the point of seeing the term *kala* being today considered by common rural Burmese people as a mere tribe or people (*kala lumyo* or "kala people").

Various Burmese words have also put the diverse Chinese communities into linguistic boxes. We have described earlier for the pre-colonial and colonial eras the use of *Letshe* or *In-gyi-she* (long sleeve) for the Fujianese, and *Leto* or *In-gyi-to* (short sleeve) for the Cantonese. *Panthay* for the Yunnanese Muslims (called *Hui* in Yunnan) has also long been common. But nowadays, *Tayoke* (from ta, meaning "one," and *yok*, meaning "face," or most probably derived from *Turk/Taruk*, or the great Mongols that invaded Burma in the thirteenth century)[25] is the more popular term designating the Chinese or people of Chinese origin in Burma. All those terms are far less derogatory compared to the *Kala* appellation for Indians and Muslims. What's more, in post-colonial diplomatic exchanges, educated Burmese people have tended to use the term *pauk phaw* or *swemyo paukphaw* to designate their "northern" neighbours. The word finds its origin in "born out of the same mother" or "of the same race," but it is today commonly understood as "senior brother," meaning one who is elder, stronger, potentially more annoying, but who can also be quite easily accommodated by the younger brother (the Burmese). Designating both the object (the Chinese) and the dual relationship, the term *paukphaw* is methodically used by Burmese and Chinese leaders during official meetings and declarations, be it U Nu, Ne Win or Than Shwe, or Mao, Zhou Enlai or Hu Jintao. It proves in fact that the Burmese are fully aware of the necessity to deal with this "big elder brother," to acknowledge his higher status. The Burmese are nonetheless prompt in recalling the way they managed to rebuff Chinese imperial troops in the past or only paid a tributary respect to the Qing dynasty for less than one century (late eighteenth, early nineteenth).[26]

Middlemen or (Sub)-colonizers? Burmese Expressions of Hostility towards Indian and Chinese Communities

Whereas the Burmese province grew richer and richer in the first half of the twentieth century, to the point of being labelled "the rice bowl of Asia," the colonial economy presented the characteristics of an oligopolistic enterprise widely controlled by and organized around a few foreign hands – Anglo-Europeans, and then Indians and Chinese – with a Burmese rural majority mostly left out of the colonial picture. The Chinese and Indian communities, as in any many parts of the globalized colonial world, often acted as middlemen between local consumers (Burmese) and outside producers or dominant governments. Since the late 1960s, academic literature on the "middlemen" minorities and their ethnic-based solidarity networks has extensively analysed this go-between function. The literature usually depicts them as more or less acculturated, and therefore stigmatized and despised by indigenous communities. It can be applied most fittingly to the Burma case in the colonial period.[27] Burmese frustrations and bitterness against imperialism (illustrated by the presence of "foreigners") nurtured an increasingly xenophobic nationalism. Its first targets logically became the Indian communities (especially the rich Chettiars) and then the British and Chinese.

In the 1890s, the British authorities reported many Burman-led anti-foreign riots. But the 1920s and 1930s witnessed the harsher anti-Indian (and to a lesser extent anti-Chinese) pogroms, most specifically in Rangoon and other urban areas (Mandalay, Pegu). The fiercest peak of Indophobic violence was reached during the May–June 1930 riots, and then in July–September 1938, with clear anti-Muslim overtones.[28] With the Great Depression as the background, the rural-based Saya San rebellion (1930–31), which was the paramount anti-foreign popular movement of colonial Burma and largely – but not exclusively – inspired by a disrobed *pongyi* (monk), Saya San, expressed years of resentment against exploitation and integration of the Burmese rural peasant majority. Crushed by colonial troops – mainly formed by Indian *sepoys* and non-Burman ethnic soldiers – the Saya San revolt bolstered Burmese nationalism and is still widely perceived as an anti-"foreign" (read, Indian and British) founding moment of the pre-independence struggle.[29] Indeed, in spite of having greatly been financed by rich Burmese Indian sponsors, the Burmese nationalist movement swiftly militated for a separation of Burma from India – which was gained in 1937 – thus widely building up its strategy along these

"Indophobic" political lines after the failure of U Ottama and U Wizara's Gandhian non-violent strategy in the 1920s.[30]

The Chinese had also been easy targets of Burmese popular anger throughout the turbulent 1930s – in January 1931 anti-Chinese popular riots erupted in Rangoon[31] – but they encountered comparatively less hostility from the Burmese psyche. Racial strife was furthered by the divisions sparked by the Japanese invasion in 1942, with Indian communities mostly remaining loyal to the defeated British and the Burmans largely welcoming (at first) the "liberation" by Nippon imperial forces. The colonial trauma thus severely affected the Burmese perceptions of Western and Indian communities.

The Salience of Xenophobic Violence in Post-Independence Burma

Once Burma's independence was granted in 1948, both Burmese Indians and Chinese had to cope with new rounds of hostile xenophobic state policies. Many Indians had already fled the Japanese invasion in 1942 along with the British forces,[32] and found it extremely difficult to come back during 1945–48. The first legal "Burmanizing" steps had already been taken by the post-1937 Burmese Legislative Council: no further Indian immigration was allowed after the separation from India and various laws were enacted to ensure the end of any "foreign" domination of Burma's land and properties.[33] These policies were furthered in the late 1940s, notably with the Union Citizenship Act and Land Nationalization Act of 1948 (the latter revised in 1953), which both proved to be strong obstacles for the Indian (and Chinese) communities to bring back their families and recover their properties after the war, or to adopt the new citizenship. The majority of Burmese Indians nevertheless tried to apply for Burmese citizenship after 1948 (while very few Chinese did) despite long and tortuous legal processes. Therefore, by the mid-fifties, about seven to eight hundred thousand Burmese of Indian origin remained in Burma (compared to around one million in pre-war times), while around three hundred thousand Burmese Chinese were now developing their socioeconomic networks there. Although greatly affected by China's internal strife (torn as it was between Chiang Kai-shek and Mao Zedong's conflicting ideologies),[34] their numbers even grew to three hundred and fifty thousand in the early 1960s, as they were in position to fill the socioeconomic vacuum left by the Indians who had departed for India, East and West Pakistan, the Malay Peninsula or the Western world.[35]

The waves of state-imposed political, cultural and economic "Burmanization" of the country were strong from the early 1960s onwards. With the advent of the autarchy and openly xenophobic military rule imposed by General Ne Win (1962–88), Indian, Chinese, Anglo-Burmese and Western communities alike, as well as non-Burman ethnic minorities, became open targets of the programmes launched by the Fabian-inspired Revolutionary Council of Ne Win.[36] While their lives were not directly threatened, their livelihoods were. Most Burmese of Indian origin panicked at the official measures announced after the 1963 Enterprises Nationalization Act. Demonetization in 1964 and the closure of foreign language schools in April 1965 were perceived as anti-Indian.

Thousands approached India's and Pakistan's embassies in Rangoon and a dramatic rush to the capital occurred in 1963 and 1964. Indian diplomats then had to figure out how to transport back to India these scores of Burmese Indians, most of whose citizenship status was still unclear.[37] Between 1962 and 1965, about three hundred thousand foreigners fled the country, most of them being Burmese Indians.[38] A majority of them settled in East and South India. A few districts near Kolkata comprising the rural towns of Subhasgram East or Barasat are now called the "Burma Colonies," as is Chennai's downtown "Burma Bazaar."[39] Several new settlements around the harbour of Visakapatnam in Andhra Pradesh also welcomed Burmese originally from Andhra and Orissa rural communities throughout the 1960s and 1970s.[40]

Once the most influential Burmese Indians had been driven out of the country, the Burmese Chinese became the new targets of the Ne Win regime. This approach was necessary to diffuse popular and internecine anger caused by the failure of the first five years of the enforced socialist revolution.[41] The Chinese had initially been far less affected by the early 1960s nationalizations, although in 1964 the Beijing-owned Bank of China and Bank of Communications were nationalized, as well as all Chinese schools in 1965. But with the impact of the Maoist Cultural Revolution spreading into Southeast Asia and Burma from 1967, Sino-Burmese *paukphaw* relations experienced a severe blow. In June 1967, the Embassy of China in Rangoon was ransacked by an infuriated Burmese mob, killing one Chinese official.[42] Anti-Chinese riots followed in June and July, mainly in Rangoon, Mandalay and Moulmein, with a clear laissez-faire attitude on the part of the Burmese authorities.[43] Ne Win even allowed the Taiwan-financed Federation of Free Overseas Chinese Association in Burma to operate, in a clear reaction to Beijing's ideological thrust.[44] After a three-year gap, official diplomatic relations between Burma and Mao's China were restored with an exchange of ambassadors in November 1970 (Beijing) and March 1971 (Rangoon).

By the early 1970s, less than half a million of the poorer Indo-Burmese or Burmanized Indians remained, while around two hundred thousand Chinese kept a visible presence in Burma despite recurrent Sino-Burmese political clashes at the highest level and noticeable migrations back to Hong Kong/Macau and Singapore.[45] Various localized anti-Muslim pogroms followed throughout the 1970s and 1980s, revealing a clear shift of Burmese resentment towards Burmese Muslims of Indian origin (especially the "Rohingya" community in western Arakan State). Finally, the Burmese Citizenship Law of 1982, which revised the 1948 act, made it even more difficult for Indian, Chinese and any other "foreigners" to be granted full Burmese citizenship rights.[46] The following 1983 census interestingly showed the low figures of 567,985 Bangladeshis, 428,428 Indians, 42,140 Pakistanis and 28,506 Nepalis – around one million Burmese of South Asian origin – remaining in Burma.[47] The same nationwide census in 1983 registered only 0.6 per cent of the 34.1 million Burmese population (0.23 million) as ethnic Chinese, which also seems a far underestimated figure. New Upper Burma–bound Yunnanese migrations had been discreetly encouraged after China's post-Mao opening-up development strategy promoted by Deng Xiaoping, and was clearly revealed during the latter's official visit to Rangoon in January 1978.[48]

Contemporary Significance of Burmese Indian and Chinese Communities

The Burmese regional and domestic context has greatly evolved after 1988 and the collapse of the Ne Win regime. Burmese Indian and Chinese communities have faced diverse fates since, with a common pattern: the strong and deep Burmanization challenge imposed by Burmese society and state authorities since the 1940s appears to have remained much in place. Today, although no reliable census data is here to assert these figures, we might argue that about two and a half to three million Burmese do have Indian origins (thus 5–6 per cent of Burma's population of fifty-five million),[49] while a larger range can be proposed for the "Burmese Chinese" or Sino-Burmese/Yunnanese: between two and four million (4–7 per cent of the population).[50] As far as the Burmese Chinese are concerned, clear evaluations are very difficult to assess, as cross-border influx and ethnic mixing have always been legion in Northern Burma. A nationwide census took place in 2014, but the data on ethnicity will be released only in 2016.

Burmanized Indians: Networks and Integration into Today's Burma

The initial waves of exiles consisted of richer Chettiars, Marwaris or Gujaratis in the late 1930s, while the poorer Burmese Indians remained in post-colonial Burma. State promotions of "Burmanization,"[51] political autarchy and a rather inclusive Burmese society have furthered their relative assimilation since the 1960s. Burmese language learnt in state schooling and the loss of Indian names when adopting more Burmese-sounding ones for their official identity papers have made them more "Burmese" than "Indian" today. Despite maintaining obvious identity markers (Hindu or Islamic practices and endogamy for instance) or still being popularly stigmatized as *Kalas* by Burmese locals, most now consider themselves "Burmese." As a Muslim lawyer, a member of the Myanmar Muslim Association of Bassein, once told me, the *de facto* enforced "Burmanization" has been a key element of the pacification of Burmese/Indian relationships since the 1960s.[52] Very few Indians in Burma had effectively maintained family linkages with the homelands of their forefathers throughout the Indian subcontinent during the Ne Win regime. After 1988, links have however been tentatively revived and even boosted after the political transition in 2011.[53]

The Manipuris/Meitheis of Western Burma (who are mostly Shaivites[54]), the Bengali Muslims, the Biharis in Zeyawadi and Kyauktaga districts and the Nepali Gurkhas seem to have been less prone to Burmanization nationwide. Strong casteist and endogamous habits among the Indo-Burmese Shaivites are still very common, while the Burmese Muslims by and large still hardly mix with Buddhists and Christians. Burmese Sikhs have on the contrary been greatly integrated to the society, as they chose, from 1947, to be registered as "Buddhists." For instance, about three hundred and fifty Sikh families still live today in Myitkyina (Kachin State), mostly doing small-scale business with Yunnan, but not at all with India or Pakistani Punjab, where they initially came from (see Figure 4).[55] Promotion of "Indian" languages has severely declined between the 1960s and 2000s,

Fig 4: Sikh Temple, Myitkyina, Kachin State © Renaud Egreteau

with only a few Hindu foundations or Sikh *gurdwaras* or *madrassas* teaching Tamil, Hindi and Urdu (or even English) through private (and discreet) donations.

The impact of Burmese Indian communities is clearly visible in the country's urban landscape, especially Rangoon and Mandalay, in the port cities of Moulmein, Bassein and Sittwe (formerly Akyab), and along the Mandalay–Toungoo–Pegu eastern corridor. Interestingly, the parallel western corridor of Mandalay–Pagan–Magwe–Pyay is almost devoid of any Indian settlements, and their subsequent architectural imprint. Gurkha (Nepali) influences are still obvious in garrison towns (Pyin U-Lwin, Kalaw, Myitkyina), while the Bengali (Muslim) presence is patent in Rangoon, Moulmein and throughout the Arakan State. Downtown Rangoon remains a fascinating Indo-Burmese melting pot that still surprises the external observer. The former capital counted around 250,000 Indians in 1941, and six decades after about 400–500,000 (around 15 per cent of its population), but again most of them are legally "Burmese" and claiming to be so. Mandalay could gather today around 100–150,000 Burmese of Indian origin (dwelling more specifically in the southwest corner and eastern side of the Royal Palace along 19th Street), but with only 30–70,000 who have effectively and strictly kept on practising Indian traditions.[56]

As part of the colonial legacy, Burmese Indians have dotted the country with thousands of religious sites, places of worship, memorials or charity buildings, whether Hindu, Muslim, Christian or Sikh. Throughout Burma, most of these buildings are today still in strikingly good condition – well repaired or refurbished through apparently large domestic donations. Evaluating the amount of private donations given to Hindu temples or societies, Sikh *gurdwaras* or Sunni/Shia mosques enables us to assert that after years of discrimination, the remaining Burmese Indian communities have managed to become a (discreet) lower urban, basically educated, middle class of shopkeepers, petty traders and manufacturers, civil servants, teachers, lawyers, pharmacists, bus drivers, etc. Far more discreet than the (upper) Chinese middle class or the richer military-linked Burmese upper class, the Burmese Indians have maintained and strengthened low-key but valuable networks throughout the country and along its borders, benefitting from transnational connections they have maintained with the few relatives who left Burma in the late 1940s.[57] One would be astonished to see the wealth accumulated by Sikhs merchants in Thai border towns, by Burmese Tamil business lords along the India–Burma borders (Manipur) or Muslim communities in the jade market of Ruili (Yunnan).

Various Burmese Indian-run institutions still carefully promote what is perceived as a distinct "Indian" identity in Burma: language (Tamil, Hindi, Urdu and Bengali mainly), religions, social traditions as well as oral history. The old revivalist and nationalist Arya Samaj set up an office in Rangoon in 1899 to bolster the literary study of Hindu culture and civilization throughout Burma.[58] Today it runs religious offices in its temple on Anawrahta Street, as well as in Mandalay and Myitkyina.[59] The Vishwa Hindu Parishad (a Hindu ideological organization funded in India in 1964) interestingly managed to enter post-independence Burma and, along with the All Burma Hindu Central Board (ABHCB) founded in 1953 in Rangoon, has ever since been trying to promote Hindu festivals (Durga Puja, Holi and others). The Tamil Hindu Society, the Rangoon-based Sri Kali Temple Trust (Figure 5) and the Ramakrishna Mission Society (renamed Shri Ramakrishna Temple Trust in 1977) all enjoy a fair amount of private donations which enables them to restore and/or construct various community-oriented charity wards, collect "Indian" documents in reading rooms and libraries, while running free dispensaries for the poorest.[60] The Hare Krishna movement is also scattered throughout Burma and provides free education to young boys.[61] The Sanatan Dharma Swayamsevak Sangh (SDSS), founded in January 1950 in Rangoon as a branch of India's Rashtriya Swayamsevak Sangh (RSS, or Hindu Association of National Volunteers, 1925), has today no such radical activities as the latter in India. The SDSS in Burma is merely apolitical, only organizing cultural events and publishing a bimonthly magazine in Burmese and Hindi (*Sabte Jyoti* [Light of truth], with a distribution of about five thousand copies).[62] It has little influence in today's Burma, at least less than is often perceived by external observers in India, mostly due to the authoritarian constraints imposed by the successive Burmese regimes.[63] A rare example of Andhra upper-caste reminiscences in Burma, the Reddy Young Men's Association also has a discreet presence in Moulmein (Mon State).

The Burmese Indian Muslims too – Sunnis (Myanmar Muslim Organization) and Shias (All Myanmar Shia Muslim Organization) – still display their faith in mosques, social trusts and funds, or community-oriented hospitals. In Rangoon, the Variav Sunni Vohra Panchayat Trust (established in 1895), the Jamiat Ulama El-Islam (1916), the Cholia Muslim Religious Fund Trust (since 1921) and the Muslim Free Hospital (built in 1937) are the oldest and still active.

Rangoon's Guru Nanak Free Dispensary and several regularly refurbished *gurdwaras* in Mandalay, Pyawbwe, Kalaw, Pyin U-Lwin (formerly Maymyo) also attest to the social and welfare activities and strength of the Burmese Sikh community. Lastly, the Christian Burmese Indians (most probably one-eighth of the total population of Burmese of

Fig 5: Kali Temple, Rangoon © Renaud Egreteau

Fig 6: Mogul Shiah Masjid, Moulmein, Mon State © Renaud Egreteau

Fig 7: Telugu Methodist Church, Rangoon © Renaud Egreteau

Indian origin) have also been allowed to maintain their places of worship countrywide, despite being supplanted by churches of Western origin or evangelist churches, especially in ethnic areas. In Rangoon, the Tamil-dominated St John's Church has been funded by the wealthy South Indian Parkavakula Welfare Society, and the Telugu Methodist Church still gathers Burmese worshippers of Andhra origin (Figure 7).

Lastly, divided but with a palpable presence, the Burmanized Indians do not mix with the tiny community of "Indian" newcomers who have settled in Burma as expatriates after 1988. Less than one thousand Indian "expats" (with foreign passports) were living in Burma in the 2000s, with around one hundred and fifty to two hundred families in Rangoon only.[64] Few are from Singapore, Pakistan and Bangladesh, but the majority represent Indian, Singaporean, Malaysian, Bangladeshi or Thai business interests; the India–Myanmar Business Club was founded in 1994, with a membership of around two hundred and fifty.[65] With the 2011 opening up of the country, however, their presence is expected to increase notably.

Yunnanese Migrations and the Lingering Rise of a "Sinophobia" in Post-1980s Burma

Although the phenomenon had been observed throughout the 1980s, the official opening-up of the Yunnan–Burma border in 1988 and the partnership established between the new Burmese junta and Beijing from 1989 have bolstered transborder links, whether political, economic, sociocultural or demographic.[66] New waves of overland Chinese (Yunnanese) migrations had been witnessed over the past two decades, in far greater proportions than colonial overseas migrations.[67] Whereas the old settled Fujianese and Cantonese minorities had mostly blended into Burmese society, speaking and writing Burmese (instead of Putonghua or Cantonese with Chinese ideograms), with men wearing *longyi* (sarongs) and puffing slim green *cheroot*, new Yunnanese migrants do not boast of such propensity for assimilation into Burmese society.

A wide international academic literature has extensively exposed the challenges offered by a new form of "Sinicization" (or "Sinonization") of post-1988 Burma.[68] Many academics, security analysts and reporters have underscored throughout the 1990s these north-originated Chinese "threats" to the Burmese society, stressing the dramatic cultural watershed initiated by waves of Chinese migrants opening new businesses, restaurants, karaoke bars and shady casinos in Mandalay, Lashio, Muse or even Rangoon, thus finding in Burma their new "Eldorado."[69] The term "Yunnanization" would be more appropriate to Upper Burma as thousands of them have flooded the region north of Mandalay and become predominantly focused on trading and transportation activities. Half of the two hundred thousand–odd population of Lashio might nowadays be of Yunnanese origin,[70] while many newcomers in Mandalay appeared to master more Chinese languages than Burmese ones. The Chinese Consulate-General in Mandalay – reopened in 1994 – gave a rough estimation of about one hundred thousand Burmese Chinese in the city (out of one million people in the mid-2000s), with its Indian counterpart estimated at a figure four times higher.[71] Chinese–Burmese associations in Mandalay have claimed that only five thousand Chinese families were dwelling in the former Burmese royal town (2009).[72]

Nevertheless, one has to temper this alarming assessment of a country certainly not fully "annexed" to Yunnan, although very well connected to it. Waves of lingering "Sinicization" have been observed in Upper Burma in post-independence years as well. When parliamentary Burma was part of the Asian Solidarity movement in the 1950s, dozens of political and diplomatic speeches of Burmese leaders, academic reports and local newspapers denounced the growing Chinese influx from post-1949 China. Beside Kuomintang forces stationed in Northern Burma, new Yunnanese migrants and traders began in the 1950s to fill in the gaps left by the Indians who had fled Burma (hence the growing number of Chinese people, from two hundred thousand in the early 1940s up to three hundred and fifty thousand in the late 1950s, a 75 per cent growth in 15 years). Later, to rebuild Mandalay after two devastating fires in 1981 and 1984,[73] Ne Win had appealed to Yunnanese traders to invest there, thus explaining the presence of numerous Sino-Burmese buildings today, displaying the years 1982 and 1985 on their front walls (Figure 8).

Nothing new then after 1988, we would argue; it is merely an illustration of the propensity of the Burmese society to assimilate the Chinese Confucian and Buddhists more easily – one immigration wave after another. It is still the case today, for the naive outsider would distinctively observe that Mandalay or Rangoon's "Chinatowns" are far more "Burmanized" and less "Chinese" than any other Chinatowns in Southeast Asia. Yet the Chinese in Burma have formed a strong (upper) middle class in the country, especially in urban areas and along the Muse–Lashio–Mandalay axis, and the promotion and cultivation of a "Chinese-ness" has clearly been revived since 1988.[74]

Fig 8: Sino-Burmese house, Mandalay © Renaud Egreteau

Fig 9: New Yunnan Buddhist Temple, Bhamo, Kachin State © Renaud Egreteau

Fig 10: Yunnanese Buddhist Temple and Association, Mandalay © Renaud Egreteau

Yunnan, Taiwan, Hong Kong and Singapore Chinese associations, donor organizations and business groupings have entered Burma since the early 1990s, financed Chinese-oriented cultural activities, promoted Chinese teaching classes (mostly Mandarin/ Putonghua) and built new Buddhist and Confucianist temples, especially in Northern Burma (Figures 9 and 10). Yunnan University (Kunming) has established extensive academic cooperation with Mandalay. Chinese students have been flooding Burmese language institutes and Confucian programmes have been set up.[75] Chinese New Year grows bigger each year in Rangoon and Mandalay, while other Chinese festivals or celebrations and places of worship are more and more openly sponsored.[76] Chinese culture is therefore thriving in post-1988 Burma, yet on lower visible scales compared to other neighbouring countries.

New Challenges for Burmese Indians and Burmese Chinese in Post-1988 Burma

The Rise of a Non-Burman Middle Class and Its Implications

For many observers, the management of Burma's rising "foreign" middle class – mainly Indians (lower) and Chinese (upper) – offers new challenges, more particularly in the case of the latter. Since the 1990s, Burmese popular psyche has portrayed quite negatively the Chinese newcomers from Yunnan, who enjoy no positive reputation among Burmese people, as the old settled Fujianese and Cantonese used to.[77] Popular perceptions portray these post-1990s (male) Chinese migrants as heavy drinkers and gamblers, looking for Burmese prostitutes in newly built and noisy karaoke bars; they prefer Chinese manufactured cigarettes to Burmese indigenous *cheroots*, speak an awful Burmese language, but have set up powerful businesses.[78] They are rich and successful, having acquired considerable commercial influence in urban areas and Northern Burma – hence their nickname *law pan* or "boss." They have generated mixed feelings among the Burmese youth. Containing potential popular anti-Chinese backlashes – like in the late 1960s – is now a top priority of the Burmese and Chinese authorities, given the highly heterogeneous patterns of the exclusive socioeconomic development of post-1988 Burma.[79] This is not the case with the lower Burmese Indian middle class, which is far more discreet and has enjoyed less visible economic success since the early 1990s.

The Burmese military rulers seem to have long been focused on not letting foreign hands back in Burma. After the 1990s, there has been a much-needed strategy to break out of isolation, aimed at attracting foreign investments. Yet, the Burmese military leadership has tended to favour Burmese (even Burman) business circles in all the most lucrative and strategic sectors of Burma's economy – including the construction of the new capital Naypyidaw ("city of kings"), built from the early 2000s with the involvement of only a very few foreign companies. Despite Burma officially being an open-market economy since 1988, liberalization there has been very limited *vis-à-vis* the outside world and the formal economy remains largely monopolistic (i.e., in Burmese military hands, whether private or state owned). There has been a tendency in Burma to "Burmanize" the economy or society whenever it is deeply subjugated by "external" or "internal" foreigners. The potential for the revival of age-old Sinophobic and Indophobic tendencies would become a new challenge if Chinese, Indian or other ethnic middle classes acquire too much influence over Burma's slowly developing economy.

This throws up new problems for political scientists and pro-democracy activists alike, as indeed, they both often put forward the need for an oppressed society to witness the rise of a richer and newly asserted middle class distinct from the ruling elite, if a democratization process is to be consolidated. In South Korea, Taiwan or Chile, an indigenous middle class, clearly de-linked to the authoritarian rulers, had been at the core of the democratic transitions of these countries. The educated middle-class circles have often initiated and then strengthened political processes of change while supporting new democratic aspirations and sustaining civil rights struggles. Theoretically, in twenty-first century Burma, with only an Indian and Chinese dominated middle class, and few ethnic groups enriched through informal cross-border trades, the desired indigenous "Burman" and urban middle class is still very much lacking.

Towards Islamophobic Trends?

While the Burmese Indian communities of Hindu, Sikh and Christian backgrounds are today facing far less violent and open hostility from the rest of Burmese society compared to the colonial or post-independence years, Burmese Muslims of Indian origin as well as the Rohingya minority – and to a far lesser extent Chinese Muslims or *Panthays* – still encounter strong colloquial patronization, administrative, political and security hurdles, if not blunt segregation and assault from the Burmese authorities and society. The derogatory term *Kala*, which nowadays almost exclusively designates the Burmese Muslims, particularly the Rohingyas of northwest Arakan State (often called *kaw taw kala* or "too black"), is still very much in use. Most of the Burmese Muslims are openly rejected or discriminated against – not only by the Burmese military administration, but also by Arakanese and Burman Buddhist-dominated societies, as well as by neighbouring countries. Hostile perceptions reviling Rohingyas and other Muslim *Kalas* are often illustrated by harsh racist discourses professed even within Burmese pro-democracy circles.[80] Many Burmese in southern Arakan or in Central Burma would proudly recall how they have rid their hometowns of the *Kalas* in the not-so-distant past.[81] This has once again materialized when, in 2012 and early 2013, Burmese Buddhist mobs burned down several Muslim quarters in the cities of Sittwe, Meikthila and Lashio.[82]

A growing "Islamophobia" has indeed been witnessed in past years in Burma, revealing recurrent tendencies of Burmese society to spontaneously react to what is first perceived as a cultural threat. By "Islamophobia" we mean the fear of the spread of Islam and of the gradual process of Islamization of culture, politics and day-to-day life of a non-Muslim society – here the Buddhist Burmese. In 1930–31, but more overtly in 1938, anti-Muslim pogroms had been fostered by Burman Buddhist communities, led by monks.[83] Various localized anti-Muslim pogroms followed after independence, especially in Arakan (bordering East Pakistan, Bangladesh after 1971) in 1946–48, 1962, 1978 and 1991. Throughout the 1970s and 1980s Central Burma witnessed various "de-Islamization" processes, with many mosques burnt down and never allowed to be rebuilt along the western Mandalay–Pagan–Magwe–Pyay transport corridor, as well as in Toungoo.[84] In Kyaukpadaung, southeast of Pagan, people proudly boast that there are no more *kala bali*, or mosques, in the area, as local oral memory recalls they had been simply washed away few decades ago.[85]

Popular violent outbreaks more easily target Indian or Muslim communities, especially when Burmese police forces or government authorities turn a blind eye to pogroms or community-aimed agitations and vandalistic outbursts. Many of the anti-Muslim pogroms which have occurred in Central Burma and Arakan since the early 2000s were clearly interpreted as a way to offer a "safety valve" to the Burmese Buddhist-dominated rural population deeply affected by poor economic conditions (in a post-9/11 context).[86] The post-1988 Burmese leadership has repeatedly denounced and resisted any rampant foreign influence, but it is towards the Burmese Muslim communities that this phenomenon remains the most blatant. In February 2009, the acerbic declarations of the Burmese consul-general Ye Myint Aung in Hong Kong further illustrated how xenophobic and insulting Burmese official declarations can be. Ye Myint Aung lambasted, as quoted in the *Bangkok Post*, the "dark brown" Rohingyas, stressing they were as "ugly as ogres" (and not Burmese at all), whereas the Burmese people – like him (*sic*) – were supposed to be of "fair and soft" complexion, and "good looking as well."[87] In 2012 and 2013, the flare-up of anti-Muslim riots in Central and Western Burma raised renewed concern about the country's democratization prospects among international and local observers.[88]

Geopolitical Implications

A few questions remain unanswered given the volatility of Burma's political situation. What is the political and diplomatic impact of this old-age "Indophobia" (or modern "Islamophobia") as well as the rising and popular "Sinophobia" witnessed in Northern and Western Burma? What is their leverage over the current Burmese military elite and how far can it influence Burma's current and future domestic and foreign policymaking? Are India's recent difficulties in gaining a credible strategic foothold in Burma and finding a gateway there to Southeast Asia rooted in these latent Indophobic tendencies and age-old anti-India fears still observed in Burma?[89] Clearly, given the historical legacies and distrust, India has struggled to enter the region. Despite New Delhi's attempts,[90] the Burmese psyche still portrays India as a potentially "imperial" threat. "The Kalas are coming back," a Burman businessman in Rangoon once said to me when discussing India's new economic policy approach to Burma. Indian policymakers know they are walking on eggshells in post-1988 Burma, and that they cannot rely on a disconnected and Burmanized Indian diaspora.[91]

But the fear of China remains now the most patent. Several Burma watchers have also argued it has influenced foreign policy changes in ASEAN and Western countries wary at seeing Burma becoming a Chinese "pawn" throughout the 1990s. But while Chinese assistance and patronage offered to the Burmese regime (and economy) is needed, the Burmese military leadership in the past two decades has been able to diversify its commercial and military partnerships enough to counterbalance Chinese domination.[92] Furthermore, Beijing's authorities have hardly any control over, or valuable knowledge about, the diverse Chinese communities newly settled in Burma, most of them being non-Han Yunnanese, Sino-Shans, Was or Kokangs.

Finally, systematic discrimination and brutal treatment of Burmese Muslims of Indian origin, or more specifically Rohingyas, has been widely described by international diplomatic, press or reports from transnational activist organizations since the massive exoduses in 1978/79 and 1991/92 to Bangladesh that these communities have experienced. This had a crucial impact on the world's perceptions of Burma, and also of its neighbours (Bangladesh and Thailand), both unwilling to welcome thousands of new "refugees." These negative perceptions have had a serious impact on the relationships Burma has established with the international community as a whole, but also more acutely with the Muslim world. As long as the Burmese do not seriously address the Rohingya issue, geopolitical tensions will linger, while Burma's peaceful national construction will remain elusive.

The impact of Burma's neighbours, India and China – both emerging giants – and their diasporic offshoots, is therefore significant to the Burmese landscape. Although being the objects of historical resentment and regular popular violence, the Burmese Indian and Chinese communities have remained a noticeable social and economic force throughout the country. Both remaining diasporas have been nevertheless fairly "Burmanized" in a post-independence context. The Indians remain easy targets of popular discrimination – especially the Muslims – while the new Chinese migrations have revived popular Sinophobic attitudes. But obvious distinctions have been made in the Burmese psyche between Indian Muslims and other Burmese Indians (Hindus, Christians, Sikhs), as well as between highly integrated Fujianese, Hokkien or Cantonese Chinese and recent Yunnanese migrants, who are far more despised. Further studies are needed to understand more deeply the construction of the identity of these yet "Chinese" and "Indian" Burmanized minorities, as well as their current impact on policymaking, beyond the usual rumours and speculations created by the Burmese sociopolitical conundrum.

Notes

1 The author wishes to thank the ISEAS-based Nalanda-Sriwijaya Centre for the invitation to present this paper at the conference held in Singapore on 28–30 January 2010. The passage was generously sponsored by HKIHSS (inc. CAS) of the University of Hong Kong.

2 For ease of linguistic simplicity and to avoid political connotation, the author has chosen to hereafter use the English terms "Burma," "Burmese," "Burman," and "Rangoon," instead of the vernacular terms of "Myanmar," "Bamar" and "Yangon," thus avoiding an awkward "Myanmarese" adjective, which is grammatically incorrect. "Burmese" then refers to the wider citizenship and common language of the people who inhabit Burma, while "Burman" (*Bamar*) more specifically designates the ethnic majority (65 per cent) of the country (hence the "Burmanization" processes further described), which also includes around 35 per cent of Burmese non-Burman ethnic minorities, such as the Karens, Kachins, Mons, etc.

3 Two of the most thorough (although dated) academic works on the Indian communities in colonial and early post-colonial periods remain Usha Mahajani, *The Role of Indian Minorities in Burma and Malaya* (Bombay: Vora, 1960); and Nalini R. Chakravarti, *The Indian Minority in Burma: The Rise and Decline of an Immigrant Community* (London: Oxford University Press, 1971). On the Chinese minorities, see the recent Mya Than, "The Ethnic Chinese in Myanmar and Their Identity," in *Ethnic Chinese as Southeast Asians*, edited by Leo Suryadinata (Singapore: ISEAS, 1997), pp. 115–46; and Tasaw Lu, Hsin-chun, "Performativity of Difference: Mapping Public Soundscapes and Performing Nostalgia among Burmese Chinese in Central Rangoon," *Asian Music* 42, no. 2 (2011): 19–55.

4 Adapa Satyanarayana, "'Birds of Passage': Migration of South Indian Laborers to Southeast Asia," *Critical Asian Studies* 34, no. 1 (2002): 89–115; Thet Lwin, "Indians in Myanmar," in *Rising India and Indian Communities in East Asia*, ed. K. Kesavapany, A. Mani and P. Ramasamy (Singapore: ISEAS, 2008), pp. 485–97; and Renaud Egreteau, "Burmese Indians in Contemporary Burma: Heritage, Influence, and Perceptions since 1988," *Asian Ethnicity* 12, no. 1 (February 2011), pp. 33–54

5 Bertie Reginald Pearn, *A History of Rangoon* (Rangoon: American Baptist Press, 1939); Tin Maung Maung Than, "Some Aspects of Indians in Rangoon," in *Indian Communities in Southeast Asia*, ed. K. S. Sandhu and A. Mani (Singapore: ISEAS, 2006), pp. 585–623.

6 See the case study developed in the 1980s by Mya Than, "Jairampur: A Profile of an Indian Community in Rural Burma," in *Indian Communities in Southeast Asia*, ed. K. S. Sandhu and A. Mani (Singapore: ISEAS, 2006), pp. 683–706.

7 The Chettiars are a distinctive Vaishya caste of southern Tamil Nadu. Among them, the Nagarathars (from Nattukottai region) have formed one of the most successful caste-based commercial networks of British India. See Mahajani, *The Role of Indian Minorities*, 16–22; Chakravarti, *The Indian Minority*, chapter 5; Michael Adas, "Immigrant Asians and the Economic Impact of European Imperialism: The Role of South Indian Chettiars in British Burma," *Journal of Asian Studies* 33, no. 3 (1974): 385–401; Raman Mahadevan, "Immigrant Entrepreneurs in Colonial Burma: An Exploratory Study of the Role of Nattukottai Chettiars of Tamil Nadu, 1880–1930," *Indian Economic and Social History Review* 15, no. 3 (1978): 329–58; and Sean Turnell, *Fiery Dragons: Banks, Moneylenders and Microfinance in Burma* (Copenhagen: NIAS Press, 2009).

8 For a comprehensive background of the Muslim communities, see Moshe Yegar, *The Muslims in Burma: A Study of a Minority Group* (Wiesbaden: Otto Harrassowitz, 1972) and Jean Berlie, *The Burmanization of Myanmar's Muslims* (Bangkok: White Lotus Press, 2008). See also on the acculturation issue: Khin Maung Kyi, "Indians in Burma: Problems of an Alien Subculture in a Highly Integrated Society," in *Indian Communities in Southeast Asia*, ed. K. S. Sandhu and A. Mani (Singapore: ISEAS, 2006), pp. 624–65.

9 Chakravarti, *The Indian Minority*, p. 15.

10 O. H. K. Spate and L. W. Trueblood, "Rangoon: A Study in Urban Geography," *Geographical Review* 32, no. 1 (January 1942): 60.

11 Chen Yi-Sein, "The Chinese in Rangoon during the 18th and 19th Centuries," *Artibus Asiae* 23 (1966): 107. A China wharf had already been reported in King Alaungpaya's Dagon (Rangoon) in the 1750s.

12 See Michael W. Charney, "Esculent Bird's Nest, Tin and Fish: The Overseas Chinese and Their Trade in the Eastern Bay of Bengal (Coastal Burma) during the First Half of the Nineteenth Century," in *China and Southeast Asia*, ed. Geoff Wade (London: Routledge, 2008), pp. 207–21; and Penny Edwards, "Relocating the Interlocutor: Taw Sein Ko (1864–1930) and the Itinerancy of Knowledge in British Burma," *South East Asia Research* 12, no. 3 (November 2004): 277–335.

13 Mya Than, "The Ethnic Chinese in Myanmar," p. 119.

14 Yi-Sein, "The Chinese in Rangoon," p. 110 and Mya Than, "Ethnic Chinese in Myanmar," p. 117. "Long sleeves" were mostly known as being involved in trading and pawnbrokering (and traditionally wore long-sleeve robes), while "short sleeves" were artisans and manufacturers.

15 Spate and Trueblood, "Rangoon: A Study," p. 64.

16 Mya Than, "Ethnic Chinese in Myanmar," p. 131.

17 Khin Maung Kyi, "Comments on Mya Than: 'The Ethnic Chinese in Myanmar and Their Identity,'" in *Ethnic Chinese as Southeast Asians*, ed. Leo Suryadinata (Singapore: ISEAS, 1997), p. 149.

18 Mya Than, "Ethnic Chinese in Myanmar," p. 118.

19 Mya Than, "Ethnic Chinese in Myanmar," pp. 139–42; and Tasaw Lu, Hsin-chun, "Performativity of Difference."

20 As detailed by the Burma-born Indian academic Walter S. Desai, *India and Burma: A Study* (Calcutta: Orient Longmans, 1954), pp. 37–8. Other Burmese (Burman) academics rather argue that *kula* derived from the Sanskrit word meaning "noble" (i.e. Buddha); see Khin Maung Kyi, "Indians in Burma," p. 640.

21 Thant Myint-U, *The Making of Modern Burma* (Cambridge: Cambridge University Press, 2001), pp. 89–90.

22 Yegar, *The Muslims in Burma*, pp. 6–7; Chakravarti, *The Indian Minority*, p. 11.

23 Mikael Gravers, *Nationalism as Political Paranoia in Burma: An Essay on the Historical Practice of Power* (Richmond: Curzon, 1999), p. 27; Khin Maung Kyi, "Indians in Burma," p. 640.

24 Yegar, *The Muslims in Burma*, p. 111; Renaud Egreteau, "Burmese Indians in Contemporary Burma," pp. 50–52.

25 Thant Myint-U, *The Making of Modern Burma*, p. 89–90. Hence the appellation *Tayok tan* for any Chinatown in Burma today.

26 Yingcong Dai, "A Disguised Defeat: The Myanmar Campaign of the Qing Dynasty," *Modern Asian Studies* 38, no. 4 (2004): 145–89.

27 Jews, Armenians and Chinese have often been taken as key illustrations. See the seminal research of Edna Bonacich, "A Theory of Middleman Minority," *American Sociological Review* 38, no. 5 (October 1973): 583–94; furthered in Ivan H. Light and Edna Bonacich, *Immigrant Entrepreneurs* (Berkeley: University of California Press, 1988).

28 See the Riot Inquiry Committee, *Final Report* (Rangoon: Government Printing and Stationary, 1939), extensively quoted by Yegar, *The Muslims in Burma*, pp. 32–8.

29 Gravers, *Nationalism as Political Paranoia*, p. 37. See also the recent analysis of the evolution of the international academic views on the rebellion by Maitrii Aung-Thwin, "Structuring Revolt: Communities of Interpretation in the Historiography of the Saya San Rebellion," *Journal of Southeast Asian Studies* 39, no. 2 (June 2008): 297–317.
30 Taylor, *The State in Myanmar*, pp. 198–201.
31 Bertie Reginald Pearn, *A History of Rangoon* (Rangoon: American Baptist Press, 1939), p. 291.
32 Around four to five hundred thousand Burmese Indians and Anglo-Europeans fled back to Assam and Bengal in 1942, according to Hugh Tinker, "A Forgotten Long March: The Indian Exodus from Burma, 1942," *Journal of Southeast Asian Studies* 6, no. 1 (1975), p. 2; Chakravarti, *The Indian Minority*, p. 170; Desai, *India and Burma*, p.75; Renaud Egreteau, *Wooing the Generals: India's New Burma Policy* (New Delhi: Authorspress, 2003), p. 21; and Taylor, *The State in Myanmar*, pp. 273–74. The figure is down to one-third of the 1941 Burmese Indian population in Gravers, *Nationalism*, p. 25 – the latter figure being in fact the most probable.
33 Desai, *India and Burma*, p. 49; Adas, "Immigrant Asians," pp. 400–401. The 1937 Burma Tenancy Bill and 1940 Land Purchase Act were indeed manifestly aimed at limiting the influence of the Chettiar community. After 1937 (and even more after 1942), the Chettiar presence in fact drastically shrunk. For the implications over the pace of the Indo-Burmese bilateral relations after the war, see Uma Shankar Singh, *Burma and India (1948–1962): A Study in the Foreign Policies of Burma and India and Burma's Policy towards India* (New Delhi: Oxford and IBH, 1979).
34 Shen-Yu Dai, "Peking and Rangoon," *China Quarterly* 5 (January–March 1961): 131–2.
35 Mya Than, "Ethnic Chinese in Myanmar," p. 119.
36 See the analysis by Robert Holmes, "Burmese Domestic Policy: The Politics of Burmanization," *Asian Survey* 7, no. 3 (1967): 188–97.
37 Author's discussion with Eric Gonsalves, retired Indian diplomat, former first secretary in India's Rangoon Embassy (1962–65), New Delhi, 27 November 2009.
38 Chakravarti, *Indians in Burma*, pp. 183–4. Taylor has it at one hundred and twenty-five to three hundred thousand: *The State in Myanmar*, p. 342.
39 Author's fieldwork conducted between 2010 and 2012: Renaud Egreteau, "The Idealization of a Lost Paradise: Narratives of Nostalgia and Traumatic Return Migration among Indian Repatriates from Burma since the 1960s," *Journal of Burma Studies* 18, no. 1 (June 2014): 137–80.
40 Such as the Burmese colonies of Kancharapalem, Ashok Nagar or Sriharipuram: see "Rebuilding Their Burma Dreams," *Hindu*, 7 July 2003.
41 In a clear "spillover effect": Mya Than, "Ethnic Chinese in Myanmar," p. 133.
42 See the recent analysis: Hongwei Fan, "The 1967 Anti-Chinese Riots in Burma and Sino-Burmese Relations," *Journal of Southeast Asian Studies* 43, no. 2 (June 2012): 234–56.
43 According to an observer of the time: John Badgley, "Burma's China Crisis: The Choices Ahead," *Asian Survey* 7, no. 11 (November 1967): pp. 753–61. See also the *New York Times*, which reported unusual demonstrations of five hundred Burmese youths in Moulmein: "Burmese Students Burn Mao Effigies," *New York Times*, 4 July 1967.
44 Robert Holmes, "China–Burma Relations since the Rift," *Asian Survey* 12, no. 8 (August 1972): 693.
45 A long-term Burma watcher, Donald Seekins (Meio University, Japan) witnessed waves of Burmese Chinese migrating back to Macau while he was a student there in 1967–68; author's personal discussion, Nago City (Okinawa), Japan, 24 February 2010.
46 Robert Taylor, "The Legal Status of Indians in Contemporary Burma," in *Indian Communities in Southeast Asia*, ed. K. S. Sandhu and A. Mani (Singapore: ISEAS, 2006), 666–82.
47 Thet Lwin, "Indians in Myanmar," p. 495.
48 Mya Than, "Ethnic Chinese in Myanmar," p. 120. See also: "China's Teng leaves Burma after Mystery Visit," *New York Times*, 1 February 1978, p. A4.
49 According to the author's successive interviews conducted at the Indian Embassy in Rangoon, and at the Indian Consulate-General in Mandalay, over the past decade. In 2001, the *Report of*

the High Level Committee on the Indian Diaspora (New Delhi: ICWA, December 2001), p. 260, stated there were 25 lakhs (2.5 million) Burmese of Indian origin, including 13 lakh Muslim, 8 lakh Hindus and 4 lakh Christians and Sikhs.

50 According to the author's various discussions held at the Chinese Embassy in Rangoon and at the Chinese Consulate-General in Mandalay between 2004 and 2008. The Chinese authorities nevertheless tend to favour the lesser figure.

51 "Indians" are not one of the 135 official "national races" recognized by the post-1988 Burmese regime, but are mostly registered as "Myanmar" or "foreigners."

52 Author's informal discussion (anonymity required), Pathein, Irrawaddy Delta, 10 November 2007.

53 Renaud Egreteau, "India's Vanishing 'Burma Colonies': Repatriation, Urban Citizenship, and (De)Mobilization of Indian Returnees from Burma (Myanmar) since 1960," *Moussons* 22 (2013): 11–34; and Renaud Egreteau, "The Idealization of a Lost Paradise."

54 Jacques Leider, "Specialists for Ritual, Magic, and Devotion: The Court Brahmins (*Punna*) of the Konbaung Kings (1752–1885)," *Journal of Burma Studies* 10 (2005): 162.

55 Author's informal discussions with Burmese Sikh shopkeepers in Myitkyina's central market, Burma, May 2005 and February 2013.

56 Author's interview with Indian Consul-General, Consulate of India, Mandalay, 5 March 2007.

57 Author's interview with the former head of the Moreh chamber of commerce, Madras, 19 August 2012. Himself a Burmese Tamil born in Mandalay in 1950, he settled in Moreh, started to organize Tamil business associations there, and has run transborder commercial operations between Northeast India and Western Burma, using much of his family connections in Mandalay.

58 Tin Maung Maung Than, "Some Aspects of Indians," p. 601.

59 Author's interview with Mr Lali, a curator at Rangoon's Arya Samaj, Rangoon, 27 November 2012.

60 Author's interview with a trustee from the Kali Trust, Rangoon, 26 November 2012.

61 Author's discussions with Brahmacharis (students) from various Hare Krishna's missions in Myitkyina (February 2013), Thanlyin (April 2013) and Nyaungchidauk (November 2012).

62 Author's interview with SDSS curator, Rangoon, 21 March 2007, and his successor, 28 November 2012.

63 "Now, Shakhas in Rangoon," *Times of India*, 1 August 2000.

64 Author's discussion with Naresh Kumar Dinodiya, president of the Indians of Myanmar Association, Rangoon, 25 January 2005.

65 Author's discussion with C. Murali, president of the India–Myanmar Business Club, Rangoon, 27 January 2005.

66 Tin Maung Maung Than, "Myanmar and China: A Special Relationship?" *Southeast Asian Affairs*, 2003: 189–210; Maung Aung Myoe, *In The Name of Pauk-Phaw: Myanmar's China Policy Since 1948* (Singapore: Institute of Southeast Asian Studies, 2011).

67 Bertil Lintner, "Rivers of Dreams: Chinese Emigrants Pour Down the Mekong," *Far Eastern Economic Review*, 22 December 1994, p. 26.

68 Mya Maung, "On the Road to Mandalay: A Case Study of the Sinonization of Upper Burma," *Asian Survey* 34, no. 5 (May 1994): 447–59; Donald Seekins, "Burma–China Relations: Playing with Fire," *Asian Survey* 37, no. 6 (June 1997): 525–39; Swaran Singh, "The Sinicization of Myanmar and Its Implications for India," *Issues & Studies* 33, no. 1 (January 1997): 116–33.

69 For a critical survey of these academic articles, see Renaud Egreteau, "India and China Vying for Influence in Burma: A New Assessment," *India Review* 7, no. 1 (2008): pp. 39–42.

70 H. Le Bail and Abel Tournier, *From Kunming to Mandalay: The New Burma Road; Developments along the Sino–Myanmar Border since 1988* (Paris: IFRI Asie Visions 25, 2010), p. 35.

71 Author's discussions in Mandalay with the Chinese Consul-General (29 April 2005) and the Indian Consul-General (5 March 2007).

72 Le Bail and Tournier, *From Kunming to Mandalay*, p. 36.

73 Mya Maung, "On the Road to Mandalay," p. 453.

74 Mya Than, "Ethnic Chinese in Myanmar," p. 142.
75 Le Bail and Tournier, *From Kunming to Mandalay*, p. 38.
76 Author's observations during the Chinese New Year in February 2013 and January 2014.
77 Mya Maung, "On the Road to Mandalay"; Seekins, "Burma-China Relations"; Singh, "The Sinicization of Myanmar"; Min Zin, "Burmese Attitudes toward Chinese: Portrayal of the Chinese in Contemporary Cultural and Media Works," *Journal of Current Southeast Asian Affairs* 31, no. 1 (2012): 115–31.
78 "Ludu Daw Amar, Respected Journalist, Dies at 93," *Irrawaddy-on-Line*. http://www.irrawaddy.org. 8 April 2008. Ludu Daw Amar popularly depicted – and denounced – in her articles and novels the rude and decaying behaviour Chinese youth had brought into Burma in the 1990s.
79 Min Zin, "Burmese Attitudes toward Chinese."
80 Author's discussions with Rakhine pro-democracy activists exiled in Dhaka, Chittagong and Cox's Bazaar, Bangladesh, October 2007.
81 Author's informal chats with local Burmese Buddhists in various rural towns of Central Burma and Arakan, March and October 2007.
82 International Crisis Group (ICG), *The Dark Side of Transition: Violence against Muslims in Myanmar*, Asia Report no. 251 (Brussels: 1 October 2013).
83 Pearn, *A History of Rangoon*, pp. 290–91.
84 Toungoo's central mosque was burned down in 2001 and still lies there half-destroyed; author's observation, Toungoo, November 2012.
85 Author's informal discussions in the cities of Kyaukpadaung and Magwe in Central Western Burma, March 2007 and April 2013.
86 See for instance a report published soon after the destruction by the Taliban of Bamiyan's Buddhas in Afghanistan: "Religious Unrest Grows amid Economic Turmoil," *Irrawaddy-on-Line*. http://www.irrawaddy.org. 24 May 2011.
87 The Burmese Consul-General had sent an open letter to his diplomatic colleagues based in Hong Kong and Macau. See: "Burma Envoy Raps Ugly, Dark Rohingya," *Bangkok Post*, 12 February 2009.
88 ICG, *The Dark Side of Transition*.
89 Egreteau, "India and China Vying for Influence," pp. 61–5.
90 I have argued this earlier: Renaud Egreteau, "It Takes Two to Tango: The Delicate Dance between India and Burma," *Asia-Pacific Bulletin*, no. 66 (Washington, DC: East West Center, 24 August 2010): 1–2.
91 Author's interview, Indian Embassy in Burma, Rangoon, 27 January 2012.
92 Egreteau, "India and China Vying for Influence."

References

Adas, Michael. "Immigrant Asians and the Economic Impact of European Imperialism: The Role of South Indian Chettiars in British Burma." *Journal of Asian Studies* 33, no. 3 (1974): 385–401.

Badgley, John. "Burma's China Crisis: The Choices Ahead." *Asian Survey* 7, no. 11 (November 1967): 753–61.

Berlie, Jean. *The Burmanization of Myanmar's Muslims*. Bangkok: White Lotus Press, 2008.

Bonacich, Edna. "A Theory of Middleman Minority." *American Sociological Review* 38, no. 5 (October 1973): 583–94.

Chakravarti, Nalini Ranjan. *The Indian Minority in Burma: The Rise and Decline of an Immigrant Community*. London: Oxford University Press, 1971.

Charney, Michael W. "Esculent Bird's Nest, Tin and Fish: The Overseas Chinese and Their Trade in the Eastern Bay of Bengal (Coastal Burma) during the First Half of the Nineteenth Century." In *China and Southeast Asia*, edited by Geoff Wade, pp. 207–21. London: Routledge, 2008.

Chen Yi-Sein. "The Chinese in Rangoon during the 18th and 19th Centuries." *Artibus Asiae* 23 (1966): 107–11.

Dai Shen-Yu. "Peking and Rangoon." *China Quarterly* 5 (January–March 1961): 131–44.

Dai Yingcong. "A Disguised Defeat: The Myanmar Campaign of the Qing Dynasty." *Modern Asian Studies* 38, no. 4, (2004): 145–89.

Desai, Walter S. *India and Burma: A Study*. Calcutta: Orient Longmans, 1954.

Edwards, Penny. "Relocating the Interlocutor: Taw Sein Ko (1864–1930) and the Itinerancy of Knowledge in British Burma." *South East Asia Research* 12, no. 3 (November 2004): 277–335.

Egreteau, Renaud. "Burmese Indians in Contemporary Burma: Heritage, Influence, and Perceptions since 1988." *Asian Ethnicity* 12, no. 1 (February 2011): 33–54.

______. "India and China Vying for Influence in Burma: A New Assessment." *India Review* 7, no. 1 (January–March 2008): 38–72.

______. "India's Vanishing 'Burma Colonies': Repatriation, Urban Citizenship, and (De)Mobilization of Indian Returnees from Burma (Myanmar) since 1960." *Moussons* 22 (2013): 11–34.

______. "The Idealization of a Lost Paradise: Narratives of Nostalgia and Traumatic Return Migration among Indian Repatriates from Burma since the 1960s." *Journal of Burma Studies* 18, no. 1 (June 2014): 137–180.

______. *Wooing the Generals: India's New Burma Policy*. New Delhi: Authorspress, 2003.

Fan Hongwei. "The 1967 Anti-Chinese Riots in Burma and Sino-Burmese Relations." *Journal of Southeast Asian Studies* 43, no. 2 (June 2012): 234–56.

Gravers, Mikael. *Nationalism as Political Paranoia in Burma: An Essay on the Historical Practice of Power*. Richmond: Curzon, 1999.

Holmes, Robert. "Burmese Domestic Policy: The Politics of Burmanization." *Asian Survey* 7, no. 3 (1967): 188–97.

Holmes, Robert. "China–Burma Relations since the Rift." *Asian Survey* 12, no. 8 (August 1972): 686–700.

Indian Council of World Affairs. *Report of the High Level Committee on the Indian Diaspora*. New Delhi: ICWA, December 2001.

Khin Maung Kyi. "Comments on Mya Than: 'The Ethnic Chinese in Myanmar and Their Identity." In *Ethnic Chinese as Southeast Asians*, edited by Leo Suryadinata, pp. 147–57. Singapore: Institute of Southeast Asian Studies, 1997.

______. "Indians in Burma: Problems of an Alien Subculture in a Highly Integrated Society." In *Indian Communities in Southeast Asia*, edited by K. S. Sandhu and A. Mani, pp. 624–65. Singapore: ISEAS, 2006.

Le Bail, H. and Abel Tournier. *From Kunming to Mandalay: The New Burma Road; Developments along the Sino-Myanmar Border since 1988*. Paris: IFRI Asie Visions 25, 2010.

Leider, Jacques. "Specialists for Ritual, Magic, and Devotion: The Court Brahmins (*Punna*) of the Konbaung Kings (1752–1885)." *Journal of Burma Studies* 10 (2005): 159–202.

Light, Ivan H. and Edna Bonacich, *Immigrant Entrepreneurs*. Berkeley: University of California Press, 1988.

Mahadevan, Raman. "Immigrant Entrepreneurs in Colonial Burma: An Exploratory Study of the Role of Nattukottai Chettiars of Tamil Nadu, 1880–1930." *Indian Economic and Social History Review* 15, no. 3 (1978): 329–58.

Mahajani, Usha. *The Role of Indian Minorities in Burma and Malaya*. Bombay: Vora & Co, 1960.

Maung Aung Myoe. *In The Name of Pauk-Phaw: Myanmar's China Policy Since 1948*. Singapore: Institute of Southeast Asian Studies, 2011.

Min Zin. "Burmese Attitudes toward Chinese: Portrayal of the Chinese in Contemporary Cultural and Media Works." *Journal of Current Southeast Asian Affairs* 31, no. 1 (2012): 115–31.

Mya Maung. "On the Road to Mandalay: A Case Study of the Sinonization of Upper Burma." *Asian Survey* 34, no. 5 (May 1994): 447–59.

Mya Than. "Jairampur: A Profile of an Indian Community in Rural Burma." In *Indian Communities in Southeast Asia*, edited by K. S. Sandhu and A. Mani, pp. 683–706. Singapore: ISEAS, 2006.

______. "The Ethnic Chinese in Myanmar and Their Identity." In *Ethnic Chinese as Southeast Asians*, edited by Leo Suryadinata, pp. 115–46. Singapore: ISEAS, 1997.

Pearn, Bertie Reginald. *A History of Rangoon*. Rangoon: American Baptist Press, 1939.

Satyanarayana, Adapa. "'Birds of Passage': Migration of South Indian Laborers to Southeast Asia." *Critical Asian Studies* 34, no. 1 (2002): 89–115.

Seekins, Donald. "Burma–China Relations: Playing with Fire." *Asian Survey* 37, no. 6 (June 1997): 525–39.

Singh, Swaran. "The Sinicization of Myanmar and Its Implications for India." *Issues & Studies* 33, no. 1 (January 1997): 116–33.

Singh, Uma Shankar. *Burma and India (1948–1962): A Study in the Foreign Policies of Burma and India and Burma's Policy towards India*. New Delhi: Oxford & IBH, 1979.

Spate, O. H. K. and L. W. Trueblood. "Rangoon: A Study in Urban Geography." *Geographical Review* 32, no. 1 (January 1942): 56–73.

Tasaw Lu Hsin-chun. "Performativity of Difference: Mapping Public Soundscapes and Performing Nostalgia among Burmese Chinese in Central Rangoon." *Asian Music* 42, no. 2 (2011): 19–55.

Taylor, Robert. "The Legal Status of Indians in Contemporary Burma." In *Indian Communities in Southeast Asia*, edited by K. S. Sandhu and A. Mani, pp. 666–82. Singapore: ISEAS, 2006.

______. *The State in Myanmar*. Singapore: NUS Press, 2009.

Thant Myint-U. *The Making of Modern Burma*. Cambridge: Cambridge University Press, 2001.

Thet Lwin. "Indians in Myanmar." In *Rising India and Indian Communities in East Asia*, edited by K. Kesavapany, A. Mani and P. Ramasamy, pp. 485–97. Singapore: ISEAS, 2008.

Tinker, Hugh. "A Forgotten Long March: The Indian Exodus from Burma, 1942." *Journal of Southeast Asian Studies* 6, no. 1 (1975): 1–15.

Tin Maung Maung Than. "Myanmar and China: A Special Relationship?" *Southeast Asian Affairs* (2003): 189–210.

______. "Some Aspects of Indians in Rangoon." In *Indian Communities in Southeast Asia*, edited by K. S. Sandhu and A. Mani, pp. 585–623. Singapore: ISEAS, 2006.

Turnell, Sean. *Fiery Dragons: Banks, Moneylenders and Microfinance in Burma*. Copenhagen: NIAS Press, 2009.

Yegar, Moshe. *The Muslims in Burma: A Study of a Minority Group*. Wiesbaden: Otto Harrassowitz, 1972.

Chapter 9

EXPRESSIONS OF FAITH IN HINDU PROCESSIONAL FESTIVALS: CASE STUDIES FROM SINGAPORE AND MALAYSIA

Gauri Parimoo Krishnan

Introduction

Religion and its practice is an expression of diasporic behaviour, and its multicultural relevance at both the social and political levels is truly the best tool to study any community or country with a huge migrant population. In the case of Singapore and Malaysia through the colonial days, their multicultural population historically has demonstrated religious tolerance, which has enabled the Hindu community to practice its religious festivals even to this day. This paper will focus on the survival, evolution and modifications these festivals, and in particular their public expression through festival processions, have undergone compared to how they were practiced in their place of origin in India. Processions are subject to innovations and their purpose can also change.[1] This paper examines the cultural and social aspects of the practice and examines the expression of devotion to Murukan among Indian and Chinese devotees as observed during processions and ritual practices for the celebration of the *kavadi* festival Thaipusam in Singapore, Malacca and Penang, as well as to Mariamman during Theemithi in Singapore.[2] Thaipusam, celebrated in the month of Thai in the Hindu calendar (occurring January–February in the Gregorian calendar), is a thanksgiving festival dedicated to the Hindu god Murukan involving asceticism and control over ones senses, while Theemithi is a ritual street theatre performance culminating in walking on burning coal.

This study analyses the way piety is expressed among worshippers observing these festivals and what inspires this piety. Many of the practices around Murukan worship are connected to the Indian diaspora that brought ritual worship to British Malaya in the nineteenth century. Many were plantation workers who brought their folk practices from the villages of Tamil Nadu and practised them in Singapore and parts of Malaysia. When and how the expression of faith went beyond the *kampong* and the Indian fold and started attracting other races,[3] especially the Chinese, requires more in-depth research. Further research is needed to understand how interracial communication happens and how members of different races come together to perform Thaipusam and Theemithi away from their country of origin. This not only helps in understanding the behavioural patterns of migrant communities but also reveals what brings these communities together. More than religion, it is language, faith, profession as well as place of residence that influences how a community behaves and how it pursues and expresses its religious faith individually and collectively. "Trading diaspora," "labour diaspora" and "professional diaspora" are all collective groupings which negotiate identities and identifications in a global world of migrations and further refine the definition of diaspora and its participation in religious activities. Setting up a temple, carrying out its renovations, temple volunteerism as well as management of temple affairs are clearly demarcated by different groups of people and reflect their economic, cultural, social as well as ethnic identity.

This paper attempts to uncover the aspirations of a heterogeneous diaspora community by exploring in depth what inspires these devotees to make the arduous journey to honour Murukan, Durga, Mariamman, Itamban, Taoist deities or to be blessed with material wealth, health and happiness. Be it some or all of the above, the process of enlargement of the scope of religious behaviour among the diaspora communities, elements of inclusiveness, parallelism and coexistence seem to be the guiding principles that explain some of the most unique expressions of faith, such as a Chinese devotee carrying *kavadi* with a Taoist deity's picture within or funding the entire cost of firewood for the Theemithi festival. However, one also has to note that Mariamman or Murukan are, after all, not as remote as we think, because they are believed to answer prayers like all other Taoist and Buddhist deities. Many parallels can be drawn to explain the similar cultural behaviour of both communities.

Based on purely situational psychology of an immigrant diaspora community, the struggle for survival often leads to religion; economic progress and success in enterprise are some of the commonly observed reasons that serve to develop community identity through temples as a congregational and a virtual unifying space. This also seems to fuel religious fervour, including a call for spiritual favours and realization beyond the material in more developed and settled immigrant societies. This psychology will also be further explored in this paper.

Murukan *Bhakti* and Its Expression in Singapore and Malaysia

In Hinduism, there are several paths to pursue one's faith. Bhakti yoga serves to worship God (Saguna *bhakti*) in human form through idol worship; Jnana yoga serves to search for the meaning of life and creation through the study of philosophical texts; Raja yoga serves in the practice of meditation upon the concept of the Brahman (Nirguna *bhakti*), while Karma yoga serves in the performance of rituals, pilgrimages and charity work. Murukan *bhakti* involves yet another aspect of devotion that involves asceticism as well as self-mortification. This requires strength of mind, body and faith attainable through *bhakti*.

Murukan or Skanda-Kumara, which in Tamil refers to youthfulness, is the son of Shiva and Parvati. Known variously as Kartikeya, Subrahmanya, and Dandayudhapani, as indicated by various myths associated with him, he stands for the sun, moon and rain; annual flooding of the rivers is associated with the arrival of Murukan. Created to be the commander of the army of the gods, he is also worshipped for his supreme knowledge of the Brahman. Murukan still symbolizes the time cycle within the larger Shaiva cult and makes the whole cosmic process of creation and dissolution, day and night, life and death, triumph of good over evil perennially meaningful. His worship involves all the four yogas of Hinduism and many ardent devotees follow these yogas at different stages of their lives.

Murukan devotees either carry *kavadis* or *palkudams* (milk pots) during the Murukan festivals.[4] A vow to carry a *kavadi* or *palkudam* may be prompted by a devotee's decision to overcome an unfavourable situation or for thanksgiving after achieving the desired result. Illness, academic success, wealth and family harmony are the popular areas which concern the vow-taking *kavadi* bearers, who fulfil their vows regardless of caste, creed, colour, religion, racial or socio-economic backgrounds. Thaipusam is a thanksgiving festival which involves asceticism and control over ones senses. Fulfilment of vows taken by devotees is generally celebrated on this day. Devotees refer to Murukan as their personal god, one who challenges them and offers them material gain. They consider carrying a *kavadi* in his honour a volunteer service; most of them have had a wish granted that makes them go through this "ordeal" again and again. For some, it is a lifetime's devotion towards gaining the physical strength to do it. Contrary to the general belief by people of non-Hindu faith, devotees do not see it as self-mortification, but a test of their faith for which they invoke Itumban's strength. Itumban is a demon of enormous faith who became the devotee of Murukan, and he is worshipped to this day alongside Murukan to invoke strength and faith among devotees. The uniqueness of Murukan *kavadis* is that devotees carry any Hindu deity as their *ishtadevata* (chosen personal god) and draw strength from the deity. It even allows Chinese and Taoist devotees to carry their own gods in the *kavadis*. *Kavadis* are carried not only in honour of Murukan but also for other Hindu deities such as Mariamman, Durga, Vinayaka, Shiva, Krishna, Rama and Hanuman. Other village and guardian deities are also invoked such as Muniandi, Munisvaran, Madurai Veeran, Sinnakarupan, Karuppanaswami and others. This reflects a democratization of divine power and freedom of expression and identity through public expression of one's faith. In this unique aspect of Hinduism that allows for collective and individualistic expression, each expression of faith is valid in its own right.

The exhibition of one's faith is not the driving force for the devotees; it is the resolve to carry the *kavadis*, year after year, with unwavering faith. Many of them carry *kavadis* well into their seventies. Some devotees I interviewed had undergone heart bypasses and other major surgeries. It is a miracle that they can walk considerable distances with this heavy superstructure over their shoulders, bodies pierced with small arrows, and in some cases, pulling a chariot hooked to their backs. The veterans of this festival – those who carry *janamakavadis* – are well known and frequently recognized in the Thaipusam festivals. They are acknowledged for their faith and commitment to their *ishtadevata*. Many old *kampong* people congregate for Thaipusam around their *kampong kavadi*. Before *kampongs* gave way to housing board flats, people of the *kampong* accompanied the devotee as a mark of solidarity as well as encouragement. Sometimes they would even fund and share the cost of the *kavadi* as well as the blessings. I had the opportunity to document one such *kavadi* from Kampong Bahru in Singapore, starting with the pre-*kavadi puja* to Thaipusam until the post-*kavadi puja*. Kampong Bahru was a small village of Indian immigrants comprised largely of port workers located near the port, which was later demolished to give way to PSA dockyards. Today, they live in different housing board estates all over Singapore, but gather together for "old times' sake" during Thaipusam. It is quite usual to see many friends and relatives joining the devotee carrying the *kavadi*, recalling their cherished memories and congregating again to relive their *kampong* spirit. With the development of Singapore's housing board flats, the old *kampongs* have disappeared, but festivals such as Thaipusam help continue the old ties, which people renew through collective prayers and festivals. Many still pay their respects to Mr Gopalaswami, the most senior member of the Kampong Bahru group.

Thaipusam is not limited to Indian participation; even Chinese Buddhist or Taoist devotees participate in this festival by carrying *kavadis* and *palkudams*. Some express great devotion to Murukan as well, draw parallels with Hinduism, and see it as service to god and humanity beyond fulfilment of their wishes. Many devotees interviewed expressed belief in the Hindu faith and the duty to extend help to others through divine work. Many are active volunteers and have chosen their path of service to humanity through this festival. Many Chinese devotees simply walk alongside their Hindu friends year after year, in the belief that they will derive good luck, prosperity and health by associating themselves in this manner with this festival. In Singapore, Penang, Ipoh and Malacca, scores of Chinese families visit the Murukan temple of the Chettiars on the day before Thaipusam to offer their prayers. They make an offering when the chariot comes through their street or *kampong* and carry the *kavadi* as well. Carl Vadivella Belle provides extensive documentation, interviews with devotees and analysis of the various centres such as the Batu Caves, Kuala Lumpur and Penang in Malaysia.[5] His work brings to light many issues regarding multicultural trends within the diaspora communities from colonial times to the present day, caste-based issues within the Hindu community and its implications in the celebration of Thaipusam, as well as interactions between the Chinese and Indian communities in Malaysia. On several occasions we have also discussed the role of the local political, economic and administrative issues that mould the festival.

Devotion to Mariamman and Its Expression in Singapore and Malaysia

Mariamman worship started as early as the nineteenth century and was brought into British Malaya by Hindu Tamil plantation workers and others from the Coromandel Coast of Tamil Nadu. From small shrines and personal worship to ward off diseases and evil spirits, congregations of larger groups began to celebrate these festivals – one of the key celebrations in Singapore being Theemithi, which is celebrated in honour of Draupadiamman. The worship of Draupadi (wife of the Pandavas in the Epic *Mahabharata*, later deified) came through boat repair workers from the village of

Vadakku Poigayoor near Nagapattinam, where this cult once flourished. Ever since, this festival has gained ground in Singapore, and people from all walks of life, races and economic backgrounds have joined in, making it a multicultural practice unique to Singapore.

Theemithi, the ritual street theatre festival, is spread over many months. Special days are allocated to the worship of mainstream Hindu gods and village gods, suggesting a unique mutation of ritual practice in a foreign land where caste and class barriers within Hinduism have been reconciled. The ritual itself has been slightly modified to suit the living conditions and cultic practices of its founders and current organizers. The presence, worship and acceptance of village gods and mainstream Hindu gods, with the former being given the centre stage, are uncommon in India as well as overseas. Such a scenario is unique to the Sri Mariamman temple[6] on South Bridge Road, the Vairavimada Kaliamman temple in Toa Payoh and Muneeshwaran temple near Queens Way, among many others in Singapore and Malaysia. The uniqueness of this combination of the iconic pantheon, which grew over several decades, suggests its devotees visit the temples from the catchment area of the nearby *kampong* (now housing board flats). This explains how Draupadiamman's worship was assimilated into the precincts of the Mariamman temple, whereas in Tamil Nadu, where her cult originates, she enjoys a special temple in her honour, as does Mariamman. However, in Singapore they are combined. This phenomenon is diametrically variant to the more Agamic Brahmanical temples such as the Shivan temple at Geylang and the Srinivas Perumal temple at Serangoon Road, which have a strictly Agamic pantheon and worship of Hindu gods related to Shiva-Vishnu families, respectively. What makes this study more interesting is its uniqueness within Singapore and its role as a new "signifier" of Hindu religious practice "signified" in an overseas context. One could cite here many synchronic phenomena from the practices of the Indian diaspora settled in Malaysia, Fiji, Mauritius and Reunion Island, to name a few. The ritual itself calls for reconsideration in conventional thinking, even on the part of a Hindu visitor to the festival. Stemming from Brahmanical as well as localized cultic stand points, the ritual is actually an enactment of the *Mahabharata* war, uniquely woven into a ritual of storytelling, re-enactment of the epic drama, ritual worship, invocation of the powerful gods including Krishna and Draupadi, vow fulfilment and personal asceticism.

The underlying aspiration in celebrating this festival is renewal, cleansing, and to remember the great sacrifice of warriors like Aravan and Abhimanyu and the strength of the vow taken by Draupadi in the epic *Mahabharata*. Reviving some of these archetypal heroes and renewing the values that they stood for, the devotees walk on fire and pray for themselves and their families.

Devotee participation in this festival is remarkable. Volunteer groups are divided up and assigned to different days, rituals and aspects of the festival, making them an important part of the festival. Many devotees walk on fire, while some also perform *kumbhidudandam*, in which they either perform *adipradakshina* prostration after every step or take several steps (3, 5 or 7) before prostrating. Many Chinese devotees are seen participating in these prayers as well as carrying *palkudams* and *mavilukkus* (flour lamps).

What is it that draws them to perform this hardship? Is it hardship at all? Is this fossilized Hindu religion? Has tourism contributed glamour to this village practice? Do all of them who walk on fire actually understand the roots of this tradition and what it stands for? Is it just showmanship and peer pressure or are the devotees genuine in their ritual performances and dedication? What is its practical relevance to Hindu society and religious practice today? Arguably, increasing belief in the goddess and the number of devotees walking on fire relates to the turbulent global economy of recent years. Besides, it is an excellent example of multiculturalism at play, where devotees from Indian and Chinese communities come together on a festive occasion and participate with equal fervour. What started as a village tradition has taken on a completely new garb, preserving the sanctity of the original purpose within the group of volunteers and veterans who have been involved in this prayer ceremony for years. Interviews with some of them who play the part of Draupadi and Krishna, chief volunteers tying the *karagam* (an auspicious pot decorated with *neem* leaves and flowers which is carried by the chief priest of the temple) and those walking on fire have provided insight into the devotion and commitment involved in the role play and enactment of the epic myth.[7]

Festive Procession and Visible Expression of Faith

The practices of Thaipusam and Theemithi in Singapore and Malaysia, although not conducted the same way, involve similar scenes and expressions of faith. However, the scale and public expression of these practices in urban public spaces are a far cry from that in India, where they are performed in rural and remote pilgrimage centres, leaving the urban public completely unaware of their existence. In both Singapore and Malaysia, the participants walk through the main streets in their complete traditional (in many cases larger-than-life) *kavadi* attire in full public view. The temporary takeover of public space, the public expression of faith in a manner that suits the personal worship of their *ishtadevata*, and being seen and supported by one's relatives and the general public is an exhibition of the power of personal faith and its predominance in the adopted homeland. The practice of lifting the deity or an offering aloft to the temple (in the case of Thaipusam, it is a milk pot) momentarily makes the public space sacred and enables the divine to be seen by everyone. At the same time, it allows the devotee full freedom to express his own devotion publicly, with many of them dancing vigorously and falling into a trance. It appears both conventional and unconventional at the same time. In considering the visibility of the Diaspora, new elements in decoration are added every year; the procession enlarges, and changes occur constantly. In Singapore, the *arigandi kavadi* (a spiked *kavadi* that pierces into the flesh of the torso) is one such example which was evolved by one Vaiti of Kampong Bahru, who was the first to try and design it. This was subsequently imitated and modified by many others.[8]

The Thaipusam procession also involves playing traditional music while the festival is conducted. Thus observers can spot a traditional *kavadi* from afar by the accompanying music and singing. *Kavadi cindu* is an important and integral part of the Thaipusam festival where devotees are accompanied by drummers and singers, particularly a choir that sings devotional songs dedicated to Murukan and other deities. This is to keep the devotee's mind fixed on his goal as well as to create a sacred atmosphere. This peaceful but spiritual journey is sometimes marred by youths in carnival mood, disturbing the original intent and purpose of the procession. It is the arduous pre-*kavadi* rituals and strict faithful self-abstinence that prepare the devotees for the arduous journey to safely reach their destination: the Thandayudhapani temple on Tank Road in Singapore. The frivolous may or may not reach their destination, as their aim is exhibitionism and not to seek Murukan's blessings.

In Singapore, traffic regulations and security are of utmost concern to the organizers and urban authorities. However, in Malaysia, this is much more relaxed and one can see a lone *kavadi* or a group surrounding a *kavadi* devotee from any corner of the city heading towards the Murukan temple designated for worship. This was observed during documentation visits to Penang and Malacca in the late 1990s. The Singapore authorities issue road closure notices in the newspapers and alert road users of the constraints as the pre-*kavadi* preparations begin several days prior to the actual Thaipusam day. In the past, when the chariot was pulled by a bullock cart, participants in the procession celebrated with much fanfare. Now it is done using a motorized vehicle in Singapore, but in Penang and Malacca the chariot procession continues to be pulled by a bullock cart.

In Singapore, the inconvenience to other road users is kept to a minimum, and in the case of Theemithi, fire walking has been switched to past midnight in order not to affect other road users during the day. Interestingly, the recent intrusion of F1 racing – and the related hassles it has caused to businesses,[9] road users and office workers in the downtown area over a period of almost a week – is not seen as an inconvenience by the transport authorities. The negotiation with authorities over the use of public space by different parties is an important facet of multiculturalism in Singapore which may be considered as an area of further research. Suffice it to say at this point that minority communities have learnt to negotiate the circumstances in order to continue their traditional faith and its public expression, as long as the necessary permits are granted for its continuity. The fact that the Theemithi festival continues with the same fervour and fire walkers are undeterred by walking at night is a testament to its popular following and increasing multicultural participation. Many Chinese devotees are also reported to participate in this festival.

Many older devotees recall with fondness how the temple chariot procession for Murukan used to go around the city with acrobats, dancers and musicians performing in front of the chariot. It appears from popular narratives that on Market Street, where many Chettiar *kittangis* were located (the area has since been completely redeveloped), devotees from the first floor of their shophouses used to hang floral garlands on ropes across the street, and the priest would pull the garlands down from the rope and place them on the deity inside the chariot.[10] This spectacular action used to draw large crowds who would congregate to see the procession. All these anecdotal reminiscences indicate that the procession at present is not as attractive as it once was, save for the lights and the decoration.

As an expression of their faith, many devotees still follow the chariot and walk the whole distance on foot. According to Vineeta Sinha:

> "Singaporean Hinduism" is subject to a variety of regulative, administrative and disciplinary mechanisms particularly in its public and official manifestation. The bureaucratic logic often at work is conditioned by the call for a specific kind of Hinduism appropriate for Singapore and Singaporean Hindus, given the nature of

> Singapore society as multi-ethnic and multi-religious, and her citizens as modern, urban, rational and literate. These articulated self perceptions culminate in the insistence that Hinduism in Singapore must be constituted and presented in a certain mode, one that distances its current construction from any superstitious, overly ritualistic or emotional dimension. While these features may have been normal and legitimate for previous generations in India or Singapore of the old days, they have no place in modern Hinduism and modern society. I argue that in this regulation and disciplining process exercised through Hindu administrative bodies, management committee of temples, and elites of the Hindu community, there is an embedded ideological position about what is "real" Hinduism. If put into practice, such a stance may potentially eradicate a variety of ritual practices that are deemed legitimate by other sections of the Hindu community in Singapore.[11]

Here, the idea of pluralism and syncretism is underscored; it is a defining factor of how Hinduism in Singapore has evolved in the last two hundred years. For village gods to survive and find new meaning in the urban and multicultural society of Singapore indeed needs further research on religious identity in a multifaith, multi-ethnic society where holding onto one's beliefs is seen as a matter of natural selection and a reflection of economic and social background.

Interfaith and Multicultural Practices Between Indian and Chinese Diaspora Communities

Popular religion, trance performances and belief in spirit mediums are common practices among Indians (mainly Hindus) and the Chinese diaspora in Singapore and Malaysia. As observed and summarized by Jean DeBernardi, these are oral, improvisational and evanescent. Colonial administration and missionaries found these practices weird, uncanny and ghastly looking. Indians, Chinese and Malays all practiced forms of spiritual possession during late nineteenth century in the face of British rationalism and scepticism.

> Some of these practices have no analogue in contemporary China or are only found in Taiwan and China's southern coastal provinces. They do resemble, however, Hindu devotional practices, including both fire-walking and the body piercing that is so conspicuous a part of the Thaipusam festival as performed by Indian communities in Malaysia and Singapore.[12]

The Mariamman and Murukan worship in Singapore is a testament to religious tolerance and understanding, the coexistence of people of different faiths in a foreign land called "home" for mutual benefit. Populated mainly by migrants from the Indian subcontinent and South China who have settled in the markets around what is now called Chinatown, today it stands not only for its iconic architectural marvels, but also as symbolic of the earliest area of congregation and worship among Indians (Hindus and Muslims) and Chinese. Mutual understanding has led the various communities to thrive here, including the Jamae Mosque started by the Chulia, the Tamil Muslims, a few metres away.

The participation of Chinese devotees in fire walking rituals during Theemithi as well as in other festivals at this temple is remarkable. Between fifty and a hundred Chinese devotees walk on fire and a handful of them also volunteer in the fire pit area.[13] There are many Chinese families with businesses in the vicinity who donate firewood and lemons, and support *ubayam* festivals and preside over functions, as their faith draws them to the temple. Those devotees residing in the Chinatown area or who have their businesses there also visit the temple regularly and have contributed to its rebuilding. They may not be familiar with scriptures and the practice of Hinduism themselves, but what motivates them to continue coming to Hindu temples is their utmost devotion and spirituality. They worship Guan Yin and Durga with equal sincerity, and this comes with an open-mindedness and simplicity of conviction.

Many Sikh as well as Chinese devotees take a veteran from the Tamil community as their guru and learn the procedures around Thaipusam for several years.[14] Recently, we interviewed Mr Vairavan and his son Agilan, residing in Yishun, who had trained and provided leadership to a Chinese group that wanted to learn the right "procedure" for *kavadi*. Several Sikh devotees interviewed during my research period in late 1990s had chosen a Tamil veteran as their guru and decided to carry *kavadi* for some years. Many veterans of the Tamil community also offer their services free of charge to devotees during Thaipusam by piercing their foreheads with the tiny *vel* (Murukan's personal weapon, shaped like a spear) in honour of Murukan or the elaborate *arigandi kavadi*. Such expression of mutual support and service can only exist in diasporic communities where everyone has a similar sense of belonging and expectations from each other.

In Penang and Malacca, thousands of devotees throng the temple precinct of the Murukan temple before Thaipusam carrying offerings of fruits, flowers and lighted lamps. They congregate in the temple with a ceremonial air of familiarity and commitment, as Murukan is also perceived with great respect and devotion by the Chinese. In a migrant country, seeing two completely different communities originating from different civilizational backgrounds uniting around the worship of village gods like Mariamman, Draupadiamman, Murukan, Itumban, Munisvaran and the Taoist gods only suggests the parallels that can be seen between these deities, who grant wishes and are approachable through worship and propitiation.

More research needs to be done on the trends of commonality between Taoist and Indian village deities of a militaristic and fierce nature.[15] However, due to China and India's ancient connections, it may be assumed with some certainty that new research into anthropological and iconographical cultures and their pantheon will reveal many interconnections. Generally invoked for protection and survival, these practices reveal the psychology of diaspora communities. To begin with further researches in this direction, I would propose studying commonalities between Mazu, the goddess of the sea, Guan Yin and Mariamman, the three protective goddesses who command a huge following in Singapore and Malaysia from their early nineteenth-century beginnings. Situating these studies in the holistic background of the immigrant societies would bring to light unknown aspirations and experiences which have given rise to new iconographies and understandings unique to the region.

Fig 1: A family group preparing for Palkudam procession. Singapore © Asian Civilisations Museum, Singapore

Fig 2: A Chinese devotee carrying kavadi, Singapore © Asian Civilisations Museum, Singapore

Fig 3: Members of the Chettiar community dancing with kavadis outside the Chettiar temple, Penang. © Asian Civilisations Museum, Singapore

Fig 4: Kavadi puja of the Kampong Bahru group, Singapore © Asian Civilisations Museum, Singapore

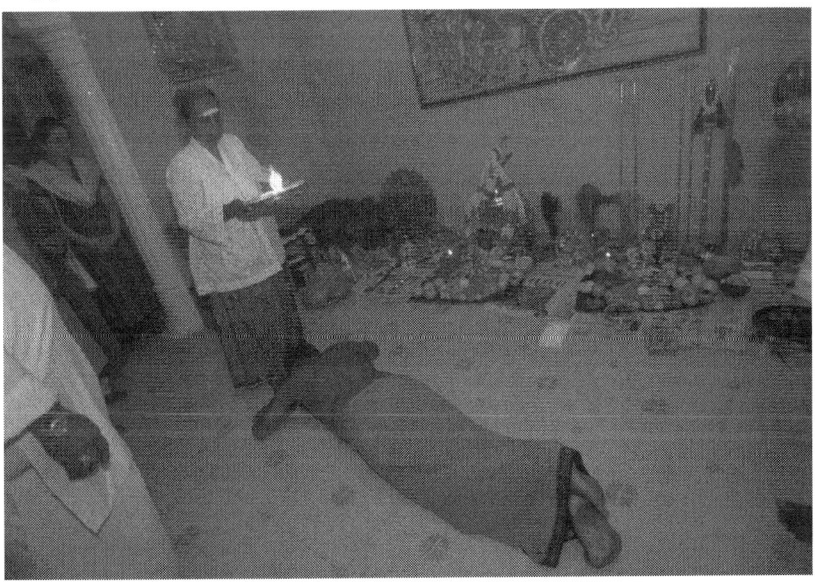

Fig 5: Chinese devotees throng the Chettiar temple on the eve of Thaipusam festival, Penang © Asian Civilisations Museum, Singapore

Fig 6: Multi-racial volunteers of the Aravan Sannidhi of the Mariamman temple during Theemithi, Singapore © Asian Civilisations Museum, Singapore

Fig 7: Senior priest of the Mariamman temple walks on the fire carrying the *karagam*, Singapore © Asian Civilisations Museum, Singapore

Fig 8: Multi-racial volunteers of the fire pit area getting ready for Theemithi, Singapore © Asian Civilisations Museum, Singapore

Notes

1 Knut A. Jacobsen, ed., *South Asian Religions on Display: Religious Processions in South Asia and in the Diaspora* (London and New York: Routledge, 2008), p. 6.

2 These two festivals were documented in Singapore and Malaysia as part of a broader project on the documentation of Indian rituals and festivals as an ongoing concern for studying living traditions from 1995–2002.

3 See for instance, Carl Vadivella Belle, "Thaipusam in Malaysia: A Hindu Festival Misunderstood?" (unpublished manuscript copy from Asian Civilisations Museum library, gifted by the author in 2008).

4 For fuller details on when *kavadis* are carried, the history of the Thaipusam festival as well as its practice in detail, see my online article, "Following Murukan: Tai Pucam in Singapore," http://murugan.org/research/gauri_krishnan.htm. 13 September 2014.

5 Belle, "Thaipusam in Malaysia".

6 For further details on the cult of Draupadiamman and the fire-walking festival of Theemithi, see my unpublished article, "Theemithi: Re-enacting the Great Ritual-Drama honouring Draupadiamman at Singapore," 2004. The Hindu Endowments Board manages this temple as well as the Theemithi festival every year. Construction of the Mariamman temple began in 1827 in the Chinatown area, where the first Chinese temple Thian Hock Kheng dedicated to the Goddess of the Sea was built in 1821 and the Jamae Mosque of 1826 was built by the Chulia Muslims from the Coromandel Coast in South India, where members of all early immigrant communities interacted.

7 Many of these veterans were interviewed by the Asian Civilisations Museum, Singapore, These interviews can be accessed on the interactive computers in the galleries.

8 Conveyed to me during my documentation by PSA group veterans Mr Jaybalan, Mr Rajaram and many other veterans of *Arigandi kavadi* in Singapore.

9 On twitter and other social media websites, a number of citizens have expressed their views, with many of them not favouring the race as it affects traffic, businesses and the general public.

10 Conveyed to me by many devotees during oral interviews between 1995 and 2002, especially by Subbiah Lakshman himself, a Chettiar who grew up in Market Street; this practice continued till the 1950s.

11 Vineeta Sinha, *A New God in the Diaspora? Muneeswaran Worship in Contemporary Singapore* (Singapore: NIAS Press, 2005), pp. 268–9.

12 Jean DeBernardi, *The Way That Lives in the Heart: Chinese Popular Religion and Spirit Mediums in Penang, Malaysia* (Singapore, NUS Press, 2006), p. 25.

13 Conveyed to me during an interview with Mr Yip, a Chinese devotee in his forties in 2009 who has been very active in the fire-walking festival, volunteering in the fire pit area, a very crucial and difficult task for which lots of experience, will power, physical strength and patience are required.

14 I accompanied Karpal Singh and his guru Jayabalan to Penang in late 1990s and interviewed both of them, and followed the entire ritual prayer and the procession to the hilltop Murugan temple.

15 Based on my literature survey, I notice, most scholars of Chinese popular religion among the overseas Chinese focus on Chinese practices exclusively, making only passing references to Hindu and Malay practices in Malaya although recognizing common threads which are yet to be unearthed.

Glossary of Indigenous Terms:

Adipradakshina: a way to circumambulate the temple or deity by taking short steps the length of one's foot. People take a vow for the fulfilment of a wish and are seen doing *Adipradakshina* during Theemithi when their wishes are granted.

Agama/Agamic: a body of scriptures which consists of philosophy, rules and disciplines related to worship, image making and temple building. They vary from sect to sect in Hinduism.

Arigandi kavadi: besides traditional kavadi, some people also carry belt kavadi or spike kavadi. Spike *kavadi* pierce into the flesh of the torso and the entire superstructure is supported by four upright poles fixed into the flesh around the waist. An experienced person is required to pierce the wearer in this manner.

Ishtadevata: personal god or deity one has chosen to worship, not necessarily what one has inherited from one's lineage.

Janamakavadis: *janamakavadis* are *kavadis* taken for life or as long as physical strength allows. Such devotees are well recognized and loved by the larger community of the temple-going crowd, who will cheer such a devotee on when they spot him in the crowd.

Kampong: "village" in Malay. Early migrants settled in *kampongs* and based on their linguistic and cultural backgrounds began celebrating festivals together. From these festivals the *kampong* spirit developed and continues to bind many of them in modern Singapore even though the *kampongs* are long gone.

Karagam: an auspicious pot decorated with *neem* leaves and flowers symbolizing fertility and the fulfilment of wishes; it is carried by the chief priest of the Mariamman temple in Singapore.

Kavadi: *kavadi* or *kavad* (in Hindi and many North Indian languages) is a horizontal pole by which a heavy weight is lifted with baskets hanging from two ends. It is used by labourers, vendors and coolies to lift heavy loads by resting the horizontal pole on the shoulder and tying the weight equidistant on each side. Traditional *kavadi* bearers carry milk pots to Murugan temples usually situated on hilltops.

Kavadi cindu: traditional Tamil songs set to music, sung during the Kavadi festival throughout Tamil Nadu and countries where Tamil diasporas are living today. Today not many people can sing the authentic songs, so recorded *kavadi cindu* songs are also played.

Kittangis: Chettiar business house; alternates as an office and residence for Chettiar moneylenders who live away from their families in male dormitories which are attached to their moneylending offices. Market Street in Singapore had many such *kittangis*, which are now demolished. In Malacca, one can still see these buildings.

Kumbhidudandam: a type of prostration in which a devotee walks and prostrates after a few steps around the temple, circumambulating it as part of a personal vow fulfilment.

Mavilukkus: oil lamps made from flour; some devotees light these on Tuesdays and Fridays in the Mariamman temple in Singapore and Malaysia as part of a vow fulfilment ritual.

Nirguna bhakti: worshipping the deity in abstract form according to Hinduism.

Palkudam: milk pot carried by devotees in Tamil Nadu as part of a special ritual ceremony.

Saguna bhakti: worshipping the deity in human form according to Hinduism.

Ubayam: special festivals celebrated in Tamil Hindu temples on designated days of the year based on the Tamil almanac. Many devotees collectively sponsor these festivals and participate in them to derive divine blessings.

References

Belle, Carl Vadivella. "Thaipusam in Malaysia: A Hindu Festival Misunderstood?" (unpublished manuscript copy from Asian Civilisations Museum library, gifted by the author in 2008).

DeBernardi, Jean. *The Way That Lives in the Heart: Chinese Popular Religion and Spirit Mediums in Penang, Malaysia* (Singapore, NUS Press, 2006).

De Groot, Jan Jacob Maria. *The Religious System of China*. Leiden: E. J. Brill. Reprint: Taipei: Literature House, 1964, 6 vols.

Jacobsen, Knut A. *South Asian Religions on Display: Religious Processions in South Asia and in the Diaspora*. London and New York: Routledge, 2008.

Kapferer, Bruce. *A Celebration of Demons: Exorcism and the Aesthetics of Healing in Sri Lanka*. Bloomington: Indiana University Press, 1983.

Kesavapany, K., A. Mani and P. Ramasamy, eds. *Rising India and Indian Communities in Southeast Asia*. Singapore: Institute of Southeast Asian Studies, 2008.

Rai, Rajesh and Peter Reeves, eds. *The South Asian Diaspora: Transnational Networks and Changing Identities*. Oxon: Routledge Contemporary South Asia Series, 2009.

Sacred Sanctuary: The Sri Mariamman Temple. Singapore: Kumbabishekam souvenir, 2009.

Sinha, Vineeta. *A New God in the Diaspora? Muneeswaran Worship in Contemporary Singapore*. Singapore: NUS Press, 2005.

Chapter 10

BEYOND BOUNDARIES? HINDU SPACES IN THE CHINATOWNS OF KOLKATA AND SINGAPORE

Jayani Bonnerjee

This paper brings together two comparative contexts, situated in South and Southeast Asia, for the study of interactions between Indian and Chinese communities, particularly through the presence of Hindu spaces in the Chinatowns of Kolkata (formerly known as Calcutta) and Singapore. It locates the space of interaction in two Hindu temples in the Chinatowns – a Kali temple in Kolkata and the Mariamman Temple in Singapore – and analyses the history and practices of interaction between the communities in these spaces within two areas of wider theoretical concern. Firstly, the paper interrogates the idea of Chinatowns as closed and bounded spaces. Intra-ethnic interactions in Chinatowns are generally perceived in terms of the neighbourhood being "consumed" and becoming the space of the other, and focus on how these spaces have a visual imagery of the exotic and forbidden. Moving beyond the racialized processes that are often behind the creation of Chinatowns in Western cities, and also the notion of the neighbourhood as a singular space, this paper presents a comparison of two Chinatowns in Kolkata and Singapore. While interactions across religious traditions also occur in spaces and sites beyond Chinatown, this paper highlights the interactions within this space to destabilize a unified and singular image of Chinatown, and also to argue that the idea of Chinatown itself plays a role in influencing these interactions. Secondly, the paper situates the comparative contexts of Kolkata and Singapore within recent concerns about highlighting the importance of "other global cities."[1] In contrast to economic and financial flows that have been the focus of Saskia Sassen's idea of "global city,"[2] *The Other Global City* situates the Asian city as part of the topography of interconnected regions, and focuses on everyday forms of interactions and cosmopolitanisms. Yet there are considerable variations within these "other global cities." Through a focus on the Hindu temples as sacred spaces in Chinatowns, this paper interrogates to what extent religion facilitates the creation of a "diaspora space"[3] and whether these shared sacred spaces can be a suitable framework for comparison across Chinese and Indian immigrant communities. Although Chinese and Indian communities form a significant proportion of the diasporic population worldwide, and despite a long history of interaction between China and India, there is little comparative research across the two communities.

Before discussing the empirical contexts, however, I outline other research on religious space and the city that has also shaped the ideas presented in this paper.

Religion, Urban Space and Cosmopolitanism

The key focus of this paper is on the practices of interaction across Indian and Chinese immigrant communities through religious spaces. The paper brings together two different urban contexts of such interaction in Kolkata and Singapore. While in Singapore both communities are diasporic and their interactions are mediated through an official image of the city-state as multicultural, in Kolkata the interaction is principally along a majority–minority axis, and takes place in what is seen as a predominantly "Bengali" city. How do communities interact through religious spaces? How do religious spaces facilitate these encounters? How do religious spaces in the city modify the idea of "community"? These are some of the questions this paper addresses. The focus, therefore, is not on the mythological, religious or even practical reasons for this interaction, but rather on the factors behind the creation and maintenance of that shared space.

Both South and Southeast Asia form rich comparative contexts to analyse the intersections between religion, migration and everyday space in the city. An increasing interest in religion in diasporic contexts has not only focused on transnational connections within these two regions[4] but also on the transformation that religious practices undergo in and through migration.[5] A significant part of these connections and transformations has focused on urban sites and the ways in which towns and cities, acting as nodes in the migratory trajectory, influence encounters across religion. Writing about the implications of modernity on "Chinese" religion, for example, Tong and Kong remark that earlier literature on religion by geographers did not unpack "the inner workings of religion nor consider explicitly the interrelations between social and spatial change."[6] While some have focused on the "politics and poetics" of religion,[7] and analysed how conceptions of "sacred space" are negotiated,[8] others have explored how urban space and politics promotes "mixity."[9] In an overview of studies on religion and urban space in Asia and Africa, Hancock and Srinivas[10] point out that scholars of these regions have long focused on both the "sacralization of cities" as well as the "urbanization of sacred spaces." So, for example, just as cities like Madurai or Varanasi in India developed around shrines and temples,[11] other research has studied the effect of modernization on religion.[12] Migration, in these literatures, besides exploring connections between places, has also been addressed through the presence of shared sacred spaces. In Southeast Asia the mixing across religion has been studied in terms of syncretic practices and how religion itself has undergone changes to reflect the effect of migration and multicultural policies.[13] In South Asia, on the other hand, shared sacred spaces, while also involving concepts of migration,[14] have been interpreted in the context of communalism and community identity.[15]

Building on this research on religion, urban space and migration, the paper also contributes to notions of "alternative"[16] and "vernacular"[17] cosmopolitanisms. An important characteristic of such cosmopolitanisms, as explained by Ashis Nandy[18] in the context of Cochin's history, is the presence of an alternative narrative of cosmopolitanism constructed through community interaction. Such alternative cosmopolitanisms are different from public narratives of cosmopolitanism in the sense that these also include an ambivalence or even animosity towards other communities,[19] reflecting "intimate histories of cosmopolitan being" in "other global cities."[20]

Setting the Contexts: Chinatowns in Kolkata and Singapore

The Chinatowns in both Kolkata and Singapore not only frame the contexts of this comparative study, but their history also informs the practices of interactions between Chinese and Indian communities in both cities. Just as both Chinatowns have developed through the migration of the Chinese community to these cities, so have their characteristics been influenced by the way urban development has intervened in the interaction between Chinese and Indian communities.

Kolkata (Calcutta) Chinatown[21]

Chinese migration to Kolkata began during the late eighteenth century. Kolkata is one of very few cities in the world to boast of two Chinatowns. These two Chinatowns are also unique in the sense that they differ significantly from the typical idea of Chinatowns elsewhere. Enmeshed within the urban fabric of Kolkata, the Chinatowns in this city are not separate, touristic entities, but uphold a way of living alongside diverse communities.

The first Chinatown in Kolkata took shape in the vicinity of Tiretta Bazaar in central Kolkata during the mid-nineteenth century. Often known as Tiretta Bazaar Chinatown or "Cheena Para" or even "Calcutta Chinatown,"[22] this locality was then home to several Chinese sailors who stayed back, waiting for their ships to return. Situated in the heart of colonial Kolkata, the Chinese population added to the cosmopolitan nature of the city. This neighbourhood developed as a Chinatown in the 1930s and 1940s when there was a significant influx of migration from mainly South China.

There are several historical references to the Tiretta Bazaar Chinatown. One of the earliest references is in an article by C. Alabaster which appeared in the *Calcutta Review* in 1858.[23] Apart from describing in detail the temples, the graveyards, the opium dens and the living quarters of the Chinese, Alabaster notes the different groups of Chinese living here: "the shoe-makers, ship-carpenters and hogslard-manufacturers."[24] Being a tiny community at that time, the Chinese intermarried among the different subgroups (mainly Cantonese and Hakka) and also with others living in the same neighbourhood, mainly "Hindustanis" and also "Eurasians":

> Properly speaking, they are two distinct colonies, belonging to distinct races, carrying on distinct trades, and speaking different languages; but community of interests, the manufacture of hogslard, opium-smoking, and Hindustani have almost merged them into one; and constant intermarriage threatens to annihilate the difference between the shoe-makers and ship-carpenters notwithstanding the still existing obstacles to such complete union in the great disparity of wealth of the two communities.[25]

Things began to change in Chinatown in the late 1950s when the Calcutta Improvement Trust decided to build a huge thoroughfare cutting across its centre. Chattawala Gully, Phears Lane and Blackburn Lane, which used to wind through Chinatown, were fragmented. The impact of the 1962 Sino-Indian conflict was also great on the central Kolkata Chinatown. Most Chinese living there were Cantonese who worked as carpenters. Since they worked as "ship-fitters" in the dock areas and also in private companies, they lost their jobs and were compelled to emigrate. Many Hakkas living there also chose to move to Tangra, the other Chinatown. Fragments of Chinatown still exist in and around Tiretta Bazaar. Bentinck Street, near Lalbazar, continues to have Chinese shoe shops, though much fewer in number. There are a number of shops selling Chinese groceries. The Sunday morning market continues with a smaller breakfast fare, while road names like Sun Yatsen Street and Lu Hsin Sarani hold on to the Chinese presence in this area of Kolkata.

Chinatown in present day Kolkata refers to Tangra, which is located in the eastern part of the city. Although most Chinese in the city live in this neighbourhood today, Tangra was at the margin of Kolkata in its early years. The neighbourhood began to take shape around 1910 when some Chinese shoemakers decided to process leather for their business and moved to the area, also called Dhapa.[26] Tangra in its early days was a marshy area with very few permanent settlements around. Although there are hardly any historical references to Tangra, when compared to Tiretta Bazaar Chinatown, the evolution of this neighbourhood mirrors the history of the Chinese community in Kolkata very well. While Tiretta Bazaar was inhabited mainly by the Cantonese (although pockets of Hakka population did exist), Tangra grew as a predominantly Hakka neighbourhood.

The initial years in Tangra were hard for the Hakka Chinese and the poverty of the neighbourhood stood out in stark contrast to the golden days of Tiretta Bazaar Chinatown.[27] The fortune of Tangra turned gradually after the Second World War with an increase in the demand for rawhide. More Hakka Chinese entered the tannery business and permanent structures were put in place. Hakkas being a close-knit community, Tangra Chinatown developed almost completely secluded from outside influence. Community organizations played an important role in the overall physical development of the area. Pei May School was set up on community initiative. Most cemeteries, both Cantonese and Hakka, are located here too. Tangra, inhabited mainly by the Chinese, appeared more insular in contrast to the cosmopolitan Tiretta Bazaar area.

The Sino-Indian conflict in 1962 was a point of disjuncture in the history of the Chinese in Kolkata and other parts of India. Border disputes between India and China, which began in 1959, culminated in a war in 1962.[28] Many Chinese holding PRC passports and associated with pro-communist schools and associations were deported and many were taken to an internment camp in Rajasthan.[29] In Tangra, tannery owners faced great difficulty in reaching the rawhide markets located in central and northern Kolkata because of restrictions on their movement. Tangra was located outside Kolkata municipal boundaries and hence the Chinese needed permission each time they had to travel beyond Tangra. But with business booming through the 1970s and 1980s, the Hakkas became more prosperous than the Cantonese and those who remained in Tiretta Bazaar Chinatown, and carved a more permanent place for the community in Kolkata.

Singapore Chinatown

Unlike Kolkata, Singapore's Chinatown occupied an officially designated area from the time of its inception. The 1828 master plan drawn by Lieutenant Philip Jackson put in place Sir Stamford Raffle's idea of allocating areas according to the different ethnic communities. At the same time, Singapore's Chinatown was never an exclusively Chinese place. The presence of places of worship of other communities, like the Nagore Durgha Shrine, the Jamae Mosque built by the Chulia Muslims, as well as the Mariamman temple, point to a mixed demography. With increasing migration from South China, the area soon developed a dense network of *huiguans* (clan associations) of different dialect groups, secret societies and Chinese businesses. The diverse dialect groups were associated with different occupations and settled in different parts of Chinatown.[30] So for example, the Hokkiens, who were engaged in trade and finance, settled around Amoy, Telok Ayer and Hokkien Street; the Cantonese, who specialized in carpentry, tailoring and the gold jewellery business, owned properties around Temple, Pagoda and Mosque Street; the Hainanese settled in Middle Road and Purvis Street; and the Hakkas, who were shoemakers, blacksmiths and ran Chinese herbal shops, settled in Upper Chin Chiew, Upper Hokkien and Upper Cross Street.[31] By the early twentieth century, Chinatown had become overcrowded and the then Singapore Improvement Trust initiated public housing projects in Tiong Bahru to relieve pressure on Chinatown. As migration continued, and the population went through waves of change, Chinatown evolved, but at the same time its material conditions deteriorated. The campaign in the 1960s by Singapore's ruling party, the People's Action Party, against "so-called 'yellow culture' and vice, gambling, prostitution, secret societies, and later hygiene" altered the face of Chinatown to some extent.[32] Finally, in 1980 the Urban Redevelopment Authority (URA) redeveloped large parts of Chinatown and the Singapore Tourist Board Plan, launched in 1998, also introduced significant revisions.[33] The idea of Singapore as a "global city" impinged on the everyday interactions between communities, and as Yeoh and Kong argue, "State-initiated efforts to create a sense of community replaced old, spontaneous, interpersonal ties and the strength of vernacular associations."[34]

Hindu Temples in Chinatowns

The nature of interaction between Chinese and Indian communities in the Chinatowns of both cities, as shown in the previous section, has changed with urban development. While in Kolkata a "mixed" Chinatown in the central part of the city has given way to a more uniform Chinatown in Tangra, in Singapore the vestiges of a "mixed" Chinatown remain as an emblem of the city's official multicultural policies. The presence of the Hindu temples in these cities and the manner in which they affect interactions between Chinese and Indian communities thus need to be interpreted in this context. Although both the Kali temple in Kolkata and the Mariamman Temple in Singapore represent a shared religious space that marks interactions between both communities, these spaces are located within the politics of community identities.

"For this Kali, Bhog is Noodles and Chopsuey"[35]

The Chinese diaspora in Kolkata, much like Chinese diasporas elsewhere in Asia, have incorporated multiple religious beliefs in their everyday lives. There are no historical records to suggest how and when the Chinese community in Kolkata began worshipping Kali. An article by Hassan Ali[36] on religious practices of the community mentions that the some members of the community in the 1940s and 1950s visited the famous Kali temple in Kalighat to offer animal sacrifices. Kali is a popular goddess in Eastern India, and is said to be the patron goddess of Kolkata. But rather than an adoption of, or being influenced by the Hindu belief system, the Chinese community in Kolkata probably started worshipping Kali through what I would like to call chance encounters and matters related to "miracles."

There are two Chinese Kali temples in Kolkata – one is located in Cheena Para, the old Chinatown, and the other in Tangra, the relatively newer Chinatown. The temple in old Chinatown goes by the name of Cheena Kali, where its Chinese connection stops. It is probable that the small temple was built by the Chinese, but the community does not have many links with this temple in the present. The old Chinatown, as mentioned earlier, was (and indeed still is) a melting pot of various communities. The Chinese in this part of the city have long shared space with lower-caste Hindus and Dalits. Many of the Dalits are involved in the pig-slaughtering business, and are great devotees of Kali. It could be that the Chinese, who had links with this Dalit community through sharing residential as well as business spaces, were influenced by their religious beliefs. Although the Cheena Kali temple has faded in importance for the community, ties with the *dosads* (pig slaughterers) continue in the present through the latter's participation in Chinese New Year festivities.

The other Chinese Kali temple is in Tangra, and is more widely known by this name. The temple site is over sixty years old[37] and was set up by Li Quansheng, a Burmese man who was sold to and brought up by a Hakka family.[38] Many stories abound as to the reasons why this shrine was set up. Some accounts say that this site was a dumping ground for local tanneries and Li Quansheng along with a Bihari person set up a temple around what were perceived to be Shiva lingams. Zhang Xing[39] writes that the Chinese probably started worshipping Kali as a fertility goddess, because there was none in their pantheon, but it remains unclear as to whether this belief was connected to the construction of this shrine. Another story, recounted by Ison Chen, who manages the temple and has done so for the last 11 years, describes how at the location of this shrine, there were a couple of vermillion-smeared black stones which were worshipped by the local Biharis, and the Chinese followed suit.[40] A 10-year-old Chinese boy, who was extremely ill, was brought to this place when the doctors had given up hope, and after his parents prayed for several nights, he was cured.[41] The site then became special for the community. Besides these stories of "miracles" around the construction of the temple, other stories perpetuate and help continue the Chinese belief in Kali. As Zhang Xing mentioned, the goddess is closely linked to fertility rituals and many women in Tangra pray to Kali for a child.[42] The temple, in its current form, was also rebuilt based on a miracle story. A Chinese man from Tangra, Guo Rensheng, rebuilt this temple entirely as a marble structure after his prayers for a Canadian visa (which was rejected thrice) were eventually successful.

Although such stories around the Kolkata Chinese community's belief in Kali do not indicate a total adoption of Hindu religious beliefs, it is interesting to note how the beginnings of Kali worship are often rooted in local, neighbourhood stories, rather than belief in a wider religious system. The temple continues to play an important role in the neighbourhood, as the Chinese New Year parade is usually preceded by a *puja* (worship) at the temple. It is also interesting that this is a case of a community taking on the responsibility of carrying out the practices of worship, rather than just participating in the activities of a "Hindu" temple. As a result, the practices of worshipping have acquired a "Chinese" character. The community arranges for a Brahmin priest to come and do the *puja* every Tuesday and Saturday, as well as during the big annual festival of Kali Puja held in October–November each year. At the same time, they have also introduced particular practices of some Chinese traditions, like lighting tall candles, burning Chinese incense sticks and paper money.[43] Some refrain from eating beef if they are praying, and some like Ison Chen, who is in charge of the temple, take a holy dip in the Ganges before the *puja*, and is enthusiastic about continuing what he calls "an ancestral *puja*."[44]

Religious "Mixity" in Singapore

The Mariamman Temple in Singapore's present Chinatown was built in 1825 by Naraina Pillay, a government clerk working with the East India Company, who is reputed to have come to Singapore on the same boat as Stamford Raffles. The land for the temple was granted to him in 1821. The area around South Bridge Road, where the temple is located, was then called Kampong Kling – "Kling" referring to the immigrant Indian population. The story goes that Pillai's workers approached him to build the temple for a Mariamman idol that they had carried from India. Mariamman, a rain and fertility deity, is revered for her powers to cure tropical diseases like smallpox, and is an important goddess for the South Indian labour diaspora. Shrines and temples of Mariamman have been set up throughout Southeast Asia in Bangkok, Penang, Kuala Lumpur and Medan, as well as in South Africa and Fiji. In recent times, Mariamman has also been worshipped in countries in Europe, including Belgium and France.[45] Although Mariamman is an important deity for the Tamil-speaking population of Singapore, Fred Clothey[46] remarks that the Mariamman Temple was built by a cross-section of Indians drawn from different castes and regions. As he writes, "This pattern of reciprocity and alliance was to be an important feature of temple space in Singapore, as neighbourhoods became increasingly heterogeneous."[47] In Singapore, the temple, since its inception, has played an important social role in the life of the Indian community. Besides acting as a site of worship, the temple provided shelter to the migrating population, while the priests officiated weddings, and acted as arbitrators in solving disputes within the community. The temple also provided wartime shelter to the local population during the Second World War.[48] The temple was initially managed by the Caulker community, from the Cuddalore area, from where Naraina Pillay also hailed.[49] The Mohammedan and Hindu Endowments Board took over responsibility for the temple in 1907, and it was ultimately passed onto the reconstituted Hindu Endowments Board in 1968, an administrative arrangement that continues to the present. The fire-walking ceremony or Theemithi, the second most important Hindu festival in Singapore after Thaipusam, is held at the temple each year. Gazetted as a national monument in 1973, Mariamman Temple remains an important part of Singapore's and indeed Chinatown's landscapes.

Although the location of the Mariamman Temple in Chinatown was a result of a combination of colonial land policy and the urban history of migration to Singapore, another Mariamman Temple in Kuala Lumpur is also located in the city's Chinatown. In Singapore, the local Chinese community in Chinatown has been involved with the temple since its earliest days. In an interview, officials of the Hindu Endowments Board[50] mentioned that temple records, which are now kept in the national archives, show donations of oil and other necessities needed for the worship of Mariamman by members of the Chinese community. The community continues to take part in the temple's activities, and some are even members of the core management group. Many take part in the annual fire-walking ceremony, and officials claim that the numbers have significantly increased over the years. The temple also plays its part in this interaction by organizing community events during Chinese New Year.

How does one explain this great devotion of the Chinese to Mariamman? Indeed, how does one interpret it? A range of people interviewed in Singapore gave answers such as "all gods are the same," or referred to Singapore's identity as a multicultural and multifaith city-state. Geraldene Lowe-Ismail, in her book *Chinatown Memories*, writes that she was surprised at the number of Chinese persons visiting and praying at the Mariamman temple:

> In fact all the old goldsmith shops opposite believed that Sri Mariamman, the Hindu mother goddess, was the same as Kuan Yin, the Chinese Goddess of Mercy, who brings good luck [...]. Over the years I have observed many Asians pray to every deity both as a mark of respect and so as not to anger any of the gods and bring bad fortune on themselves.[51]

This observation has also been made by Ara Wilson in the context of another Southeast Asian city, Bangkok.[52]

Although there could be mythological reasons as to why Mariamman is a popular Hindu deity among the Chinese community in Singapore, and indeed across Southeast Asia, it is interesting to analyse the contexts in which these interactions across communities take place in the religious sphere. Vineeta Sinha's[53] work on Hinduism in Singapore has shown that everyday Hindu religiosity in the city is characterized by "mixing and matching" and that there are several instances where "different" sacred spaces have merged. Sinha explores how Taoist and Hindu spaces have merged in a temple in Yishun (Hock Huat Keng/Veeramuthu Muneeshwaran temple) and explains this merging of sacred spaces through the demands of the secular space of urban planning. However, as PuruShotam[54] notes, religions in Singapore are ethnicized and "raced." So discourses around Hinduism are ultimately linked to "Indian-ness" and Taoist practices to "Chinese-ness." Indeed, as Sinha writes, "The amazement that greets contemporary evidence of such religious encounters is to be partly located in the role of the nation-state and the multiracial paradigm which it has generated to structure ethnic relations in Singapore since the 1960s."[55] The role of Mariamman temple in Chinatown and also the participation of the Chinese community in the religious and social activities of the temple thus need to be interpreted in the space that shapes the interaction between the "sacred" and the "secular."

Beyond Boundaries? Some Conclusions

At the beginning of the paper, I raised questions around the use of religion as a space for interactions between Indian and Chinese communities and also about the importance of shared sacred spaces as evidence of "alternative" cosmopolitanisms in the city. My aim in this paper was to explore how communities interact through religious spaces, how religious spaces facilitate these encounters and how religious spaces in the city reflect ideas and practices of cosmopolitanism. A comparison of practices of cosmopolitanisms, as I shall term these interactions across religions, between Kolkata and Singapore show significant differences in the way the Chinese communities in both cities engage with Hinduism. If in Kolkata the interaction is more about a peripheral engagement within "Chinese"-created spaces, in Singapore such interactions assume and are indeed narrated through wider discourses around race and ethnicity. The official location of the Mariamman temple within Chinatown in Singapore then assumes a lesser importance than the actual interactions that take place between the two communities. At the same time, these cosmopolitan practices are shaped by the minority position of both communities. In Kolkata the Chinese engage with Hinduism as a minority community, and their engagement is shaped by their residential proximity to other marginal groups like the Dalits. In Singapore, however, the Chinese form the majority ethnic community and their engagement with Hinduism takes a more negotiated form. It is also important to note that social differences in Kolkata operate more on religious lines, making such an engagement on the part of the Chinese at best tenuous and somewhat exceptional, whereas in Singapore ethnicity marks the difference between communities, and the conversation across religious boundaries takes on a more central role in defining social life. Wider questions can also be raised around Chinese practices of adopting Hindu religious beliefs as a sign of interaction with Indian communities. But as I have argued in this paper, the adoption of syncretic religious practices needs to be mediated through the politics of urban space and migration.

Notes

1 Shail Mayaram, ed., *The Other Global City* (London: Routledge, 2009).
2 Saskia Sassen, *The Global City: New York, London, Tokyo* (Princeton, NJ: Princeton University Press, 1991).
3 Avtar Brah, *Cartographies of Diaspora: Contesting Identities* (London: Routledge, 1996).
4 Sunil Amrith, *Migration and Diaspora in Modern Asia* (Cambridge: Cambridge University Press, 2011).
5 Rajesh Rai, "Homogenisation and Fragmentation, Inclusivism and Exclusivism in the Development of Hinduism in Singapore," *South Asian Diaspora* 1, no. 1 (March 2009): 3–17.

6 Tong Chee Kiong and Lily Kong, "Religion and Modernity: Ritual Transformations and the Reconstruction of Space and Time," *Social and Cultural Geography* 1, no. 1 (2000): 29–44 (p. 30).
7 Lily Kong, "Mapping 'New' Geographies of Religion: Politics and Poetics in Modernity," *Progress in Human Geography* 25 (2001): 211–33; also see Lily Kong, "Global Shifts, Theoretical Shifts: Changing Geographies of Religion," *Progress in Human Geography* 34, no. 6 (2010): 755–76.
8 Lily Kong, "Negotiating Conceptions of 'Sacred Space': A Case Study of Religious Buildings in Singapore," *Transactions of the Institute of British Geographers* 18, no. 3 (1993): 342–58.
9 Vinita Sinha, "'Mixing' and 'Matching': The Shape of Everyday Hindu Religiosity in Singapore," *Asian Journal of Social Science* 37 (2009): 83–106.
10 Mary Hancock and Smriti Srinivas, "Spaces of Modernity: Religion and the Urban in Asia and Africa," *International Journal of Urban and Regional Research* 32, no. 3 (2008): 619.
11 Hancock and Srinivas, "Spaces of Modernity," p. 619.
12 Peter van der Veer, *Imperial Encounters: Religion and Modernity in India and Great Britain* (Princeton, NJ: Princeton University Press, 2001).
13 Rai, "Homogenisation and Fragmentation," 2009; and Sinha, "'Mixing' and 'Matching.'"
14 Henn, for example, studies how cultural, social and physical mobility has led to "syncretistic" worship of Our Lady of Vailankani and Shri Dev Damodar in roadside shrines of Margao, Goa. Alexander Henn, "Crossroads of Religions: Shrines, Mobility and Urban Space in Goa," *International Journal of Urban and Regional Research* 32, no. 3 (2008): 658–70.
15 See for example, N. K. Das, ed., *Culture, Religion and Philosophy: Critical Studies in Syncretism and Inter-faith Harmony* (Jaipur: Rawat, 2003); Peter Van der Veer, "Syncretism, Multiculturalism, and the Discourse of Tolerance," in *Syncretism/Anti-syncretism: The Politics of Religious Synthesis*, ed. Charles Stewart and Rosalind Shaw (London: Routledge, 1994).
16 Ashis Nandy, "Time Travel to a Possible Self: Searching for Alternative Cosmopolitanism of Cochin," in *Japanese Journal of Political Science* 1, no. 2 (2000): 295–327.
17 C. Breckenridge et al., *Cosmopolitanism* (Durham, NC: Duke University Press 2002).
18 Nandy, "Time Travel to a Possible Self."
19 Nandy, "Time Travel to a Possible Self."
20 Mayaram, *The Other Global City*, p. 8.
21 Calcutta was renamed Kolkata in 2001, I have continued to use the latter name to refer to the city for consistency.
22 A name acquired much later with the establishment of a second Chinatown in Tangra, further east of the city.
23 C. Alabaster, "The Chinese Colony in Calcutta," in *Calcutta: People and Empire, Gleanings from Old Journals*, ed. P. Chaudhury and A. Mukhopadhyay (Calcutta: India Book Exchange, 1975).
24 Alabaster, "The Chinese Colony in Calcutta," p. 137.
25 Alabaster, "The Chinese Colony in Calcutta," p. 138.
26 Ellen Oxfeld, *Blood, Sweat and Mahjong: Family and Enterprise in an Overseas Chinese Community* (Ithaca, NY: Cornell University Press, 1993).
27 Julien Berjeaut, *Chinois a Calcutta: Les Tigres du Bengale* (Paris: l'Harmattan, 1999).
28 J. Cohen and S. Leng, "The Sino-Indian Dispute over the Internment and Detention of Chinese in India," in *China's Practice of International Law: Some Case Studies*, ed. A. J. Cohen (Cambridge, MA: Harvard University Press, 1972), pp. 268–320.
29 Cohen and Leng, "The Sino-Indian Dispute."
30 National Heritage Board, *Discover Singapore on Foot: Heritage Trails* (Singapore: National Heritage Board, 2006).
31 National Heritage Board, *Discover Singapore on Foot.*
32 Karl Hack, "Chinatown as a Microcosm of Singapore" (2000). http://www.hsse.nie.edu.sg/staff/blackburn/ChinatownHistory.pdf. 13 September 2014.
33 Karl Hack, "Chinatown as a Microcosm of Singapore."

34 Brenda S. A. Yeoh and Lily Kong, "Reading Landscape Meanings: State Constructions and Lived Experiences in Singapore's Chinatown," *Habitat International* 18, no. 4 (1994): 17.
35 J. Mukherjee, "For This Kali, Bhog Is Noodles and Chopsuey," *Times of India*, 17 October 2009. *Bhog* refers to food offering made to the goddess.
36 Hassan Ali, "The Chinese in Calcutta: A Study of a Racial Minority," in *Aspects of Society and Culture in Calcutta*, ed. M. K. A. Siddiqui (Calcutta: Anthropological Survey of India, 1982).
37 *Times of India*, 17 October 2009.
38 Zhang Xing, "Creating a New Cultural Identity: India-Related Religious Practices among the Chinese Community in Kolkata," *China Report* 45, no. 1 (2009): 53–63.
39 Zhang Xing, "Creating a New Cultural Identity."
40 *Times of India*, 17 October 2009.
41 *Times of India*, 17 October 2009.
42 Zhang Xing, "Creating a New Cultural Identity."
43 *Times of India*, 17 October 2009.
44 S. Das, "Chinese Kali Puja," *Kolkata Mirror*, 16 October 2009.
45 Hindu Endowments Board (HEB), *Sacred Sanctuary: The Sri Mariamman Temple* (Singapore: HEB, 2009), p. 32.
46 Fred Clothey, *Ritualizing on the Boundaries* (South Carolina: University of South Carolina Press, 2006), p. 63.
47 Clothey, *Ritualizing on the Boundaries*, p. 63.
48 HEB, *Sacred Sanctuary*, p. 14.
49 HEB, *Sacred Sanctuary*, p. 14.
50 Interview date, 11 July 2010.
51 Geraldene Lowe-Ismail, *Chinatown Memories* (Singapore Heritage Society, 1998), p. 38.
52 Ara Wilson, "The Sacred Geography of Bangkok's Markets," *International Journal of Urban and Regional Research* 32, no. 3 (September 2008): 631–42.
53 Sinha, "'Mixing' and 'Matching.'"
54 Nirmala PuruShotam, *Negotiating Language, Constructing Race: Disciplining Difference in Singapore* (Berlin: Mouton de Gruyter, 1998).
55 Sinha, "'Mixing' and 'Matching,'" p. 103.

References

Alabaster, C. "The Chinese Colony in Calcutta." In *Calcutta: People and Empire, Gleanings from Old Journals*, edited by P. Chaudhury and A. Mukhopadhyay, pp. 137–57. Calcutta: India Book Exchange, 1975.

Amrith, S. *Migration and Diaspora in Modern Asia*. Cambridge: Cambridge University Press, 2011.

Berjeaut, J. *Chinois à Calcutta: Les Tigres du Bengale*. Paris: l'Harmattan, 1999.

Brah, A. *Cartographies of Diaspora: Contesting Identities*. London: Routledge, 1996.

Breckenridge, C., S. Pollock, H. Bhabha and D. Chakrabarty, eds. *Cosmopolitanism*. Durham, NC: Duke University Press, 2002.

Cohen, J. and S. Leng. "The Sino-Indian Dispute over the Internment and Detention of Chinese in India." In *China's Practice of International Law: Some Case Studies*, edited by A. J. Cohen, pp. 268–320. Cambridge, MA: Harvard University Press, 1972.

Clothey, F. *Ritualizing on the Boundaries*. South Carolina: University of South Carolina Press, 2006.

Das, N. K. ed. *Culture, Religion and Philosophy: Critical Studies in Syncretism and Inter-faith Harmony*. Jaipur: Rawat, 2003.

Das, S. "Chinese Kali Puja." *Kolkata Mirror*, 16 October 2009. http://kolkatamirror.com/index.aspx?page=article&sectid=139&contentid=200910162009101517152695 3ac1ca2a4&sectxslt=. 20 July 2010.

Hack, K. "Chinatown as a Microcosm of Singapore." 2000. http://www.hsse.nie.edu.sg/staff/blackburn/ChinatownHistory.pdf. 13 September 2014.

Hancock, M. and S. Srinivas. "Spaces of Modernity: Religion and the Urban in Asia and Africa." *International Journal of Urban and Regional Research* 32, no. 3 (2008): 617–30.

Hassan, Ali. "The Chinese in Calcutta: A Study of a Racial Minority." In *Aspects of Society and Culture in Calcutta*, edited by M. K. A. Siddiqui, pp. 85–97. Calcutta: Anthropological Survey of India, 1982.

Henn, A. "Crossroads of Religions: Shrines, Mobility and Urban Space in Goa." *International Journal of Urban and Regional Research* 32, no. 3 (2008): 658–70.

Hindu Endowments Board (HEB). *Sacred Sanctuary: The Sri Mariamman Temple*. Singapore: HEB, 2009.

Kong, L. "Global Shifts, Theoretical Shifts: Changing Geographies of Religion." *Progress in Human Geography* 34, no. 6 (2010): 755–76.

______. "Mapping 'New' Geographies of Religion: Politics and Poetics in Modernity." *Progress in Human Geography* 25 (2001): 211–33.

______. "Negotiating Conceptions of 'Sacred Space': A Case Study of Religious Buildings in Singapore." *Transactions of the Institute of British Geographers* 18, no. 3 (1993): 342–58.

Lowe-Ismail, G. *Chinatown Memories*. Singapore: Singapore Heritage Society, 1998.

Mayaram, S. ed. *The Other Global City*. London: Routledge, 2009.

Mukherjee, J. "For This Kali, Bhog is Noodles and Chopsuey." *Times of India*, 17 October 2009. http://www.allvoices.com/s/event-4416011/aHR0cDovL3RpbWVzb2ZpbmRpYS5pbmRpYXRpbWVzLmNvbS9pbmRpYS9Gb3ItdGhpcy1LYWxpLWJob2ctaXMtbm9vZGxlcy1hbmQtY2hvcHN1ZXkvYXJ0aWNsZXN ob3cvNTEzMjk0Ni5jbXM=. 20 July 2010.

Nandy, A. "Time Travel to a Possible Self: Searching for Alternative Cosmopolitanism of Cochin." *Japanese Journal of Political Science* 1, no. 2 (2009): 295–327.

National Heritage Board. *Discover Singapore on Foot: Heritage Trails*. Singapore: National Heritage Board, 2006.

Oxfeld, E. *Blood, Sweat and Mahjong: Family and Enterprise in an Overseas Chinese Community*. Ithaca, NY: Cornell University Press, 1993.

PuruShotam, N. S. *Negotiating Language, Constructing Race: Disciplining Difference in Singapore*. Berlin: Mouton de Gruyter, 1998.

Rai, R. "Homogenisation and Fragmentation, Inclusivism and Exclusivism in the Development of Hinduism in Singapore." *South Asian Diaspora* 1, no. 1 (March 2009): 3–17.

Sassen, S. *The Global City: New York, London, Tokyo*. Princeton, NJ: Princeton University Press, 1991.

Sinha, V. "Merging 'Different' Sacred Spaces: Enabling Religious Encounters through Pragmatic Utilization of Space?" *Contributions to Indian Sociology* 37 (2003): 459–94.

______. "'Mixing' and 'Matching': The Shape of Everyday Hindu Religiosity in Singapore." *Asian Journal of Social Science* 37 (2009): 83–106.

Tong, C.K. and L. Kong. "Religion and Modernity: Ritual Transformations and the Reconstruction of Space and Time." *Social and Cultural Geography* 1, no. 1 (2000): 29–44.

Van der Veer, P. "Syncretism, Multiculturalism, and the Discourse of Tolerance." In *Syncretism/Anti-syncretism: The Politics of Religious Synthesis*, edited by Charles Stewart and Rosalind Shaw, pp. 185–99. London: Routledge, 1994.

______. *Imperial Encounters: Religion and Modernity in India and Great Britain*. Princeton, NJ: Princeton University Press, 2001.

Wilson, A. "The Sacred Geography of Bangkok's Markets." *International Journal of Urban and Regional Research* 32, no. 3 (September 2008): 631–42.

Yeoh, B. S. A. and L. Kong. "Reading Landscape Meanings: State Constructions and Lived Experiences in Singapore's Chinatown." *Habitat International* 18, no. 4 (1994): 17–35.

Zhang, Xing. "Creating a New Cultural Identity: India-Related Religious Practices among the Chinese Community in Kolkata." *China Report* 45, no.1 (2009): 53–63.

Section III

INDIANS IN CHINA AND CHINESE IN INDIA

Chapter 11

LAW AND ITS IMPACT ON DIASPORIC PHILANTHROPIC INSTITUTIONS: THE PRACTICES OF *SINCHEW* AND THE *WAQF* IN THE STRAITS SETTLEMENTS

Stephanie Chung Po-yin

Since the middle of the nineteenth century, with the increase of British colonial activities in maritime Asia, the British legal system had been applied and enforced in various regions in Asia in varying degrees of intensity. Contrary to the popular interpretation that the British colonial administrators always stayed away from matters of *native* religions and customs, the British officials were in fact heavily involved in the religious lives of their colonial subjects in Asia.[1] Through a reconstruction of legal disputes found in the Straits Settlements, this paper discusses how the British legal system interacted with Asian customs and in particular, the Islamic *waqf* and Chinese *sinchew* (神主 *shen zhu*) practices during the late nineteenth and early twentieth centuries. The imposition or customization of colonial laws on indigenous practices underlined not only the fundamental cultural differences between the East and the West on wealth management and its transference, but also the power competition between various diasporic groups and the emerging colonial powers.

Rule against Perpetuity in the Historical Context

In traditional Asian societies, economic activities were always embedded with political and religious forces under the disguise of communal temples and family groups.[2] In Indian, Islamic and Chinese societies, it was common for wealth to be retained and accumulated in the form of religious and charitable endowments, or in the names of deceased ancestors or patron deities.[3] Economic activity was a segment of the complicated web of kinship, religious activities and personal relations. However, with the increase of British colonial activities starting from the nineteenth century, the presence of the British legal system in Asia gradually undermined the material interests of many of these endowments. The traditional practices of holding properties in the name of ancestors and deities were challenged by British legal ideas, in particular the "rule against perpetuities."[4]

By the nineteenth century the incorporation of business entities into the legal form of the corporation was embedded in British society. In 1862, the Companies Act consolidated earlier piecemeal legislation which guaranteed legal protection and limited legal liability for the corporation, and registration under company law had become a right rather than a privilege. The decision in *Saloman v. A. Saloman Co. Ltd* (1897) AC 22 accepted that "entrepreneurs acting through companies should have the benefit of distinct legal personality as well as limited liability granted to them by statute."[5] This was the product, however, of a long history in Britain, and Western Europe more generally, of gradually sloughing away the suspicions of powerful rulers of any organization which sought to tie up property, particularly land, in perpetuity, with its attendant possibilities for the avoidance of feudal duties. These early suspicions gave rise to the rule against perpetuities, which particularly affected another legal mechanism – the trust (or in its earlier form the *use*) – that had emerged by the thirteenth century as a key means of elite family land holding in England. Statutes of Mortmain were enacted in 1279 and 1290 providing that no estate should be granted to a corporation without royal assent, with the exception of the charitable trust. Modern versions were contained in the Mortmain and Charitable Uses Acts of 1888 and 1891, such that unauthorized conveyance into mortmain made the land liable to forfeiture by the crown. Although abolished in Britain in 1960, the principles remain in the complex perpetuity rules governing private trusts in England and Wales, which have only recently been through another process of reform (but not abolition).[6]

Over the past two hundred years, the British Courts in Asia have handed down a series of decisions regarding the legitimacy of an endowment whose expressed objective was to finance worship of ancestors and deities. In the Straits Settlements, it has been held that English rule against perpetuities (which provided that no contingent or executory interest in property could be created unless it was necessarily vested within the maximum period of one or more lives in being and 21 years afterwards) applied in the cases of Muslim and Chinese wills and settlements. This paradox, between Asian customs and the British rules against perpetuities, is addressed in this paper with legal cases from the Straits Settlements. These legal records highlight a peculiar historical development in modern history; they reflect the interaction and blending of several conflicting legal traditions in Southeast Asia.

The Straits Settlements as a Frontier Society

English voyagers were active in Malayan waters in the sixteenth century. Penang is regarded as one of the first English settlements in Peninsular Malaysia. The official history of Penang under the British East India Company (EIC) can be traced back to the year 1786, when Captain Francis Light (a naval officer turned merchant adventurer) obtained for the EIC a cession of the island from the Sultan of Kedah. After Penang became a British trade centre, traders from various regions gathered and settled down on the island. Within three years of its founding as a British port, it had a population of about ten thousand people. Since Penang Island is situated on the trading route of the Straits of Malacca, the settlement attracted people of all descents: Europeans, Chinese, Indians, Bugis and Arabs. In the early days of Penang, Georgetown functioned as a port town, where regional traders brought in products such as nutmeg, pepper, clove and textiles. Among these early immigrants were two prominent groups, the Indian Muslims and the Chinese, who took Malay wives and became a part of the earliest permanent community. The two communities were known as Peranakan Jawi (Indian Muslim) and Peranakan Cina, also known as the Baba-Nyonya (Straits Chinese). More Chinese and Indians were drawn to the Straits Settlements during the second half of the nineteenth century by the booming tin and rubber industries.[7]

The British EIC was interested in trade, not governance. For decades, it did little to organize law and administration. In 1792, Captain Light authorized local headmen to administer justice to their own people. Later, some limited criminal regulations were published. In 1826, along with Malacca and Singapore, Penang became part of the British Straits Settlements. Against this political background, several legal traditions amalgamated to form the legal foundation of the Straits Settlements. Notable among these legal traditions are native or indigenous law (*adat*), Muslim law and English law. After British intervention into the Malay States, British colonial officials claimed that they would grant recognition to local religion and custom.[8] But as will be shown, the British courts frequently meddled in the interpretation of Islamic and Chinese religious practices, always trying to regulate Muslim and Chinese "charitable" institutions within the realm of British law.

Chinese Sinchew *Cases*

In the Straits Settlements, a frontier society in which each migrant group had its own place of worship, various religious groups flourished. Mosques, temples, clan houses, shrines and other endowments were established by the immigrant communities. But it is not always clear where the borderline runs between customary observances and religious ceremonies. To the colonial courts, the Chinese practice of *sinchew* was one of these confusing traditions.

Trusts for burial ground and trusts for the performance of ancestral worship (*sinchew*) were two of the most common types of Chinese customary perpetual trusts in Peninsular Malaysia and Singapore.[9] From the nineteenth century, the British courts also passed down legal precedents that these perpetual trusts violated the British rule against perpetuities.[10] Four major cases of *sinchew* have been found in the law reports of the nineteenth century.[11] All of them were concerned with the administration of estates with provisions which set aside rents, profits, land and other properties and income for the performance of religious ceremonies in honour of the deceased and his wife or wives. The bulk of the inheritance was tied up in family estates, with directions that the rents and profits of the estate be used to support the *sinchew* ceremony. In three of these cases, the judges were of the opinion that such provisions were void as they did not conform to the rule against perpetuity. This law states in effect that property cannot legally be tied up for longer than a period of a life or lives in being at the time of the bequest, and 21 years afterwards.

In the classical case of *Choa Choon Neoh v. Spottiswoode* (1869), Sir Benson Maxell, CJ, had to consider whether the rule against perpetuities applied to the colony. The British judge believed that the rule was "of great economical importance, and as well fitted for a young and small community" and thus should be applied to the Straits Settlements. He said:

> In this Colony, so much of the law of England as was in existence when it was imported here, and as is of general (and not merely local) policy, and adapted to the condition and wants of the inhabitants, is the law of the land; and further, that law is subject, in its application to the various alien races established here, to such modifications as are necessary to prevent it from operating unjustly and oppressively on them. Thus in questions of marriage and divorce, it would be impossible to apply our law to Mahomedans, Hindoos, and Buddhists, without the most absurd and intolerable consequences, and it is therefore held inapplicable to them. Tested by these principles, is the rule of English law which prohibits perpetuities either of local policy, unsuited to an infant settlement, or inapplicable by reasons of the harshness of its operation, to people of oriental races and creeds? The rule is not founded by any Statute, but is a rule of general and fundamental character, of great economical importance, and as well fitted for a young and small community of a great state, for both are interested in keeping property, whether real or personal, as completely as possible an object of commerce, and a productive instrument of the community at large.[12]

This legal dispute was related to a Peranakan Cina (Straits Chinese) family with the surname Choa. Mr Choa Chong Long was born in 1788 in Malacca. He went to Macau in 1838 and was murdered by some burglars. Mr Spottiswoode was the executor of his will, which contained a clause allocating certain of Choa's properties for the formation of an estate for the purpose of financing the *sinchew* ceremony (this involved engraving Choa's name on a wooden tablet). Male descendants were required to visit the tablet frequently and present food offerings on the table in front of it. His descendants challenged this clause and filed a lawsuit in the British court in the Straits Settlements, and the nature of the *sinchew* ceremony was called into question.

Sir Maxwell was unfamiliar with the custom of *sinchew*. After examining "several Chinese men of learning" for "the purpose of ascertaining what are the nature and object of this devise," Maxwell provided the definition of the concept of *sinchew*: "The word *Sinchew* is composed of *Sin*, which means a spirit, soul or ghost, and *Chew*, which means ruler; and the composite word means the spirit ruler, or spiritual head of the house."[13] Sir Maxwell then ruled that the term describes the rituals of ancestor worship and made the following comment: "The primary objective of the ceremony is to show respect and reverence to the deceased, to preserve his memory in this world, and to supply his wants in another."[14]

The term *sinchew* thus refers to the spirit tablets of the ancestors as well as to the ceremonies held for their worship.[15] Sir Maxwell made history when he delivered the verdict. The British court had to rule whether accumulating properties for the purpose of the *sinchew* ceremony was an infringement on the rule against perpetuities.[16]

The argument was about whether the bequest could be considered charitable. The British judge believed it could not. The judge, Sir Maxwell, spelled out the rationale of his verdict:

> The food [for the *sinchew* ceremony] is [...] removed, and eaten or otherwise disposed of by the relatives, but there is no distribution of it in charity or among the poor. Indeed, the Chinese have a repugnance to food which has been offered in this way, except when they are members of the family. The [offering] papers which are burnt supply the spirit with money and clothing, the gold and silver tinsel turning into precious metal. No prayers are offered to the spirit; the person who makes the offering of food asks for nothing whatever. The primary object of the ceremony is to show respect and reverence to the deceased, to preserve his memory in this world, and to supply its wants in the other.[17]

The British judge believed that the *sinchew* ceremony had little to do with "general public utility." He also gave an elaborate description of the ceremonies connected with such a bequest. *Sinchew*, as the British judge understood, was not a charity. He defined it as a sacred ceremony in memory of a deceased person. Participants of the ceremony who were members of the same family would then share the food offered to the deceased. There was no distribution of those sacrifices among the poor thereafter. Also, *sinchew* was performed solely for the benefit of the deceased and thus it was neither a charity for public welfare, nor a religious activity.

As the British judge saw no element of charity in the *sinchew* ceremony, the court declared that money and property maintained for the purpose of *sinchew* should not be exempt from the rule against perpetuities. This verdict was reaffirmed in *Ong Cheng Neo v. Yeap Cheah Neo & Ors* in 1872–75.[18]

In *Ong Cheng Neo v. Yeap Cheah Neo & Ors* (1872), a Chinese trust of house and land for the enjoyment of one's family members and their descendants was declared void for perpetuity. The judge decreed that any perpetual trust without any element of public welfare was not a charity. Also, the performance of *sinchew* was not considered a charitable activity since it only involved members of a particular family and any benefit of the performance was not extended to the public. Any perpetual trust for that purpose was not recognized as a charitable trust and hence was void for perpetuity. The perpetuity rule was part of the law of the Straits Settlements. It was stressed that the incorporation of the perpetuity rule into the law of the colony was for the public good. Applying the rule in the Straits Settlements was beneficial to the general public, and as part of the public policy it was programmed for the development of the community as a whole. Again the performance of *sinchew* was not regarded as a charity or a religious activity, but a private ceremony. The case went to the Privy Council, which upheld the verdict of Sir P. Benson Maxwell, CJ, in the case of *Choa Choon Neoh v. Spottiswoode* (1869):

> Whilst the English Statutes relating to superstitious uses and Mortmain ought not to be imported into the law of the Colony, the rule against perpetuities was to be considered a part of it. This rule, which certainly has been recognized as existing in the law of England independently of any statute, is founded upon considerations

> of public policy, which seem to be as applicable to the condition of such place as Penang as to England, viz., to prevent the mischief of making property inalienable, unless for objects which are in some way useful or beneficial to the community. It would obviously be injurious to the interests of the Island, if land convenient for the purposes of trade or for the enlargement of a town, or port could be dedicated to a purpose which would for ever prevent such a beneficial use of it. The law of England has, however, made an exception, also on grounds of public policy, in favour of gifts for purposes useful and beneficial to the public, and which, in a wide sense of the term, are called charitable uses; and this exception may properly be assumed to have passed with the rule into the law of the Colony.[19]

The above two cases, and particularly the verdict of *Choa Choon Neoh v. Spottiswoode* (1869) had significant repercussions on legal debates involving other ethnic groups (e.g., the Muslim community) in the colony. Notable among these cases is *Fatimah v. Logan* (1871), which involved a prominent Tamil Muslim family in Penang.

Muslim Waqf *Cases*

Before the British EIC established its control over the Malay Peninsula, Indian Muslim traders were influential in the courts of Kedah, Aceh and in the Straits of Malacca. The establishment of the East India Company government in Penang created new opportunities for these traders. Along their route of migration, these migrants transplanted their traditions to the newly settled colony. Notable examples include the setting up of *waqf*.

The institution of *waqf* (*awaqf* in plural) has a venerable history in most Islamic communities from the Middle East to Asia. For centuries, Muslims have fulfilled their social responsibilities and served their societies with an institution known as *waqf*. In its generic form, *waqf* conveys the idea of restriction, of setting aside for specific purposes. The ownership of the *waqf* property is transferred to God – that is to say, such property ceases forever to be subject to the rules of private proprietorship. In practice, a wide range of applications of the *waqf* idea have emerged over time and space, usually under the administration for mosques, schools and cemeteries. The legal validity of this institution has created a number of legal disputes in the Straits Settlements.[20]

Since the days when the British port of Penang was established in 1786, the largest *waqf* community in Penang has been centred around the Capitan Kling Mosque. The Indian Muslim community living around this mosque consists mainly of Tamil Muslims. A number of legal disputes questioning the legal validity of *waqf* can be found in this migrant community. Among them was a case involving a Muslim family: *Fatimah v. Logan & others* (1871).

Mohamed Mercian Noordin arrived in Penang from Nagore in the 1820s. He utilized his links of kinship and language with communities across the Indian Ocean. Eventually, he built up an extensive business network from South India to Aceh and China. He was reported to be a landlord in Penang, holding many shops and houses, and a large estate in Province Wellesley. He had a large family. Among his wives were a Malay, a European, an Indian and a Chinese woman.[21]

In 1869, Mahomed Noordin created a large family endowment through his will. The will was drafted with the help of a Western lawyer, Daniel Logan, and he appointed Daniel Logan, his sons and his son-in-law as his executors and trustees. He gave to them on trust all the residue of his real estate in Penang, Province Wellesley or elsewhere to be divided into 24 shares, such shares to be held in trust for the benefit of his descendants.

In addition to the private family trust, Noordin also created a public *waqf* of 11 pieces of land. To ensure that his *waqf* would be properly managed, he set up the *waqf* along the lines of modern foundations. He endowed 11 pieces of land and 31 shophouses altogether on Chulia Street, Prangin Road, Beach Street and China Street, all built up and expected to fetch decent rents. To ensure the upkeep of the *waqf*, Noordin specified that necessary expenses should be deducted for the maintenance of all the properties.[22]

Noordin also had a family tomb built for his mother by Indian masons. The vestibule of the tomb accommodated one of the first schools for the Muslim community. Noordin wished the family vault to be constantly well illuminated, having provided for the cost of lighting the "Mosque or burial-place of my deceased mother and the school rooms thereto adjoining." Noordin also stated in his will that he endowed it with $20 per month "for the learning of English, Hindoostanee, Malay, Tamil, Malabar and the Alkoran." The first objective of the *waqf* was to pay "to the Managing body of the School built by me in Chulia Street, adjoining the compound of the Capitan Cauder Mohuddeen's Mosque, for the learning of English, Hindoostanee, Malay, Tamil, Malabar, and the Alkoran."[23] In addition, Noordin stipulated that $60 per month was to be paid to his eldest daughter and her legitimate offspring.

Mohamed Noordin then willed that the residue of the rents and profits of his *waqf* should be expended upon an annual 10-day *kenduri arwah* consisting of "Kenduri and entertainments for me and in my name [...] according to the Mohammedan religion or custom," an annual 10-day *kenduri maulud* for the poor "in the name of all the prophets," including lighting, to the extent of $300, and a feast (Malay, *kenduri*; Tamil, *kanturi*; probably from a Persian term for "tablecloth", also spelled as "Kandoorie" in British law reports) to the poor once every three months to the extent of $100. Any surplus would go to purchasing clothes for distribution to the poor.[24]

In 1869, Mohamed Merican Noordin died at the age of 92 (the surname Merican Noordin was passed to future generations). Almost immediately after Noordin's death, the will was challenged by some of his beneficiaries in a case called *Fatimah v. Logan & others* (1871).[25] Mahomed Noordin's ex-wife, Fatimah, his daughter and son-in-law filed a petition for equity. The defendants were Daniel Logan and the other executors of Mahomed Noordin's estate. The court case was significant. Firstly, the protagonist involved in the case was a prominent family in Penang. Secondly, the case raised an important constitutional question, "whether the capacity of the deceased to make a Will was to be decided by the Mahomedan or by the English law."

Justice William Hatchett, who presided over the case, ruled according to the logic laid down by Sir Benson Maxwell in *Choa Choon Neoh v. Spottiswoode* (1869) that the British rule against perpetuities applied to the Straits Settlements. On this foundation, he set out to examine whether the clauses in the will could satisfy the "charitable test." Among other things, Justice Hatchett ruled that the trust for the school was a good charitable bequest, but the gifts for *kenduri* (*kandoorie*) were not charitable gifts.[26]

During the course of the judgement, Justice Hatchett claimed that he was unfamiliar with the custom of *kenduri* and likened it to "ceremonial entertainments." "The purpose of this trust seems to be of a ceremonial, religious, and also of a festive nature." Referring to a particular section of Noordin's will "to expend for the yearly performance of *Kandoories* and entertainments for me and in my name to commence on the anniversary of my decease according to the Mohammedan religion or custom, such *Kandoories* to continue for ten successive days every year," the judge said:

> No evidence was given to show the nature and object of these feasts and *Kandoories*, and whether they are enjoyed by the Mohammedan religion and I am therefore left to form my opinion from the words of the will itself and I confess that looking at the description of the objects of the testator's bounty in the most liberal manner, it does not appear to me that they can in any sense of the word be called charitable. I do not see how it can be of any public utility to give feasts even when these feasts are to be enjoyed by the poor. For although it would be good charity to give alms to a poor, a feast can scarcely be regarded in the same light. On the whole I am of opinion that the gifts are not charitable, and that they are therefore void.[27]

As illustrated by the above judgment, one of the most debatable issues arising from Tamil Muslim bequests was whether the *waqf* for *kenduri* was a "charitable" gift. The judge ruled that it was not. As the gift was to last forever, it was considered void as it tended to perpetuity.

The legal validity of *waqf* for *kenduri* was also disputed in the 1882 court case of *Mustan Bee & Ors. v. Shina Tomby & Anor*. According to the law report, an Ibramsah died in 1864, leaving a will in 1863, declaring among other things that a shop at 13 Market Street "should not be sold by any one, but its rents should go for its repairs, and the balance should be spent for *Kandoories* for the testator." It was explained that "these *Kandoories* were feasts given to the friends of the deceased, and the poor generally, during which feasts, alms were given, and sometimes prayers recited: these were considered to benefit the testator's soul." Again, the British court held that the trust was void as it tended to perpetuity.[28] The shop as a device for *waqf* was held to be void, following *Fatimah v. Logan & others* (1871). In another case, *Ashabee v. Mohammed Hashim* (1887), a bequest of $400 for maintenance of the testator's wife and to be spent in *kenduri* – without demonstrating how much of it was for maintenance and how much for *kenduri* – was held to be void for uncertainty and tending to perpetuity. So, in a series of cases in the Strait Settlements, the British courts consolidated the view that a trust for *kenduri* was not charitable and therefore void, as it tended to perpetuity.

Asian Customs and Western Law: Mutual Adjustments

While the British courts in the Straits Settlements were ruling on the legal validity of gifts donated for financing Chinese *sinchew* and Muslim *kenduri* practices, crucial economic changes were taking place on the Malay Peninsula. These changes gradually forced the colonial government to adjust its policy in Southeast Asia.

As early as the 1840s, the discovery of tin mines in inner parts of Perak gradually changed the political geography in the region. Whereas downstream chiefs, enjoying larger volumes of traffic, were previously more powerful than upriver chiefs, the discovery of tin in the interior began to upset the settled political order. The British seized this opportunity in forming allies. James Birch and Frank Swettenham, for instance, were busy travelling along the river regions liaising with different Malay chiefs and Chinese miner leaders. As the economic importance of the Malay Peninsula gradually increased, the administration of the Straits Settlements was severed from the India Office in 1867. The British colonial power became more concerned with intervention into the "Malay States." This period saw a great influx of new migrants to Penang, which became fragmented under numerous competing groups. The Chinese community was split into dialect and secret society groupings, while the Muslim societies, notably the "Red Flag" and "White Flag" societies, allied themselves with the Chinese groups. These tensions gradually led to the Penang Riots of 1867 where the Red Flag allied itself with the Tua Pek Kong and the White Flag with the Ghee Hin.[29]

In 1867, a bloody riot involving fighting between rival Sino-Malay groups broke out in Penang. After the riots, the colonial government reinforced its belief that it was better for the Malays and Chinese and Indians not to mix too much. Starting from the 1870s, an Inspectorate of Police was established (1872); indirect rule through headmen ended in the Straits Settlements and secret societies were regulated and later disbanded (1885). The British introduced a series of restrictive laws – the Commission of Inquiry on the Penang Riots of 1867 recommended Ordinance XIX of 1869 "for the registration of certain societies and the prevention of unlawful assemblies." This was amended to the Dangerous Societies Ordinance of 1882, which was modified in 1885. The conclusion to this series of legislations was the Societies Ordinance of 1890, when all societies were assumed illegal until approved for registration. All social organizations were secret societies unless their books were open to the government. From the Penang Riots of 1867 to the Pangkor Treaty of 1874 to the Societies Ordinance of 1890, the consolidation of colonial rule over the Peninsular Malaysia gradually led to the dismantling of combined multi-ethnic power, and the creation of racially segregated administrative units along "ethnic" lines. The government reinforced its divide-and-rule policy.[30]

By the turn of the twentieth century, political events also persuaded the colonial authorities to reconsider their policy towards the local Muslim community. The outbreak of the Balkan Wars stimulated expressions of loyalty by Muslims worldwide to the Ottoman Empire. In 1912, funds were raised by the Muslims of Penang for the Ottoman Empire, for those who had shed blood for the cause of Islam. During the First World War, Turkey's position as Germany's ally affected Muslim attitudes towards the British, symbolized by an insurrection of Indian sepoys in the 5th Light Infantry in Singapore in 1915. In response to these political events, the colonial government in Singapore reacted by establishing a Mohammedan Advisory Board as an "emergency measure" in 1915.

A similar board was set up in Penang in 1916. Like the Singapore committee, it was chaired by a British officer from the Malayan Civil Service. The British colonial government was keen on strengthening its supervision over the local religious groups.

In China, the Qing government was overthrown in 1911 and a new republic was established. Under a new young Republican government, deliberate attempts were made by Chinese officials to mobilize "nationalist feeling" among the overseas Chinese communities. In the twenty-five years or so after 1912 the Chinese legal system also experienced a revolution. Old legal ideas were discarded and replaced by new codes on Western lines. The growth of communist activities in China also had strong repercussions among the overseas Chinese communities.

Parallel to the above developments, British colonial governments in Asia also adjusted their policies towards various religious groups. Through decades of political interaction, different religious traditions (Christian, Muslim, Buddhist) were also adjusting themselves in the colonial context. These changes, among other examples, were reflected by a number of legal cases and new legislations found in the Straits Settlements.

By the turn of the twentieth century, in the Straits Settlements, elite status was always achieved through patronage, burnished by images of piety and charity. Since the nineteenth century, the leaders of various migrant communities endowed landed property for various religious purposes, designating their management to be continued by their descendants. With the passage of time, financial, business and charitable issues were becoming confused. Starting from the 1860s (especially after the abolition of the British EIC), the ill-recorded accumulation of property donations had left a trail of legal tangles. The overwhelming majority of cases on religious gifts that came before the courts were from the Muslim or Chinese communities. Many problems arose because of:

1) the confusing relationship between religious observances and filial piety;
2) whether gifts contained a sufficient element of public benefit to be charitable; and
3) the blurred distinction between worship and customary festivity, ceremony or ritual.[31]

By the end of the twentieth century, issues of urban planning also muddied the boundaries between religious and earthly domains. Municipal authorities contested the Islamic concept of a trust in perpetuity, as opposed to the British preference for 99-year contracts. The authorities also considered taking over *awaqf*, regarded as fostering slum conditions amid a prospering settlement. In 1903, the government appointed a commission of enquiry and this resulted in the passing of Ordinance no. XVII of 1905, under which was constituted a corporation called the Mahomedan and Hindu Endowments Board. Financed by income from the *waqf* lands, the Endowments Board played its role in reinventing mosque architecture in the image of the empire and modelling Muslim settlements on Western town-planning ideals. Starting from the 1910s, for instance, a number of new mosques were built and designed by European architects employed by the colonial government. This was followed by a wave of comprehensive redevelopment of the *waqf* settlements in the 1930s, with the publication of the *Hand Book of the Mohamedan and Hindu Endowments Board* in 1932. The opening paragraph of the handbook reiterates the rationale for the establishment of the board:

> In the early days of Penang the East India Company gave considerable portions of land for the purpose of the founding and maintenance of Mohammedan Mosques and Indian Temples. Subsequently a number of similar dedications were made by private persons. With the development of George Town these areas became very valuable as building sites. Rows of Chinese shops were built and much of the land was sold under circumstances which were often obscure and occasionally of doubtful validity. Further, a lack of business men among the managers of the endowments led to considerable confusion in financial matters.[32]

Other than the introduction of the above legislative measures to better "manage" the *waqf* community, the colonial courts in the Straits Settlements also claimed that it would adopt a more "liberal" view towards local religious ideas. By the 1930s, for instance, the British courts had already grown accustomed to more religious practices relating to *waqf* (e.g., to equate feasts commemorating the dead with *kanturis*). In 1936, in *Re Abdul Guny Abdullasa*, the British judge took reference from the two classic cases (*Fatimah & Others v. Logan*, *Aishabee & Others v. Mohamed Kassim & Others*), but claimed that the courts would construe the will as liberally as possible. The judge noted that according to the previous cases, *kandoories* were not usually charitable because of the lack of public benefit, but gifts for the recital of prayers in the names of certain Mohammedan saints, with feasts, could be upheld as a good charitable gift.

In *Re Abdul Guny Abdullasa*, the testator divided his bequest of one-third share for the purpose of three charities, with details at the end of the clause about how much was to be expended on each one:

> Out of the one share set apart for my charity expenses, 12 marakals (gantangs [a cubic measure]) of boiled rice shall be purchased for the ceremony of reciting prayers in the name of the Saint Mohamed on the night of the 17th Rabialawal and 11 marakals of boiled rice for the ceremony of reciting prayers in the name of Katubul Aktabu Saidena Mohaideen Abdul Kader Jailanee on the night of the 17th Rabial-Akir and 10 marakals of boiled rice for the ceremony of reciting prayers in the name of Nagor Syed Hamid on the night of the 17th of Jamadil-Akir. The rice is to be cooked with ghee, flower[s], Sandalwood paste, rosewater, Indian joss sticks, etc. shall be purchased and prayers should be recited through Lebays [a professional class of people who pray for remuneration for their services], after this each Lebay shall be made to recite a prayer in the name of each of the souls of the dead persons and Katam in the name of each of the Saints. In the end alms in money shall be given to the Lebays and to the poor and food (rice) shall be distributed to everyone present including the Lebays. For the first charity (ceremony) about Rs. 15 shall be expended including the value of rice, etc. for the second charity about Rs. 131/4 shall be expended and for the third charity about Rs. 121/2 shall be expended.

The judge related the ceremony to *kenduri* and took reference from previous verdicts:

> It was contended on behalf of the plaintiff that the ceremony enjoined was in the nature of a Malayan "kandoorie" and that following the decisions in Fatimah & others v Logan 1 Kyshe 269 and Aishabee & others v Mohamed Kassim & others 4 Kyshe 212, therefore the trust was void. There is, I think, a clear distinction between the ceremony enjoined and "kandoories," which are feasts in honour of a deceased attended by his relations and are held on the anniversary of the testator's death. Moreover, the deceased in the present case was not a Malay. The ceremonies envisaged are not in perpetuation of the name of the deceased nor are his relatives enjoined to attend, and although food is to be distributed at the conclusion it does not appear to me that the main object is of a festive nature.[33]

The British judge also claimed that "I must confess that I am not sufficiently versed in Mohamedan religious observances to say exactly what it does mean," but he spelled out in great details "what purposes are charitable." His standard was based on the principles of English law:

> Although there may be no definition of the word "charity" in its popular sense, yet in its legal sense it comprises four principal divisions, namely:
>
> (a) trusts for the relief of poverty,
> (b) trusts for the advancement of education,
> (c) trusts for the advancement of religion, and
> (d) trusts for other purposes beneficial to the community not falling under any of the preceding heads.
>
> Trusts under the last heading are no less charitable in the eye of the law because incidentally they benefit the rich as well as the poor, and indeed, every charity that deserves the name must do either directly or indirectly.[34]
> [...]
> Further, one might add that where there is an expressed charitable intention to be found in a will, as in this case, Courts will construe the will as liberally as possible so as to give effect to such intention and, if necessary, will apply the *cy pres* doctrine.[35]

According to the principles of the English Law of charities, a purpose is not charitable unless for the public benefit, with a minor exception in the case of relief of poverty, in that a gift to the donor's poor relatives is charitable. The British judge held that "the will, being a trust created for the holding of a religious ceremony in honour of and in the name of certain Mohamedan Saints, is valid as a whole and that it creates a trust for a charitable object, namely, the advancement of religion." His rationale was:

> Applying these [English] principles to the first charity or ceremony one can, I think, uphold the trust as being one for the advancement of religion. It appears to be a trust

> for the recital of prayers on certain specified dates in the names of certain specified Mohamedan Saints. It is true that the recital of prayers does not necessarily involve the expenditure of money, but I understand that Lebays are a sort of professional class of prayer who receive remuneration for their services and whether or not the fact that rice is to be purchased and cooked in a special way is part of the ceremony seems to me beside the point, as it is to be distributed "in the end" to everybody present, both rich and poor, including the Lebays and also alms in money to the Lebays and poor.[36]

As a conclusion, in this Penang case, a gift by a testator for the recital of prayers on certain specified dates in the names of certain specified Mohamedan saints was held to be a good charitable gift as it is one for the advancement of religion. Another gift for the recital of prayers in the names of each of the souls of the dead in the name of each of the saints was upheld as a valid charitable bequest, and judged as a legal trust for the advancement of religion.[37]

The above verdict had repercussions on other legal disputes in the Straits Settlements. In 1948, for instance, the Singapore Court of Appeal had in *Re Hadjee Daeing Tahira binte Daeing Tedlellah* (1948) held that a trust "to provide yearly at the date of my death in memory of my parents and my sisters and myself a feast for poor persons of the Mohammedan religion in accordance with Mohammedan custom" was charitable, overruling *Fatimah v. Logan & others* (1871). The judge presiding the case said, "In the present case the proposed expenditure is substantially in nourishment and as it is limited to the poor it is a charitable expenditure if it can be considered as a form of relief of poverty." Referring to the old precedent, *Fatimah v. Logan & others* (1871), the judge concluded:

> While the relief of poverty constitutes one of the types of charity recognized by the law it does not follow that every form of expenditure on the poor is charitable e.g. a fund to pay for admission to dog races would not be charitable and we can imagine meals of a type that would not be charitable. In other words the relief of poverty means the provision of the more ordinary necessities of life. However I do not consider that the mere use of the word "feast" suggests that the type of meal contemplated is of necessity one that brings it outside the scope of charity. While this sort of relief is not an ideal or even a satisfactory method of relieving the poor in the absence of any regular system of poor relief, it cannot be said that it lacks that element of public utility which is a necessary part of charity in the legal sense. On this point I am prepared to overrule the case of Fatimah v. Logan & others.[38]

Accordingly, the ruling given in *Fatimah v. Logan & others* (1871) was overruled in 1947.[39]

In the 1940s, the overruling of *Fatimah v. Logan & others* (1871), a classic case related to Muslim *waqf*, found its counterpart in legal cases related to Chinese *sinchew* practices. As illustrated by the above discussion, trust established to sustain *sinchew* practice for the testator's soul in accordance with Chinese custom had been consistently held as not charitable (e.g., in *Choa Choon Neoh v. Spottiswoode* [1869], *Ong Cheng Neo v. Yeap Cheah Neo & Ors* [1872]). From the British court's point of view, trusts established for *sinchew* purposes could not be charities; the gift which formed the subject of the charitable trust had to be of a public rather than a private nature, thus excluding observances which "can lead to no public advantage, and can benefit or solace only the family itself."[40]

The debates continued for decades. In the 1940s, although the court still held that no trust was charitable unless it was for the "public benefit" (or for the benefit of a section of the community), the British judges gradually recognized that much Chinese piety was based on the family or the clan (姓 *seh*, i.e., all persons with a common surname) and the scope of "public benefit" could be interpreted in a more "liberal" manner. This debate is illustrated by the following court case.

In 1948, in *Lim Chooi Chuan v. Lim Chew Chee*, the judge needed to determine whether a trust to found a "temple" (a "Yong Ghee Kong Soo") dedicated for ancestral worship for members of a Chinese *seh* (surname) contained a sufficient element of public benefit to be charitable.[41] Mr Wylie (federal counsel) representing the attorney general, claimed that:

> It is clear from Choa Choon Neoh v Spottiswoode 1 Ky 216 that both religious rites and sacrificial offerings are involved in Chinese ancestral worship. It has also been held that trusts to carry out Sin-Chew ceremonies are not charitable because they do not benefit any section of the public. But I am of opinion that a trust to found a Temple where all the members of a Chinese "Seh" (that is, all having one surname) may carry out ancestral worship may be a charitable trust [...]. While I agree that if a man establishes a trust for ancestral worship for the benefit of his own soul it is not a charitable trust, yet, if he provides a temple for the benefit of the public or a section of the public (e.g. the members of a Chinese "Seh") then it seems to me that the element of charity is inserted into the trust even though each member of the "Seh" carries out in the Temple ancestral worship for his own benefit.[42]

During the debate, it was clearly established that a clan (or *seh*) was a sufficient section of the community for the purpose of charity but the family was not. The court held that a trust for the purchase of burial ground was a valid charitable trust as the use of the property was for members of the same *seh* only. The justification for this was that a *seh* is a public charity since it is set up to provide burial and worship facilities for its members. Trusts made for the establishment and upkeep of temples and worshipping places (for the public) have been considered valid.[43]

As a conclusion, in *Lim Chooi Chuan v. Lim Chew Chee* (1948–49), a trust providing for the carrying out of *sinchew* by the members of one *seh* was held charitable in that it benefitted one part of the public. Gifts to household divinities are not charitable, but a temple house open to the public is. The provision of a temple where all the members of a clan sharing the same surname (*seh*) may carry out ancestral worship was regarded as a charitable object. The provision to the public or a clan (a *seh*) of a burial ground was considered charitable, but a private burial ground for members of a family was not. In this manner, the court construed the testator's will "as liberally as possible."

This verdict further (and indirectly) penalized property supporting "family *sinchew*" practice for "household divinities" and formally endorsed the legal status of property supporting *sinchew* practice beyond the family and placed under the control of "public ancestral temples."[44]

Conclusion

"Non-interference" was a cornerstone of British imperial policy, but this policy has been challenged by works done in the Straits Settlements, a frontier society where various migrant communities were negotiating their economic and political roles in a colonial context. Given the diverse cultural background, the British administration did not find it easy to rule the colony. After the Penang Riots in 1867 (involving fighting between rival Sino-Malay groups), the British reaffirmed its policy of "divide-and-rule." As illustrated by the above discussion, the British were frequently intervening in what they saw as the non-religious aspects of religious institutions in the Straits Settlements. The move was loaded with political and economic calculations.[45] In this process, the British colonial government was backed by the police, the courts and a series of ordinances, targeting different ethnic groups. The Societies Ordinance of 1890 (targeting the Chinese communities) and the Mohammedan and Hindu Endowments Ordinance of 1905 (targeting the Muslim and Hindu communities) were products of such cross-currents.

Through a reconstruction of the legal disputes surrounding the conflicting traditions of property holding found in the Straits Settlements (highlighted by the ideas of Chinese *sinchew*, Muslim *waqf*, and the British rule against perpetuity), this paper suggests that different cultures have developed different institutions to amass "wealth" for religious, charitable and economic purposes. Under British colonial rule, Chinese and Muslim "charitable" institutions entered a protracted process of legal negotiations, between informal traditional norms of the family estate and the formalities of the British courts concerning the idea of charities, the rule against perpetuities and the concept of "mortmain." The blurred distinction between worship and customary festivity, ceremony or ritual created a series of legal debates regarding what was to be regarded a "public" charity.

Starting from the late 1860s, after the withdrawal of the British EIC in the Straits Settlements, those objects of Muslim and Chinese charity that did not agree with English law (e.g., the idea of "public" benefit) were declared null and void in the colonial courts. But after decades of adjustment under a new administration (the Malayan Civil Service), and after a number of legislative measures were gradually introduced, the British judges adopted a more "liberal" view to interpreting local religious ideas; the scope of "public" benefit embedded in the practice of Chinese *sinchew* and Muslim *waqf* was gradually widened.

It is interesting to draw a comparison of the *sinchew* practice and the *waqf* as a trust, holding land and property and being a focus of financial and commercial networks of two important diasporas: the Chinese and the Indian Muslims. There was one major difference: as trusts established for the purpose of family, *sinchew* was repeatedly voided by the British judges, while Muslim *awaqf* eventually gained legal recognition by the British courts. British intervention in *waqf* was unique in several ways. It created a new legislation of *waqf* in its bid to bring these "trusts" under control. A non-Muslim bureaucracy incorporated them under central administration. Britain awed its subjects through municipal reform and magnificent architecture. With this "centralization/ bureaucratization" of *waqf* property, the reputation of the original dedicators has fallen into obscurity.[46] Nowadays, *waqf* property is largely placed under government supervision (via appointed trustees and government representatives). For the Chinese *sinchew*, the tradition survived with an interesting adjustment. No formal legislation or statutes were passed to supervise property donated to support Chinese *sinchew* practice. The law governing these properties is essentially a judge-made law. Property donated to support "family *sinchew*" practice was voided by the British courts and failed to gain legal protection in the colony. But property donated to "*seh* temples" for *sinchew* practice was granted full legal recognition. With this legal protection, Chinese immigrants continued to donate to "public ancestral temples" and carried out their *sinchew* practices as a clan (sharing the same surname, but not necessarily the same ancestors). Even nowadays, Penang has a large ensemble of Chinese ancestral temples (*kongsi*) for individuals with the same surname. Khoo, Cheah, Yeoh, Lim and Tan Kongsi were known as the "five big clans" that formed the backbone (maintaining the power balance) of the Chinese community of Penang. We learn from the above story that British law has exerted great influence on the philanthropic institutions of diasporas; other than injecting new meanings to old religious practices, British law has redrawn the political contour of these native "charitable institutions."

Notes

1 See Vanaja Dharmalingam, "The British and the Muslim Religious Endowments in Colonial Malaya" (MA dissertation, Department of History, Faculty of Arts, National University of Singapore, 1995).

2 See Louis Dumont, *From Mandeville to Marx: The Genesis and Triumph of Economic Ideology* (Chicago: University of Chicago Press, 1977); Karl Polanyi, *The Great Transformation* (Boston: Beacon Press, 1957); see also his *The Livelihood of Man* (New York: Academic Press, 1977); Gregory C. Kozlowski, *Muslim Endowments and Society in British India* (Cambridge: Cambridge University Press, 1985); John Robert Barnes, *An Introduction to Religious Endowments in the Ottoman Empire* (Leiden: E. J. Brill, 1986).

3 The most prominent of these examples include *Tong* (translated by the British courts as "ancestral trust") in China and the Hindu Joint Family in India. See for example, Denis Twitchett, "The Fan Clan's Charitable Estate, 1050–1760," in *Confucianism in Action*, ed. David Nivison and Arthur Wright (Stanford: Stanford University Press, 1959), pp. 97–133; David Faure, "The Lineage as Business Company: Patronage versus Law in the Development of Chinese Business," in *Chinese Business Enterprise: Critical Perspectives on Business and Management*, vol. 1, ed. Raj Brown (London: Routledge, 1995), pp. 82–106; Myron L. Cohen, "Shared Beliefs: Corporations, Community and Religion among the South Taiwan Hakka during the Ch'ing," *Late Imperial China* 14, no. 1, 1993, pp. 1–33. See also H. R. Chakraborty, *Commentary on Hindu Religious Endowments* (Calcutta: S. C. Sarker, 1986).

4 We find in Roger Bird, *Osborn's Concise Law Dictionary* (London: Sweet & Maxwell, 1983), p. 252, the following: "The rule against perpetuities forbids any disposition by which the absolute vesting of property is or may be postponed beyond the period of the life or lives of any number of persons living at the time of the disposition."

5 A. Hudson, *Equity and Trusts* (London and New York: Routledge Cavendish, 2010), p. 186.

6 See Perpetuities and Accumulations Act 2009. See also John Chipman Gray, *The Rule against Perpetuities* (Holmes Beach, FL: Gaunt), 2000.

7 Yeoh Seng Guan, ed., *Penang and Its Region: The Story of an Asian Entrepôt* (Singapore: NUS Press, 2009).

8 Roland St John Braddell, *The Law of the Straits Settlements: A Commentary* (Kuala Lumpur: Oxford University Press, 1982).

9 M. B. Hooker, "The Relationship between Chinese Law and Common Law in Malaysia, Singapore, and Hong Kong," *Journal of Asian Studies* 28 (1969): 723–42.

10 Stephanie Po-yin Chung, "Western Law vs. Asian Customs: Legal Disputes on Business Practices in India, British Malaya and Hong Kong, 1850s–1930s," *Asia Europe Journal* 1, no. 4 (2003), pp. 527–39. See also Choa Choon Neoh v. Spottiswoode (1869), in R. C. Woods, A Selection of Oriental Cases Decided in the Supreme Court of the Straits Settlements (Pinang: S. Jeremiah, 1869), Appendix, pp. 1–102.

11 Choa Choon Neoh v. Spottiswoode (1869); Ong Cheng Neo v. Yeap Cheah Neo (1875); and Tan Jiak Kim and another v. Tan Jiak Kim and others, *Straits Settlements Law Report* 12 (1911): 1–10.

12 Braddell, *The Law of the Straits Settlements*, pp. 74–5.

13 Choa Choon Neoh v. Spottiswoode (1869), p. 3.

14 See also J. D. Vaughn, *The Manners and Customs of the Chinese of the Straits Settlements* (Kuala Lumpur: Oxford University Press, 1971), p. 26–7.

15 Song Ong Siang, a historian of Southeast Asian history, wrote in 1923 his idea of *sinchew*. In reporting the completion of the assembly hall and temple of the Tan clan, he wrote, "One portion of the premises has been used as the repository for the sin-chew or ancestral tablets of the men of that clan." Song Ong Siang, *One Hundred Years' History of the Chinese in Singapore* (Singapore: University of Malaya Press, 1967), p. 186.

16 Choa Choon Neoh v. Spottiswoode (1869), pp. 5–9.

17 Choa Choon Neoh v. Spottiswoode (1869), pp. 5–9. See also S. Buang, *Malaysian Legal History: Cases and Materials* (Kuala Lumpur: Ministry of Education, Malaysia, 1993), p. 19.

18 Yeap Cheah Neo v. Ong Chen Neo, Law Reports, Privy Council Appeal Cases (1875) 6: 381. Doubt has been raised in other cases. In Malaysia and Singapore, some ancestral worship trusts have been upheld as "valid purpose" trusts. For instance, in Re Khoo Cheng Teow (1932) *Straits Settlements Law Report* 226, a testamentary gift for the ancestor's memory was upheld. The report discusses the analogy with masses for the dead.

19 Quoted from Braddell, *The Law of the Straits Settlements*, p. 76.

20 Siti Mashitoh Mahamood, *Waqf in Malaysia: Legal and Administrative Perspectives* (Kuala Lumpur: University of Malaya Press, 2006).

21 Khoo Salma Nasution, "Colonial Intervention and Transformation of Muslim Waqf Settlements in Urban Penang: The Role of the Endowments Board," *Journal of Muslim Minority Affairs* 22, no. 2 (October 2002): 299–315.

22 Fatimah & Ors v. Logan & Ors (1871), in James William Norton-Kyshe, *Cases Heard and Determined in Her Majesty's Supreme Court of the Straits Settlements 1808–1884*, vol. 1, *Civil Cases (Undated)* (Somerset: Legal Library [Publishing Services], 1885), p. 255. See also *Hindu and Mohamedan Endowments Board Handbook* (Penang, 1905), pp. 19–21.

23 *Hindu and Mohamedan Endowments Board Handbook*, pp. 38–9.

24 *Hindu and Mohamedan Endowments Board Handbook*, p. 20.

25 Fatimah & Ors v. Logan & Ors (1871), p. 255.

26 The *Kenduri* was a popular religious ritual feasting on the death anniversary of a saint or the birthday of the Prophet. An important event in the Tamil Muslim calendar, it can take the form of elaborate festivals lasting for many days. See Torsten Tschacher, "The Impact of Being Tamil on Religious Life among Tamil Muslims in Singapore" (DPhil dissertation, National University of Singapore, 2006), pp. 50–51; Susan Bayly, *Saints, Goddesses and Kings: Muslim and Christians in South Indian Society 1700–1900* (Cambridge: Cambridge University Press, 1989), pp. 85, 143.

27 Fatimah & Ors v. Logan & Ors (1871), p. 269.
28 Mustan Bee & Ors v. Shina Tomby & Anor (1882), in James William Norton-Kyshe, Cases Heard and Determined in Her Majesty's Supreme Court, vol. 1, pp. 580–81.
29 See, for instance, Engseng Ho, "Gangsters into Gentlemen: The Breakup of Multiethnic Conglomerates and the Rise of a Straits Chinese Identity in Penang," paper presented at the Penang Story International Conference, Penang, 18–21 April 2002.
30 Ho, "Gangsters into Gentlemen." See also Wong Yee Tuan, "The Rise and Fall of the Big Five of Penang and Their Regional Networks, 1800s–1900s" (PhD thesis, Australian National University, 2007).
31 C. W. Keeton and L. A. Sheridon, The Comparative Law of Trust in the Commonwealth and the Irish Republic (London: Barry Rose, 1976), pp. 301–20.
32 *Hand Book of the Mohamedan and Hindu Endowments Board*, pp. 1–2.
33 Re Abdul Guny Abdullasa (1936) 5 M. L. J. 174.
34 Commissioners for Special Purposes of Income Tax v Pemsel (1891) App Cas 531 at p. 583.
35 Re Abdul Guny Abdullasa (1936) 5 M. L. J. 174.
36 Re Abdul Guny Abdullasa (1936) 5 M. L. J. 174.
37 See Tschacher, "The Impact of Being Tamil on Religious Life," pp. 50–51.
38 Estate of Haji Daing Tahira (1948), M. L. J. 62.
39 Estate of Haji Daing Tahira (1948), M. L. J. 62; see also Ibrahim, *Towards a History of Law*, p. 59.
40 Yeap Cheah Neo & Ors v. Ong Cheng Neo (1875), 381.
41 The will spelled out that "only those of the Chinese race and bearing the surname of Lim shall be and are eligible to attend the Temple for the purpose of worship." Lim Chooi Chuan v. Lim Chew Chee (1948–49) M. L. J. 66–7.
42 Lim Chooi Chuan v. Lim Chew Chee (1948–49) M. L. J. 66–7.
43 Lim Chooi Chuan v. Lim Chew Chee (1948–49) M. L. J. 66–7.
44 Lim Chooi Chuan v. Lim Chew Chee (1948–49) M. L. J. 66–7.
45 Dharmalingam, "The British and the Muslim Religious Endowments."
46 Khoo, "Colonial Intervention," pp. 299–315. See also Michael G. Peletz, *Islamic Modern: Religious Courts and Cultural Politics in Malaysia* (Princeton, NJ: Princeton University Press, 2002), pp. 48–9.

References

Ahmad Ibrahim. *Towards a History of Law in Malaysia and Singapore.* Kuala Lumpur: Dewan Bahasa dan Pustaka, Ministry of Education Malaysia, 1992.

Barnes, John Robert. *An Introduction to Religious Endowments in the Ottoman Empire.* Leiden: E. J. Brill, 1986.

Bayly, Susan. *Saints Goddesses and Kings: Muslim and Christians in South Indian Society 1700–1900.* Cambridge University Press: Cambridge, 1989.

Braddell, Roland S. *The Law of the Straits Settlements: A Commentary.* Kuala Lumpur: Oxford University Press, 1982.

Buang, S. *Malaysian Legal History: Cases and Materials.* Kuala Lumpur: Ministry of Education, Malaysia, 1993.

Bird, Roger. *Osborn's Concise Law Dictionary.* London: Sweet & Maxwell, 1983.

Chakraborty, H. R. *Commentary on Hindu Religious Endowments.* Calcutta: S. C. Sarker, 1986.

Chung, Stephanie Po-yin. "Western Law vs Asian Customs: Legal Disputes on Business Practices in India, British Malaya and Hong Kong, 1850s–1930s." *Asia Europe Journal* 1, no. 4 (2003): 527–39.

Cohen, Myron L. "Shared Beliefs: Corporations, Community and Religion among the South Taiwan Hakka during the Ch'ing." *Late Imperial China* 14, no. 1 (1993): 1–33.

Dharmalingam, Vanaja. "The British and the Muslim Religious Endowments in Colonial Malaya." MA dissertation, Department of History, Faculty of Arts, National University of Singapore, 1995.

Faure, David, "The Lineage as Business Company: Patronage versus Law in the Development of Chinese Business." In *Chinese Business Enterprise, Critical Perspectives on Business and Management*, vol. 1, edited by Raj Brown, pp. 82–106. London: Routledge, 1995.

Gray, John Chipman. *The Rule against Perpetuities*. Holmes Beach, FL: Gaunt, 2000.

Hand Book of the Mohamedan and Hindu Endowments Board, Penang. Penang: Criterion, 1932.

Hindu and Mohamedan Endowments Board Handbook, Penang. 1905.

Ho, Engseng. "Gangsters into Gentlemen: The Breakup of Multiethnic Conglomerates and the Rise of a Straits Chinese Identity in Penang." Paper presented at the Penang Story International Conference 2002, 18–21 April 2002, Penang.

Hooker, M. B. (1969). "The Relationship between Chinese Law and Common Law in Malaysia, Singapore, and Hong Kong." *Journal of Asian Studies* 28: 723–42.

Keeton, C. W. and L. A. Sheridon. *The Comparative Law of Trust in the Commonwealth and the Irish Republic*. London: Barry Rose, 1976.

Khoo, Salma Nasution. "Colonial Intervention and Transformation of Muslim Waqf Settlements in Urban Penang: The Role of the Endowments Board." *Journal of Muslim Minority Affairs* 22, no. 2 (October 2002): 299–315.

Kozlowski, Gregory C. *Muslim Endowments and Society in British India*. Cambridge: Cambridge University Press, 1985.

Kyshe, James William Norton. *Cases Heard and Determined in Her Majesty's Supreme Court of the Straits Settlements 1808–1884*, vol. 1, *Civil Cases (Undated)*. Somerset: Legal Library (Publishing Services), 1885. Peletz, Michael G. *Islamic Modern: Religious Courts and Cultural Politics in Malaysia*. Princeton, NJ: Princeton University Press, 2002.

Polanyi, Karl. *The Great Transformation*. Boston: Beacon Press, 1957.

______. *The Livelihood of Man*. New York: Academic Press, 1977.

Siti, Mashitoh Mahamood. *Waqf in Malaysia: Legal and Administrative Perspectives*. Kuala Lumpur: University of Malaya Press, 2006.

Song, Ong Siang. *One Hundred Years' History of the Chinese in Singapore*. Singapore: University of Malaya Press, 1967.

Torsten, Tschacher. "The Impact of Being Tamil on Religious Life among Tamil Muslims in Singapore." DPhil dissertation, National University of Singapore, 2006.

Vaughn, J. D. *The Manners and Customs of the Chinese of the Straits Settlements*. Kuala Lumpur: Oxford University Press, 1971.

Woods, R. C. *A Selection of Oriental Cases Decided in the Supreme Court of the Straits Settlements*. Pinang: S. Jeremiah, 1869.

Wong, Yee Tuan. "The Rise and Fall of the Big Five of Penang and Their Regional Networks, 1800s–1900s." PhD thesis, Australian National University, 2007.

Yeoh, Seng Guan, ed. *Penang and Its Region: The Story of an Asian Entrepôt*. Singapore: NUS Press, 2009.

Chapter 12

INDIAN SOLDIERS AND POLICEMEN IN CHINA IN THE COLONIAL PERIOD

Madhavi Thampi

There are many grounds for drawing comparisons between overseas Indian and Chinese communities, particularly those that emerged in the colonial era. Major dislocations and changes in socio-economic conditions in the nineteenth and twentieth centuries in these countries gave rise to huge outflows of population. Indian and Chinese communities came to be established not just in neighbouring regions of Asia but also in far-flung regions of the world, in the Pacific and Caribbean islands, in Europe and Africa, and in North, Central and South America. Apart from the traditional presence of merchants, indentured labour was a predominant feature of these communities: the conditions under which Indian and Chinese labour were recruited and transported overseas and under which they toiled were essentially the same. The laws governing their immigration into foreign countries and the discrimination they faced there were also similar in nature.

However, the Indian community in China in the colonial era differed from the general pattern of overseas Indian and Chinese communities in one major respect: it consisted of a high proportion of men from the security services – soldiers, policemen and watchmen. Particularly after the 1880s, anywhere from 50–85 per cent of the Indians in Hong Kong, Shanghai and the treaty ports of East China came from this category.[1] This pattern was not replicated in virtually any other Indian or Chinese immigrant community.

This paper explores why the Indian community in China in the colonial period consisted of such a high proportion of soldiers, policemen and watchmen. In particular, what brought such a large number of young males from the rural areas of particular districts of Punjab province to China? What sustained this trend of migration for so many decades, and what brought it to an abrupt end in the 1940s? The paper will also examine the role of China as a transit point for these Indians, as they sought to migrate to other parts of the world, and also when they sought to return to India for economic or political reasons. Next, it will try to establish the connection between the high proportion of soldiers and policemen in the Indian community in China and its emergence as a major base for militant nationalist groups and activities in the twentieth century. And finally, it will put forward some tentative conclusions on the possible impact of this group of migrants on Chinese perceptions of India and Indians in the modern era.

Colonial Recruitment and Deployment of Indians in China for Military and Policing Duties

It is a fact of India's modern history that the British established their political domination over the country using forces drawn mainly from different Indian communities and regions. Starting with the establishment of the First Bengal Native Regiment by Robert Clive in 1757, the three British presidencies of Bengal, Madras and Bombay recruited, trained and deployed Indian regiments to wage their battles against hostile Indian rulers and rival European forces, and to expand their domain in India, resulting in their more or less complete domination of the subcontinent by the middle of the nineteenth century.

From this, it was but a short step to deploying Indian soldiers for overseas tours of duty. British political and military engagements in different parts of the world far exceeded the ability of forces drawn from Great Britain itself, and therefore tried and tested Indian regiments were a natural choice for deployment overseas. It was in 1801 that Governor-General Wellesley first sent Indian soldiers abroad to Egypt to take part in the campaign against Napoleon. The Napoleonic Wars also provided the occasion for the first dispatch of Indian soldiers to China. Rear Admiral Drury landed in 1808 with 600 Bengal soldiers in Macau, allegedly to prevent it from falling into French hands. Needless to say, the Qing emperor was incensed, and the British admiral deemed it prudent to withdraw from Macau hastily rather than risk a confrontation with the Chinese at this time. However, when the First Opium War broke out in 1839, Indian soldiers were again used by the British. Apart from actual fighting and patrolling duties, they were also used to garrison places occupied by the British, including the island of Hong Kong. About 2,700 Indian soldiers were present at Britain's takeover of Hong Kong on 26 January 1841.[2]

The year 1849 saw the end of the Anglo-Sikh wars which brought the whole of Punjab in Northwest India under British domination. Military service was a traditional and respected form of employment for Sikh and other young males from rural Punjab. Initially, British authorities were reluctant to recruit the vanquished Sikhs into their armed forces, even though they admired their military prowess. However, their experience during the great countrywide rebellion of 1857, in which the British dominion in India was virtually saved by the regiments from Punjab, changed their attitude. British military authorities thereafter were virtually unanimous in their praise for the bravery, reliability and excellent physique of Punjabi and particularly Jat Sikh soldiers. Between 1862 and 1914, the number of Punjab regiments in the British Indian Army more than doubled from 28 to 57.[3] The recruitment of Punjabis and especially Sikhs was justified by the "martial races" theory, which held that certain communities in India were particularly qualified to bear arms by virtue of tradition and certain inherent qualities. At the same time, social and economic conditions in Punjab in the later nineteenth and early twentieth century made military service for younger sons a particularly attractive economic proposition for rural families, as a way of supplementing their income.[4]

As Britain's military involvement in China grew in the later nineteenth and early twentieth century, young men recruited directly from certain districts and villages in Punjab were increasingly attracted to serve in China. It was no coincidence that the same districts which produced the largest section of Indian emigrants to the Far East were also the ones that provided the largest proportion of recruits for the British Army.[5] After the First Opium War, Indians were deployed again in the Second Opium War, the campaign against the Taiping Rebellion, the suppression of the Boxer Rebellion, and in the garrisoning of Hong Kong and certain parts of China at different times.

With the consolidation of the British occupation of Hong Kong, Indians were also recruited to man the police service on the island. For the same reasons that they were recruited for military engagements in China, Sikh and other groups from Punjab were deemed to be particularly suitable for police duties in Hong Kong. From 1845, the ranks of the Hong Kong police force began to consist of almost equal numbers of Indian, Chinese and European men. Many of the Indians were later shifted to jail duties when the policy of increasing the proportion of Chinese in the police force began to be implemented from the late 1870s. The red-turbaned, bearded Indian policeman came to be a familiar sight on the streets of Hong Kong, Shanghai and other treaty ports in the later nineteenth and early twentieth century. A judge of the Supreme Court of the International Settlement at Shanghai in 1906 noted that "The opinion is held here that Sikhs make cheap and efficient police for the rougher work of keeping order among the Chinese in the streets, and that they have done very well in cases of riot."[6] Pay and service conditions in the police force were attractive compared to those prevailing in the army.[7]

The number of Indians employed as police in Hong Kong, Shanghai, Hankou and other Chinese cities was roughly matched by the number employed as private watchmen. Very often, those retired or discharged from the army or police services stayed on to serve as watchmen in factories, shops and restaurants, and other private establishments. This was particularly true in the smaller towns and treaty ports where the foreign concessions were too small for them to have their own police forces. However, lack of security of tenure, often leading to destitution, was a major problem among Indian watchmen in China. Correspondence between the colonial authorities in Hong Kong, India and the British government in London indicates that there was some anxiety about how to handle Indian watchmen who had exhausted all their resources and were unable to make their way back to India or even to the larger cities where they might have got help from other members of their community. However, all attempts to stem the flow of Indians with uncertain job prospects from coming to China in search of employment were, by and large, unsuccessful.

China as a Transit Point for Forward Migration

Claude Markovits has pointed out that the concept of "circulation" rather than migration might be a more appropriate way to characterize the movement of Indians abroad in the colonial era.[8] It has been estimated that as much as 90 per cent of the Indians who went abroad in the colonial era eventually returned home.[9] In the case of the Indians who went to China as well, a large number returned home at the end of their careers or when their service contract was over. But apart from return migration, there was also the practice of forward migration. As new employment opportunities opened up further afield, particularly in the Pacific region and the Americas, places like China became stepping stones for Indians who sought to reach those places.

The greatest concentration of Indian security personnel in China was in Hong Kong and Shanghai. The most comprehensive survey of Indians in Hong Kong, in the 1911 census conducted by P. P. J. Wodehouse, listed a total of 375 policemen, 50 jailers and 388 private watchmen from India. By comparison, only 233 people were listed as being employed in the commercial sector.[10] In Shanghai, the overwhelming majority of those Indians who were employed were to be found in the security services. In 1912, 449 Indians were listed as policemen, 400 as watchmen and 76 as jailers.[11] While service conditions of Indian policemen and jailors in China were better than what they were in India, their pay and promotion prospects were considerably inferior to those of their European counterparts, with very few rising above the rank of sergeant. Also, less than 5 per cent were able to bring over their families to join them. Most of them led very isolated lives, with almost no intermingling with either the local Chinese or the Europeans in the force.[12] All this led to increasing frustration and resentment among them. In 1907, the Indian police of the Shanghai International Settlement went on strike for the first time. Men who were getting paid 16 to 22 yuan per month as salary in Shanghai became agitated on learning from their friends in America that they were earning as much as the equivalent of 60, 80 or even 100 yuan.[13] Ultimatums were issued to the authorities there and in Hong Kong, resulting in a spate of mass resignations among the police and jailors in the Chinese treaty ports and Hong Kong. To the dismay of the British, some Indians also sought passports to proceed to Russia, where it was feared they would be recruited into the military forces of the Russian Empire, which was locked in a bitter rivalry with Britain in the Far East.[14] The British were seriously worried. "Something will have to be done," wrote the secretary of state for the colonies in 1910, "if the present terms don't keep men in the service or attract newcomers."[15]

Hundreds of other Indians made their way from China to other places that were ill-prepared to receive them. In July 1907, the British consul at Lima, Peru, reported the arrival of what he called an "invasion" of 200 Indians from Hong Kong, most of whom he declared were destitute and in poor health, and were unfit for work of any kind. In 1908, another batch arrived in German New Guinea, where they found conditions not to their liking, and so returned to Hong Kong.[16] Apparently, agents of steamship companies seemed to have played some role in the often ill-advised passage of Indians from China and the Far East to the Americas. In some cases, the companies they worked for offered them a commission for each passenger, and so they are reported to have painted rosy visions of profitable employment in the New World in order to attract more Indians on board.

However, starting from 1908, Canada and the United States, as well as other countries, began to impose restrictions to drastically curtail Indian immigration. In just a couple of years, the tide of onward migration of Indians from China to North America had begun to reverse itself. The 1911 Census of the Indian Population of Hong Kong stated that emigration to America was "practically at a standstill." It listed 115 Punjabi males as "unemployed," presumably referring to those who were waiting either to proceed to North America and other destinations or to return to India.[17] The authorities in Hong Kong issued warnings to their counterparts in India to publicize widely that the scope for employment in Hong Kong was drying up. The returning wave of unemployed Indians combined with the continuing flow of migrants from India, waiting for their chance to set sail from China, produced a situation of growing frustration and unemployment.

The Rise of Militant Nationalism

There is a direct connection between the conditions prevailing among Indians in transit in Hong Kong and China, and what has come to be known as the *Komagata Maru* episode of 1914, which inflamed nationalist sentiments among Indians against British rule. The Japanese ship *Komagata Maru* carried 337 Indians from China and Japan to Vancouver, Canada, where they were denied entry. After a standoff lasting several weeks in which they had to remain on board the ship and were denied basic facilities, the passengers were eventually forced to sail back to India, where many were killed and wounded during a protest march from the docks after they disembarked in Calcutta. The Indian businessman Gurdit Singh, who had chartered the *Komagata Maru*, later attributed his decision to the pathetic conditions he saw prevailing among the Indians in Hong Kong:

> When I came to Hong Kong for some private business in January 1914, I could not bear the grief and hardship of the Vancouver emigrants who had been waiting in the Sikh temple in Hong Kong. It was a matter of injustice and darkness, I thought, because our brethren were passing their days in a miserable state for the hope of arriving at Vancouver while staying here for one year and spending money for their eating from their own pockets.[18]

It has been said that in the early twentieth century, China was second only to the United States as an overseas base of militant nationalist activities among Indians.[19] There were three main peak periods of such activities: one around the time of the First World War, the second during the turbulent years in China of 1925–27, and the third during the Second World War. All three upsurges in revolutionary activity in the Indian community can be linked to the predominance of the army and police personnel within the community. This is ironic, considering that these same men had been sent out to China in the first place to defend the interests of the British Empire.

The first phase of militant nationalism, in the years following the *Komagata Maru* episode, was related to the seething discontent and frustration of aspiring Indian emigrants who were either unable to proceed to Canada and the United States, or else were forced to return from there. The British authorities in Hong Kong and Shanghai were well aware that the local Sikh temples (*gurdwaras*), which sheltered many such men, were seething cauldrons of unrest. Knowing that there were close ties of community, religion and even kinship between these men and those serving in many of the Indian regiments deployed in China, the British tried to prevent contact between their soldiers and Indian civilians, particularly in the *gurdwaras*. But they were unsuccessful. The situation became particularly serious for the British because of the mobilization among these sections carried out by the Ghadar Party, a revolutionary nationalist group formed among Indian workers in North America, which was recruiting men and arms overseas to carry out the overthrow of British rule in India by force of arms. The Ghadar Party also had some links with Germany, Britain's enemy in the First World War. The British authorities in China carried out mass arrests and deportations of Indians whom they suspected of seditious activities, but had a hard time on their hands until the defeat of the Ghadar Party's conspiracy in India in the later part of 1915 that ended this particular phase of revolt among Indians in China.

The second high tide of nationalist activity was triggered off by British attempts to use Indian policemen and soldiers during the upsurge in the Chinese nationalist movement in the stormy years of 1925 to 1927. The shooting of striking Chinese workers at Canton in the summer of 1925, in which Indians were used, was condemned by nationalists in India and abroad. Indian troops, who were being rushed to China in August 1927 as reinforcements, were met practically at the docks by political organizers who were already active among the Indian military personnel in China to dissuade them from firing on Chinese. The regiment had to be hastily disbanded and sent back home. Refusals to fire on Chinese and desertions from the Indian to the Chinese side began to occur. Seventy Indian members of the Hong Kong police force resigned en masse and offered their services to the governor of Guangdong, while in Hankou the revolutionary government offered to train and employ 1,000 Indians from the Shanghai police force.[20] Activists of the Ghadar Party set up a network of infiltrators and propagandists within the Indian police force and troops, and its journal, *Hindustan Ghadr Dhandora,* was widely circulated among them. Eventually, a combination of heavy-handed repression by the British authorities, waning Chinese official support and infighting within the community led to the tapering off of revolutionary activities by 1931.

When Japan launched its invasion of China in the 1930s, Indian nationalists, both in India and in China, were vehement in their denunciation. However, the rapid Japanese advance in Southeast Asia after 1941, the fall of British-ruled Hong Kong, Singapore and Malaya, and the news of the Japanese approaching India through Burma led to rising support in the Indian community in China once again for a military overthrow of British rule in India. Support for the Indian National Army (INA) led by the fiery Subhash Chandra Bose, which collaborated with the Japanese in its efforts to march to India, grew rapidly. The INA and its military programme had particularly strong appeal among the soldiers, police and watchmen, many of whom joined its ranks and also handed over their entire savings to the organization. The political wing of the INA, the Indian Independence League, assumed a position of prominence in the social life of the Indian community in China, and had branches in several cities and towns of East and Central China, including those with smaller numbers of Indians such as Beijing, Hankou and Tianjin. However, the defeat of Japan, and the mysterious death of Subhash Chandra Bose in a plane crash near the end of the war, left the movement rudderless and demoralized. Large numbers of Indians in China were rounded up at the end of the war and deported as "collaborationists." This situation, as much as the dismantling of foreign concessions in China in the 1940s, meant that there was no room for Indians from the security services in China at the end of the war. Writing home about his situation, Indian security guard Narain Singh lamented: "Jobless, penniless and friendless in a faraway land of fantastic prices is a dreadful situation. Viewed from whatever angle, the future looks dismal."[21]

Conclusion

The presence of Indian soldiers, policemen and watchmen in China lasted for almost exactly one century, from the middle of the nineteenth to the middle of the twentieth century. Despite the fact that in any given year they did not number more than a few thousand, there is evidence that their presence significantly coloured the Chinese perception of India and Indians in the modern era.

From the time that Indians began to land on China's shores as troops and camp followers of the British, the Chinese were bemused and disdainful of those whom they called *heiyi* or *heigui* (black barbarians or black ghosts). At worst they were seen as "savage" or "wild," and at best as pawns merely doing the bidding of their masters. The role of Indians in policing Chinese cities meant that a wider section of the Chinese populace had experience of their rough and ready methods of maintaining "law and order." That the negative image of Indians did not substantially change even well into the twentieth century can be seen in the words of the poet Xu Zhimo, who wrote regretfully in 1923 that "I dare say when we look at an Indian we do not pity him, we despise him. I think Indians are the most misunderstood people there are; although they are in Asia, too, most people think of them as the same as the red-turbaned Sikh policeman on the streets."[22] Nationalist Indians, who sought to reach out to the Chinese, were acutely aware of this perception. The Comintern representative in China, M. N. Roy, wrote that "the rickshaw coolies and street urchins stand in greater fear of the Indians than of the English or other foreigners."[23] Others, like Rash Behari Bose, said in anguish that he hung his head in shame when he heard of his countrymen being used to shoot down Chinese.[24]

The rise of anti-imperialist activities among the Indian community in China in the early twentieth century, and the forging of ties with nationalist Chinese groups and leaders in the process, had the potential to reverse this stereotype of Indians in the minds of Chinese. It appeared that, finally, Indians and Chinese were fighting on the same side against a common enemy. However, the developments during the Second World War, when a substantial proportion of the community sided with the Indian National Army, which was associated with Japan, prematurely terminated this trend. Indians in China at the end of the war were once again seen as having collaborated with China's enemies and few in China would have regretted seeing them leave China's shores for good in the mass repatriation organized in the late 1940s.

Notes

1 See "A Note on the Indian Population in China," Appendix A, in Madhavi Thampi, *Indians in China: 1800–1949* (New Delhi: Manohar, 2005), pp. 231–7.

2 K. N. Vaid, *The Overseas Indian Community in Hong Kong* (Hong Kong: Centre of Asian Studies, University of Hong Kong, 1972), p. 15.

3 Stephen P. Cohen, *The Indian Army: Its Contribution to the Development of a Nation* (Bombay: Oxford University Press, 1971), p. 44.

4 For a discussion of this, see W. H. McLeod, "The First Forty Years of Sikh Migration," in *The Sikh Diaspora: Migration and the Experience beyond Punjab*, edited by N. Gerald Barrier and Verne A. Dusenbery (Delhi: Chanakya, 1989); and Joyce Pettigrew, "Socio-economic Background to the Emigration of Sikhs from Doaba," *Punjab Journal of Politics* 1, no. 1 (1971): 48–81.

5 A. E. Barstow, *Handbooks for the Indian Army: Sikhs* (New Delhi: Government of India, 1899, reprint 1940), p. 33.
6 Foreign/External-B/March 1909/40–41. National Archives of India (NAI), New Delhi.
7 In 1908, the pay of a soldier in the Indian Army was Rs 9 per month, as compared to the Rs 26–30 earned by an Indian policeman in China. NAI, Foreign/External-B/March 1909/40–41.
8 Claude Markovits, *The Global World of Indian Merchants, 1750–1947: Traders of Sind from Bukhara to Panama* (Cambridge: Cambridge University Press, 2000), p. 6.
9 K. S. Sandhu, "Sikh Immigration into Malaya during the Period of British Rule," in *Studies in the Social History of China and South East Asia*, edited by Jerome Ch'en and Nicholas Tarling (Cambridge: Cambridge University Press, 1970), pp. 348, 352–3.
10 Report of the Census of the Indian Population of Hong Kong taken on 20 May 1911. *Hong Kong Census Reports, 1841–1941* (Hong Kong: Hong Kong Census Department: 1965).
11 Thampi, *Indians in China*, Appendix A, p. 235.
12 Henry Lethbridge, *Hong Kong: Stability and Change* (Hong Kong: Oxford University Press, 1978), p. 178; and Colin Crisswell and Mike Watson, *The Royal Hong Kong Police (1841–1945)* (Hong Kong: MacMillan, 1982), p. 78.
13 *Shanghai Yanjiu Ziliao* 上海研究资料 [Materials for research on Shanghai] (Shanghai: 1984), p.100.
14 NAI, Foreign/Secret-E/March 1907/96–98; CO 129/353, p. 455, 11 December 1908.
15 Great Britain Colonial Office – Hong Kong: Original Correspondence, CO 129/365, no. 101, pp. 564–72 (microfilm).
16 CO 129/344, pp. 512–15, and CO 129/341, no. 249, p. 444.
17 *Report of the Census of the Indian Population of Hong Kong Taken on Twentieth May, 1911* (Table XLI), 103 (56).
18 CO 129/410, 8 April 1914, p. 286.
19 Don Dignan, *The Indian Revolutionary Problem in British Diplomacy, 1914–1919* (New Delhi: Allied, 1983), p. 31.
20 See Thampi, *Indians in China*, pp. 191–5.
21 Letter of S. Narain Singh to the then foreign secretary of the government of India, dated 9 September 1949. NAI, MEA/1949/F. no. 826-CJK/49 (Sec.).
22 Cited in Stephen N. Hay, *Asian Ideas of East and West: Tagore and His Critics in Japan, China and India* (Cambridge, MA: Harvard University Press, 1970), p. 241.
23 Sibanarayan Ray, ed., *Selected Works of M. N. Roy, vol. 2 (1927–1937)* (New Delhi: Oxford University Press, 1988), p. 574.
24 Sohan Singh Josh, *Hindustan Ghadar Party: A Short History*, vol. 2 (New Delhi: People's Publishing House, 1978), pp. 259–61.

References

Primary Sources

Great Britain Colonial Office Records – Hong Kong: Original Correspondence (C.O. 129 series).
Hong Kong Census Reports, 1841–1941. Hong Kong: Census Department, s.n. 1986.
National Archives of India, Proceedings of the Foreign Department, Foreign and Political Department and External Affairs Department.

Secondary Sources

Barstow, A. E. *Handbooks for the Indian Army: Sikhs*. New Delhi: Government of India, 1899, reprint 1940.
Cohen, Stephen P. *The Indian Army: Its Contribution to the Development of a Nation*. Bombay: Oxford University Press, 1971.

Crisswell, Colin and Mike Watson. *The Royal Hong Kong Police (1841–1945)*. Hong Kong: MacMillan, 1982.

Dignan, Don. *The Indian Revolutionary Problem in British Diplomacy, 1914–1919*. New Delhi: Allied, 1983.

Hay, Stephen N. *Asian Ideas of East and West: Tagore and His Critics in Japan, China and India*. Cambridge, MA: Harvard University Press, 1970.

Lethbridge, Henry. *Hong Kong: Stability and Change*. Hong Kong: Oxford University Press, 1978.

Markovits, Claude. *The Global World of Indian Merchants, 1750–1947: Traders of Sind from Bukhara to Panama*. Cambridge: Cambridge University Press, 2000.

McLeod, W. H. "The First Forty years of Sikh Migration." In *The Sikh Diaspora: Migration and the Experience beyond Punjab*, edited by N. Gerald Barrier and Verne A. Dusenbery, pp. 29–48. Delhi: Chanakya, 1989.

Joyce Pettigrew. "Socio-economic Background to the Emigration of Sikhs from Doaba." *Punjab Journal of Politics* 1, no. 1 (1971): 48–81.

Ray, Sibanarayan ed. *Selected Works of M. N. Roy, vol. 2 (1927–1937)*. New Delhi: Oxford University Press, 1988.

Sandhu, K. S. "Sikh Immigration into Malaya during the Period of British Rule." In *Studies in the Social History of China and South East Asia*, edited by Jerome Ch'en and Nicholas Tarling, pp. 335–54. Cambridge: Cambridge University Press, 1970.

Shanghai Yanjiu Ziliao 上海研究资料 [Materials for research on Shanghai]. Shanghai: 1984, p. 100.

Thampi, Madhavi. *Indians in China: 1800–1949*. New Delhi: Manohar, 2005.

Vaid, K. N. *The Overseas Indian Community in Hong Kong*. Hong Kong: Centre of Asian Studies, University of Hong Kong, 1972.

Chapter 13

NEW INDIAN MIGRANTS IN GUANGZHOU AND ITS VICINITY

Jia Haitao

With the continuous development of China's economy, more and more foreigners have come to China as short-term visitors or travellers. Meanwhile, an increasing number of foreigners have settled down or set up enterprises in the local area. Among them, Indians have become a noticeable group with a rising population. The last ten years have witnessed the immigration to and settlement in China of people from developing countries and the phenomenon is becoming increasingly intense. Migrants have swarmed into China because, from their point of view, China is a "paradise" full of opportunities: free and open, safe and friendly, and convenient and easy to make money in. Running at the forefront of China's reform of opening up and as one of the most economically developed areas, Guangdong has always fascinated foreign migrants and investors. Guangzhou, the capital city of Guangdong Province, is especially appealing to them, being renowned as an international metropolitan city and an exciting economic hub. Nowadays, foreigners can be seen everywhere on the streets of Guangzhou. Among them, the proportion of migrants from developing countries is expanding and their number has surpassed that from developed countries. There are many foreigners living in residential districts, as well as in the outskirts of Guangzhou. The increase of immigration from developing countries has not only brought vitality to the Guangdong economy, but also resulted in many problems. Many of these people are illegal migrants and overstayers engaged in criminal activities. The Indian migrants are different from migrants from both developing and developed countries. This group presents its own characteristics which are worthy of special attention.

This paper aims to provide a systematic and comprehensive description of the Indian migrants in Guangzhou and its vicinity on the basis of fieldwork. There are many Indians living in Shenzhen, Dongguan, Zhongshan and Sanshui. Due to Sanshui's proximity to Guangzhou, the livelihood and business activities of Indians living there can be regarded as part of the larger Guangzhou metropolis. The other three cities, all within the Pearl River Delta, are not far away from Guangzhou. Therefore, the lives, social and business activities of the Indians living there are similar and linked closely to those in Guangzhou. Time constraints did not permit further investigation of the Indians living in these three cities outside Guangzhou. The Indian immigrants discussed here are mainly those resident in Guangzhou and Sanshui. Indians in Shenzhen, Dongguan and Zhongshan are included in the discussion only for reference.

Basically, "Indian Migrants" here refer to the long-term stayers or residents of China. However, short-term visitors are sometimes included in this category because some of the statistics here, provided by the local governmental organizations, also include them and make no distinction between them and the long-term stayers. Regretfully, certain difficulties exist in obtaining some information and relevant data, and a number of the distributed questionnaires remain unanswered. A few Indian friends and an Indian restaurant, Vastu, helped me distribute the questionnaires in November 2009. Mr Deepak Gupta, retired director of Procter & Gamble, now CEO of Guptas Group Ltd (Hong Kong) and the owner of the restaurant, and an Indian student named M. Srinivasan collected some of the questionnaires for me. I hereby express my sincere gratitude to them. This paper provides a basic but comprehensive description of the feedback, citing some specific comments from it. In addition, materials and figures obtained through my personal interviews are also incorporated.

A Surge of Indian Migrants Settling in the Pearl River Delta: The Cities of Guangzhou, Shenzen and Sanshui

Since ancient times, there has been cultural exchange and trade contact between China and the Indian subcontinent, but almost all of the recorded names known today were Buddhists of the two regions – for example, Kashyapa Matanga, Dharmaraksha, Buddhabhadra, Jinabhadra, Kumarajiva, Paramartha, Jinagupta and Bodhidharma from India, and Faxian, Xuanzang and Yijing and others from China. None of them were traders. As Jawaharlal Nehru tells us, "It was through Buddhism that China and India came near to each other and developed many contacts."[1] However, Amartya Sen argues, "As it happens, Buddhism is not the only vehicle of Sino-Indian relations, which began almost certainly with trade. Indian traders were engaged in importing goods from China for re-export to Central Asia more than two thousand years ago."[2]

It is generally held that, in the past, there were no detailed records on Indians actively participating in Sino-Indian communications and Indian settlement in China, nor has this history been systematically studied. Amarjit Kaur maintains, "Yet this contemporary movement/migration of Indians in East Asia remains little understood principally because of its recent nature and scarce data."[3] A. Mani points out, "The period of modern Indian immigration dates from the entry of Western nations into Southeast Asia for trade and colonization."[4]

The large-scale overseas immigration from the subcontinent dates back to the 1830s,[5] when Indians appeared in China during the Sino-British Opium War. Indian sepoys participated in the war and some Indians served as policemen and employees in British-occupied territories and concessions such as Hong Kong and Shanghai. As A. Mani describes, "Indian soldiers and traders had travelled to China and Japan during the colonial period. Three major cities that attracted sizeable number of Indians were Hong Kong, Shanghai and Nagoya."[6] However, the success of the Chinese communist revolution in 1949 resulted in the withdrawal of foreign powers, and Indians thereupon also left China.

After the Opium War, the number of Indian traders and businessmen in China increased and they mainly dwelt in the newly acquired British colony of Hong Kong and the "Treaty Ports" of Shanghai and other cities. "By the early 1930s, the tentative estimate of the total number of Indians was about 10,000, of which approximately 5,000 were in Hong Kong, 3,000–4,000 in Shanghai and other cities and towns of eastern China, and about 1,000 in Xinjiang."[7] It is believed that a number of Indians were living in Tibet during that time, especially in Lhasa. However, this number is hard to verify now. From the 1950s to the 1970s, the number of Indian migrants to China gradually declined and reached a negligible level. In the 1980s, despite the changing situation, the number of Indians coming to China was still very limited. With the further advance of China's economic development, China now draws an increasing number of Indian visitors and business migrants. Many tourist visa holders have commercial purposes instead of tourism. Some Indians on short-term visas are engaged in Sino-Indian trade and commerce, cultural study or academic, cultural or educational exchanges and visits. There are permanent residents (who have obtained a right of abode of more than one year) actively adapting to Chinese society as businessmen, entrepreneurs and foreign students, or accompanying their relatives. "According to Indian Embassy estimates, the community numbered only about 4,000 in 2005, located mainly in Beijing, Tianjin, Shanghai, Guangdong (particularly in Shenzhen city), Liaoning, Zhejiang and Jiangsu Provinces."[8]

An Indian government survey tells us, "While concentrated on the enormous foreign trade sector, some Indians have set up manufacturing units in Shenzhen in China and increasingly, a large number of highly educated professionals are seeking employment in banking, finance and information technology sectors."[9] Currently these figures are outdated. The Indians in China today are mainly concentrated in Shenzhen, Beijing, Shanghai, Guangzhou, Yiwu, Foshan and so on. Indians residing in the capital of Guangdong province, Guangzhou, now outnumber those in Shenzhen.

Guangzhou, as an international metropolis, plays a very important part in the economic development of China and is South China's most significant economic centre, where many foreigners visit and live as residents. Guangdong Province, with its highly industrialized economy of the Pearl River Delta including developed cities like Shenzhen, Guangzhou and Dongguan – as well as its proximity to Hong Kong and Macao – attracts even more foreign visitors and residents. The statistical data of the Guangdong Entry–Exit Inspection and Quarantine Bureau shows that Guangdong Province has one of the largest numbers of foreigners' entry and exit among all provinces and autonomous regions in China. In the first half of 2009, the number of foreigners entering and exiting via Guangdong Immigration and Customs reached 6.15 million, accounting for 30.4 per cent of the total number for the country. There are 1.147 million temporary residents and 57,793 permanent residents in Guangdong, and 37,100 foreign nationals from 181 countries are employed there. According to the statistical data of the Guangdong Entry–Exit Inspection and Quarantine Bureau, by the end of first half of 2009, Japanese, South Koreans, Americans, Indians and Filipinos were the top five in terms of the number of permanent foreign residents in Guangdong province.[10]

Based on the statistics from the Visa and Immigration Section of the Embassy of the People's Republic of China in India, China officially issues 400,000 visas to Indian citizens annually,[11] the majority of which are for short-term visits, tourism, business trips, trade negotiations and purchasing activities. Of these, the number of people who have obtained residential permission and taken jobs in China are beyond our knowledge, as we have no access to statistics on the various types of visas. We have not acquired any relevant data on the movement of Indians from the Guangdong Entry–Exit Inspection and Quarantine Bureau. The number of Indians passing through customs in Guangdong, the types of visa they are holding and other related information is incomplete. The departments in charge face problems of data management or missing records. According to the residential registration statistics collected by the Tourism and Public Security Departments, from 2001 to September 2008, the number of Indian visitors or temporary visitors in Guangzhou was 103,415, of whom 95,658 were males; from September 2008 to November 2009, the number was 68,059, of whom 54,036 were males.[12] The data are far from accurate due to the use of inappropriate statistical methods. There are some visitors who do not stay in hotels, but in the houses or apartments of their relatives or friends. Many of them do not report to the local police stations either. There are some private hotels that do not require their foreign guests to register their passport numbers and nationalities. Thus, it is not easy for the Tourism and Public Security Departments in Guangzhou and other cities to collect accurate figures of foreign stayers. It could be said that the data are usually collected by these government organizations in a random or casual way. The comparison of the numbers of Indian visitors – between nearly 70,000 people in less than 14 months from September 2008 to November 2009 and 103,415 people in eight years or so from 2001 to September 2008 – does not demonstrate as such a recent sudden increase in visitors from India, but illustrates how unreliable the statistical data for 2001 to September 2008 is. In fact, the numbers of Indians coming to settle in China declined after the financial crisis.

We tried to obtain the statistics for each year and even each quarter, only to find that the sum of statistics for each quarter does not match closely with the annual statistics, and the sum of annual statistics also does not match the total. Therefore, what is presented here is just a rough list of general data, instead of a more detailed and specific one. The two groups of data serve as a comparison point. However, the statistics between September 2008 and November 2009 are basically credible.

Based on the research carried out on the statistics of the Foreigners Management Department of the Guangdong Entry–Exit Inspection and Quarantine Bureau and other agencies, we discovered that some Indians reside permanently in Guangdong using their tourist visas. There are also some who conduct businesses or make a living through other means in an illegal way. These agencies do not however possess accurate statistics about Indian visitors and the overstaying population. The outbreak of the global financial crisis had a strong impact on China's economy, which in turn affected Sino-Indian trade. In 2009, the number of Indians coming to China decreased, while the number of Indian permanent residents in China dropped substantially. It was estimated that in 2007, before the financial crisis, the number of temporary and long-term Indian residents in Guangdong reached between seven and eight thousand people,[13] including

Table 1: The Population and Demographic Distribution of Indian Permanent Residents in Guangdong Province (By June 2008)

City	Population
Guangzhou	1882
Foshan	160
Shenzhen	519
Dongguan	277
Zhuhai	82
Zhongshan	48
Other cities	427
Total	3394

Source: Foreigners Management Department of the Guangdong Entry–Exit Inspection and Quarantine Bureau in November 2009

permanent residents (who obtain right of abode for one year or more), illegal overstayers with expired passports and a number of medium and short-term tourists or visitors.

According to the statistics from the Foreigners Management Department of the Guangdong Entry–Exit Inspection and Quarantine Bureau, the Indian permanent residents in Guangdong (those who had obtained permanent right of abode) numbered 3,394 by the first half of 2008 and they mainly lived in Guangzhou, Shenzhen, Foshan, Dongguan, Zhuhai and Zhongshan.[14] Detailed information is provided in Table 1.

Based on the information provided by the Consulate General of India in Guangzhou to *Guangzhou Daily*, the number of Indian permanent residents in Guangdong totalled 3,394, which basically coincides with the data we gathered above. However, the demographic distribution we obtained from the Consulate General of India doesn't exactly match the above table. The details are as follows: Guangzhou, 1,755; Shenzhen, 845; other cities, 794. According to what we have learned from the consulate, despite its small number of Indian migrants, Foshan possesses the largest group of foreign nationals.[15]

Basic Classifications and Professions of the Indians in Guangzhou

It is difficult to ascertain the exact number of companies established by Indians in Guangdong, for many of them are registered in the name of Hong Kong trading companies or third-country companies. According to our survey, there are only 86 registered Indian companies (foreign capital enterprises whose titles include "Indian") in Guangdong. These companies operate in the pharmaceutical, packaging, catering, import and export industries, etc. Some of the more famous ones include Bank of India, Bank of Baroda, Araco Manufacturers Ltd, and Real Oriental Diamond Product Co. Ltd. Even India's most famous entertainment television station, Zee TV, has set up a bureau in Guangzhou. Most of the above companies are located in Guangzhou and Shenzhen, while there are some in the cities neighbouring Guangzhou, such as Sanshui and Foshan.[16]

Table 2: Indian Companies and Corporations in Guangdong Province

Name	Location
Ranbaxy Limited	Guangzhou
Essel Packaging Ltd	Guangzhou
KGK Diamond Co. Ltd	Shenzhen
Prosperos Channels	Guangzhou
Stainless Limited China Representative Office	Guangzhou
Sparkle Way limited	Shenzhen
Bank of India	Shenzhen
Bank of Baroda	Guangzhou
H. Daya International Co. Ltd	Shenzhen
Real Oriental Diamond Product Co. Ltd	Pany, Guangzhou
J&M International (HK) Ltd	Shenzhen
Promise Asia HK	Shenzhen
Rasbova International (FE) Co.	Shenzhen
Remix Elect Ltd	Shenzhen
Seven Ocean Impex (HK) Ltd	Shenzhen
M/S Sealord Exports	Shenzhen
Luck World Trading	Guangzhou
Hallimax (Fareast) Limited	Guangzhou
KB Group Ltd	Shenzhen
Expert International Trade Ltd	Shenzhen
Brilliant Standard Ltd	Shenzhen
Tim industries Ltd	Shenzhen
Akashi Export Ltd	Shenzhen
Picasso Company Limited	Shenzhen
Araco Manufacturers Ltd	Guangzhou
Sanwin Watches and Electronics Ltd	Guangzhou
Oriental Overseas Ltd	Guangzhou
Shakti International Ltd	Guangzhou
Po Wai Industrial Co.	Guangzhou
KB China Ltd	Guangzhou
Component and Equipments Ltd	Guangzhou
Tectfield Investment Ltd	Guangzhou
Day's Impex Limited	Guangzhou
PNS International	Guangzhou
Prime International (Guangzhou Branch)	Guangzhou
Super Merry industries Ltd	Guangzhou
Vin Mart Canada Inc.	Guangzhou
Victex International	Guangzhou
Argain Trading Co.	Guangzhou

Name	Location
Triveni Exports Co. Ltd	Guangzhou
Nagrani (HK) Ltd	Guangzhou
China Export Ltd	Guangzhou
Aspinet Limited	Guangzhou
Badar Co. Ltd	Guangzhou
Ballon Marketing (China)	Guangzhou
Lamos International (China) Ltd	Guangzhou
Concord Asia (Mfg&Exporters)	Guangzhou
Efficentask Limited	Guangzhou
Jackie's Guangzhou Office	Guangzhou
Fone International Co. Ltd	Guangzhou
JB International	Guangzhou
Indo Manu Trading Co. Ltd	Guangzhou
Success Electronics Limited	Guangzhou
Trang Overseas	Guangzhou
Zee TV	Guangzhou

Source: Information provided by Consul Muraly Nair of the Indian Consulate General in Guangzhou on 22 January 2010.

In Guangzhou, the number of Indian restaurants is increasing. Currently, there are 16, including eight bigger ones and one opened by a Nepali. The most expensive one is located in the Asian Hotel and is characterized by luxurious decor and song and dance performances.

Indians in Guangzhou can be grouped into three categories according to statistics provided by the Indian Consulate General in Guangzhou: white-collar workers and senior managers in Indian, multinational or foreign capital enterprises, business people mainly engaged in trading, and Indian students specializing in medicine.[17] These statistics are more or less the same as the results of our survey, except that we list the categories according to their numbers.

The results of our survey indicate that the majority of Indians in Guangzhou are business people engaged in trading. The second largest group consists of medical students studying at Sun Yat-sen University, Southern Medical University, Jinan University, etc. The third group is made up of white-collar workers and higher-ranking managers in Indian, multinational, foreign capital and Chinese enterprises. Of course, families of these Indian business people and workers constitute a large proportion of the total Indian population. Students excluded, Indians dealing with trade in Guangzhou and Guangdong province are mainly males, with some of their spouses doing odd jobs. Besides, there are some Indians with expired visas or without any certificates of identification who not only reside illegally, but also occasionally take part in or get involved in illegal activities.[18] However, most Indians live a comfortable and stable life with promising businesses. As a result, many Indians in Guangzhou are better off compared with other immigrants from developing countries in terms of both business and living conditions. However, some Indians left China with the onset of the economic crisis because they found it hard to maintain their businesses.

Among the Indians living in Guangzhou and Guangdong Province, the Sindhis, Gujaratis, Tamils and Telugus occupy a larger proportion of the total. Geographically speaking, most of them came from Bombay, Chennai, Delhi, Calcutta and Kerala.[19] Most of the Indians who live in Guangzhou and Guangdong Province are successful businessmen, among which the Sindhis are the most outstanding. The Sindhi people are usually compared to Chinese businessmen from the Wenzhou and Chaoshan area, because they are perceived to be frequent world travellers and "born businessmen." Nowadays, many Sindhis who have settled down in China are from Taiwan (about thirty to thirty-five families).[20] They used to do business in Taiwan, and then moved to Mainland China because there are more opportunities there. Many Sindhis have already become residents of Guangzhou and other cities in Guangdong province.

According to the statistics obtained,[21] the employed population of Indians in Guangdong was 1,858 in May 2009 (with 1,108 family members), among whom 831 work in Guangzhou (with 628 family members). In 2008, the number of Indian students in Guangdong was 428. These students mainly majored in medicine schools of Southern Medical University, Jinan University and Sun Yat-sen University. A few others were studying in South China Normal University, Shantou University and Shenzhen University, among others.

Most of the Indian students in China are self-sponsored, and only a few are government-sponsored or exchange students.

> There are twenty Indian students studying in China under the government scholar exchange scheme, nine in Shanghai, seven in Beijing, and two each Guangdong Provinces. Besides this, there are about 700 self-sponsored Indian students enrolled in Chinese universities to pursue international medical degree courses in 2005.[22]

Indian students who pursue education in China at their own expense mostly specialize in medicine, and few study other majors. How do we explain this phenomenon? The Indian educators who were interviewed by the *Global Times* claimed that Indian students rush to study medicine in China because the education quality of the medicine major in China is considered excellent and the tuition fee is relatively low. It was estimated that in 2005 there were nearly two thousand Indian students studying in China through international education agencies, such as the famous Asian Education Consultancy in South India.[23] Some medical colleges or universities with medical departments recommended by Indian agencies are prestigious institutions, while some may be less well known to Chinese people.

According to our present knowledge, there are a number of reasons that Indian students seldom pursue majors other than medicine in China. One is the language barrier. Another is the quality of education offered by Chinese universities, which are considered less advanced than their Western counterparts due to the poor internationalization of Chinese higher education. Except those students involved in Chinese language study, most overseas students find it difficult to adapt themselves to the local teaching environment: most majors and courses of Chinese universities are taught in Chinese, using Chinese textbooks and reference books, all of which act as a huge obstacle for overseas students who know little or nothing about Chinese languages. In Guangzhou, Indian students who study medicine also face language problems, although this issue is being addressed.

Some overseas students holding student visas are engaged in illegal employment or participate in trading or other activities. However, most Indian students focus on their studies and they are not often involved in employment or other activities, much less in illegal activities.

Indian students in Guangzhou are a special group, and they differentiate themselves from other Indians. Research shows that most Indian students are basically satisfied with their learning experiences in China, but are not without problems. Some are quite disappointed mainly because of the treatment they receive and because the study conditions are not as good as advertised by admission agencies. This is not to criticize the facilities and living conditions of Chinese universities, but it is more about problems related to instructors and language barriers. As reported by the *Hindu*, while all universities enrolling Indian students claim to offer full English classes, in reality, the situations vary among these universities.[24] Actually, hardly any Chinese university is capable of teaching medicine entirely in English. Some universities usually recruit temporary Indian teachers, while most Chinese teachers seldom shoulder teaching tasks. Even worse, in order to reduce expenses, the few Indian teachers employed often teach many courses and even work as part-time teachers teaching Indian students in other universities.

There are other problems existing in Indian students' daily life and study in China. For example, a number of Indian students do not adapt to local cuisine. Vegetarians, especially, find it difficult to stick to their eating habits, owing to there being few genuine vegetarian restaurants in China. Indian students' communications with Chinese students also face some minor obstacles, among which the biggest problem is that they cannot really integrate into the campus culture or truly participate in the activities of Chinese students. The administration or faculty members of the universities have little experience in getting foreign students involved in academic or other kinds of activities on campus, which leads to Indian students' relatively inactive lifestyles. Some Indian students also encounter difficulties when they have finished their courses and pursue internships. Some universities promise to offer internship opportunities for English-speaking people during enrolment, but fail to do so. Moreover, some hospitals do not provide internships for those Indian students who speak Chinese less fluently. Therefore, many Indian students have to go back home to find internships, which results in great inconvenience for them.

The Living Conditions of Indians in Guangzhou and Their Promotion of Sino-Indian Trade

Guangdong Province, especially the Pearl River Delta, has one of the fastest growing economies in China. It is also among the most developed and prosperous provinces in China. The delta, dotted with cities like Guangzhou, Shenzhen, Dongguan, Foshan, Zhongshan, Sanshui and other cities, is China's leading area for implementing economic reforms and attracting foreign capital. It is also one of the regions with the largest number of foreign-funded enterprises. China is often referred to as the "factory of the world," mainly because of the concentration of powerful manufacturing and widespread foreign-funded enterprises or joint-venture factories in the delta. Therefore, this area boasts a huge number of foreign visitors and foreigners settlers. Furthermore, due to its role as the "factory of the world," there exists a huge international labour market in the delta. Ten years ago, foreigners in the Pearl River Delta mostly came from advanced economies such as Western countries or Asian countries like Japan and Korea. Nowadays, people from developing regions like the Middle East, South Asia and Africa also pour into China, and their number has surpassed that of people from developed regions.

According to media reports, since 1996, the number of foreigners working and doing business in Guangzhou has increased yearly. Foreigners in Guangzhou live in concentrated areas, which can be geographically classified into four major districts:

(1) The area around Huan Shi Dong Lu, including the Xiu Shan Building, Tao Jin Lu, Garden Hotel and Jian She Liu Lu. Foreigners in this area are mostly African merchants, working staff from European and Japanese consulates, and nationals of India.
(2) The area surrounding Tian He Bei Lu, including Ti Yu Dong Lu, Tian He Lu, Long Kou Xi Lu and Lin He Zhong Lu. There are many offices of foreign organizations in the CITIC Plaza building. Foreigners in this area are mainly businessmen from Japan, America and Europe.
(3) There are also large residential districts with complete facilities in Panyu District, including Clifford Estate, Riverside Garden and the Star River Hotel Apartments, where foreigners are mostly from Asian countries like Japan, Thailand and Malaysia.
(4) The area around San Yuan Li, including Jin Gui Village and Ji Chang Lu. Most of the foreigners here are African businessmen who deal with clothing and shoes. Currently, some Koreans involved in Sino-Korean trade have also begun to gather and scttlc in this area.

With the increase in the foreign population, illegal foreign immigrants, overstayers and employees also increase. Illegal business operations – that is, those operating without business licenses – are also included here. According to news reports, the illegal groups mentioned above mainly come from South Asia, the Middle East and Africa. In the past, few illegal immigrants chose China as their destination, and thus the Chinese government paid little attention to this issue. However, more recently this has become a serious social problem. Statistics show that the proportion of foreigners illegally involved in business and employment without an Aliens Employment Permit or a Foreign Experts Certificate is as high as 69 per cent, and many illegal employments concentrate on education (English training), culture (commercial performance), sports, housekeeping, leisure services and so on.[25] The problems of illegal overstaying and employment also exist among the Indian population. Some Indian restaurants are found without licenses and some cooks without labour permits. There are also some Indians working in other professions without labour permits.[26]

Illegal overstaying, illegal employment or illegal business operations were once rampant among Indians living in Guangzhou and the surrounding areas. Nowadays, the situation has been improved to a certain degree. As early as 2006, an Indian called Vee by reporters said in an interview that he knew that many Indian restaurants operated illegally, because these operators did not have business licenses, tax certificates or hygiene permits. Furthermore, foreign employees in these restaurants did not hold green cards and labour permits. He also showed business cards of these illegal restaurants to reporters. He further pointed out the illegal exchange of foreign currencies and renminbi in these restaurants, the Indian owners of which had registered companies in Hong Kong. He felt that these Indians seriously affected the reputation of the whole Indian population. However, the Chinese law enforcement authorities paid little attention to these issues, or they simply imposed a fine, which did not root out the problem.[27]

It is only in the last twenty years that China has become a hotspot for foreign immigration. Consequently, China lacks experience in immigration management and has not set up a complete framework of related laws and regulations. Nevertheless, the surge of illegal immigrants, overstayers and employees compels many local governments to start thinking about the issues brought about by foreign immigration. Guangdong province precedes other provinces in tackling these issues. Nonetheless, the related regulations in Guangdong are still in their initial stage and far from perfect. Furthermore the implementation of relevant national regulations is still under consideration. Undoubtedly, the establishment of specific laws or regulations will not only combat foreign illegal immigration, overstaying and employment, but also specify the conditions under which foreigners can live and work in China. These in turn provide convenience for their long-term stay and employment in China.

On 24 November 2009, the government of Guangdong Province issued the "Service Regulations on Strengthening the Management of Foreigners in Guangdong Province" (second version of the "Proposed Draft for Discussion"). It stipulates that foreigners who have been working or studying in China for over one year can purchase housing properties in Guangdong province in the name of an organization or a person, but for private use only. According to the report of the *Guangzhou Daily*, the draft also specifies that citizens, legal persons and other organizations are prohibited from providing housing to foreigners with invalid passports or expired visas. Moreover, it strictly stipulates the obligations and liabilities of the lessors, real estate agents, property companies, employers and so on who provide housing services to foreigners.[28] According to the draft, when foreigners check in at a hotel, the staff should verify their identifications and require them to go through the proper registration procedures. The lessors who provide housing for foreigners should also verify their identification to see if they have permission to stay. Some Indians stay illegally in China and some of them have bought property here, but most of them live in rented accommodation. Indian students mainly live on campus, while a few rent houses outside the university and even fewer buy property.

Compared to Africans or even immigrants from industrialized countries, Indians living in Guangzhou and surrounding districts are regarded as relatively successful. Actually, they quite enjoy their lives here because they have adapted themselves well to the local environment. They get along quite well with Chinese people, and thus have few limitations and suffer little discrimination here. The Chinese government helps protect the rights of the Indians, and the Chinese citizens are friendly to them.

Wang Gungwu correctly points out, "Unlike the Chinese, the Indians did not undergo any assimilation process in the counties of their adoption."[29] Indians in Guangdong are gregarious and prefer to live together with other Indians. Indians are closely related to each other and gather together and form their own chambers, clubs, guilds and other associations. They celebrate every Indian festive occasion together and once held an open-air festival on the busiest road of Guangzhou; the local government reacted positively and allowed it. Furthermore, the local TV station broadcast the pageant live.[30] From this we can see that Indians are willing to actively display their Indian cultural identities and characteristics without any hesitation or worry.

The Indians in Guangzhou tend to club together in their own organizations, such as the Indian Chamber of Commerce and the Guangzhou Indian Women's Association. They have also organized clubs, guilds and other informal associations. But most Indians in China do not like to talk about them with outsiders, since foreigners are not allowed to register this kind of organization and the Chinese government deems their existence illegal.

Of course, Indians also take part in all the other foreign organizations which accept other nationalities. An example of this is the Progressive Group, an organization for all the foreigners in Guangzhou, regardless of their nationality or gender. Compared with other foreigners in Guangzhou, Indians are relatively good at communication. Most of them can speak English fluently, which provides more convenience in joining social activities. Indian women in Guangzhou energetically take part in all kinds of activities, and most of them have a close relationship with the Guangzhou International Women's Association.[31]

Because of the sensitivity to foreigners' participation in political activity, the Chinese government has a prudent policy in the application and registration of foreign organizations in China: all foreign organizations have to go through a complicated and strict procedure before they are allowed to register with the Chinese government. However, the Indian organizations in Guangzhou are non-governmental organizations, and so are the other foreign organizations in Guangzhou. It is beyond any question that the purpose of forming these organizations is only to establish a platform for information sharing, social gatherings, communication and helping each other, definitely not for illegal purposes, and certainly not directed against the Chinese government. Some organizations are only founded in order to learn more about Chinese culture, while others are founded for business purposes. Of course, Indians do not have to organize activities or hold meetings in the name of associations or organizations. The Indian's way of communication and cooperation is highly internationalized and diversified, which may be an example for Chinese to learn from.

The living environment of the Indian people in Guangzhou is relatively comfortable, safe and convenient. Most Indian people have their own houses, and live in very good housing conditions. The district areas in which Indians live are shown in Table 3.

Makarand Paranjape maintains, "The Indian Diaspora has become an important economic force to India."[32] They have become the driving force of Sino-Indian trade.

Table 3: The Residential Areas of Indians in Guangzhou

District	Community
Panyu	Qifuxincun, Biguiyuan, Lijiang Garden, Olympic Garden, etc.
Tianhe	Longkou Dong Road, Longkou Xi Road, Longkou Zhong Road, Tianhe Bei Road, Huating Road, Linghe Street, Huayang Street, Huangpu Avenue, Shuiyin Road, etc. Mainly reside in Park View Court, Huijing New Town.
Yuexiu	Taojing, Huanshi Dong Road, Songfengxi Road, Lijing Road, Mingyue Road, Siyouxin Road, etc.
Haizhu	Bingjiangdong Road, Chigang, etc.
Liwan	Zhongshanqi Road, Baohua Road, etc. Mainly residing in Liwan Squar, Dongjunliyua, Fuli Square.
Baiyun	Jinghu Garden, Fulitaoyuan, etc.
Huadu	No Indian residents.
Nansha	No Indian residents.

Source: Based on information obtained from the local public security bureaus in November 2009

It is through their efforts that the volume of Sino-Indian trade skyrocketed. According to the information provided by Muraly Nair, consul of the Consulate General of India-Guangzhou, in 2008, the total trade volume between India and Guangdong reached US$7.027 billion.[33] Between 2004 and 2008, Guangdong's exports to India increased at an average annual rate of 93.2 per cent. In 2007, telephone and related components had become Guangdong's largest export items to India, with total export value of US$429 million; followed by batteries, whose total exports reached US$185 million. In addition, automated data analysers and air conditioners also accounted for a large proportion of Guangdong's export to India. In 2007, aluminium ore, copper and iron ore were India's main exports to China.

The Perceptions of China by Indians based in Guangzhou and Their Integration with Chinese Society

For the following part, I will start by analysing the completed questionnaires as well as primary materials gained through my personal interviews and investigations. Then, after citing some materials obtained from newspapers and magazines, I will conduct a more systematic discussion of the attitudes of Indians in Guangzhou towards China and their integration with the local community. First, allow me to make a brief introduction of the informants participating in the interviews and investigations. The number of collected questionnaires amounted to 34 and the number of face-to-face interviews totalled 17. Most of them were permanent residents living in China for more than one year. Ten of them were students, while others had different careers.

My surveys and interviews showed that most Indians in Guangzhou were satisfied with their lives and the investment or commercial environment in China. Their impressions of Chinese people were generally positive. Chinese people are praised as hard working. "Disciplined," "kind-hearted," "friendly," "enthusiastic," "hospitable" and "helpful," were the most frequently mentioned descriptions. A few Indians regard Chinese as astute and practical.

Though some Indians considered it difficult to communicate with Chinese or to integrate into local society because of personal factors, most respondents experienced smooth and successful integration with their local environment. Nevertheless, the language barrier posed a great challenge to many of them, since most Chinese cannot communicate with Indians in English. Consequently, they – and this includes those Indian students pursuing medical majors – hold a relatively low opinion of Chinese education. With regard to Sino-Indian relationships, their opinions varied. Some perceived problems and barriers. Some were quite satisfied with the current situation.

The survey showed that the Indians in Guangzhou did not have any difficulties or experience any discrimination. They obtained visas relatively easily and gained quick access to China, and this was especially convenient for students. In a word, Indians have experienced smooth transitions and enjoyed successful livelihoods and career development in Guangzhou. In fact, Indians were more likely to succeed a few years ago because at that time the Chinese government had few restrictions on foreigners' immigration, housing, employment and business operations. Now, the management of these areas is becoming more and more standardized.

Like many entrepreneurs from developing countries, Indians discovered opportunities in China and made China their entrepreneurial paradise. Many Indians, especially the early settlers and investors, found it easy to make a fortune or succeed in China. More and more Indians poured into China to realize their dreams of becoming rich – dreams that are difficult to achieve in their motherland or other countries. They also refer to it as the "China Dream" – China being the ideal place to fulfil their dreams and create miracles. This "'China Dream' had started to lure more Indians across the Great Wall."[34] In the early period, it was quite easy to try one's luck in China because illegal settlement, employment or business operations in Guangzhou did not arouse the attention of the Chinese government, and many people came to China just holding tourist visas. At that time, Indians faced no limitations in working locally.

In February 2004, 27-year-old Banu Kumar came to Guangzhou alone and worked for his friend. Today, he has his own company and two houses, as well as a beautiful Chinese wife and a lovely daughter. Kumar came from Hyderabad, a South Indian city, and only held a high school diploma. In 2005, at the suggestion of a Chinese friend, he began to buy computer accessories in Guangzhou to resell back to India. In February 2007, he rented an apartment in Hong Kong and registered his own company. A year later, he bought an apartment in Guangzhou for office use and moved the company to Guangzhou. Today, his company has become the supplier of many Indian software companies. His stories and wedding photos were published in the famous newspaper *Guangzhou Daily* and he himself has become a celebrity in Guangzhou.[35]

Ashok Amarnani is another Indian with a family in Guangzhou. He and his wife Neeta, along with three young daughters, began formally residing in a house bought in Regal Court, Longkou West Road in Guangzhou in April 2000. He opened the first

Indian restaurant in Guangzhou, named "Jewel of India." He now has many branches in Guangzhou and the Pearl River Delta and enjoys a booming business and great publicity. Through catering operations, he has made many friends in China and provided useful information for those Indian newcomers or Indians living in Guangzhou. Ashok is always pleased to offer assistance. Under his influence, many Indians have chosen to settle in the residential district where he lives, and thus Regal Court now has one of the largest Indian populations. In 2003, there were more than a hundred Indian families living in the district.[36] The majority of these people are very successful businessmen and entrepreneurs. They have close contact with each other and contribute to a rich Indian culture in the community.

Nowadays, Ashok not only takes care of his chain of restaurants, but also operates other businesses. His wife Neeta Amarnani works in an English school in Guangzhou and his three daughters studied in Guangzhou International School. The girls are all proficient in Chinese, and this makes him and his wife feel very proud. Presently, two elder daughters are studying in renowned universities in Canada and Australia respectively, while the younger girl is studying at high school in Guangzhou.[37] Ashok has already become a personage among both Indians and Chinese and his entrepreneurial story was published in the newspaper some time ago. In 2003, when he was interviewed in a local newspaper, he mentioned that, "In Guangzhou, new companies are registered by Indians on a weekly basis."[38]

In an interview with a Chinese journalist, an Indian businessman known as Sam noted that "China is a better place for doing business. In India, official corruption, low efficiency and high cost make business operations highly difficult. A similar situation won't be found in China."[39] He found large markets and factories producing various commodities of high quality with reasonable prices everywhere in China. He particularly emphasized Guangzhou's role as the factory of the world and spoke of the Canton Trade Fair. Sam's assessment of Guangzhou can be concluded as follows: infinite business opportunities, convenient life and little discrimination in religious belief. With regard to eating habits, he still prefers Indian food and the numerous Indian restaurants in Guangzhou provide great convenience for him.

Vee, the Indian businessman mentioned earlier, originally conducted business in Nepal and later came to Chengdu, China. After six months in Chengdu, he moved to Guangzhou and served as the business representative of a Hong Kong company. He married a Chinese woman and has a son. His work mainly involves purchasing commodities and collecting marketing information for reports to send to the headquarters in Hong Kong. He had been staying in Guangzhou for nearly ten years when he gave his first media interview in 2006. He was quite satisfied with the business environment in Guangzhou and has taken it as his second hometown. He believes that the living conditions of Guangzhou are much better than those in India, and almost all local infrastructure, such as the air-conditioned buses, is superior to that in India.[40]

However, Vee had a negative impression of Guangzhou's public security, because both he and his wife had been robbed. He also complained about the increasing appearance of counterfeit money in Guangzhou. Furthermore, he felt that some Chinese businessmen lacked credibility. He was cheated once in Dongguan and lost a prepayment of US$6,000 because of the counterpart's bankruptcy. Another Indian businessman, Sam, had a similar experience. From his perspective, not all companies are dishonest and large companies are better than small companies. However, since they cannot acquire all their desired goods from large companies, they have to deal with smaller ones.[41]

Research shows that Indians have no objection to Sino-Indian marriages. Many people believe that as long as both parties are happy with one another, congenial marriage is the natural consequence. Many people hold a positive attitude, noting that transnational marriages enable Indians to adapt more easily in China. Among the Sino-Indian transnational marriages, most cases are of Indian men marrying Chinese women. The proportion of Indian women marrying Chinese men is very small, with only two cases in Guangzhou. Many Indians find this hard to explain. Some Indians believe this phenomenon is due to the number of Indian men coming to China, which surpasses that of Indian women (nearly 90 per cent of them are men).[42]

Among Sino-Indian marriages, that of an Indian with Malaysian nationality named Sathya Moorthy is the most well known. It is widely held that he married a mayor in Hunan Province and that his father-in-law is a senior officer serving in the central government. He is mainly engaged in educational exchanges between China and India and personally runs a company called Sino-India Education and Technology Alliance in China. Moreover, he serves as India's first dean of the Confucius Institute, affiliated to VIT, a university located in Tamil Nadu, India.[43] He has various other business interests as well.

Some overseas students from the Sino-Indian exchange projects easily succeed in China. They are often picked by Indian companies as representatives in China for their language skills and familiarity with the Chinese community. Once they became familiar with the business and the market, they quickly establish their own enterprises, which grow rapidly into large groups. Sagnik Roy, Shahul Hameed and K. G. Sridevi are each examples of this. They are also married to Chinese women and enjoy a happy family life.

Sagnik Roy was considered the most successful Indian businessman in China by the *Times of India* newspaper. He is from Calcutta and came to study in China through an ICCR student exchange program in 1990. Later, he worked for several US companies in China and became an agent for an Indian pharmaceutical company in China. He established his own enterprise after he married a Chinese trader named Tian Fu. His company now has total assets valued at over US$600 million. The company is jointly owned by him, his wife and some of their relatives. He has also planned a project worth US$11 million to build a factory producing computer hardware in his hometown of Kolkata.[44]

Shahul Hameed lives in Shenzhen, Guangdong province. He graduated from Jawaharlal Nehru University as a PhD student specializing in Chinese studies. He obtained a scholarship sponsored by the Chinese government during his academic years and studied Chinese in Beijing for two years. He was selected by the Ministry of Commerce of India as its representative in China in 1997, and three years later founded his own company. His wife is Chinese and they have two daughters. He serves as the managing director of Huge Mark Corporation Ltd. The headquarters of his group is located in Shenzhen, where he now lives. He also has factories in other areas of China.[45]

K. G. Sridevi is one of the only two known cases of Indian women who married a Chinese in Guangzhou. She studied overseas and was an MPhil student specializing in Chinese language at Jawaharlal Nehru University. She studied Chinese at a Chinese university in Beijing sponsored by governmental grants. She fell in love with a Chinese youth and finally decided to settle in China. She and her husband jointly opened a company called Sundial Metals & Minerals, specializing in the import and export of metal ores. Their business is booming. According to her, she focuses less on business and more on taking care of her family and organizing activities for foreign women's associations in Guangzhou. She is very active and popular among foreign women in Guangzhou. Her fluent Chinese is considered the best among Indians there; many Indians believe the level of her Chinese even exceeds that of most Chinese people. She is passionate about China and satisfied with her life in Guangzhou and China. She specifically called China a "paradise" for foreigners and Indian entrepreneurs. Her parents also live with them. She has very good marital relations with her husband, with differences only in terms of their eating habits.[46]

The lives of Indians in Guangdong, especially in Guangzhou, is colourful, and the majority of them are reluctant to go back to India. They have maintained their individuality and their own cultural traditions, but also live in harmony with the local community. This is in part due to their appreciation of Chinese culture and the friendly and kind-hearted nature of Chinese people. It is important to point out here that China's economic and foreign policies have played a most crucial role. Over the past thirty years, China has always attached great importance to attracting foreign investment and has been dedicated to the protection of its investment environment. This is conducive to the survival and development of foreign investors, including Indians. Additionally, the minor fluctuations in Sino-Indian bilateral relationships have had no significant impact on Indians' investment and daily life in China. On the other hand, in recent years, the Indian government has imposed many restrictions on Chinese investment locally. Chinese projects in India and Chinese workers involved in some projects have constantly been facing problems such as project termination and labour repatriation. However, the Chinese government did not adopt corresponding policies in response. This is likely a key factor contributing to the success of Indian business people and entrepreneurs in China.

Conclusion

The Indians in Guangdong are a unique group. They live, study or expand their businesses in their own way. They maintain their distinct lifestyles and behaviour patterns, preserve their own cultures and manifest these remarkable features in every aspect. Indian corporations in Guangdong have unique corporate cultures and modes of operation. In a nutshell, Indians, whether individually or otherwise, whether working for companies or running personal businesses, can adapt to China's social environment quite well and are adept at dealing with Chinese people and government departments at all levels. Indians are smart businessmen and are born social activists or diplomats. They are highly sociable and acquainted with all kinds of international etiquette and rules. They possess sound commercial awareness and speak fluent English. They pay attention to communicating with Chinese people, not only with the intention of fitting into Chinese society and developing social relationships, but also to skilfully maintain extensive contacts with local foreigners from other countries, especially those from developed countries.

Their outstanding communication skills and business development capacity as well as excellent English language skills help them delve deep into the various Chinese and foreign networks in Guangdong. In terms of the above qualities, Indian immigrants outstrip most those from less-developed economies and are on a par to those from developed economies. The Indians in Guangdong enjoy a high independence and social profile; they not only share powerful internal cohesion and solidarity, but also have a strong self-protection awareness and ability. Compared to the migrants from developed and developing countries, Indians in Guangdong live a dynamic and comfortable life with successful businesses. Both businessmen and investors are quite satisfied with their local operations.

The commercial success and the opportunities acquired by Indians in China provide a great contrast to the Chinese living in India. The situation of the latter group makes them envious and even indignant. Many Indians consider China to be "paradise" for life and business and are willing to live in China permanently. They work hard to expand their businesses and advance their careers, thus attracting their Indian counterparts to join them. There is no doubt that the number of Indians in China, especially those in Guangdong, will continue to increase, and this will further contribute to the rising number of Sino-Indian marriages. This situation will have a major and even substantial impact on every aspect of Sino-Indian relations. Undoubtedly, the Indians in China provide a great impetus to the development of Sino-Indian trade, the deepening of Sino-Indian cultural exchange and facilitating the overall improvement of Sino-Indian relations. Whether it is subjective due to emotional linkages or objective due to business demands, the majority of Indians in China hope that China and India can live in harmony and strengthen mutual cooperation. These people are the driving force of Sino-Indian communications. There is a strong possibility that, because of their presence, a qualitative change in Sino-Indian friendship and Sino-Indian relations will no longer be an unrealistic dream.

Appendix I: Questionnaire on living Conditions of Indians in China

This survey is organized by the Institute for Chindian Studies of Jinan University, for the purpose of academic research and international symposium. Your name is required in this survey with the view of avoiding repetition or reuse of personal data and keeping continuity of statistics accumulation. We will not publish your name in our questionnaire report or academic papers (except with individual permission). Your personal information will be kept strictly confidential. If you are not comfortable with any questions, you can leave the questions blank. Should you have any problems, please refer to the enclosed documents or contact us (telephone number: 15817058267, 85228343, e-mail: tjiaht@sina.com).

Table 1: Personal Information

Name (optional)	Age	Occupation	Sex	Marriage status	Nationality of spouse	Visa type	Length of stay in China

Table 2: Evaluation of working and living environment (degree of satisfaction)

	Extremely satisfied	Satisfied	Just so so	Dissatisfied	Extremely dissatisfied
Overall satisfaction degree of life in China					
The friendliness degree of the Chinese					
A sense of security					
The satisfaction degree of Chinese education					
Chinese investment and business environment					
Convenience of access to and from China					
Your career development in China					
Evaluation of China's overall development					
Evaluation of living conditions of Chinese					
Evaluation of current Sino-Indian relationship					
Communication and socialization with Chinese					

Appendix II: Detailed and in-depth questions (Please attach an additional sheet if you need more space to continue your answers).

1. Is it easy to make money in China? Why? How do you evaluate the investment and business environment in China? Have you ever encountered bribe solicitation or been intentionally spited by others?
2. How do you evaluate China's overall development? What is your biggest obstacle here?
3. How do you evaluate China and the Chinese people? What impressed you the most?
4. What is the biggest difference between China and India (Chinese and Indian people)?
5. How do you evaluate Sino-Indian relations? What is the obstacle to the further improvement of Sino-Indian relations? Does the fluctuation of Sino-Indian relations affect your business or career?
6. What is your reason for working/doing business or studying in China?
7. Is it easy to obtain a visa? Is entry or exit of China convenient?
8. Did you apply for your study in China through an agency or other channels? What's your opinion of Chinese education and the university you currently stay in?
9. Is it easy for Indians to get themselves integrated into Chinese society? Why?

10. Are you in favour of intermarriages with Chinese people? What are the attitudes of Indians towards these intermarriages?
11. What is the reason for the imbalance existing in Sino-Indian intermarriages? (There are more Indian men marrying Chinese women than Chinese men marrying Indian women.) Why are there intermarriages with Chinese people?
12. Is the concept of caste held strongly among Indian people? What are the linkages and channels of communication between Indian people? What community do you belong to?
13. What are the major categories of Indians in China in terms of language and geography?
14. What specific measures should be taken by Chinese and Indian governments to expand bilateral trades and enhance economic and cultural exchanges mutually?

Notes

1 Jawaharlal Nehru, *The Discovery of India* (New Delhi: Jawaharlal Nehru Memorial Fund, 1981), p. 192.
2 Amartya Sen, *The Argumentative Indian* (New Delhi: Penguin, 2005), p. 166.
3 Amarjit Kaur, "The Movement of Indians in East Asia: Contemporary and Historical Encounters," in *Rising India and Indian Communities in East Asia*, edited by K. Kesavapany and A. Mani (Singapore: Institute of Southeast Asian Studies, 2008), p. 28.
4 A. Mani, "Community Formations among Indians in East Asia," in *Rising India and Indian Communities in East Asia*, edited by K. Kesavapany and A. Mani (Singapore: Institute of Southeast Asian Studies, 2008), p. 49.
5 High Level Committee on Indian Diaspora, "The Indian Diaspora." http://www.Indiandiaspora.nic.in. 14 September 2014.
6 Mani, "Community Formations," p. 50.
7 Brij V. Lal, Peter Reeves and Rajesh Rai, eds, *The Encyclopedia of the Indian Diaspora* (New Delhi: Oxford University Press, 2007), p. 211.
8 Ji Ping, "China: Indians' New Found Land," in *Rising India and Indian Communities in East Asia*, edited by K. Kesavapany and A. Mani (Singapore: Institute of Southeast Asian Studies, 2008), p. 199.
9 High Level Committee on Indian Diaspora, *Report of the High Level Committee on the Indian Diaspora*, p. xxiii. http//www.Indiandiaspora.nic.in. 14 September 2014. All data in this paragraph are cited from "Statistics from Ministry of Public Security: In 2009 the Total Number of Entries and Exits of Passengers Amounted to 34.8 Million," http://www.gov.cn/gzdt/2010. 14 January, 2010.
10 Wang Pan, Kong Bo and Che Xiaohui, "The Employment and Livelihoods of Millions of Foreigners Pose a Great Challenge to Chinese Immigration Policies," *Economic Information Daily*, 14 October 2009. All figures of the statistics in this paragraph are cited from this report.
11 Interview with Sathya Moorthy, 20 January 2010. Moorthy maintains a good relationship with the Chinese embassy. He told me that he obtained this figure from the Chinese ambassador.
12 Statistics of the Bureau of Tourism and the Guangdong Entry–Exit Inspection and Quarantine Bureau in November 2009, obtained in November 2009.
13 This estimation is based on my overall survey.
14 The account in this paragraph and the statistics of Table 1 are based on the information obtained from the Foreigners Management Department of the Guangdong Entry–Exit Inspection and Quarantine Bureau in November 2009.
15 Lu Yun, "Nearly 2,000 Indians in Guangzhou," *Guangzhou Daily*, 16 October 2009.
16 The basic information about Indian companies and corporations in Guangzhou, including the list of such companies, were provided by the Indian Consulate General in Guangzhou, on 4 November 2009 and 22 January 2010.

17 Lu, "Nearly 2,000 Indians in Guangzhou." The following account of this paragraph is also based on this report.
18 Interview with the policemen of the Foreigners Management Department of the Guangdong Entry–Exit Inspection and Quarantine Bureau in November 2009.
19 Interview with K. G. Sridevi, 20 January 2010.
20 Interview with Mr Govind Vidhani, 16 November 2009.
21 Statistics in this paragraph were obtained from the Foreigners Management Department of the Guangdong Entry–Exit Inspection and Quarantine Bureau, in November 2009.
22 Ji, "China: Indians' New Found Land," p. 200.
23 Ren Yan, "Indian Students Rushed to Study Medicine in China," *Global Times*, 4 November 2005.
24 Pallavi Aiyar, "Indian Doctors – Made in China," *Hindu*, 17 May 2006.
25 Wang Pan, Kong Bo and Che Xiaohui, "The Employment and Livelihoods of Millions of Foreigners Pose a Great Challenge to Chinese Immigration Policies," *Economic Information Daily*, 14 October 2009.
26 Interview with the policemen of the Foreigners Management Department of the Guangdong Entry–Exit Inspection and Quarantine Bureau in November 2009.
27 The account in this paragraph is based on Su Hui and Peng Minggang, "Love and Hate: Indians in Guangzhou," *World View*, no. 9, 2006.
28 Lian Qingqing, "Foreigners Who Have Been Working or Studying in Guangzhou over One Year Can Purchase House Property in Guangdong," *Guangzhou Daily*, 25 November 2009.
29 Wang Gungwu, "India and Indians in East Asia: An Overview," in *Rising India and Indian Communities in East Asia*, edited by K. Kesavapany and A. Mani (Singapore: Institute of Southeast Asian Studies, 2008), p. 7.
30 Su and Peng, "Love and Hate."
31 The account in this paragraph is based on my interview with K. G. Sridevi, 20 January 2010.
32 Makarand Paranjape, preface to *In Diaspora: Theories, Histories, Texts*, edited by Makarand Paranjape (New Delhi: Indialog), p. v.
33 Lu, "Nearly 2,000 Indians in Guangzhou." The following account of this paragraph is also based on this report.
34 Pallavi Aiyar, "Indians' Gold Rushing in China," trans. Wang Wan Ying, *News of the World*, 10 April 2007.
35 The account of this paragraph is based on Wen Junhua, "Indian Businessman Kumar: My Home Is in Guangzhou," *Guangzhou Daily*, 16 October 2009.
36 Liu Youcai, Sun Ying, Kuai Lehao and Tian Shuangyue, "Indians Registered a New Company Every Week," *Southern Metropolis Daily*, 23 September 2003.
37 Interview with Ashok Amarnani, 19 June 2010.
38 Liu, Sun, Kuai and Tian, "Indians Register a New Company Every Week."
39 Su and Peng, "Love and Hate." The account is based on this report.
40 Su and Peng, "Love and Hate."
41 Su and Peng, "Love and Hate."
42 Interview with Govind Vidhani, 16 November 2009; interview with Deepak Gupta, 9 March 2010.
43 Interview with Sathya Moorthy, 20 January 2010.
44 Saibal Dasgupta, "An Indian Student Achieved Great Business Success in Chinese Market," *Times of India*, 8 September 2006.
45 The account of Shahul Hameed in this paragraph is based on my discussions with him in November 2008 and October 2009.
46 The account of this paragraph is based my interview with K. G. Sridevi, 20 January 2010.

References

Aiyar, Pallavi. "Indian Doctors – Made in China." *Hindu*, 17 May 2006.

______. "Indians' Gold Rushing in China." Translated by Wang Wan Ying. *News of the World*, 10 April 2007.

Chen, Xiang, Gong Xuan, Huang Yuelin. "Guangzhou Police Has Launched a Series of Special Campaigns Aiming at Cracking Down on Illegal Immigrations." *Guangzhou Daily*, 21 May 2009.

Dasgupta, Saiber. "An Indian Student Achieved Great Business Success in Chinese Market." *Times of India*, September 8 2006.

Ji, Ping. "China: Indians' New Found Land." In *Rising India and Indians in East Asia*, edited by K. Kesavapany and A. Mani, pp. 195–206. Singapore: Institute of Southeast Asian Studies, 2008.

Kaur, Amarjit. "The Movement of Indians in East Asia: Contemporary and Historical Encounters." In *Rising India and Indians in East Asia*, edited by K. Kesavapany and A. Mani, pp. 27–48. Singapore: Institute of Southeast Asian Studies, 2008.

Lal, Brij V., Peter Reeves and Rajesh Rai, eds. *The Encyclopedia of the Indian Diaspora*. New Delhi: Oxford University Press, 2007.

Lian, Qingqing. "Foreigners Who Have Been Working or Studying in Guangzhou over One Year Can Purchase House Property in Guangdong." *Guangzhou Daily*, 25 November 2009.

Liu, Youcai, Sun Ying, Kuai Lehao and Tian Shuangyue. "Indians Registered a New Company Every Week." *Southern Metropolis Daily*, 23 September 2003.

Lu, Yun. "Nearly 2,000 Indians in Guangzhou." *Guangzhou Daily*, 16 October 2009.

Mani, A. "Community Formations among Indians in East Asia." In *Rising India and Indians in East Asia*, edited by K. Kesavapany and A. Mani, pp. 49–70. Singapore: Institute of Southeast Asian Studies, 2008.

Nehru, Jawaharlal. *The Discovery of India*. New Delhi: Jawaharlal Nehru Memorial Fund, 1981.

Paranjape, Makarand. Preface to *In Diaspora: Theories, Histories, Texts*, edited by Makarand Paranjape, pp. i–vi. New Delhi: Indialog, 2002.

Ren, Yan. "Indian Students Rushed to Study Medicine in China." *Global Times*, 4 November 2005.

Sen, Amartya. *The Argumentative Indian*. New Delhi: Penguin, 2005.

Su, Hui and Peng Minggang. "Love and Hate: Indians in Guangzhou." *World View*, no. 9 (2006).

Wang, Gungwu. "India and Indians in East Asia: An Overview." In *Rising India and Indians in East Asia*, edited by K. Kesavapany and A. Mani, pp. 3–11. Singapore: Institute of Southeast Asian Studies, 2008.

Wang, Pan, Kong Bo and Che Xiaohui. "The Working and Living of Millions of Foreigners Pose Great Challenge to Chinese Immigration Policies." *Economic Information Daily*, 14 October 2009.

Wen, Junhua. "Indian Businessmen Kumar: My Home Is in Guangzhou." *Guangzhou Daily*, 16 October 2009.

Chapter 14

WHO IS A CHINESE-INDIAN? SEARCH FOR THE CULTURAL IDENTITY OF THE CHINESE-INDIANS IN KOLKATA, SIHUI AND TORONTO

Zhang Xing

Introduction

Scholars from several disciplinary perspectives have discussed the issue of ethnic and cultural identity among "diasporic" and immigrant communities. Stuart Hall, for example, offers two ways of looking at cultural identity. "The first position," he writes, "defines 'cultural identity' in terms of one, shared culture, a sort of collective 'one true self,' hiding inside the many other, more superficial or artificially imposed 'selves,' which people with a shared history and ancestry hold common."[1] The second definition, Hall notes, recognizes that "there are also critical points of deep and significant *difference* which constitute 'what we really are'; or rather – since history has intervened – 'what we have become.'"[2]

This issue of defining cultural identity is relevant for examining who, in a wider diasporic context, is "Chinese" and, in a specifically Indian context, who is a "Chinese-Indian" or "Indian-Chinese"?[3] But it should be noted, as Tan Chee-Beng points out, that there is a

> distinction between cultural identity and ethnic identity. Ethnic identity refers to ethnic identification with a particular ethnic category; cultural identity refers to cultural expression. Individuals identifying with the same ethnic category may emphasize different cultural traits in expressing their ethnic identity. An approach to the study of ethnicity is to see how individuals identify themselves ethnically and then study how they express ethnic identity culturally; in other words, how people use cultural features to express ethnic identity.[4]

During the early history of China, the region around the Yellow River Valley formed the core of Chinese civilization. It was around this area, during most part of the first millennium BCE, that the concept of a common culture, comprising shared behaviour, institutions, and beliefs, was formulated.[5] This was the place to which Han Chinese in general trace their descent, specifically to the legendary Yellow Emperor. With the teachings of Confucius officially propagated during the Han dynasty (206 BCE–220 CE) and the standardization of the script before that, a sense of homogeneity and core Han Chinese culture took shape, and, according to Myron L. Cohen, "a unified culture" that "provided standards according to which people identified themselves as Chinese" developed.[6] Cohen explains how the actions of the Chinese state, especially with the emphasis on education and examination system, led to the spread of these core cultural values, rituals and Confucian etiquette into the local society. He writes,

> Rituals firmly linked China's common people to a national culture through their emulation of local elites. This process was facilitated by the local-level social mobility that by late traditional times was institutionalized in many different ways: through partible [*sic*] inheritance, the pronounced commoditization of land and other valued goods, the examination system, and the strong deemphasis of hereditary status discriminations implied by all of these. As to the elites, even those living in rural communities were immersed in much larger social networks based on marriage, commercial ties, the examination system, and many other elements. The social universe of the elite was united by a culture largely colored by both etiquette and ritual precisely because involvement in that culture had to be based primarily on norms recognized and accepted in China as a whole.[7]

Viewed thus, it was, at least in theory, these core cultural practices, that developed in ancient China and permeated into local levels that the Chinese immigrants carried with them to foreign lands. However, as Tong Chee-kiong and Chan Kwok-bun have noted in their study, explaining what constitutes "Chinese" is, in fact, not always obvious or easy for the Chinese overseas. For these – mostly *not* from among the cultural elite – Chinese identity, either self-perceived or imposed by others, could, rather, be explained through physical features, biological descent, Chinese-language abilities, cultural practices, and other attributes. In their survey of the Chinese in Singapore, Tong and Chan show that those who call themselves "Chinese" are actually not very clear about what makes them Chinese. Giving an example of this ambiguity pertaining to one of their informants, they point out that when asked about the attributes of being Chinese, the person "was slightly stunned; except for the fact that he knew he was 'Chinese,' he confessed he could not articulate what it was that made him Chinese."[8]

Explaining this sort of reaction, Tong and Chan write, "In fact, one characteristic of our informants during the interviews, particularly the younger ones, was the combination of deep confusion, painful self-examination, and rationalization when confronted with the exercise of defining their Chineseness." They also note that there were "many inconsistencies and contradictions" among the respondents. "One English-educated Chinese informant," they write, "claimed that the Chinese language is the central marker of ethnic identity, but she herself does not speak Chinese at all. Yet she saw no problem in calling herself Chinese."[9]

The first-generation Chinese immigrants seem to be relatively clear about their Chineseness. Calling themselves the "Tang people" (*tangren* 唐人; i.e., people of the Tang dynasty, 618–907 CE), one of the golden ages of Chinese history, these people, mostly from South China, identified with their place of origin. For them, Tong and Chan suggest, "ethnic identity is anchored in territoriality and grounded in the historicity of China. Their sense of ethnicity is tied to 'place,' 'locality,' or 'community.'"[10]

Tong and Chan also explain the role of state in ascribing ethnic identity to the Chinese living in Singapore. The Singapore government classifies people according to their race and ethnicity, which then appear in their birth certificates and identity cards. Children of mixed marriages are classified based on the father's ethnicity. This official classification has significant impact on the education choices of the children of mixed marriages because, under the country's educational system, they are required to learn their "mother tongue" according to the ascribed ethnic identity.[11]

The research undertaken by Tong and Chan indicates that most people considered birth and descent as the main criterion for Chineseness. "If you are not born Chinese, you can't become Chinese," said one of their informants. Some also considered appearance, an attribute also related to birth and descent, as another main reason for a Chinese identity. One person arguing for this "decisive factor" said, for example, "I think as long as your *face* is Chinese, even if you do not speak Chinese, you are *still* a Chinese."[12] Although other informants questioned why someone lacking knowledge of Chinese language and customs should be considered Chinese, saying, "I think Chinese who do not speak Chinese are not really Chinese Chinese,"[13] the authors come to the following conclusion:

> Birth, appearance, and descent set the first parameters. A Chinese cannot unbecome himself/herself racially. However, as we have tried to show in this essay, there is still plenty of room left for the ethnic actor to move around. Human agency is still very much alive and well. Now, is the ethnic actor free or not free? Is ethnicity involuntary or voluntary? In the case of the Chinese in Singapore, the answer is: It is not either/or; it is both. It is both non-negotiable and negotiable. Ethnic actors have indeed increased their degree of freedom over the years but are best reminded of the limits.[14]

Likewise, the Chinese in India are not a unique community in regard to their notion of Chinese identity. Similar to other Chinese overseas communities, they are also ambiguous about it; like some other groups in Southeast Asia, they too have suffered political persecution and marginalization; and in emigrating to a third country or returning to China, they follow the patterns seen among other immigrant Chinese communities. There is, however, a distinction, as will be noted below, between those who settled in Kolkata, and those who live/lived in other parts of India. The Chinese in Kolkata, especially those who live in Tangra, rarely indicate processes of assimilation and acculturation. Those who live in other areas of Kolkata and India, on the other hand, have had more intimate interactions with the local host communities. Indeed, as I have argued elsewhere, the Chinese community in Tangra, comprising mostly of Hakkas, is distinctive in regard to their preservation of Chinese ethnic and cultural identities.[15]

It must also be pointed out here that unlike some other countries, such as in Singapore, India does not generally record the ethnic affiliation in their official documents. This applies to the Chinese with Indian nationality and generally also to others.[16] Thus, there is an absence of state pressure to officially opt for a certain ethnicity, or be forced to have one. It is possible that this has bearing on "Chinese-ness" in India. However, it is not possible to delve deeper into this matter in this essay. In any case, similar to the Chinese communities overseas discussed above, the Chinese in Kolkata also find it difficult to answer what makes them Chinese. They likewise emphasize biological descent and ancestry, the ability to speak a Chinese language, and cultural practices and beliefs as the main elements of their Chinese identity. But they also claim to be Indians at the same time. For them the Indian identity comes from the fact that they were born in India and, in some cases, their Indian citizenship. Thus they call themselves "Chinese-Indians" or "Indian-Chinese."

In this essay, I attempt to examine this complicated issue of hybrid identity among the Chinese in Kolkata. The term "Chinese-Indian" (or "Indian-Chinese") is not only used by the people in this community, it is also a name given to a unique style of hybrid cuisine originating in Kolkata that has become popular across the globe. While it is maybe easier to identify the Chinese and Indian ingredients of this hybrid cuisine, explaining who is a Chinese-Indian or Indian-Chinese could be an arduous task. Matters have become more complex because many Chinese from India were deported to China during the India–China conflict in the early 1960s. A substantial number have also emigrated to Canada during the 1970s and 1980s. These two groups are sometimes called "Chinese-Indian-Chinese" and "Chinese-Indian-Canadians" respectively. Such multi-hyphenated designations are not unique. Rather it is part of a common phenomenon in a globalized world, where people migrate and remigrate within few generations. In addition to explaining what the term "Chinese-Indian" signifies to the Chinese immigrants in Kolkata and those now living in China and Canada, I will also try to find the "Indian" element(s) among these three groups of Chinese-Indians who are linked through their shared experiences in India.

Being Chinese-Indian in Kolkata, India

A Bengali-language magazine pointed out recently that the Chinese in Kolkata when asked about their identity stated that they were "Indians," but as far as their customs are concerned they emphasized that they were "Chinese."[17] Indeed, there are people among the Chinese immigrant community in India, such as Paul Chung, the president of the Indian Chinese Association for Culture, Welfare and Development in Kolkata, who insist that they are Indians first. Paul Chung is assertive about his Indian nationality, insisting on using the term "Indian-Chinese" instead of "Chinese-Indians" when referring to the Chinese community in India. In his cultural practices and beliefs, however, Paul Chung rarely shows any indication of Indian influences, except that he can converse in Hindi. For him, "Indian-Chinese" is a person with Indian nationality and Chinese ethnicity, a view seemingly shared by many other Chinese in Kolkata.[18] This hybridity is perhaps what the Bengali-language magazine was trying to convey.

From the late eighteenth century, the time they started settling in Kolkata, until the early 1960s, the Chinese immigrants successfully preserved their "Chinese" identity through endogamy, especially within the same dialect group, cultural practices, distinctive educational system and confined dwelling places. Interactions with the local Indian population were largely limited to business dealings and other work-related activities. In fact, during the early stages of their migration to India, the Chinese preferred, even in their business dealings, to associate with the British living in India rather than the locals.[19] Most of these early immigrants were attracted to British India for economic reasons and wanted to return to China after a few years of work. There were others who regularly sojourned between China and India. Indeed, a majority of early immigrants, mostly consisting of male labourers, saw India as a temporary residence and not a new homeland.

During the early twentieth century, when chaotic situations in China caused by civil wars also forced women and children to migrate to India, the Chinese community in Kolkata was transformed dramatically. For the first time, issues such as communal welfare, education and other social matters became a concern for the community. Such concerns led to the establishment of Chinese-medium schools, cultural associations, Chinese-language newspaper offices and other institutions. Even at this time, India was perceived as a temporary dwelling place. This perception can be discerned from the curricula at the Chinese-medium schools established in Kolkata and other Indian cities, where all courses were about China and the stated goal of education was to one day return to China and contribute to the construction of the "motherland."[20]

The multicultural and multi-ethnic society of Kolkata was conducive to the Chinese maintaining their exclusivity and pursuing their own way of life without much interference by the British government. Even after the independence of India in 1947, neither the West Bengal state nor the central government made any efforts to assimilate the Chinese community. The Chinese-medium schools were allowed to function even when they did not follow any of the existing Indian education systems. Officially, however, there was ambiguity about the status of Chinese immigrants. Many Chinese immigrants came and lived in India without any form of identification documents. Even those born in India did not have a clear idea about their citizenship or nationality, or of new political concepts that came to the forefront in the post-colonial world. Intelligence files from the British and the post-independence periods indicate that the government authorities perceived the Chinese residing in India as foreign nationals to be closely watched by the police and intelligence officers. The files, containing the reports of these officers, were categorized and marked as belonging to "Chinese nationals."

This ambiguity in the official status of the Chinese immigrants in India and their attempt to preserve their "Chinese" identity proved disastrous for the community during the India–China conflict in the early 1960s. It was more devastating for those who had applied for passports from the embassy and consulates of the People's Republic of China (PRC) in India (others had taken either Taiwanese "citizenship," or remained people with "no nationality"), which had opened shortly after the establishment of diplomatic relations between the PRC and India in 1950. When the relations between the two countries deteriorated in the late 1950s, many of these Chinese immigrants were perceived as agents of communist China and interned. Eventually, about three thousand of them were deported from India. The official exchanges of letters between the Indian and Chinese governments regarding the treatment of these immigrants are revealing.[21] Both governments perceived Chinese immigrants as Chinese nationals who had either lived in India for a long time or been born in that country.

In the days leading to the India–China war of 1962, the Indian government placed all immigrants of Chinese origin under the "Foreigners Act" and made it mandatory for them to register and regularly report to the local police stations. It also put various other restrictions on the Chinese, including denying them employment in "sensitive" government positions. These actions and policies of the Indian government forced a large number of Chinese immigrants to seek livelihoods outside India, especially in North America. This experience also left a deep emotional scar on them. Even though most had never thought of themselves as Indian, the actions of the Indian government made it apparent that they did not belong to that country.

In Kolkata, the deportation and the later emigration of the Chinese has reduced their population from about fifteen thousand in the mid-1950s to fewer than four thousand in recent years. This resulted in the closure of many of the associations, Chinese-language newspapers and Chinese-medium schools that were established in the first half of the twentieth century. The effect has been more pronounced in the Bowbazar Chinatown, where the decrease in the Chinese population was accompanied by the influx of a large number of Muslims from other parts of India. Constructions of new buildings and urban development projects have also transformed the space in which the Chinese immigrants used to dwell and work. This change, however, has also facilitated interactions between the Chinese and other ethnic groups living in the Bowbazar area. Some, including the two daughters of Paul Chung, have even married non-Chinese. Others have gradually forgotten their varieties of Chinese language and converse only in Hindi, English or Bengali. Although they may still be practising Chinese traditions at home, such as ancestor worship and certain funerary rituals, outside, they identify more closely with Indian culture, sports and cuisine. In fact, one person from the Bowbazar area who went to Shenzhen to work found that she was very different from the local Chinese in regard to the ways of thinking, cultural practices, eating habits, etc. She even introduced herself as an "Indian" to her colleagues in Shenzhen.

The situation is different with most of the Chinese immigrants living in the Tangra area, which has emerged as the main dwelling place of the Chinese in India. The Hakkas, who established tanneries and other leather businesses in this area, built a walled community for themselves. Often their residences are right above or next to their tanneries. Tall walls separate the tannery-cum-residences of the Chinese from other ethnic groups in the neighbourhood. Moreover, the fact that their workplaces are within this same area makes it unnecessary for them to travel to other parts of the city or interact with other ethnic groups. They still emphasize endogamy, the preservation of "Chinese" traditions and cultural values, and remain fearful of being assimilated into Indian society. Even when they relish Indian snacks and enjoy Indian TV and films, they usually distance themselves from local Indians and are critical of those Chinese who marry outside the community.

However, among the Tangra residents too there are those who call themselves "Chinese-Indians" or "Indian-Chinese" because they were born in India. This is evident in a survey I conducted in Kolkata in August 2008 of about fifty Chinese immigrants. Given a choice among "Chinese," "Indian," "Chinese-Indian," "Indian-Chinese," "Hakka" and "Cantonese" to describe their ethnic identity, most of the respondents picked "Chinese-Indian" (15) or "Indian-Chinese" (25). Five said that they were "Hakka," two wrote that they were "Chinese," and one answered that she was an "Indian." Most of those who picked "Chinese-Indian" or "Indian-Chinese" explained that they chose the option because they were born in India. They either "sometimes" or "never/almost never" attended Indian cultural events or ceremonies, but "often/always" attend Chinese cultural events. The common "Indian" activity of these people was eating Indian food.

The survey above seems to confirm the point made at the beginning of this section, i.e., that the "Indian" part of the hybrid "Chinese-Indian" or "Indian-Chinese" identity is frequently associated with the place of birth, possibly also the nationality or citizenship acquired through birth in India. There are very few Chinese immigrants in Kolkata, mostly living in the Bowbazar area, who, due to mixed parentage and influence from non-Chinese ethnic groups, have become ethnically or in appearance different from the majority in the community. Thus, the word "Chinese-Indian" (or "Indian-Chinese"), in the context of Kolkata, could be used to describe 1) a Chinese immigrant who was born in India (and maybe holds Indian citizenship); or 2) a handful of Chinese immigrants who have ethnically assimilated into Indian society mostly because of mixed parentage. The lifestyles of these two groups, however, can vary significantly. While the first group has retained most of the practices and beliefs brought to India by previous generations and can usually speak their regional language, those belonging to the second group cannot speak any Chinese languages and seldom engage in traditional Chinese religious and cultural activities.

Being Chinese-Indian in Sihui, China

In the late 1950s and early 1960s, many Chinese immigrants living in different parts of India were rounded up and sent to internment camps, including one at Deoli in Rajasthan. These people were charged with (or simply suspected of) activities detrimental to the national security of India. From the internment camps, about three thousand Chinese were taken to Chennai, in South India, where ships sent by the PRC Government waited to take them to China. Many of these Chinese were born in India and had never been to China and did not speak any of the Chinese languages. When they arrived at Chinese ports, they were screened for transmittable diseases and, depending on the local language they spoke (if any), housed in one of the *nongchangs* 農場 (farming villages) in the South Chinese provinces of Guangxi, Guangdong and Yunnan. While some of these so-called *Yindu guiqiao* 印度歸僑 (returned overseas Chinese from India) continue to live in these villages, others have resettled in their ancestral towns or relocated to various urban cities around China.

Mr Mao 毛 is one such person who lived in the *Laibin nongchang* 來賓農場 in Guangxi province after coming to China from India with his deported parents. According to him, the *Yindu guiqiao* who later migrated to Hong Kong have formed their own association, which organizes annual gatherings. At these gatherings, cultural festivities such as singing of Indian songs, dancing and the consumption of Indian food take place. Videos produced at the gatherings are distributed among the community in Hong Kong and elsewhere in China. Mr Mao, who now lives in Guangzhou, also informed me about the Diwali celebrations that are organized at the *Laibin nongchang* in Guangxi province. Here too, the *Yindu guiqiao* engage in singing, dancing, making and eating Indian food, and reminiscing about their lives in India. Children and grandchildren of these individuals, some of whom were born in the *nongchang*, also participate in these celebrations.

Mr Mao's descriptions of these activities were confirmed by a group of *Yindu guiqiao* I met in Sihui county, about sixty kilometres from Guangzhou. During my two-day fieldwork in the county in February 2009, I met about twelve individuals who had settled in the county after coming from India. The chairman of the Sihui Qiaolian 四會僑聯 (Sihui overseas Chinese association), a person named Chen Jianhua 陳建華, is himself a *Yindu guiqiao*. Mr Chen was born in Kolkata and studied at a local Chinese-medium school until the sixth grade. He organized my meetings with other "returnees" from India. Some of these individuals came from Kolkata and others had lived in the northeastern regions of India. After coming to China all of them were initially accommodated at the *Yingde nongchang* 英德農場 in Guangdong province, where they lived for a number of years and even married other *Yindu guiqiao*. Almost everyone I interviewed had fond memories of their lives in India and were concerned about the present situation in the Indian city or town they came from. Mr Chen, for example, called India his "second home." None of them have visited India after returning to China but hope that one day they will have the opportunity.

Among these individuals, two middle-aged women named Tan Enmei 譚恩美 and Zhou Yulian 周玉蓮 are different from the other *Yindu guiqiao* I met during my fieldtrip. The two women, who lived in Northeast India, are more attached to their Indian past and enthusiastically express their liking for India, despite the fact that they were deported. Zhou Yulian does not speak Mandarin and prefers to talk in Cantonese or Hindi. Her husband, whom I interviewed on the phone, in addition to Hindi, also knows Bengali. Tan Enmei, who speaks good Hindi, pointed out that she and Zhou Yulian frequently cook Indian food, with spices brought from Hong Kong, and converse in Hindi. They also have a collection of Hindi films on VCDs and DVDs. Tan Enmei even tries to teach Hindi words to her granddaughter. Both of them want to go back to India, not necessarily to resettle there, but to relive their old memories. Others I interviewed in Sihui do not show similar affection and longing for India although they meet occasionally and talk in Indian languages. They seem to belong to a third category of Chinese-Indians: those, such as Chen Jianhua, who were born in India and now live in China, hold Chinese citizenship and have integrated into the Chinese society. They have more or less disassociated themselves from their Indian past.

Tan Enmei and Zhou Yulian, on the other hand, have genuinely incorporated Indian cultural elements into their daily routines. Indeed, the Indian connection for them is more than just their birth and experience in that country. In fact, in this regard they are also different from those in Kolkata who call themselves "Chinese-Indians" or "Indian-Chinese" only because of their Indian citizenship. Tan Enmei and Zhou Yulian seem to have been acculturated by Indian society before coming to China. Even after living in China for more than forty-five years they are attempting to come to terms with their Chinese surroundings. At the same time, they have strived to preserve Indian customs, practices and memories. Thus, they, and perhaps also some of those celebrating Diwali in the *nongchang*, would come under a fourth category of "Chinese-Indians": those who were born in India and are trying to live an Indian life in a Chinese county or village as Chinese citizens.

Being Chinese-Indians in Toronto, Canada

Unlike a majority of the *Yindu guiqiao* in China, the Chinese from India who went to Toronto were not as a rule forced to leave the country. They voluntarily emigrated to Canada to find better prospects and livelihood.[22] The treatment of the Chinese by the Indian government and restrictions on employment opportunities in India were, as mentioned above, some of the main factors that led to the search for an alternative abode. Toronto was not the only foreign destination for the Chinese from India looking for better livelihood; some also emigrated to Europe and Australia.

In the early 1980s, when the Chinese from India arrived in Toronto, they were given accommodation in a public housing project in the St Jamestown neighbourhood of the city, near the Toronto Chinatown.[23] Since the buildings in the project were painted in red, the dwelling is remembered as the "Red Buildings" and "a place where the history of the Chinese-Indian-Canadians began." There were numerous Hakka families from Kolkata who lived in this project, so much so that Ellen Oxfeld comments that the "social life in St Jamestown might partly replicate that of Dhapa."[24] When they were able to afford their own accommodation in Toronto, most of these Kolkata Chinese decided to relocate to the Brimley McCown neighbourhood in the eastern suburbs of the city known as Scarborough. In fact, some in the community call the neighbourhood "Second Dhapa" because of the concentration of the Hakka migrants from Kolkata. However, it is neither as cohesive nor as culturally vibrant as the neighbourhood in Kolkata.

Today, Toronto has about ten thousand Chinese who have emigrated from India, more than the population of the Chinese settled in Kolkata. Ellen Oxfeld has noted that the "most important social ties" of these people in Toronto were and still are with other Kolkata Chinese, "either those who have migrated and live in Canada, or those who remain in India."[25] Indeed, there are at least three associations that foster such social links among the Kolkata Chinese living in Toronto. These are the Yinhua Association, founded in 1990; the Meizhou Association of Eastern Canada, established in 1998; and the Hakka Helping Hands, which started operating in 2000.[26] The Yinhua Association is the most active among these.

There are also other social activities that bring the Chinese immigrants from Kolkata and elsewhere in India together every week. On every Wednesday and Friday, from 9 p.m. to midnight, Chinese immigrants from Kolkata, who are mostly in their forties and fifties, meet at a Tim Horton's coffee shop to discuss miscellaneous topics that are often related to their lives in Toronto and sometimes also focus on India. On Saturdays, older men in their sixties have a similar gathering from 7 a.m. Women immigrants in the same age group meet from 9 a.m. onwards. Often there are thirty to forty people who attend these gatherings and enjoy Indian desserts and snacks.

When asked about their cultural identity, most respondents point to their Indian birthplace, Chinese ethnicity and Canadian citizenship. One person named Linda Liu explained, "I am a CIBC – Canadian India-born Chinese. I have three identities. I am proud to be a Canadian, to be Indian born and to be a Chinese." Another person called Steven Huang says, "I am a Chinese first, Indian second, then Canadian." He admits that he calls himself Indian because he was born there; otherwise he thinks he is more influenced by Canadian society than either Chinese or Indian. For Kwai-Yun Li, the author of *The Last Dragon Dance: Chinatown Stories*, the Indian elements in her "triple identity" include India as the birthplace, her liking for Indian food and movies, and her ability to speak an Indian language.

But there are other individuals who are bitter about their experience in India. One person I interviewed was born in China but grew up in India; she later migrated to Taiwan, from where she came to Canada. When asked if she would call herself Chinese-Indian or Chinese-Indian-Canadian, she replied that she was just a Chinese. The Indian government had refused to give her citizenship or a passport, so, she asked, why would she call herself an Indian? Similar resentment was expressed to Shirley Chiu, who undertook an excellent comparative study of the Indian-Chinese and Caribbean-Chinese in Toronto. Two of her respondents, Mark and Monica, gave the following answers respectively:

> Considering the past (Sino-Indian conflict), India is not a good place for the Chinese. Even though I was born in India, I wasn't treated as an Indian citizen, but a second-class citizen [...]. I know a lot of university graduates who didn't get jobs because they were Chinese-Indian.
>
> There was no protection for visible minorities like us. We were a visible minority. Discriminatory actions were taken by local politicians and police officers that made us stand out.[27]

In fact, during my fieldtrip in Toronto in November 2009, I found that many of my interviewees were reluctant to acknowledge that they had come to Canada from India even though they admitted India as their birthplace. Even among the former Chinese residents of Kolkata who have weekly meetings at Tim Horton's, India or their experiences in that country are not the main themes of their conversations. Rather, they want to socialize with people who had previously shared the same space with them. The fact that this space happened to be in India does not necessarily appeal to them.

Conclusion

For the Chinese whose families have lived in India for over two hundred years, "Chinese-Indian" (or "Indian-Chinese") is just one of their many identities. As the discussion above indicates, the word "Indian" in this hybrid identity generally indicates the birthplace rather than ethnic assimilation, acculturation, or the integration of the Chinese with the local society of Kolkata or other regions of India. This is at least how those who call themselves "Chinese-Indians" (or "Indian-Chinese") explain the hybridity. Indeed, the fact that they were born in India is something they cannot deny, even though for the most part of their history, the Chinese in Kolkata had tried to preserve their distinctiveness and distance themselves from the local Indian society. In fact, as Jennifer Liang has explained, they were fearful of becoming Indian. It is possible that the birthplace explanation is used to minimize their association with India.[28]

This is evident from the Chinese who have emigrated from India to Toronto. Although they usually avoid references to India in their social interactions with each other, it is the links formulated in an Indian city that knit them together. In fact, when they find it difficult to adjust or find a decent livelihood in Toronto, the place they return to is India. Even for marital relations, prospective brides and grooms are sought in Tangra rather than in China.[29] However, this is perhaps due to the fact that Tangra is perceived as an exclusive settlement of the Chinese that preserves Chinese culture and heritage, with limited, if any, impact from the surrounding Indian society. So it can be argued that the links those in Canada maintain are not with India per se, but with a specific neighbourhood of Kolkata inhabited by the Chinese. It is also true that the "Chinese-Indians" living in Toronto, like many Chinese residing in Tangra, reveal little influence of Indian society and culture. There are some who can speak Indian languages, enjoy eating Indian food and have Indian friends. But these are not sufficient traits to indicate any profound Indian impact on their lives. As a result, in their case "Chinese-Indian" could only mean, as they themselves explain it, an ethnic Chinese born in India.

There is another dimension to this explanation, relating to how the Indian people and Indian government perceive the ethnic Chinese. The India–China conflict clearly revealed that the Indian government (and to some extent, the people) saw the Chinese as outsiders. Ellen Oxfeld has argued that they are perhaps the most marginalized immigrant group in India.[30] "Their status as foreigners associated with a country that has been engaged in hostilities against India," she writes, "combined with their association with a particularly degraded occupation (leather making), lend certain uniqueness to their role and give them even more of an outsider status than other migrants to Calcutta."[31] Indeed, if the Chinese, particularly those in Tangra, have segregated themselves from the Indian society, the Indian government and people have also contributed to this isolation by preventing them from integrating into the Indian society and workforce. Thus, specifying India as their birthplace may be the only way the hybrid identity could be explained by those in Kolkata and Toronto.

By contrast, the situation with those who were deported to China in the 1960s is somewhat complex. Life in India for many of them had ended abruptly. When they arrived in China, the economic condition was poor and the living situation was not as good as in India. Thus, despite the internment and forced deportation, some of these people have fond memories of India and Indian customs, some of which they try to replicate even today. For some of these *Yindu guiqiao*, "Chinese-Indian" signifies more than just Chinese ethnicity and the idea of India as only their birthplace. They seem to have affection, memories and cultural attachment to India. Many who feel this did not reside in Kolkata before they were deported.

Had they been in Kolkata, pressure from the community might have prevented frequent interactions with local Indians; in other parts of India such exchanges seemed to have thrived. These interactions and exchanges between the immigrants and members of the host community could have been responsible for generating fond memories of India and giving them a different sense of being Chinese-Indian. Many indeed seem to have had a sense of belonging that they are trying to find again in China.

Notes

1 Stuart Hall, "Cultural Identity and Diaspora," in *Identity: Community, Culture, Difference*, edited by Jonathan Rutherford (London: Lawrence & Wishart, 1990), p. 223.
2 Hall, "Cultural Identity," p. 225. Chinese scholars in their study of the Chinese overseas also frequently use Stuart Hall's views on identity. See, for example, Liu Hong's edited work called *Haiyang yazhou yu huaren shijie zhi hudong* 海洋亞洲與華人世界之互動 [Maritime Asia and the interactions with the world of the Chinese overseas] (Xinjiapo: Huayi guan, 2007).
3 While the term "Chinese-Indian" emphasizes the Chinese ethnicity of these people, "Indian-Chinese" highlights their Indian nationality, which they were able to acquire in the 1990s. In this study I have used "Chinese-Indian" as the term for the ethnic Chinese who have resided in Kolkata for several generations or migrated to India before 1962; some of these people may have acquired Indian citizenship, others have passports that belong to a third country such as Canada. I also prefer to use the term "Chinese-Indian," instead of "Indian-Chinese," because of the importance the preservation of "Chinese identity" seems to play in this community.
4 Tan Chee-Beng, *Chinese Overseas: Comparative Cultural Issues* (Hong Kong: Hong Kong University Press, 2004), p. 26.
5 Myron L. Cohen, "Being Chinese: The Peripheralisation of Traditional Identity," in *The Living Tree: The Changing Meaning of Being Chinese Today*, edited by Tu Wei-ming (Stanford: Stanford University Press, 1994), p. 89.
6 Cohen, "Being Chinese," p. 89.
7 Cohen, "Being Chinese," p. 94.
8 Tong Chee-kiong and Chan Kwok-bun, "One Face, Many Masks: The Singularity and Plurality of Chinese Identity," *Diaspora* 10, no. 3 (2001): 364.
9 Tong and Chan, "One Face, Many Masks," pp. 364–5.
10 Tong and Chan, "One Face, Many Masks," p. 365.
11 Tong and Chan, "One Face, Many Masks," p. 366.
12 Tong and Chan, "One Face, Many Masks," p. 370.
13 Tong and Chan, "One Face, Many Masks," p. 378.
14 Tong and Chan, "One Face, Many Masks," p. 386.
15 Zhang Xing, "The Chinese Community in Calcutta: Preservation and Change," PhD dissertation, Martin Luther University, Halle-Wittenberg, 2011.
16 Note that this applies to ethnicity not nationality.
17 Unfortunately, I do not have the publication details for this article, which was given to me by a Chinese in Kolkata.
18 Interview on 23 January 2008.
19 See Jennifer Liang, "Migration Patterns and Occupational Specialisations of Calcutta Chinese: An Insider's History," *China Report* 43, no. 2 (October–December 2007): 397–410.
20 I have discussed this issue in detail in *Preserving Cultural Identity through Education: The Schools of the Chinese Community in Calcutta, India* (Singapore: Institute of Southeast Asian Studies, 2010).
21 For a detailed study of this issue, see Leng Shao-chuan and Jerome Alan Cohen, "The Sino-Indian Dispute over the Internment and Detention of Chinese in India," in *China's Practice of International Law*, edited by Jerome Cohen (Cambridge: Harvard University Press, 1972), pp. 268–320.

22 Shirley S. Chiu, "Ethnic Identity Formation: A Case Study of Caribbean and Indian Hakkas in Toronto," MA thesis, York University, Toronto, 2003.
23 Ellen Oxfeld, *Blood, Sweat, and Mahjong: Family and Enterprise in an Overseas Chinese Community* (Ithaca, NY: Cornell University Press, 1993).
24 Oxfeld, *Blood, Sweat, and Mahjong*, p. 251.
25 Oxfeld, *Blood, Sweat, and Mahjong*, p. 244.
26 Chiu, "Ethnic Identity Formation," pp. 34–6.
27 Chiu, "Ethnic Identity Formation," p. 100.
28 Jennifer Liang, "The Chinese in Calcutta: An Insider's History," unpublished paper (Microsoft Word document, accessed December 2011).
29 Ellen Oxfeld, "Cross-Border Hypergamy? Marriage Exchanges in a Transnational Hakka Community," in *Cross-Border Marriages: Gender and Mobility in Transnational Asia*, edited by Nicole Constable (Philadelphia: University of Pennsylvania Press, 2005), pp. 17–33.
30 This may, however, be debated by drawing attention to descendants of black African slaves, particularly in West India. This issue needs to be studied comparatively.
31 Oxfeld, *Blood, Sweat, and Mahjong*, p. 38.

References

Bose, Basanta Kumar. "A Bygone Chinese Colony in Bengal." *Bengal Past and Present* 47 (1934): 120–122.

Chiu, Shirley S. "Ethnic Identity Formation: A Case Study of Caribbean and Indian Hakkas in Toronto." MA thesis, York University, Toronto, 2003.

Cohen, Myron L. "Being Chinese: The Peripheralisation of Traditional Identity." In *The Living Tree: The Changing Meaning of Being Chinese Today*, edited by Tu Wei-ming, pp. 88–108. Stanford: Stanford University Press, 1994.

Hall, Stuart. "Cultural Identity and Diaspora." In *Identity: Community, Culture, Difference*, edited by Jonathan Rutherford, pp. 222–237. London: Lawrence & Wishart Limited, 1990.

Leng, Shao-chuan and Jerome Alan Cohen. "The Sino-Indian Dispute over the Internment and Detention of Chinese in India." In *China's Practice of International Law*, edited by Jerome Cohen, pp. 268–320. Cambridge: Harvard University Press. 1972.

Li, Kwai-Yun. *The Last Dragon Dance: Chinatown Stories*. New Delhi: Penguin Books Ltd, 2008.

Liang, Jennifer. "Migration Patterns and Occupational Specialisations of Calcutta Chinese: An Insider's History." *China Report* 43, no. 2 (October-December 2007): 397–410.

______. "The Chinese in Calcutta: An Insider's History." Unpublished paper.

Liu, Hong 劉宏. *Haiyang yazhou yu huaren shijie zhi hudong* 海洋亞洲與華人世界之互動 [Maritime Asia and the Interactions with the World of the Chinese Overseas]. Xinjiapo: Huayi guan, 2007.

Oxfeld, Ellen. *Blood, Sweat, and Mahjong: Family and Enterprise in an Overseas Chinese Community*. Ithaca: Cornell University Press, 1993.

______. "Cross-border hypergamy? Marriage exchanges in a Transnational Hakka Community." In *Cross-border Marriages: Gender and Mobility in Transnational Asia*, edited by Nicole Constable, pp. 17–33. Philadelphia, Pennsylvania: University of Pennsylvania Press, 2005.

Tan, Chee-Beng. *Chinese Overseas: Comparative Cultural Issues*. Hong Kong: Hong Kong University Press, 2004.

Tong, Chee-kiong and Chan Kwok-bun. "One Face, Many Masks: The Singularity and Plurality of Chinese Identity." *Diaspora* 10, no. 3 (2001): 361–389.

Zhang, Xing. *Preserving Cultural Identity Through Education: The Schools of the Chinese Community in Calcutta, India*. Singapore: Nalanda-Sriwijaya Research Series, Institute of Southeast Asian Studies, 2010.

______. "The Chinese in Calcutta: Preservation and Change." Ph.D. dissertation, Martin Luther University, Halle-Wittenberg, 2011.

Section IV

ACROSS THE GLOBE: INDIAN AND CHINESE DIASPORAS

Chapter 15

OVERSEAS INDIAN AND CHINESE COMMUNITIES IN FILM: DEFINING IDENTITIES THROUGH POPULAR HINDI FILM AND TRANSNATIONAL CHINESE AND INDIAN FILMS, 1990s ONWARDS

Coonoor Kripalani[1]

The Diasporic Communities and the Films

The global population of Indians overseas is estimated at over 17 million. Of these over 2.5 million are estimated to be in the United States (constituting 0.92 per cent of the US population), while Singapore's Indian population constitutes officially 9.2 per cent of the nation's population, including citizens, permanent residents (over 330,000) and expatriate workers (over 100,000). The global population of Chinese overseas is estimated at 40 million, over twice the number of overseas Indians. An estimated 30 million are living in Southeast Asia, while in the United States persons of Chinese descent number approximately 3.6 million, comprising 1.2 per cent of the US population.

Both these populations were subject to the global demands for migrant labour in the nineteenth century, when the colonial powers took workers as indentured labour to other colonies – to work on plantations and in mines, and in some cases to assist in junior administrative posts. Many of these migrant workers did not return, making these new lands their home. Political and economic instabilities of the post-colonial era created the next wave of migration from both countries.[2] It is the latter group of migrants during the last six decades who have kept close ties with the motherland, particularly in the Indian case. The communities of Indians and Chinese overseas, old and recent, provide both the subject matter as well as the audiences for films that depict the Indian and Chinese diasporic communities.

Members of diasporic communities often struggle with their identities.[3] Are they Indian, Indian-American, or American, Chinese, American-Chinese, Fijian, Fijian-Indian, Canadian, Canadian-Chinese, and so on? What makes a person living in North America, for instance, Indian or Chinese? Is it their parentage, their values, the food they eat, the language they speak (or are expected to speak at home)? Is it in their blood? Is it their ethnicity? Is it their culture? Are they American in their homeland, and Indian or Chinese in North America? Are they foreign everywhere? Much scholarly work has been done on multicultural identities in overseas communities.[4] This paper looks at how film defines these identities. It demonstrates that popular Hindi film reaches out to the diaspora, incorporating the overseas population into the utopian nation. In comparison, the auto-ethnographic films made overseas which look at the diasporic communities as their subjects, provide a more introspective and critical look at themselves. These films provide an insight into the conflicted identities of these communities, as second, third and fourth generations adapt to their new homelands. Taken together, filmic representations of the overseas Indian and Chinese depict the struggles for identity within these communities.

This paper firstly examines the portrayal of the Indian diaspora in popular Hindi films of the 1990s onwards, through selected works that particularly focus on Indian families living overseas where Indian family values, culture and tradition are negotiated in alien lands. The films are *Dilwale Dulhaniya Leh Jayenge* (The brave heart will win the bride, 1995), *Pardes* (Foreigner, 1999), *Kabhi Khushi Khabie Gham* (Sometimes happy, sometimes sad, 2001), *Kal Ho Naa Ho* (Tomorrow may or may not happen, 2003), *Kabhi Alvida Naa Kehna* (Never say goodbye, 2006), *Namastey London* (Hello London, 2007) and *Dostana* (Friendship, 2008), while *New York* (2009) offers a view of the problems faced by South Asians post 9/11. Films such as *Swades* (My country, 2004), *Aaja Nachley* (Come dance, 2007), *Namastey London*, *Delhi-6* (2009) and *3 Idiots* (2009) explore the return of the immigrant to the homeland. The common thread of nationalistic and patriarchal values in these commercial films are evidence of the way the film industry embraces the diasporic Indian nation.

These films are compared with Chinese films from the same period that look at diasporic communities such as *The Joy Luck Club* (1993), *The Wedding Banquet* (1993), *Double Happiness* (1994), *Song of the Exile* (1990), *Farewell, China* (1990), *Full Moon in New York* (1990), *Comrades: Almost a Love Story* (1996), *The Gua Sha Treatment*, 2001) and *The Flight of the Red Balloon* (2007). While acknowledging that these Chinese films are not exactly comparable to popular Hindi (Bollywood) films, they are instructive of and insightful into the lives of migrant Chinese. These films specifically address the struggles of immigrants and the push and pull factors that lead to out-migration from China.

Viewing these films as "transnational Chinese films,"[5] it is also appropriate to compare them with transnational Indian/South Asian films – for example, *My Beautiful Laundrette* (1985), *East is East* (1999), *Bhaji on the Beach* (1993), *Mississippi Masala* (1991), *The Journey* (1997), *Monsoon Wedding* (2001), *Bend It Like Beckham* (2002), *Bride and Prejudice* (2004) and *The Namesake* (2006). These films are offerings from the diasporic community itself, and provide us an insider's view of the issues within this community and the issues faced in interaction with the host community.

The Indian Diaspora in Popular Hindi Film

The consumption of cultural products from the home country is not only important in retaining links with the homeland, but also provides a familiar zone during leisure time. Screenings of popular Hindi films have been popular with Indian communities globally from the 1950s onwards. The arrival of home videos in the late 1970s saw a decline in theatre screenings, but these revived in the 1990s with a new production format from Bollywood.

Dilwale Dulhaniyan Leh Jayenge (*DDLJ*, 1995) was one such pivotal film. It opens with Baldev Singh, the father of the heroine, delivering a soliloquy as he feeds pigeons in London's Trafalgar Square early in the morning. His solemn voice informs the audience that even after living in England for 22 years, he feels alien. One day, he vows, he will return to his country. A rather stern and traditional Indian father, Baldev Singh faces the challenge of raising his two young daughters in England.

Stern, traditional fathers are also the linchpins of the next two films examined, *Pardes* (1999) and *Kabhi Khushi Khabie Gham* (*KKKG*, 2001), as it is through them that the patriarchal values of these communities are demonstrated. Just like Baldev Singh in *DDLJ*, who wishes to arrange the marriage of his daughter Simran to Kuljit, the son of his friend in the Punjab, in *Pardes*, Kishorilal in the United States decides to arrange the marriage of his son Rajeev to Ganga, the daughter of his childhood friend Suraj Dev in India. In *KKKG*, it is the stern Yashvardhan Raichand who disowns his son, Rahul, when he marries Anjali (a girl of a lesser social standing) against the wishes of his father. Raichand's wife Nandini stands by helplessly, unable to intervene or dissuade her husband as Rahul and Anjali are compelled to leave the family home for the United Kingdom.

The common trope in each of these films is marriage to the right partner, and is the driving force of the intra-family relationships depicted. It is a common idiom and needs no elaboration to Indian audiences. In each of the three instances, the chosen partner of the protagonist has to prove his/her worthiness to the family to gain acceptance. This worthiness is demonstrated by upholding "Indian" values.

In *DDLJ*, Simran cannot even broach the subject of Raj Malhotra, her chosen partner. A short encounter between him and her father leaves Baldev with a poor impression of

Fig 1:

the young man, and so Raj has to claw back his respect. The film portrays his core as Indian, with an externally Western (smart) image. Raj's morals are irreproachable, and he does not take advantage of Simran when he is alone with her for a night – he keeps her *izzat* (honour). Nor will he spirit her away (even with her mother's encouragement) without her father's consent; he says he is "Indian" and will marry Simran only when her father willingly agrees to it – as a respectable Indian boy would.

While upholding the glory of Indian values and culture (note that even Raj's father, who inserts himself into the wedding party to support his son, points out his Indian-ness when he says, "Everything is available [in England], but not this culture. [...] I carry India in my heart"), the film stands in contrast to earlier productions, like Manoj Kumar's *Purab aur Pachhim* (East and West, 1970). These invariably depict the overseas Indian to be materialistic, showy, dressed Western style and lacking Indian values (and often even morals), with little or no understanding of India. In *DDLJ*, it is quite the reverse. It is the local Indian boy, Kuljit, who is a cad and up to no good – a quite unsuitable husband for the heroine, Simran.[6]

Similarly, in *Pardes*, Rajiv, the partner chosen for Ganga, is a cad – he parties, smokes, drinks and womanizes, and attempts to rape her. It is his Indian adopted brother, Arjun, who becomes her saviour, and it is only after Rajiv's worthlessness is proved that Ganga can unite with her true love, Arjun.[7] Throughout this film, Indian rituals and values are extolled and contrasted to the hollowness of a materialistic Western culture.

In *KKKG* (2001), Indian values are embodied in Anjali, the objectionable daughter-in-law. She proves her worthiness by saying her morning prayers in her London home and paying respect to a photo of her parents-in-law (since they are not there in person) – set to the tune of "Sare Jahan se Achha Hindustan Hamara" (The best in the whole world is our Hindustan). Anjali seeks to impart Indian ideals and inform her son about India by singing Indian songs (e.g., "Mere Desh ki Dharti" [The soil of my land]) to him. Despite their comfortable life (big house and garden, fast new cars, etc.), Anjali and Daijaan, the family retainer, long for their home.

A striking feature of both *DDLJ* and *KKKG* is that while these Indian families are living well materially, there is little social interaction with their host community (and in Anjali's case in *KKKG*, she feels the lack of sincerity of her neighbour, who makes a convenience of them by leaving her child in their care). They live in longing for their homeland. In *Pardes*, though Rajiv is able to party with his international group of friends, the social influences are depicted as un-Indian and undesirable.

Kal Ho Naa Ho (*KHNH*, 2003), a story of Indians living in New York, likewise features minimal contact with non-Indians. Except for the song sequences – in which passers-by are called in to join the exuberant rendition of "Pretty Woman," and in the disco, "It's the Time to Disco," where we see interaction with a mixed population – the story is confined to Indians. The film deals with the domestic and financial troubles of Naina's family, and the wealth and comfort of Rohit's home (they even have a domestic helper from India), giving the audience a peek at the diversity of the lifestyles and regional cultures of Indians living in New York. With some gay humour and many light-hearted moments that reflect Aman's big personality, the film carries viewers through many emotional ups and downs.

The challenge of raising an Indian girl who boldly interacts with the host community is brought out in *Namastey London* (2007), a twenty-first century remake of *Purab aur Pachhim* whose tagline is "A British brat meets a Funjabi boy." Jasmeet ("Jazz") the anglicized daughter of Manmohan Singh, is bent upon marrying her English boyfriend, Charlie Brown, while her father tries to get her married to a suitable Indian boy, Arjun. It is only when Charlie's friends insult India and Arjun delivers a diatribe against the British, while extolling the greatness and virtues of India, that Jazz became convinced of his worthiness.

Another two films set in New York, *Kabhi Alvida Na Kehnaa* (*KANK*, 2006) and *Dostana* (2008), deal with extramarital affairs and divorce, and homosexuality, respectively. *Dostana* pays homage to Indian women in the hit song "Desi Girl," personified by Neha, the overseas Indian woman.

> *Ain't nobody like my desi girl*
> *Dekhi lakh lakh pardesi girl* [I've seen lakhs of foreign girls]
> *Sab toh soni saadi desi girl* [The best of them all is my desi girl]
> *Who's the hottest girl in the world?*
> *My desi girl, My desi girl*

This is a significant change from films of previous decades, which question the morality and values of girls raised overseas.

Neither of these films really needed to be located in New York, but one can speculate that the themes of infidelity, extramarital relations, divorce and homosexuality can be framed more comfortably in an alien territory, among an overseas population. Vijay Mishra's analysis would agree with this:

> What Bombay Cinema keeps representing is never the diasporic Other but its own and India's (mis)reading of the diaspora. Part of this "misreading" reflects a center–periphery understanding of the homeland–diaspora nexus in which the diaspora becomes sites of permissible (but controlled) transgressions while the homeland is the crucible of timeless dharmik virtues.[8]

New York, the 2009 Bollywood offering, is a departure from the rosy picture of Indians in the films cited so far. *New York* presents the racial profiling of Indian Muslims in the wake of 9/11, and how their unfair and unwarranted detention serves only to push them the other way into terrorist activities. This film concerns working-class men of South Asian origin who struggle for their livelihoods and yet are willing to undertake acts of terrorism in retaliation against unwarranted punitive actions by the US government.

The Return of the Native

Here let us consider the films that centre around the return to India of Indians living overseas: *Swades* (2004), *Aaja Nachley* (2007), *Delhi-6* (2009) and *3 Idiots* (2009). The first three deal with overseas Indians returning home and facing the distrust of locals, who view them as having no commitment. The locals feel that they return to make speeches and point out flaws but do nothing about them, as they are only back for a short while and have the option to leave again for foreign shores. In contrast, the returning Indian plainly sees discrimination, poverty, superstition and corruption, and steps up to confront these social ills.

In *Swades*, when NASA scientist Mohan returns to India after an absence of 12 years, he encounters both joyous moments as well as some harsher aspects of non-progressiveness – caste discrimination, poverty, illiteracy and an aversion to change. His interventions and views are not well received locally, as he is seen as little more than a visitor from the United States. Despite this, he intervenes successfully in some of the practical and social issues. Mohan finds satisfaction in helping villagers build a reservoir and a hydroelectricity plant, and he knows he will return after finishing his NASA project.

Diya faces similar criticism and harassment in *Aaja Nachley*, when she returns to her native town, Shamli, to save her former dance school, Ajanta, which is under threat of demolition. She is harshly judged for having married an American and gone to live in the United States. Taunted by the residents, politicians and local authorities over her aim to save the school, she nevertheless takes the challenge in hand. She confronts the obstacles thrown across her path by the local constabulary, who act as the arm of the local politician, and ultimately succeeds in winning a reprieve of the demolition order, saving Ajanta.

Delhi-6 tells of a young man, Roshan, born and raised in the United States, bringing his grandmother, Annapurna, back to her home in Chandni Chowk in Delhi. Initially warmed by the affection of the extended family, Roshan is respectful of the traditions and rituals of daily life. As delighted as Annapurna is to be home, Roshan is bewildered at the police brutality, political corruption, casteism, superstition, fear, communalism and discrimination he encounters. He is ridiculed as a half-half (his mother is Hindu and his father Muslim) and his American values are not appreciated. Roshan develops a love interest in the girl next door, Bittu, who has dreams of making it big in Mumbai (on a TV reality show). His intervention in undoing a match that her father tries to arrange for her earns him her father's wrath. But with his values and heart in the right place, Roshan wins the girl and the support of the community.

The portrayal of Chatur Ramalingam in *3 Idiots* reveals the homeland's attitudes towards its foreign-born offspring. Ramalingam, a nerdy high achiever and a product of the diaspora from Uganda, is introduced at the beginning of the film, boasting to his old college rivals 10 years after graduation. He shows them images on his smartphone of his perfect suburban home, beautiful wife and fast car. He boasts of his huge salary, compared to the pittance he assumes they earn. Ramalingam is highly competitive, and thinks of his three former classmates as losers. Achievement to him is defined by the money a person earns and he has returned to India only to ingratiate himself with a noted inventor. In comparison to his Indian-born classmates, he is shown to have less EQ and a willingness to do anything to succeed.

Imaging of the Diasporic Nation

These images of the diasporic nation show Indians abroad as generally having attained a very high standard of living, residing in plush accommodations and denied no material wants. Their main problem is marrying off Westernised children, particularly girls, to good Indian spouses who uphold the right Indian values, who will guide these offspring of the diaspora back into the fold of Indian cultural mores and values. The nucleus of values is seen to be the family unit, and everything is done to preserve it in the Indian way.

In a departure from films in previous decades, the Indian residing overseas is not portrayed as wicked (with the exception of Rajiv in *Pardes*); on the contrary, their hearts are shown to be purer than those of the home-grown characters, such as Raj in *DDLJ*, Mohan in *Swades*, Diya in *Aaja Nachley* and Roshan in *Delhi-6*. However, they are mistrusted by the local community and are perceived as meddlers who can simply return overseas after stirring up problems. The first generation of Indians living overseas, such as Baldev Singh in *DDLJ*, Anjali in *KKKG*, Kishorilal in *Pardes* and the grandmother Annapurna in *Delhi-6*, long for the homeland. They are eager to have their offspring share the same love of the motherland and to imbibe Indian values. When they return to India, the lush green fields of their villages stand in sharp contrast to the urban landscapes they have come from.

These films completely ignore the masses of migrant labour from India, who go overseas to seek menial work (domestic helpers, cleaners, gardeners, waiters/waitresses, etc.) or perform hard labour (construction workers, security guards, builders, etc.). This is a large group scattered around the globe that faces untold misery and slave-like conditions to earn a few hundred dollars to send home. They remain mostly unseen on the glossy screens of Bollywood. Only in passing do we see the Indian maid in *KHNH*, during a comedic scene between Rohan and Arjun.

In this respect, the 1970 film *Purab aur Pachhim* is striking for fleshing out such a life in the character of Lalchand, a domestic worker in the home of Mr Sharma, father of the protagonist, Preeti, an Indian girl who has grown up in Britain and adopted Western style and dress. Bharat, a young man visiting from India, addresses him as "Lalchand-ji,"[9] and Mr Sharma, struck at this demonstration of respect, says he has never before had this suffix added to his name. Lalchand came to work with Mr Sharma when he was still a boy. His father told him never to leave Mr Sharma, to treat him like a god, and to stick with him like Hanuman stuck to Rama. So he never left Mr Sharma, and as the latter did not go back to India, neither did Lalchand. He says he has a wife whom he has not seen for 40 years, as they were married off as children, but his bride awaits his return. Finally, towards the end of the story, when Lalchand is reunited with his wife, Preeti's brother, a Hare Krishna devotee, says to his sister, "Only in India will a wife wait 40 years for her husband. I have understood, Preeti. Now you should also understand." Thus, loyalty is also presented as a *dharmik* virtue.

New York gives us a look at migrant workers, but here it is mainly related to the fallout of 9/11, and how this type of stereotyping leads to the opposite effect – the victims band together to seek revenge, and fall prey to extremist philosophies.

The Chinese Diaspora in Film

When seeking to compare Chinese and Indian diaspora films, it is difficult to find a category of Chinese film that is exactly comparable with the Indian films detailed above.

The popular perception of "Chinese films" is that of kung fu (Chinese martial arts) – Bruce Lee, Shaolin Temple, and flying monks and daggers immediately spring to mind. How can we describe a "popular" Chinese film? And which Chinese dialect would it be in – Mandarin, Cantonese or some other? Where would it be made – Hong Kong, Taiwan, Mainland China, Singapore or Hollywood?

The films selected here were made in a variety of places, all by Chinese directors, some of whom have found a place in Hollywood, but each in some way defining the lives of Chinese overseas. These "autoethnographic"[10] films are also described here as "transnational," meaning "those that exceed the boundaries of any single national territory."[11]

The groundbreaking narrative of *The Joy Luck Club* (1993) contrasts the lives of four Chinese women who have grown up and lived in China with those of their American daughters, making apparent the tension of the two cultures and two generations. Having fled from times and events of great upheaval, the personal lives of each of the four members of the Joy Luck Club, who regularly play mah-jong together, tell of the suffering and dislocation of people due to wars and natural disasters in China, compounded in the sufferings of women due to their unequal position in society. Their rebellious daughters answer back to their mothers and yet their psyches are shaped by their mothers' influence. Their stories give them their Chinese identity and strength of character. Raised in the United States, their daughters do not identify with this type of Chinese suffering and their childhood clashes continue into adulthood, but they come to realize the wisdom of their mothers holds good for all human relationships.

Mina Shum's *Double Happiness* (1994) also examines intergenerational rifts among overseas Chinese, and what it means to be Chinese in North America. In the opening scene, Jade, an aspiring actress, informs the viewer that she wants to tell them about her family, omitting the fact that they are Chinese. However, as the movie unfolds, the viewer

Fig 2:

is made to realize that the story is really about what it means to be Chinese. Jade faces discrimination at both ends: she is subtly denied entry into a popular nightclub in town on the one hand, and on the other is berated by a Hong Kong talent recruiter during an audition when she cannot read the Chinese script. "Are you really Chinese?" screams the talent scout. Her parents strive to cultivate Chinese values in their children, which means primarily that the children must respect and obey their parents. The children are expected to appreciate the sacrifices made by their father to give them this comfortable life in Canada. Educated as an architect, his language deficiency in Canada forced him to settle for a blue-collar job.

In these two Chinese films, there is no looking back to the motherland as a utopia – no hankering to return or to extol its virtues, as in the case of popular Indian films. A premium, however, is put on Chinese culture. It is to be preserved, especially in aspects of filial piety, hard work, respecting traditional norms and succeeding and achieving in their new homes through competition. Indian films depict Indians overseas as mainly living very affluent lives, and this element of struggle to achieve as depicted in Chinese films is hardly ever a factor in Indian ones. What they do share is the goal of finding the right partners for their children, with whom they can continue to uphold their cultures and value systems. Intergenerational conflict is a common feature in both Indian and Chinese films, as the older generation seeks to preserve its cultural moorings while the younger generation rebels against the tradition that sets them apart in their overseas homes.

Clara Law's *Farewell, China* (1990) and Peter Chan's *Comrades: Almost a Love Story* (1996) both tell of the pressure on young Chinese migrants to make a successful life overseas, and of the difficulties and pitfalls that lie along that road. The former tells of the hardships Li Hong endures in the United States, including a gang rape by African Americans. The financial and emotional costs (she leaves behind her husband, Nansan, and her baby) seem all too much, as we witness Hong's descent into madness and paranoia. The viewer is also presented with vignettes of other Chinese like Jane, a 15-year-old runaway who works as prostitute. Like the American daughters of *The Joy Luck Club*, she denies her Chinese-ness. She hates having Chinese parents, hates being Chinese. She dyes her hair blonde so as not to look obviously Chinese. "Now I'm happy. I'm free," she says. We also get a glimpse of a Chinese migrant who has attained the American dream, when the down-and-out Nansan goes to Scarsdale to contact his sponsor.[12] The man who opens the door wants nothing to do with him. His frantic search for Hong is set against dirge-like background music of an old Chinese song about people migrating from China – markedly distinct from the nationalistic background music of Hindi films.

In contrast, set to the sweet love songs of Teresa Teng, *Comrades*, too, tells a tale of Chinese immigrants trying to fit in. Hong Kong is the foreign territory to begin with, where Mainlanders try hard to lose their identity and emulate the urbanity of a "Honkie" (a person from Hong Kong). As Li Xiaojun arrives in Hong Kong, he is befriended by Li Qiao, a savvy English-speaking Mainlander, trying hard to conceal her identity as a "China girl." Her entrepreneurship (recruiting immigrants for language school, investing in the stock market, acting as a proxy for flat sales, etc.) and quick moneymaking schemes stand in contrast to Xiaojun's slow "country" way of interacting with his new urban environment. Li Qiao is proud to have shed her "China girl" identity and become a "Honkie."

Stanley Kwan's *Full Moon in New York*[13] is the story of three Chinese women in New York. Wang Hsiung Ping is an actress from Taiwan, Li Feng Jiao an entrepreneur from Hong Kong, while Zhao Hong is from Mainland China and married to an American-born Chinese. The friendship of these three women can be seen as a metaphor for Chinese reunification,[14] as well as a commentary on cultural identity among diaspora populations. Although seemingly well adjusted as New Yorkers, the friendship between the three women is a way to hold on to their Chinese roots. Made at a time (the late 1980s) when a number of Hong Kong directors, like Clara Law, Ann Hui, Mabel Cheung and Alex Law, were inspired to make films about migration to the United States, this offering from Stanley Kwan is very much a reflection of the times.[15]

These three films show how Chinese migrants negotiate life in foreign lands with their wits about them, relying on each other and the types of employment opportunities available to them. For her livelihood, Li Qiao in *Comrades* works in a McDonald's, a massage parlour and then as the moll of gangster Pao, while Xiaojun works as a Chinese chef's assistant. In *Farewell, China*, Hong works as a waitress in a Chinese restaurant, and then ends up prostituting herself, while Nansan pimps for his young friend Jane. The dehumanizing strain of migration leads Hong to go insane. Like Jade in *Double Happiness*, Hsiung Ping in *Full Moon in New York* goes from audition to audition, trying to establish herself as an actress. With these types of jobs, negotiating one's status in an alien land becomes difficult.

With the exception of *Full Moon in New York*, mainstream Hindi films do not depict this aspect of job seeking. Overseas Indians are shown as entrepreneurial, and in almost every film they work at their own companies or shops. The nature of their businesses is not disclosed, but it also neatly sidesteps the issue of racial bias in the job market, as well as the whole issue of the problems of settling in a foreign land. Almost never are there characters in Indian films doing the jobs that Nansan and Hong or Li Qiao and Li Xiaojun are shown doing.

The Diaspora in the Homeland

In the 1990s, with the approaching return of Hong Kong to the Mainland, the theme of conflicted identities, together with the dynamics of overseas residents returning to China, was explored by the Hong Kong film director Ann Hui.

In *Song of the Exile* (1990), 25-year-old Hueyin, a student in the United Kingdom, is prevailed upon by her Japanese mother, Aiko, to return for her sister's wedding in Hong Kong. Hueyin is Anglicized and clashes with her mother, eventually giving in on her dress and hairstyle. Hueyin's father was a Chinese doctor working in Northeast China and her parents married during the war. Her Chinese grandparents never fully accepted their Japanese daughter-in-law, always treating her as an outsider. When Aiko decides to visit her hometown in Japan, Hueyin accompanies her. Unable to speak the language, she gets into scrapes and misunderstandings and gains a better understanding of her mother's experiences of settling into an alien environment. Aiko too comes to realize her preference for her Hong Kong lifestyle and Cantonese food. With a better understanding of each other, both Aiko and Hueyin come to learn that home is located in an emotional space rather than a geographical one.[16] On a visit to her grandparents now living on the Mainland, where they returned to serve the motherland, Hueyin finds her grandfather ailing, victimized by the Red Guards for purchasing Song poetry to send to Hueyin.

My American Grandson (1991) shows an eager Mr Ku preparing for the arrival of his grandson, Ming, from the United States. His parents, scientists on an official US programme, send him back to China for a few weeks while they travel for work. Ming is a complete brat and unable to cope with life in China. He finds the neighbours intrusive, is shocked he doesn't have his own room, or a toilet in the flat, and prefers KFC meals to fresh home-cooked ones. Grandpa Ku spends his meagre savings and borrows money so that Ming can eat American meals and play in video game parlours, and to put him up in a hotel where he can shower like he is used to, watch TV and help himself to sodas from the minibar. Mr Ku rationalizes these expenses as "in the interests of Sino-American relations!" A misadventure in a rural area finally puts Ming back in touch with his Chinese self and he learns the pride of being Chinese.

In an older film, *Homecoming* (1984), directed by Yim Ho, an urbanized Hong Kong woman, Shan Shan, returns to her village across the border for a visit. She visits her friend Ah Zhen, who is now married to her ex-boyfriend Tsong. The rural quality of their home and lives stands in stark contrast to her urban life in Hong Kong. She buys Tsong a pair of rubber boots to wear in the flooded fields, and invites Ah Zhen to bring the village school children for a visit to Hong Kong, leading Ah Zhen to express how little she likes cities. The visit shows Shan Shan what she has given up by leaving her hometown – not just the rural life but the emotional ties of family.

Each of these three films elaborates the political undertones and physical discomfort faced by overseas residents on their return to China, and describes their ties to their homeland in emotional terms. There is a pointed contrast between their chosen homes and the homes they have left behind. This aspect is also featured in the films of the returning overseas Indian. Like Ming when he returns to his grandfather in Beijing, Jazz in *Namastey London* stands apart from her relatives when she visits her home village in the Punjab, clearly not enjoying being at such close quarters with others or dealing with their inquisitiveness. In *Swades*, *Aaja Nachley* and *Delhi-6*, the returnee is filled with an urge to improve society, correct ills and contribute to the betterment of their former homes. They are seen to be giving up a better life for the love of their home country. This feature is absent in the Chinese films.

The Freedom of Living Overseas

Ang Lee's *The Wedding Banquet* (1993) is a good example of the dual lives led by overseas citizens. Outside the network of social structures in his native Taiwan, Gao Wai-tung is free to pursue his personal life in the United States, where he lives with his Caucasian gay lover, Simon. His mother frequently requests him to marry as she wants grandchildren. Simon suggests a sham wedding for Wai-tung to his tenant Wei-wei, an impoverished Mainland Chinese artist, who needs a green card and money to stay in the United States. The overjoyed parents arrive in New York by surprise and organize a wedding banquet. Here we observe the lavish banquet and numerous Chinese customs and ribaldry, aimed at the fecundity of the bride, transposed to the United States. As the bride is from Shanghai, Mr Gao looks upon this marriage as a bridge between the Mainland and Taiwan. When Wai-tung informs his mother that he is gay, they decide it must be kept a secret from his father. But Mr Gao has figured it out already and presents a red packet to Simon, acknowledging him as part of the family and swearing him to secrecy. He doesn't want to let on to the others that he knows the truth. It is his compromise for getting his grandchild.

The solution here is characteristically Chinese, as pointed out by Cynthia Liu.[17] Simon's position is akin to the concubine: he cooks, cleans and looks after Mr Gao when he is unwell – his place in the family is privately acknowledged.

The ability to live where one desires and go where one wants is an overwhelming freedom, as Nansan's friend informs him in *Farewell, China*. "This is America. You don't need the party's permission to move," he shouts as he throws him out. This liberty applies to a traditional family structure as well, where movement without family approval would be restricted. Wai-tung is able to live with his gay lover, as he is living outside the boundaries of traditional Chinese society.

Living overseas also raises the issue of cultural clashes, as depicted in *The Gua Sha Treatment* (2001),[18] an offering from Mainland director Zheng Xiaolong. Xu Datong is a brilliant video game designer living the American dream in the United States with his wife and his young son, Dennis. Datong's father is visiting them from China and treats his grandson with *gua sha*.[19] As the story progresses, the *gua sha* marks on Dennis are misinterpreted by health workers as child abuse, and immediately the Child Welfare Agency removes Dennis from his own home and the care of his parents. In court hearings, the cultural divide is played up by a clever lawyer. He makes Datong's video games seem violent and barbaric, linking them to his cultural heritage through a deliberately ridiculous interpretation of *Journey to the West*, a Chinese classic. Raking up an incident where Datong publicly struck his son, he is deemed to be abusive and unfit as a father,

Fig 3:

and cannot be reunited with his son. Datong explains that he struck his son "to give face" to John, with whom his son Dennis had an altercation. It is ultimately resolved by John, who proves to the court what *gua sha* really is.

The last Chinese film to consider is Hou Hsiao-hsien's *The Flight of the Red Balloon* (2008). Here we see Song Fang, a film student in Paris, working as a nanny to Simon, whose single mother leads a frantic life. Suzanne is shown mostly ranting about her woes – absent husband, a tenant who isn't paying rent, setbacks at work – while in contrast, Song Fang is calm and controlled. While we learn so much about the personal life of Suzanne, we learn no more about Song Fang. As she accompanies Simon to all his after-school activities, she makes a documentary following a red balloon travelling through the city of Paris. The gentle pace of this is at odds with the frenetic life of Suzanne.

The freedom of living overseas is frequently shown as a transgression in commercial Hindi cinema. Divorce (*KANK*), homosexuality (*KHNH*), relationships that transgress social norms (*Purab aur Pachhim*, *Namastey London*, *Dostana* and *Pardes*) are all shown to exist outside the motherland. These transgressions are righted eventually by the *dharmik* culture of India. Sometimes the freedom of not having the state, family or culture dictating behaviour and movement is confusing, for instance when Nansan is thrown out of his friend's house, and in Indian films, when girls switch from Western to Indian clothes, depending on the occasion.

Transnational Indian Films

It is useful to consider transnational Indian films, made by the diaspora community, which provide an introspective look. These "autoethnographic" films provide a counterbalance to Bollywood offerings on the diaspora. These films are generally made in English for the viewership of an international market.

Two early British productions about the South Asian community are useful for comparison: *My Beautiful Laundrette* (1985) and *East is East* (1999), which both depict gay relationships. In contrast to the Bollywood productions that show "faux" gays, these characters are genuinely so. In *My Beautiful Laundrette*, British-born Omar tries to make a go of his uncle's defunct laundry, together with his boyfriend, Johnny. They face racism and attacks from the skinheads of London, while Omar has to deal with the dynamics of a South Asian family – his alcoholic, failed intellectual father and crafty, entrepreneurial uncle. *East is East* deals with the mixed marriage of a Pakistani man, George Khan, and a British woman, Ella. Ironically, George wishes his children to conform to the Islamic way and discourages their mixing with Caucasians, but the children's dress and behaviour conforms more to British youth culture than Mr Khan would like. He tries to arrange the marriages of his sons, but the eldest, Nazir, runs away. It turns out he is gay, and as in *The Wedding Banquet*, the others in the family decide it best not to share this information with the father. The younger sons also rebel against their father, who then turns on Ella. It is a story of domestic abuse, all in the name of religion and conformity.

Gurinder Chadha's *Bhaji on the Beach* presents slices of lives of Indian women in Britain who confront tradition, such as Ginder, an abused wife, who has run away with her son, and Hashida, whose pregnancy (with her black boyfriend) brings the censure of

Fig 4:

the older women. The theme of interracial relations is developed more thoroughly in *Mississippi Masala*, through Meena's relationship with Demetrius, an African American. The colour bias of Indians is depicted vividly, even more so than the bald statements in *Farewell, China.*

Bend It Like Beckham is a brilliant film that again brings to the fore the concern with quickly marrying off girls in the diaspora to promising young men approved by their families, and looks at the intersection of the diasporic presence within the West. Jess, the daughter of a conservative Sikh family in West London, is football mad and secretly joins a semi-pro women's football team. Her English friend, Jules, is her mentor. Jules's mother is as perplexed about her daughter's choices and lack of boyfriend as are Jess's parents about her activities.

If one were to assume that the big fat Indian wedding is as intrinsic to Indian films as kung fu is to Chinese films, then *Bend It Like Beckham* qualifies just as well as do *Monsoon Wedding* and *Bride and Prejudice.* Although *Monsoon Wedding* is the story of a family wedding in Delhi, the groom with whom the match is arranged is from Houston, Texas. Indian enough that he has agreed to marry Aditi by this arrangement, Hemant Rai also wins over his bride as a modern man should. Aditi is having an affair with her married boss, and when Hemant discovers this, he talks it over with Aditi, until she resolves that she wants to go ahead with the marriage. There is a marked difference in how this overseas Indian handles the situation and to what would be the likely reaction of the Indian alpha male in a Bollywood production – possibly he would go on the rampage, beat up the married lover and refuse to marry the girl who has been "sullied." In this introspective look by an overseas director, the film also raises the issues of incest and child abuse, issues rarely viewed in slick Bollywood productions.

Chadha's adaptation of Jane Austen's *Pride and Prejudice* lends itself perfectly to the quest for wealthy eligible husbands for the daughters of Indian parents. In her film,

Bride and Prejudice, the story is imposed on contemporary Indian society, shifting to the diaspora, and climaxing in scenes of a colourful Punjabi wedding.

The final two films selected tell realistic stories of Indians overseas. *The Journey* is the story of a retired widower, Kishan, who goes to live with his son, American daughter-in-law and granddaughter in the United States. He grows close to the child, but after he is separated from her on one of their outings, the daughter-in-law becomes less tolerant of him. Kishan moves out, thus shattering his "American dream" of joining his son.

The Namesake is the story of a young couple, Ashok and Ashima, who make their lives in the United States. It gives us many insights into what new migrants have to cope with as they settle in a foreign land. While Ashok is fully engaged in his academic work, Ashima, a classical singer, spends many lonely hours negotiating an alien culture. Their children are born there and naturally imbibe the American lifestyle. Their son, Gogol, the namesake, attempts to assume the WASP persona through his girlfriend (like the girls in the Chinese movies, Gogol denies his ethnicity), and only after the sudden death of his father does he revert to his Indian roots. With her husband gone, Ashima sells their home and returns to India to continue her career in music.

The Indian transnational films discussed here reflect a concern for the family unit and the suitable marriages of girls, just like popular Hindi films and the Chinese films *The Joy Luck Club* and *Double Happiness* do. Protection of ethnicity and culture is portrayed as being vested in ensuring that females stay within the community. Race relations are more of an issue in these films, which keenly focus on this aspect, which is also the case in the Chinese films. Indian women's relations with non-Indian males are not encouraged. The films also look at intergenerational issues – like the father in *The Journey*, coming to stay with his son and his family in the United States, the visit of Ming to his grandfather in Beijing in *My American Grandson*, and the clash between Gogol and his parents in *The Namesake* – which translate into cultural clashes as well, as the younger generation imbibes and mimics the culture of the host country.

Preserving Indian and Chinese Culture Overseas

> *I was raised the Chinese way. I learnt to swallow my own misery and eat others' bitterness.*
>
> (Ying-ying in *The Joy Luck Club*)

A strong feature of the Chinese films is the depiction of suffering (*shou ku*) and angst, which is quite absent in the case of the Hindi films. There is a great emphasis on the enormous suffering of the first generation that migrated, who suffered war and physical privation, factors that drove them to seek new locations. This occurs in depictions of both the generation that migrated in the first half of the twentieth century as well as the younger generation of the later part of the century, as in the films, *Farewell, China* and *Comrades*. This suffering is relived in *Gua Sha*, in which common cultural practices are perceived through Western eyes as draconian abuse. This feature of suffering is much less of a factor, if not entirely absent, in commercial Hindi films. The transnational film, *The Namesake*, shows Ashima as a young bride suffering loneliness and alienation as a result of her relocation to the United States. But *DDLJ*, *KKKG* and even *KHNH*, despite the melodrama of personal relationships and emotional sadness, are in the main joyous and full of fun, and we experience some of this joyful flavour during the banquet scene in *The Wedding Banquet.*

On the other hand, the strong feature of nationalistic feeling in the popular Hindi films is absent in the transnational Chinese and Indian films selected here, with the exception of *Full Moon in New York*, which suggests a full realization of Chinese-ness rests in reunification. The hankering for the homeland is lacking in these films, painting a more realistic picture of those who left to seek a better life not looking back. This paper suggests that the popular Hindi films create an idealized portrait of the overseas Indian community, to embrace it in its nationalist agenda.

Like the Indians overseas wanting to preserve their Indian-ness, the Chinese overseas are depicted as wanting to preserve their Chinese-ness. This entails maintaining the family, respect for one's elders, obedience and producing children. In the first two films discussed, *The Joy Luck Club* and *Double Happiness*, there is an emphasis on Chinese-ness and the wish to see the children happily married within their community. While this is shown to be achieved in the Indian examples (both Hindi and transnational), in the Chinese films we see the triumph of the individual. Jade in *Double Happiness* leaves the family nest to strike out on her own, and each of the daughters in *The Joy Luck Club* finds her own personal balance. It is only June, Su-yuan's daughter, by seeking out her twin sisters in China, who finds her family – still it is not in the sense of creating her own nuclear family. In all the Indian films, the fulfilment of the individual is seen to be when he/she embraces the whole social enterprise – family and community.

We see the same values reiterated in *The Wedding Banquet*, by Wai-tung's mother. In the end, Wai-tung finds his individual satisfaction by being with the partner of his choice, as well as fulfilling the norms of creating his own nuclear family. In this sense, *The Wedding Banquet* is different from depictions of homosexuality in Hindi film, as in the latter they are all shown to be spurious. They are either for comic effect (*KHNH*) or for purely practical purposes (*Dostana*), perhaps because audiences are deemed not ready for the real thing. The South Asian transnational films, however, do depict real gay relations in both *My Beautiful Laundrette* and *East Is East.* However, in all cases, for real or otherwise, homosexuality is located outside the boundaries of the nation – as that is perhaps where it can most comfortably be located.

Among depictions of the returning diaspora, in both cultures we are shown fairly similar reactions. The returnees seem like fish out of water, looking at everything like outsiders, sometimes critical and sometimes reflective. The locals are not always tolerant and feel like Dong San in *My American Grandson*, describing Ming as "the fake foreigner." Similarly, in the Hindi films *Swades*, *Delhi-6* and *Aaja Nachley* the efforts of the foreign-returned citizens are greeted with resentment and resistance. These feelings are reversed in both the Chinese and Indian cases, when the visitors have settled in and proved themselves. In *Song of the Exile* we have the example of Hueyin's grandparents returning to China to serve the motherland, but we are informed that their efforts were not appreciated. The Hindi counterparts demonstrate the success of the contributions from India's overseas sons and daughters.

The struggle to preserve one's identity in a foreign culture is present in both the Indian and Chinese films, centred especially on women. It is through the marriage of young women to appropriate partners that cultural mores and traditions can be ensured. As Marchetti says:

> Race and racism are intimately connected with sex and gender in these films. If they can be read as cautionary tales for the Chinese abroad as well as celebrations of the enduring power of Chineseness, then they can also be read as cautionary tales for Chinese women and as celebrations of patriarchal tradition.[20]

This applies equally to the Indian films. Just as Li Hong is threatened by the African Americans in *Farewell, China*, Ganga's purity in *Pardes* is threatened by her fiancé, Rajiv, located in the foreign "other," Meena's is under threat in *Mississippi Masala*, and Jazz faces menace in *Namastey London*. In each of the films *DDLJ*, *KHNH* and *Namastey London*, the focus is on arranging a suitable marriage for the daughter, within safe cultural parameters.

To sum up, in their filmic representations, both the Indian and Chinese overseas communities aim to protect their ethnicities and culture through the marriages of their offspring within the same groups. Girls are particularly targeted in fulfilling this function, as patriarchy strives to assert itself. While the material conditions in their new home countries are obviously better, the ethnic culture is deemed superior. Sometimes the clash of cultural values has devastating results, as in *Gua Sha*. There is an emphasis on religious ritual, respect of the family elders and conformity to culture-appropriate mores. The suffering of Chinese immigrants is a key factor in their overseas culture, while among the overseas Indians the rot of the sociopolitical structure is pervasive. And finally, there is a certain freedom in the filmic representations of overseas communities, in which characters break free of cultural and political restraints: freedom to be gay, to have marriages based on love, to divorce, to cross racial and cultural boundaries, but most of all to improve the quality of their lives.

Filmography

Popular Hindi Films:

3 Idiots (2009)
Director: Raj Kumar Hirani

Aaja Nachley (Come dance, 2007)
Director: Anil Mehta

Delhi-6 (2009)
Director: Rakesh Omprakash Mehra

Dilwale Dulhaniyan Leh Jayenge (The brave heart will win the bride, *DDLJ*, 1995)
Director: Aditya Chopra

Dostana (Friendship, 2008)
Director: Tarun Mansukhani

Kabhi Alvida Na Kehnaa (Never say goodbye, *KANK*, 2006)
Director: Karan Johar

Kabhi Khushi Khabie Gham (Sometimes happy, sometimes sad, *KKKG*, 2001)
Director: Karan Johar

Kal Ho Naa Ho (Tomorrow may or may not happen, KHNH, 2003)
Director: Karan Johar

Namastey London (Hello London, 2007)
Director: Vipul Amritlal Shah

New York (2009)
Director: Kabir Khan

Pardes (Foreigner, 1999)
Director: Subhash Ghai

Purab aur Pachhim (East and West, 1970)
Director: Manoj Kumar

Swades (My country, 2004)
Director: Ashutosh Gowarikar

Transnational Chinese Films:

Comrades: Almost a Love Story (1996)
Director: Peter Chan

Double Happiness (1984)
Director: Mina Shum

Farewell, China (1990)
Director: Clara Law

Full Moon in New York (1990)
Director: Stanley Kwan

The Gua Sha Treatment (2001)
Director: Zheng Xiaolong

My American Grandson (1991)
Director: Ann Hui

The Flight of the Red Balloon (2007)
Director: Hou Hsiao-hsien

The Homecoming (1984)
Director: Yim Ho

The Joy Luck Club (1993)
Director: Wayne Wang

The Song of the Exile (1990)
Director: Ann Hui

The Wedding Banquet (1993)
Director: Ang Lee

Transnational Indian Films:

Bhaji on the Beach (1993)
Director: Gurinder Chadha

Bend It Like Beckham (2002)
Director: Gurinder Chadha

Bride and Prejudice (2004)
Director: Gurinder Chadha

East Is East (1999)
Director: Damien O'Donnell

Monsoon Wedding (2001)
Director: Mira Nair

Mississippi Masala (1991)
Director: Mira Nair

My Beautiful Laundrette (1985)
Director: Stephen Freares

The Journey (1997)
Director: Harish Saluja

The Namesake (2006)
Director: Mira Nair

Notes

1 Grateful acknowledgements to the HKIHSS (including the Centre of Asian Studies), University of Hong Kong, and the Nalanda-Sriwijaya Centre, ISEAS, Singapore, for their support of this research; and to AMIC and Lorraine Perreira for the use of resource materials.

2 For more details, see Brij V. Lal, Peter Reeves and Rajesh Rai, eds, *The Encyclopedia of the Indian Diaspora* (Paris: Editions Didier Millet, 2006); Lynn Pan, ed., *The Encyclopedia of the Chinese Overseas* (Singapore: Archipelago Press and Landmark Books, 1998); Wan Lu Tang's introductory video to the Hua Song Museum, Singapore, and other general historical readings.

3 Wang Gungwu, "Introduction: Migration and New National Identities" and "Upgrading the Migrant: Neither Huaqiao nor Huaren," in *The Last Half Century of Chinese Overseas*, ed. Elizabeth Sinn (Hong Kong: Hong Kong University Press, 1998), pp. 1–33. The paradoxes discussed by Wang here can be applied to the Indian diasporic community as well.

4 See for instance the works of Brij Lal, *Chalo Jahaji: On a Journey of Indenture through Fiji* (Suva: Fiji Museum, 2000); Rajagopalan Radhakishnan, *Diasporic Mediations: Between Home and Location* (Minneapolis: University of Minnesota Press, 1996); Chan Kwok Bun, *Chinese Identities, Ethnicity and Cosmopolitanism* (London: Routledge, 2005); Wang Gungwu, *The Chineseness of China* (Hong Kong: Oxford University Press, 1991); Billy K. L. So et al., *Power and Identity in the Chinese World Order: Festschrift in Honour of Professor Wang Gungwu* (Hong Kong: HKU Press, 2003).

5 Chris Berry and Mary Farquhar, *China on Screen: Cinema and Nation* (New York: Columbia University Press, 2006), p. 4; see also the discussion in Gina Marchetti, *From Tian'anmen to Times Square: Transnational China and the Chinese Diaspora on Global Screens, 1989–1997* (Philadelphia: Temple University Press, 2006).

6 See also the discussion of this film in Coonoor Kripalani, "Coming of Age: Bollywood Productions of the Nineties," *Asian Cinema* 12, no. 1 (Spring/Summer 2001).

7 Kripalani, "Coming of Age."

8 Vijay Mishra, *Bollywood Cinema, Temples of Desire* (London: Routledge, 2002), p. 267.

9 In India, the suffix "ji" is used as a mark of respect when addressing people who may be senior or have a high status.

10 Mary Louise Pratt, quoted in Benzi Zhang, "Re-siting the Global/Re-sighting the Local: The Politics of Cultural Diaspora," in *Sights of Contestation: Localism, Globalism and Cultural Production in Asia and the Pacific*, ed. Kwok-kan Tam, Wimal Dissanayake and Terry Siu-han Yip (Hong Kong: Chinese University Press, 2002), p. 42.

11 Berry and Farquhar, *China on Screen*, p. 4.

12 Generally applicants applying for a US visa need a sponsor to vouch for them financially. In Nansan's case, his sponsor was a family acquaintance.

13 Thanks to Dr Geoff Wade of the Nalanda-Sriwijaya Centre, ISEAS, Singapore, for recommending this film.

14 Stephen Teo, "Full Moon in New York," *Senses of Cinema*, January 2001. http://archive.sensesofcinema.com/contents/cteq/01/12/newyork.html. 31 March 2010.

15 Marchetti, *From Tian'anmen to Times Square*, p. 6.

16 Janet Maslin, review of *Song of the Exile* (1990), "Review/Film: Finding Home in Emotional, Not Geographical, Terms," *New York Times*, 15 March 1991. http://movies.nytimes.com/movie/review?res=9D0CEFD8153FF936A25750C0A967958260. 21 January 2010.

17 Cynthia Liu quoted in Berry and Farquhar, pp. 178–9.

18 Thanks to Professor Jia Haitao, director, Institute of Chindian Studies, Jinan University, Guangzhou, for suggesting this film.

19 A remedy for treating common ailments by rubbing oiled skin with a coin or ceramic spoon. This treatment often leaves temporary welts on the back.

20 Marchetti, *From Tian'anmen to Times Square*, p. 203.

References

Books

Berry, Chris and Mary Farquhar. *China on Screen: Cinema and Nation*. New York, Columbia University Press, 2006.

Chan Kwok Bun. *Chinese Identities, Ethnicity and Cosmopolitanism*. London: Routledge, 2005.

Lal, Brij. *Chalo Jahaji: On a Journey of Indenture through Fiji*. Suva: Fiji Museum, 2000.

Lal, Brij, Peter Reeves and Rajesh Rai, eds. *The Encyclopedia of the Indian Diaspora*. Paris: Editions Didier Millet, 2006.

Marchetti, Gina. *From Tian'anmen to Times Square: Transnational China and the Chinese Diaspora on Global Screens, 1989–1997*. Philadelphia: Temple University Press, 2006.

Mishra, Vijay. *Bollywood Cinema, Temples of Desire*. New York, London: Routledge, 2002.

Pan, Lynn ed. *The Encyclopedia of the Chinese Overseas*. Singapore: Archipelago Press and Landmark Books, 1998.

Radhakishnan, Rajagopalan. *Diasporic Mediations: Between Home and Location*. Minneapolis: University of Minnesota Press, 1996.

Sinn, Elizabeth, ed. *The Last Half Century of Chinese Overseas*. Hong Kong: Hong Kong University Press, 1998.

So, Billy K. L. et al. *Power and Identity in the Chinese World Order: Festschrift in Honour of Professor Wang Gungwu*. Hong Kong: HKU Press, 2003.

Tam, Kwok-kan, Wimal Dissanayake and Terry Siu-han Yip, eds. *Sights of Contestation: Localism, Globalism and Cultural Production in Asia and the Pacific*. Hong Kong: Chinese University Press, 2002.

Wang Gungwu. *The Chineseness of China*. Hong Kong: Oxford University Press, 1991.

Articles

Kripalani, Coonoor. "Coming of Age: Bollywood Productions of the Nineties." *Asian Cinema* 12, no. 1 (Spring/Summer 2001): 29–48.

Wang, Gungwu. "Introduction: Migration and New National Identities." In *The Last Half Century of Chinese Overseas*, edited by Elizabeth Sinn, pp. 1–12. Hong Kong: Hong Kong University Press, 1998.

_______. "Upgrading the Migrant: Neither Huaqiao nor Huaren." In *The Last Half Century of Chinese Overseas*, edited by Elizabeth Sinn, pp. 15–33. Hong Kong: Hong Kong University Press, 1998.

Zhang, Benzi. "Re-siting the Global/Re-sighting the Local: The Politics of Cultural Diaspora." In *Sights of Contestation: Localism, Globalism and Cultural Production in Asia and the Pacific*, edited by Kwok-kan Tam, Wimal Dissanayake and Terry Siu-han Yip, pp. 35–56. Hong Kong: Chinese University Press, 2002.

Websites

Maslin, Janet. Review of *Song of the Exile* (1990), "Review/Film: Finding Home in Emotional, Not Geographical, Terms." *New York Times*, 15 March 1991. http://movies.nytimes.com/movie/review?res=9D0CEFD8153FF936A25750C0A967958260. 21 January 2010.

Teo, Stephen. "Full Moon in New York." *Senses of Cinema*, January 2001. http://archive.sensesofcinema.com/contents/cteq/01/12/newyork.html accessed 7 May 2010.

Video

Wan Lu Tang's introductory video to the Hua Song Museum, Singapore.

Chapter 16

THE "OTHER" NRIs: THE CASE OF LOW-WAGE INDIAN MIGRANTS IN THE GULF

Laavanya Kathiravelu

The Indian state's relationship with its overseas residents has been extensively theorized.[1] This literature primarily addresses the significance of remittances and knowledge, which are channelled back to the homeland through its middle-class NRIs (non-resident Indians). In these formulations, low-wage migrants are often left out. Analysis of low-wage migrants' relationship to India is instead limited to macroeconomic formulations at village/state levels,[2] anthropological accounts of reintegration and quotidian experiences of living abroad.[3] Their relationship as transnational subjects caught between regimes of sending and receiving countries has yet to be effectively addressed. Based on fieldwork conducted in Dubai in 2008, this paper demonstrates that this group is largely excluded from initiatives of non-resident citizen benefits, while constructed primarily as empowered free agents in a capitalist global economy. This results in a situation where neo-liberal markets are assumed to effectively regulate labour, and sending and receiving nations abdicate responsibility for ensuring rights and welfare of the migrant. However, both countries continue to reap economic benefits of their labour as productive subjects.

Introduction

In current academic as well as popular and media discourses, much has been made of India's recent "rise." In addition to the subcontinent's rapid economic growth, significant attention has been paid to ethnic Indians living outside the country's borders while contributing to its cultural as well as economic influence. With an estimated twenty million people of Indian origin living outside the country today,[4] their relevance in developing understandings of the Indian nation-state as well as of transnational communities should not be overlooked. This research, in bringing those two elements together, shows that the Indian state is often discriminatory in providing for the welfare of its overseas citizens. While middle-class NRIs are courted through investment policies and visa categories to maintain cultural and economic links with the motherland, the less privileged migrant is relatively neglected in terms of welfare and rights provisions.

They are thus more vulnerable to harsh governance regimes in receiving countries, given the temporary and circular nature of their migrations. This inequality results in victimizing low-wage migrants while seemingly celebrating their agency as free agents in a neo-liberal global marketplace. As this paper shows, in Dubai, migrants' rights are effectively unregulated. Thus, a reliance on NGOs and migrant networks has developed to deal with rights, claims and everyday problems faced by low-wage migrants relegated to the bottom of the socio-economic hierarchy. This examination of low-wage migrant welfare is indicative of the processes that characterize the handling of migrants in other GCC (Gulf Cooperation Council)[5] states and has potential implications in shaping future policy initiatives in both sending and receiving countries.

Non-Resident Indians, Remittances and the Indian State

> The term NRI emerged in the 1970s when the Reserve Bank of India (RBI) marketed specific savings and investment instruments to the successful Indian community abroad, especially those based in North America, Europe, South-east Asia and the Middle East.[6]

Other scholars[7] have dated it to the early 1980s. It is generally agreed that the term originated as a way to describe people of Indian origin who had moved to developed countries and established themselves in their adopted environments as successful immigrants. These were typically middle-class Indians who frequently maintained familial as well as cultural ties to the homeland. With the rolling out of India's economic liberalization policies in 1991, state monopoly of many industries ended and the investment of foreign capital in most sectors of the economy was encouraged.[8] As a strategy to draw foreign capital into India and combat effects of a brain drain, the NRI policy in a climate of economic liberalization was highly successful, allowing savings to be kept in foreign currencies and lessening the risk of converting to an unstable Indian rupee. Scholars writing about NRIs have emphasized discourses of cultural affinity and nationalist sentiment that the Indian state draws upon to solicit such injections into the Indian economy. However, what is significant to note here is that these particular investment policies were targeted primarily at what the state defined as *successful* overseas Indians. The low-wage migrant is not similarly addressed by Indian state discourses as being valuable to its growth, although their contributions make up a significant portion of annual remittances. Their patterns of migration also follow a longer and more stable trajectory, which is not dependent on stimulus by the state or triggered by India's integration into the global economy. Opportunities for low-skilled or unskilled Indians remain limited despite India's accelerated economic growth with working class socio-economic positions not improving at the rates of the middle-class. Migration is still seen as offering relatively more opportunities for social mobility and capital accumulation than remaining in India.

In the year 2008, total remittances to India amounted to USD52 billion, which placed it as the top recipient of overseas transfers in the world.[9] Undocumented capital networks, which low-wage migrants more typically utilize, further inflate that number.[10]

These remittances represent about 3 per cent of the country's GDP, a portion higher than even revenues from India's software exports.[11] In Kerala, where the overwhelming majority of emigration is to the Gulf States, remittances constitute 22 per cent of the state domestic product. Remittances to this part of South India have had a positive impact on per capita incomes, standards of living and in the reduction of poverty levels.[12] In fact, indicators demonstrate a level of development closer to nations in Western Europe and North America than to the rest of India.[13] Remittances from overseas Indians have also greatly aided in the improvement of India's balance of payments deficit and accounts for more than the total amount of international development aid India receives. "There is no denying that the dependence of the Indian economy on this commoditized human transfer has allowed it to maintain a conventional trade imbalance and, at the same time, post record foreign exchange reserves (over USD71 billion in 2002/03)."[14] The economic importance of migrant remittances to the Indian state is undisputable. But while macro economic impacts of remittances have been analysed extensively in the literature,[15] the relationship between the Indian state and the contributors of such overseas capital has primarily been limited to assessments of how NRIs in North America and Europe maintain connections with the home country.[16] Gulf migration in this aspect has thus far been largely overlooked.

It is estimated that about USD14 billion, or more than a quarter of India's combined remittances, comes from the Gulf region. Within this region, the UAE and Saudi Arabia are the states with highest remittances. With the financial crisis, remittances from the Gulf have even overtaken those from North America.[17] Migration to the Gulf is primarily low-wage and temporary, of a substantively different nature to the highly skilled migration to North America, which often ends up in permanent settlement. And although the portion of remittances by low-wage migrants is decreasing in comparison to investments by wealthy NRIs, their savings ultimately result in less reliance on welfare payments, new infrastructure and a better-educated population, thereby reducing a reliance on the state to provide such initiatives. Long-term consequences of labour migration and remittances thus have significant positive outcomes for the Indian state. In that context, Walton-Roberts says, "In light of India's commitment to engage with NRIs, it must be asked whether the state has effectively mobilized to protect the interests of the very people from whom it has derived the greatest financial returns."[18] This paper suggests that in the instance of the low-wage migrant, it has not. Subject to different regulatory regimes and rhetoric in both sending and receiving states, this already marginalized group receives relatively less attention from both scholars and state policies, compared to middle-class NRIs who are aggressively courted by the Indian government.

Indian Connections with Gulf and Dubai/UAE

Dubai, one of the seven emirates that form the United Arab Emirates (UAE), shares a long history of trade and interaction with India. Due to the city-state's strategic geographical position, it has been for centuries a trading post for routes between Europe, Africa and Asia. The British colonial period, where trade routes to India were secured, marked an intensification of the trade ties between India and Dubai.[19]

Dubai's intimate links with India are further evidenced by the fact that in the early decades of the twentieth century, Dubai was the key entrepôt centre for goods from India, which were then re-exported to Persia and the neighbouring states. This close interdependency continues to this day, where India is not just a source of labour, but continues to function as a market for goods re-exported from Dubai's ports. In the first half of 2008, India topped the list of Dubai's main trading partners in import, export and re-export sectors.[20] In fact, Dubai today is characterized as more of an "Indian cultural space" than an Arab one.[21] Despite these historic cultural and economic links, Indians in the UAE do not enjoy any special consideration or treatment. Instead, they are relegated to the base of a hierarchy structured along lines of "race" and nationality.[22] They face structural as well as more quotidian forms of discrimination, from restricted employment opportunities to refusal of entry to leisure spaces. Low-wage Indian migrants are further marginalized by their class positions and fall at the bottom of the socio-economic ladder due to their disadvantageous position across multiple vectors of discrimination. The autocratic nature of the UAE government, in addition, adds complexity to a situation where the Indian state must balance the maintenance of strategic economic links with the need to put pressure on the host government to comply with workers and human rights conventions, to ensure that the welfare of its citizens is adequately looked after. These issues of the transnational management of labour rights will be elaborated in the following sections.

Indians in the UAE

Indians in the Gulf make up 19 per cent, almost a fifth of the total number of persons of Indian origin living outside India today.[23] They are estimated to number about four million in all. (The reluctance of Gulf governments to publish breakdowns of their resident populations based on nationality contributes to the difficulty of arriving at a precise number.) Unlike diasporic Indians in North America, Europe and Southeast Asia, almost all in the Middle East continue to maintain migrant status, regardless of the length of time they have lived in their adopted countries. Half of those migrants come from the state of Kerala in South India.[24] In the UAE itself, Indians number more than one million (in 2001; these numbers are bound to be higher today)[25] out of a total population of four million.[26] In Dubai itself, Indians make up more than half the resident population, amounting to more than half a million. A majority of these Indians in the UAE originate from the South Indian states of Kerala, Tamil Nadu and Andhra Pradesh.

The bulk of migration to the Gulf from India took place in the mid-1970s in order to cope with the creation of jobs associated with the oil boom. While many of these early migrants came to work in unskilled manual positions, others filled managerial and entrepreneurial gaps, as the local Emirati population was not adequately trained to undertake such work. Although there is still a high demand for migrant labour in the Gulf, diversification of migration trends has resulted in incorporation of more migrants from other parts of the Arab world, South Asia and North Asia, although Indians still form the majority group of residents in the UAE at present. This movement away from the recruitment of South Asians is one of the effects of the regional policy of Arabization (Emiratization in the UAE), which aims to increase the numbers of citizens in the work force, especially within the private sector, which has historically been dependent on large numbers of both skilled and unskilled migrants. This move has been associated with the increasing fear of dominance by a majority foreign population and their taking over of jobs as well as a resultant loss of traditional (Islamic) values due to the modernizing effects of globalization and concurrent "Westernization." Louer[27] identifies this as a similar discourse that runs through other Gulf societies such as Bahrain. One of the objectives of such state policies has been to reduce the overdependence on one nationality (i.e. Indians). Thus increasingly, Central and North Asian labour is being sought for low-skilled work. In the UAE, however, the policy of Emiratization has been largely unsuccessful in its implementation and there is a continued dependence on unskilled and skilled migrant labour. And despite the above-described shifts, the largest group of low-skilled migrants in the UAE also continue to come from India, predominantly from the region of Andhra Pradesh.

Global Restructuring

Dubai today occupies a dynamic position within the global hierarchy of states. Prior to the GFC (Global Financial Crisis) and the declaration by Dubai World in December 2009 that it was defaulting on its loans, Dubai was seen as a fast climber, quickly losing its identity as a poor, undeveloped state through vast infrastructural investments, high levels of foreign direct investment and improving standards of healthcare and education. Boasting a higher annual GDP growth rate than even China, Dubai was perceived as perhaps the state most rapidly embedding itself within the neo-liberal world order. Dubai is also a highly appropriate example of the global restructuring that is taking place with less developed nations like China and India acquiring greater economic and political power on the world stage. These are causing shifts in international relations, disrupting and reconfiguring global power, and have implications for transnational conventions and the international regulation and movement of migrants. In the words of Datta et al.:

> Global economic restructuring [...] critically shapes transnational migration in terms of setting out the broad parameters which determine who moves, how mobility is organised and facilitated, and the rights which accompany different sets of migrant workers – which in turn determines the warmth with which they are received in host cities.[28]

Currently, profits from the sale of oil account for less than 3 per cent of Dubai's GDP, while tourism contributes 30 per cent.[29] There are increasingly many highly trained workers arriving in the UAE to address the skill shortages created by an economy that is moving towards more service-oriented industries such as tourism, finance and real estate. With the construction sector also one of the main drivers of the UAE's economic growth, most migrants from India today come to work in building and related industries. The large numbers of manual labour needed to propel the real estate boom in Dubai and the UAE mean that the majority of the Indian migrant work force comprises low-wage workers engaged predominantly in unskilled and low-skilled jobs. The lack of an appropriately trained population, combined with the reluctance of locals to undertake private sector or low-paying jobs has also created a large skilled migrant pool.[30] Many of these skilled migrants are from India's middle classes, drawn to the Gulf by higher salaries and a more stable political climate. This results in a two-tier migration system whereby long-term, higher-salaried packages, often inclusive of benefits such as housing, cars and children's education allowance, are given to skilled migrants. Shorter-term, typically two-year contracts with low salaries and no extra allowances or benefits are conditions under which most unskilled labourers migrate. This bifurcation reflects existing and widening inequalities across the world, perpetuated by processes of globalization.

Structural Violence

> The experiences of South Asians in the Gulf are best approached through the narratives of the laws that are designed to marginalise them, and that set an inflexible frame for expatriate work and family life.[31]

The Gulf States are unique as receiving countries. Although it is the region that has the highest dependence on migrant labour (with the UAE having the highest local to migrant ratio), the GCC states are also the most guarded about granting citizenship rights to migrants. Functioning as autocratic welfare states, the social contract between citizens and rulers rests upon the understanding that as long as the welfare of subjects is well taken care of, the sheikh's authority to govern is not questioned. This mode of governance, which has its roots in Bedouin tribal politics, has evolved into the current system of distribution of oil benefits and of profits from state investments.[32] In such a rentier state, citizenship is traced along patrilineal and patriarchal lines, with only children born to Emirati fathers granted Emirati citizenship.[33] Full citizenship and its benefits, such as free state education, is not offered to even long-term migrants or their children, who may have been born and lived their entire lives in the UAE. More recently, benefits previously available to all, such as free healthcare, have been limited to nationals. The intensification of the divide between citizen and foreigner is augmented by stricter immigration and visa policies, which have also become more bureaucratic and expensive.

Every labour-importing state faces the challenge of balancing the economic need for migrant labour with the political imperative to control it. In the Gulf and UAE in particular, this is achieved through a system of *kafala* or sponsorship, whereby a local Emirati partner is required for all commercial ventures. This policy, implemented in the mid-1970s, was a "restriction aimed at discouraging permanent residence." But rather than create a new class of local entrepreneurs as was hoped, the phenomenon of "silent partners" emerged – "citizens who play a minor role in the economy by merely signing contracts and completing formalities."[34]

To reside within the UAE, an individual must thus obtain a work visa for himself and a family visa from his or her employer should he want to bring his or her family. Women cannot sponsor spouses or children except in certain limited circumstances. The work visa process functions through the system of *kafala*, a formal practice of patronage that is common in the Gulf region. Most low-wage migrants are brought into Dubai through a *kafeel* or sponsor who is either an individual or enterprise for whom they will work throughout their time in Dubai. A foreigner wanting to start a business also needs a local partner or sponsor. For this, typically he/she will be charged a fee or a cut of the profits in return. The national will then normally own 51 per cent of the enterprise. Free zones are spaces of exception, where a foreigner is allowed to hold a majority share or fully own a business or enterprise. Of course, this is only an option for entrepreneurs with a sizable amount of capital, categorically excluding the low-wage migrant. When the work visa expires (at the same time as the job contract), the migrant (and his family) must leave the country. Individuals, thus, are valued only for as long as they are productive economic agents. In addition, the *kafala* system ensures that the migrant is dependent on his or her sponsor for his or her legal status. This creates a disjuncture between both sending and receiving states' articulations of migrant labour as free agents responding to demand in a global marketplace, and the system of bondage to a particular employer practised in the UAE. Should the migrant want to move to another job, a certificate of no objection must first be obtained from his or her original employer. Workers are not independently able to move to an employer who offers a better remuneration, given that supply of labour is controlled by employers. Absconding from or terminating a contract under objections from the employer/sponsor could also result in a (year-long or indefinite) ban on entry and work in the UAE. It is also common practice for employers to take possession of passports of low-wage labourers, ensuring it is impossible for the migrant to easily change jobs or even leave the country. Longva sums up the situation succinctly: "The GCC countries do not have a free labour market."[35] Most countries enforce some mode of differential exclusion, usually accepting desirable skilled immigrants for long-term permanent residency and even citizenship, while limiting the low-skilled to temporary status. The GCC states are extremes in this respect, where *all* migrants are allowed in only "within strict functional and temporal limits."[36]

The low-wage migrant, in comparison to the white-collar worker, is subject to further restrictions. This results in very different everyday experiences for different strata of migrants from India. For example, low-wage migrants are placed in situations where they cannot bring their families with them. In Dubai itself, this results in a population where there are three times the numbers of males as females.[37] This is due, firstly, to the UAE's laws that disallow migration of the family if the individual migrating for work does not earn an income that exceeds AED4000[38] per month, and secondly, because of high living costs. Most of these migrants typically come to the UAE to be employed in semi-skilled or unskilled positions and earn between AED600–2000 per month. This is, for most, sufficient only for their own maintenance and a small remittance, and is not enough to support another or multiple family members in the UAE given the relatively high rents of accommodation and costs of food, education and transport (as compared to their home countries). And, despite pressure from international rights agencies and the Indian government, at present, there is no minimum wage requirement in the UAE.[39] The motivation in going abroad for most low-wage migrants is to remit as much of their income as possible back to their families left behind, and thus the temporary hardship of separation is viewed as a necessary sacrifice. Being away from family for long periods results in social problems latent in the low-wage migrant population. These costs are not publicly acknowledged as outcomes of migration and are only apparent in the high rates of suicides and alcohol abuse among the low-wage migrant group.

Although the system of *kafala* is supposed to ensure that care of the migrant is ultimately the liability of the sponsor, in practice, the arrangement can function quite differently. Privatizing the relationship between employer and migrant employee implies that the state then has little jurisdiction or inclination to ensure that provisions for migrant rights and welfare are made. This is especially significant in the case of domestic workers who typically do not even have recourse to corporate infrastructure. Hondagneu-Sotelo explains how this results in a highly inequitable relationship:

> Workers negotiate job terms and pay without the benefit of guidelines established by government, unions, employment agencies or private firms. A labor agreement established between two lone individuals who are operating without standard guidelines heightens the asymmetry of the employer–employee relationship.[40]

This raises important issues of regulation and questions of responsibility for the welfare of the migrant when the sponsor abdicates responsibility. One way in which the system of *kafala* is regularly misused is through the selling of work visas. Despite the sponsor/*kafeel* and employer having to, by law, be the same person or entity, in reality, visas are not necessarily tied to a particular employer. They are regularly sold to migrants or agents in their home countries with the implicit understanding that someone other than the sponsor can employ the migrant worker. This illegal selling of what are termed *azad* (free) visas, is how agents are able to charge large sums to potential migrants that typically ensnare them within structures of debt bondage. Ironically, however, low-wage migrants on an *azad* visa have more freedom to move between jobs and employers, enabling them to bargain for better pay and working conditions. Not being tied to a particular employer may also mean periods of little or no work – an extremely difficult prospect for low-wage migrants in debt. Workers on the *azad* visa make up part of the flexible workforce that is also comprised of overstayers and those working on a tourist/visit visa. These illegal practices are widespread and their prevalence points to a relative tolerance by state authorities who are complicit in maintaining a flexible labour pool. However, migrants on *azad* and visit visas have to be constantly vigilant against police checks and deportation. These groups, by virtue of their irregular status also have no recourse to the labour tribunal or police in instances where they do not get paid for work they have carried out.

Contract substitution is another form of exploitation that many low-wage migrants face within the *kafala* system that is not regulated or monitored by the state. This basically refers to the substitution of the contract originally agreed upon in the country of origin with one that does not contain conditions as favourable to the worker – i.e., lower pay and housing allowance as well as longer working hours. Once the migrant is in the receiving country, they have little alternative but to sign the revised contract, having no basis on which to negotiate. Many would have borrowed large sums to finance their migration, making a refusal of the contract and return unfeasible until their loan is discharged. Many of my informants also reported not being given enough time to read the contract's terms nor having the terms explained before being made to agree. Here we see the threat of deportation being used to discipline and structurally disadvantage the low-wage migrant.

In the regulation of labour flows, the UAE is an extreme example of how "the rights of states clearly prevail over the rights of migrants, with states retaining the ultimate right to set the conditions under which foreigners may enter and reside in their territory."[41] The state, however, also has the ultimate right to determine when the migrant should leave its borders. In the UAE, this is expressed clearly in the ever-present threat of deportation or revocation of visa privileges.[42] The constant threat of deportation by the Emirati state is the most effective means of disciplining the migrant population. Especially for many low-skilled migrants, who cannot return without having repaid their incurred debt and remitted substantial savings, deportation is not just socially shameful but financially disastrous. The threat of deportation also prevents group bargaining for migrant rights, as collective protesting usually results in protestors being immediately deported. But although organizing labour unions is illegal in the UAE – a violation of the rights of migrants to free association – in recent years there have been strikes by low-wage construction labourers demanding wage increases and to be paid on time. Many of these, while gaining publicity for their cause, have not resulted in any real or sustained change. With the mass exodus of many low-wage migrants and the effects of the GFC taking their toll on Dubai's construction sector, many have been forced to leave without having been paid in months. Police and labour tribunals have also been largely ineffective or disinterested in responding to migrants' claims of non-payment or late payment. These strikes however, do point to a rising political consciousness among low-wage migrants in the UAE. They can be seen simultaneously as "*reactions* to their marginalized condition and *productive* of new forms of political belonging."[43]

Although states have developed sophisticated surveillance mechanisms, overstayers and irregular migration[44] are still common. There were 83,000 residency violators in Dubai in 2007 alone.[45] This relative tolerance and lack of urgency towards illegal migration suggests that the receiving state is complicit in ensuring the existence of this flexible, temporary workforce. Irregular migrants will typically work for lesser wages than others in their position and employers in the UAE do not have to incur the cost of visas and mandatory health insurance, thus making them an attractive component for an economy structured along increasingly neo-liberal lines. As Nicola Piper argues:

> Even in the destination (and typically more-developed) countries, as a result of their increasingly restrictive migration policies, the numbers of undocumented migrants who typically work in the informal sector of the economy are also rising. Their presence is tacitly approved but because they tend to be lower or unskilled, their contribution is officially ignored.[46]

This is echoed by Piyasiri Wickramasekara, who alludes to how host country governments play a part in sustaining undocumented migration:

> There is tacit tolerance of the presence of migrant workers in irregular status on the part of many governments during economic booms, and to sustain large informal sectors in their economies, while officially they aim to be seen as "combating" or "fighting" irregular migration.[47]

The UAE government's recent tightening of the visa extension policy was publicized as a means of addressing the widespread problem of working on tourist visas.[48] In practice, however, border hopping to renew visas continues to function as before. This lack of implementation of announced changes, while giving the impression of cracking down on illegal migration, did not, in reality, engender any effect. For overstayers, the UAE government's announcement of granting amnesty to illegal workers every few years (the previous two amnesty periods were in 2003 and 2007) has also created a level of complacency with regards to irregular migration. For some low-wage migrants, it is seen as a legitimate, state-sanctioned means of negotiating their illegal status while temporarily avoiding detection and arrest. Holding regular amnesties has been acknowledged as international good practice.[49] In the case of irregular migration to the UAE, however, they do not seem to address the root cause of the issue, which has to do with the strict hiring policies which tie migrants, via work visas, to specific employers. During the 2007 amnesty, the majority of irregular migrants who turned themselves in to the authorities were Indian low-wage workers, who had either overstayed their visas or had been working on a "visit" visa.

As a consequence of their marginality as illegals, these migrants are more susceptible to being economically exploited and socially excluded. "Above all, irregular migration is a protection problem, since migrant workers become vulnerable to extreme violations of their human and labour rights. [...] Fear of detection may keep migrant workers away from even legitimately available services."[50] Many irregular migrants in Dubai I came across during my fieldwork there, for instance, expressed reluctance in approaching embassy officials, local police or labour rights committees for fear that their illegal status would emerge and lead to immediate deportation to their home country and a future ban on working in the UAE. This often means that irregulars have limited access to healthcare and no insurance benefits. This is problematic given that many of them work in high-risk and dangerous environments on construction sites and oil rigging platforms.

Termed "guest workers" in the UAE, to underscore their reliance on the benevolence of the state, migrants are effectively placed in a position where they have very limited rights. Under circumstances where they have no access to long-term residence or citizenship, and where they are forced to leave their families behind, the low-wage migrant is placed in a position where ties to the homeland cannot be given up and must be maintained for an eventual return. The receiving country places them in a situation where they are "needed but not wanted"[51] and limits their participation in political and social spheres of urban life.

Sending states, on the other hand, utilize ties of family and political citizenship to target low-wage migrants with specific policies to ensure that they keep remitting a portion of their incomes.[52] Institutions such as the State Bank of India (SBI) have developed financial instruments specifically with low-wage migrants in mind. These initiatives are primarily to aid quicker and more reliable remittance payments. They act to formalize money transfers by low-wage migrants, who are more likely to use informal channels. The majority of workers in the Gulf, especially the low-wage migrants, are particularly important to the Indian state as their remittances are typically a larger proportion of their incomes and more frequent than that of skilled migrants who do not leave family behind. Their labour is more precarious, as they can be subject to deportation and their contracts cancelled more easily. Thus, many migrate for work for periods of a few years, returning and then leaving again after a break of a few months or years. Walton-Roberts articulates this link between the unstable and circular nature of much low-wage migration, and the increased likelihood of income being remitted. The irregular migrant, given the instability of his/her legal status, is also highly beneficial to the sending state:

> The greater the uncertainty of settlement and tenure for Indian migrants overseas, the greater the potential economic returns to India. Under the conditions of globalized labour markets, intense state regulation of international migration (including the reduction of rights accorded to temporary and undocumented workers) creates a scenario where the sending state can financially benefit from their own citizens' vulnerability. The two global movements of capital and migrants have to contend with very different regulatory regimes.[53]

Governments can thus be seen as complicit in the perpetuation of such bifurcated systems of flows, where capital moves quickly across borders while bodies remain static. This points to the need to re-examine recent discourses in migration which have celebrated the effects of return/circular migration and low-wage migrants' remittances as contributing towards development agendas, as there is a disconnect between such nation-building rhetoric and reality on the ground.[54] While depicted as transnational agents of change, the low-wage migrant is often subject to structural exploitation by receiving countries and abuse by employers.

This *kafala* system of sponsorship, agents, recruiters and people smugglers involved in these networks of migration all constitute what has been termed the "privatization of migration" – a phenomenon that is also seen as consistent with global trends of liberalization and deregulation. The state, in the case of Dubai, the UAE and other Gulf states, has minimal involvement in processes of migration. This absence of state regulation or monitoring of the mobility of labour is not, however, part of more recent neo-liberal strategies of the Emirates. As previously mentioned, the *kafala* system has been in place since the early waves of migration associated with the discovery of oil deposits. However, new laws requiring, for example, compulsory medical insurance ensured by the employer for every labour migrant entering Dubai, point to ways in which the state is further distancing itself from the responsibility of managing its large migrant population. Labour migration is dealt with as a private economic relationship between employer and employee. The system of *kafala* thus reflects the laissez-faire approach of government that Dubai espouses in its state rhetoric as a space of commercial enterprise. There are, as we have seen, various problems that arise from this perspective of looking at labour migration as a primarily and predominantly self-regulating economic phenomenon, without taking into consideration its social and political consequences.

Indian State Involvement

The beneficial outcomes reaped by the Indian state are not matched by a corresponding level of care and concern towards low-wage migrant welfare. Very recent literature acknowledges that the entire regulation of international migration by the Indian state needs an overhaul, as current regulatory practices are inadequate in ensuring migrants' welfare.[55] The inability to regulate or govern agents' recruitment fees is probably the most urgent single issue which needs to be addressed in relation to South Asian low-wage labour in the UAE and wider Gulf region. Despite legislation which stipulates that the employer should bear all recruitment fees including the cost of travel to the UAE, many low-wage migrants from India (and other less developed countries) remain in a situation where they pay large fees to an agent who finds them a job and/or work visa in one of the Emirates. Like the majority of migrants, most agents too are from India, and most of them are unregulated and unauthorized by the state or government.[56] For many working-class Indians, these agents are often the only route to becoming a migrant. They have knowledge about the process of migration and contacts with potential employers which would otherwise be inaccessible. Many mortgage or sell their homes and possessions or take on loans in order to finance this placement fee. Unscrupulous agents usually take a significant cut of the "fees" even if the employer foots the entire cost of the visa administration and airfare. The migrant is, therefore, under pretence, still made to pay for it. While in the majority of situations the promised visa and flight ticket to the UAE materialize, in some instances entire life savings may never be recovered. These payments of agents' fees often account for a large proportion of the migrant workers' wages. The level of indebtedness of foreign contract workers can thus be considered "debt bondage" as they are placed in a situation where they are trapped within a particular job for as long as their loan is unpaid. Being embedded within the *kafala* system also makes it extremely difficult to change employment. In such situations, low-wage migrants reported taking an average of one and a half to two years to clear their debts.

Another factor that complicates the debt bondage situation is that many low-wage migrants migrate through personal networks of family and friends, who in turn also demand "fees" or payment for their assistance. This "co-ethnic exploitation" is a double-edged sword.[57] While friendship and family networks can function as productive ways to achieve social mobility through migration, they may involve becoming implicated in exploitative relations. Many low-wage migrants are aware of this risk and yet agree to such arrangements, making ambivalent the position of exploiter. Marina de Regt points out that this is indicative of "the weakness of government policies of both sending and receiving countries and illustrates the blurred line between legal and illegal migration."[58] Although migration may be through legal channels, practices by agents who facilitate such mobilities are often against the law.

The regulation and policing of recruiters is perhaps the most urgent job of the Indian state, as it is the single biggest factor which would reduce the situation of debt bondage of which many low-skilled workers are victims. The widespread and continued prevalence of this phenomenon points also to a lack of educational initiatives by the Indian government to create awareness of such practices. In my interviews with low-wage migrants, the need for informing potential migrants of such practices of exploitation repeatedly emerged as an important and urgent responsibility of the Indian government. Migrants and NGO workers recommended dissemination through mass media outlets as well as more formal means of information distribution such as state arms of the labour ministry.

Joseph, a social worker in a Dubai-based voluntary organization which deals with migrant welfare issues, explains why there still exists a continual stream of low-wage migrants being cheated by agents and going to Dubai with large debts. He attributes it firstly to a lack of information about the reality of labour migration to the Gulf: "People are not educated; that is the main reason behind it. Now it is greatly reduced. Because a lot of Andhra people went back and they have seen a lot of people in a pathetic situation."

Some initiatives have recently been undertaken at the level of the individual state in India. However, their levels of success in reducing exploitation have yet to be assessed. The establishment of the Overseas Manpower Company Andhra Pradesh (OMCAP) by the state government, for example, ensures greater involvement in the training and recruitment of overseas workers. This initiative ensures that potential migrants are not just equipped with the appropriate skills, but that they are matched up with employers, thereby eliminating the agent's middleman role. The entire process of training and placement occurs at no cost to the trainee. In December 2009 the Indian state also signed an agreement with the UAE in order to centralize recruitment through one agency. The long-term effects of these announced changes remain to be seen, although the Indian embassy has reported a significant reduction in labour complaints.[59] However, given that much recruitment takes place at the very local level, mediated through kinship or friend networks, a greater grassroots campaign may be necessary to effectively deal with the issue of unscrupulous placement agencies and agents.

Beyond the regulation of recruitment, the Indian state has also shown a lack of involvement in the implementation of workers' rights in Dubai and the UAE. The withholding/non-payment of wages or underpayment and breaches of work contracts is the most significant issue with regards to migrants' employment rights.[60] Such problems of withholding salaries are widespread in Dubai, with construction labourers going unpaid for up to six months. Temporary migrant workers whose visas are linked to their contracts have little opportunity or avenues in such circumstances to air their grievances. The choice is typically between deportation, or working under the employer's conditions. The monetary investment, social and economic capital necessary to bring such wage claims to court also disables the low-wage/unskilled migrant from seeking recourse. Nicola Piper goes on to suggest that in such situations networking between NGOs as well as greater initiative by embassies, for example in providing legal support, is needed.[61]

The issue of jurisdiction here is an important one as NGOs and migrant advocacy groups based in sending countries do not have the authority to settle disputes in the receiving country, and thus are of little practical assistance to migrants.[62] They have to turn either to local NGO groups or to their embassy or consulate in the receiving state, which has the most legal and political clout in dealing with such matters. It is thus extremely problematic when embassies representing large numbers of migrants are ill-equipped and inadequate in handling migrant welfare issues. This often means that migrants turn to informal alternatives for support. As Gamburd has discovered:

> Housemaids whom I have interviewed often find services at the embassy lacking, noting insufficient staff and Spartan accommodations. Rather than rely on formal institutions in times of trouble, women often turn to informal personal networks to help them out of difficult situations.[63]

In my research, this was also a theme that surfaced regularly among NGO workers. The lack of involvement by the Indian embassy as representatives of the government in dealing with wage concerns of low-wage labourers is lamented by an activist in Dubai:

> But now they come over here, through some XYZ agent, and they can't even speak to someone. The agent will not take responsibility for non-payment of wages etc. He will say, "Come on, there are other people that are working. You're alone or what? You work!" But these fellows, they should go back and ask the government. There should be someone responsible on the government's side. That these people have been sent; they have not been paid the salaries [...]. Immediately they can call the embassy and tell them! So and so companies are not paying the salaries.

But beyond dealing with unpaid and late payment of wages, my informant goes on to point out the Indian embassy's basic inadequacies in catering for the needs of low-wage migrants, who come mostly from Andhra Pradesh, with knowledge of only their local language, Telegu, and who are not usually proficient in Hindi or English, the languages in which the embassy functions. This also seems to indicate that the embassy is practically oriented more towards catering for the needs of skilled, middle-class migrants. His criticisms are specifically of inappropriate language provisions, as well as the need for an accessible and widely known point of communication. He quotes from a conversation he had with an embassy official:

> "*You* should have the help desk for them. In the Indian embassy. I know you, so I'll call you on the mobile. But an ordinary, normal person, how will he call you? How will he inform you of his problems, his grievances?" I told him: you have to have a help desk.
>
> "We have the mobile numbers, the help desk."
>
> "What help desk? They don't speak Telegu [...]. Our people can't speak more than Telegu. So keep someone who can speak Telegu. Around 80 per cent of construction workers are from Andhra Pradesh. So you should realize that there should be someone who can speak Telegu. And not just a mobile phone, there should be a proper help desk. Where they can register their complaints."

In recent months, under pressure from organizations representing migrants, the Indian embassy has established a 24-hour help desk, a service which has been outsourced due to the difficulties of the overstretched consulate in dealing with the logistical necessities of such an undertaking. Whether information about this service is being effectively disseminated, however, still remains to be seen. Representatives of sending countries also have to bear in mind, in fighting for their citizens' rights, the disadvantageous positions in which they may be placing migrants from their country.

> An additional problem for origin countries is that, with increasing competition on the "labour export market," they have relatively little influence on the treatment

> of their nationals in the countries of destination and little bargaining power when it comes to the negotiation of bilateral agreements (BLAs) or Memoranda of Understanding (MoUs), partly because they fear losing their share in the regional or global market. [...] But not all sending countries are equally affected by this and it seems the diversification in terms of skill levels, occupations and countries of destination is one way to avoid being the victim of competition of this sort. This has been done quite successfully by the Philippines.[64]

Despite India's emergence as an important player in the global economy, its assertion of political pressure to guarantee, for example, minimum wage for its construction workers, has proved inadequate in changing labour standards in the Gulf States. A minimum wage for Indian workers would make them strategically disadvantaged compared to migrants from countries with weaker currencies and who are willing to work for less. The quest for cheap labour and moves to diversify supplies has for example already led to greater numbers of Chinese low-wage migrants in Dubai. To diversify skill levels and destinations of potential migrants calls for movement towards tighter regulation and more resources devoted to the issue by the Indian government, as opposed to the more laissez-faire approach it now adopts. However, as pointed out by Gamburd[65] and other scholars, as long as an international hierarchy exists between labour-sending and labour-receiving countries, ensuring that low-wage, low-skilled migrants receive the same levels of welfare, protection and rights as skilled migrants will be a challenge.

Reliance on Migrant Groups and NGOs

In a conservative political environment such as Dubai, it is almost impossible for low-wage migrants to set up organizations of their own, due to their temporary and precarious status in the host state, but also due to their marginal economic position, which places them at the bottom of social hierarchies and agendas. These impediments to self-organization such as legal status, type of job and lack of democratic space have been acknowledged.[66] And, as has been previously mentioned, labour unions are illegal. They have not, however, prevented more dynamic and temporary forms of collective bargaining from emerging. Strikes and riots have resulted in payment of overdue wages as well as wage hikes and improved living conditions for some low-wage workers. However, these are rare and unsustainable in the provision of rights in the long-term.

In the absence of a strong presence of sending-country embassies and lack of welfare provision by them in Dubai, it is the non-governmental agencies transcending the borders of the nation-state which largely cater to the needs of migrants and which campaign for migrant rights. "It is alternative organizations, such as migrant worker associations or NGOs working on migrant issues, that have taken on an important role."[67] These include international NGOs such as Human Rights Watch (HRW) and Amnesty International. HRW, for example, published a defamatory report in 2006 which not only brought undesirable international attention to Dubai's treatment of low-wage migrants but also put significant pressure on the local government to implement and enforce better laws to guarantee standards of living and safety at the work site. A subsequent report released in 2008 has led to consideration for stricter laws on recruitment and heftier penalties for trafficking. Pressure by Western governments to improve labour standards as a precondition to the signing of free trade agreements (FTAs) has also prompted the UAE to make some visible moves to improve low-wage migrants' living and working conditions. But as much as these international shaming practices force governments to address worker concerns, their effects are not as sustained or involved at the local level as is necessary to ensure sustained change. Efforts of international and transnational organizations have also met with only limited success, as most lack any "teeth" to enforce disciplinary measures or ensure compliance. For example, the three most significant global legal ILO conventions for the protection of migrant rights have disappointingly low rates of ratification.[68] And the states that have done so thus far are mostly labour-sending countries.[69]

As pointed out by Grugel and Piper, "while international organizations are influential, along with NGOs and some states, in shaping the framework of regulation, implementation depends on state actors and non-state actors – often different ones from the NGOs that operate at the global level."[70] In the UAE, it is middle-class, longer-term migrants who have taken up the mantle to set up voluntary and humanitarian organizations in order to take up the concerns of low-wage labour. (This is an unusual situation in that it is not nationals who have stepped up as in other politically conservative labour-importing countries like Singapore and Malaysia.) In Dubai, NGOs act as intermediaries between employers and migrant labour in resolving labour disputes as well as raise funds for the payment of *diya* (blood money),[71] hospitalization and for the repatriation or burial of dead bodies. They also act as representatives of embassies at the grassroots level, bringing grievances to the attention of authorities through established networks and lines of communication. They are transnational in their outreach, working in collaboration with NGOs from sending nations, and often maintaining contact with migrants who have been repatriated and continuing to cater for their welfare in their home states.

The nature of many of these humanitarian organizations (as they prefer to be called), are informal and they are often not officially recognized by the UAE government, although their activities are public and acknowledged. Part of the refusal of the government to officially sanction their activities and admit that there is a place for such entities is the fear of being construed as inadequate and inept in dealing with the migrant population. There is also apprehension of the potential political unrest they can instigate in concert with disgruntled migrants. Thus, activities of such groups are closely monitored and their members subject to acts of surveillance such as phone tapping and routine interrogations. Such inadequate support, in practice, for migrant rights as well as the lack of advocacy in migrant policy, have been acknowledged in the available literature.[72] The difficulties of appealing to democratic political process combined with the suppression of dissenting voices in the UAE make for an even more imbalanced situation.

In addition to a lack of encouragement from the government of the UAE, NGO workers also lament the lack of support from their own country representatives. Volunteers recount experiences of appointments with Indian embassy officials not being kept when the issue at hand was welfare provision of low-wage labour and instances of unsuccessfully trying to seek audiences with the Indian overseas minister on his regular visits to Dubai. On these visits, the minister typically meets with members of the Indian business and entrepreneurial sectors in Dubai, often to encourage stronger ties through foreign direct investment in India. Here again, we can see through grounded examples how the Indian state favours the concerns of its middle class overseas.

Given that the majority of local NGOs are also made up of (middle-class) migrants, and that these activist-volunteers are themselves vulnerable to deportation and entry bans, they are limited in their demands to and criticisms of the Dubai government. Inhabiting the place of outsider, their role in calling for political reform is restricted by their own temporary status as "guest workers" whose prescribed place in Emirati society is to be uniformly uncritical while embodying the productive worker. Unless more Emirati nationals take up rights advocacy work, civil society pressure on the government of the UAE will remain limited to liminal spaces such as Internet forums and blogs, where critics can remain anonymous.

The Abu Dhabi–based UAE Human Rights Association is one of the few Emirati-initiated organizations concerned with abuses and welfare of migrant workers. This is indicative of first steps by the national population in acknowledging that there is a need for non-state actors to address affairs of migrant rights. They have echoed calls by international human rights groups to allow trade unions and institute a minimum wage. But unless expanded in both scope and size, the impact of such organizations on state policies will remain marginal.

Conclusion: Call for Transnationalization of Rights

While it has been acknowledged that the political system of a state is the most important factor in ensuring migrant rights,[73] this paper has sought to show that working but often informal relationships between state actors and non-governmental organizations also play an important role in the implementation of rights on the ground.[74] This is especially significant in regimes such as those in the Gulf, where unionization and other forms of collective bargaining are outlawed. Even as NGOs and humanitarian groups are forced to work in informal and unofficial ways, there is a growing awareness for the need to better ensure rights of migrants as Dubai and other Gulf states are integrated deeper into the world economy, and are thus opened up to greater accountability. However, along with international NGOs, sending countries such as India need to assert greater political pressure on receiving countries to demonstrate that the contributions and welfare of their lower-skilled migrants are just as valued as those of their skilled expatriates. Above all, this means recognition of migration as more than a purely economic process, but a complex transnational phenomenon, which requires both sending and receiving countries to protect the rights of the migrants from whose labour they benefit. This requires a movement away from a focus on remittances and their impacts, and instead an increased consideration of social issues such as the provision and protection of rights.

We must then consider more than just economic factors in understanding potential migrants' motivations. International migration is fuelled by a consumerist boom in countries such as India and the creation of an aspirational class for which labour migration is a viable means to achieve desired levels of social mobility. Although for many low-wage migrants, migration to the Gulf means years of separation from family and country, it is often seen as a "rite of passage" in which one establishes oneself as a mature man and economic provider.[75] In addition to these familial and societal expectations, the modernity represented by places such as Dubai exerts a strong pull. Despite the possibilities of incurring large debts and being cheated by migration agents, as mentioned above, labour migration thus still remains an attractive option for low-skilled Indians who cannot find such avenues to break out of class and caste structures within their home country. Ultimately then, the phenomena of labour migration, especially of low-skilled labour, is transnational and dependent on the disparity between richer and poorer states. It thus needs to be understood through a broader framework than one that limits analysis to single countries – a recommendation that migration scholars have started to make regularly.

Here is where the transnationalization of rights emerges as a paradigm shift that is necessary to ensure and reflect the simultaneous responsibilities of origin and destination regions in the provision of legal rights, citizenship status and social inclusion. This means that our "conventional understanding of concepts such as citizenship and human rights need to be re-assessed for their validity or relevance."[76] Regulatory frameworks of the state are increasingly being challenged, for example, by the work of transnational NGOs. They are able to tap into more informal networks outside and across state boundaries that transcend the framework of the geographically bounded national entity. Structures of governance are becoming more difficult to conceptualize because of their increasing transnationality and informality, characterized by turning to more informal modes of governance practices and the "neoliberal agenda of state withdrawal."[77] So along with reconceptualizing institutions of governance, there is also a need to reconceptualize political identities like citizenship, as they are no longer the only basis along which governance is practised. Low-wage temporary migrant labour seeks to benefit most from such new conceptualizations.

Notes

1 Andrew M. Gardner, "Strategic Transnationalism: The Indian Diasporic Elite in Contemporary Bahrain," *City & Society* 20, no. 1 (2008); Binod Khadria, "Actors and Models of Indian Diaspora in International Relations: From Social Parasites to Economic Boon?" Asia Research Institute Working Paper Series, no. 85 (2007); Johanna Lessinger, "Indian Immigrants in the United States: The Emergence of a Transnational Population," in *Culture and Economy in the Indian Diaspora*, ed. Bikhu Parekh, Gurharpal Singh and Steven Vertovec (London: Routledge, 2003); Johanna Lessinger, "Non-resident Indian Investment and India's Drive for Industrial Modernization," in *Anthropology and the Global Factory: Studies of the New Industrialization in the Late Twentieth Century*, ed. Frances A. Rothstein and Michael L. Blim (London: Bergin & Garvey, 1992); Peter van der Veer, "Virtual India: Indian IT Labour and the Nation-State," in *Sovereign Bodies: Citizens, Migrants, and States in the Postcolonial World*, ed. Thomas Blom Hansen and Finn Stepputat (Princeton, NJ: Princeton University Press, 2005), Margaret Walton-Roberts, "Globalization, National Autonomy and Non-resident Indians," *Contemporary South Asia* 13, no. 1 (2004).

2 K. Pushpangadan, "Remittances, Consumption and Economic Growth in Kerala: 1980–2000," Centre for Development Studies Working Paper, no. 343 (2003); K. C. Zachariah et al.,

"Impact of Migration on Kerala's Economy and Society," Centre for Development Studies Working Paper, no. 297 (1999); K. C. Zachariah et al., "Socio-economic and Demographic Consequences of Migration in Kerala," Centre for Development Studies Working Paper, no. 303 (2000); K. C. Zachariah et al., "Return Emigrants in Kerala: Rehabilitation Problems and Development Potential," Centre for Development Studies Working Paper, no. 319 (2001); K. C. Zachariah et al., "Gulf Migration Study: Employment, Wages and Working Conditions of Kerala Emigrants in the United Arab Emirates," Centre for Development Studies Working Paper, no. 326 (2002); K. C. Zachariah and S. I. Rajan, "Gulf Revisited: Economic Consequences of Emigration from Kerala; Emigration and Unemployment," Centre for Development Studies Working Paper, no. 363 (2004).

3 Sulayman Khalaf and Saad Alkobaisi, "Migrants' Strategies of Coping and Patterns of Accommodation in the Oil-Rich Gulf Societies: Evidence from the UAE," *British Journal of Middle Eastern Studies* 26, no. 2 (1999); Anh Nga Longva, "Keeping Migrant Workers in Check: The Kafala System in the Gulf," *Middle East Report* 211 (Summer 1999); Anh Nga Longva, *Walls Built on Sand: Migration and Exclusion in Kuwait* (Boulder, CO: Westview Press, 1997); Magnus Marsden, "Lords of a Dubai Labour Camp: Pakistani Migrants in the Gulf," *IIAS Newsletter*, 2008; K. C. Zachariah et al., "The Impact of Immigration Policy on Indian Contract Migrants: The Case of United Arab Emirates," *International Migration* 41, no. 4 (2003).

4 Brij Lal, Peter Reeves and Rajesh Rai, *The Encyclopedia of the Indian Diaspora* (Singapore: Editions Didier Millet, 2006).

5 The GCC is composed of Saudi Arabia, Qatar, Bahrain, Kuwait, Oman and the United Arab Emirates.

6 Walton-Roberts, "Globalization," p. 58.

7 Lessinger, "Non-resident Indian Investment," p. 62.

8 Muzaffar Chishti, "The Rise in Remittances to India: A Closer Look," *Migration Information Source*, 1 February 2007. http://www.migrationinformation.org/Feature/display.cfm?id=577. 1 December 2008.

9 Dilip Ratha et al., *Migration and Development Brief* (Washington, DC: World Bank, 2009), pp. 1–10.

10 *Hawala*, an informal system of money transfer, is widespread not only because it is quick, but also because it generally pays a premium exchange rate. However, with the introduction of a market-based exchange rate by the Indian government in 1993 and stricter regulation of capital flows post 9/11, it has become less popular.

11 Chishti, "The Rise in Remittances to India."

12 Zachariah, Nair and Rajan, "Return Emigrants in Kerala"; Zachariah and Rajan, "Gulf Revisited."

13 Saseedran Pallikadavath and Chris Wilson, "A Paradox within a Paradox: Scheduled Caste Fertility in Kerala," *Economic and Political Weekly*, 9 July 2005.

14 Walton-Roberts, "Globalization," p. 58.

15 Zachariah et al., "Impact of Immigration Policy"; Zachariah, Mathew and Rajan, "Socio-economic and Demographic Consequences"; Zachariah and Rajan, "Gulf Revisited."

16 Lessinger, "Indian Immigrants in the United States"; Lessinger, "Non-resident Indian Investment"; Walton-Roberts, "Globalization."

17 Ratha et al., "Migration and Development Brief," p. 3

18 Walton-Roberts, "Globalization," p. 58.

19 Yasser Elsheshtawy, "Redrawing Boundaries: Dubai, an Emerging Global City," in *Planning Middle Eastern Cities: An Urban Kaleidoscope in a Globalizing World*, ed. Yasser Elsheshtawy (London: Routledge, 2004), p. 173.

20 "Dubai Non-oil Trade Up by 54% in H1," *Dubai Chronicle*, 8 September 2008. http://www.dubaichronicle.com/?p=1296&print=1. 8 September 2008.

21 Neha Vora, "Producing Diasporas and Globalization: Indian Middle-Class Migrants in Dubai," *Anthropological Quarterly* 81, no. 2 (2008): pp. 382–3.

22 Vora, "Producing Diasporas and Globalization," pp. 386–7.

23 Indian Council of World Affairs (ICWA), *Report of the High Level Committee on the Indian Diaspora* (New Delhi: ICWA, 2001).

24 Marie Percot and S. Irudaya Rajan, "Female Emigration from India: Case Study of Nurses," *Economic and Political Weekly*, 27 January 2007.

25 Zachariah, Prakash and Rajan, "Gulf Migration Study," p. 5.

26 *UAE Yearbook 2005* (Abu Dhabi: Ministry of Information and Culture, 2005).

27 Laurence Louer, "The Political Impact of Labor Migration in Bahrain," *City & Society* 20, no. 1 (2008): p. 33.

28 Kavita Datta et al., "Men on the Move: Narratives of Migration and Work among Low-Paid Migrant Men in London," *Social & Cultural Geography* 10, no. 8 (2009): p. 869.

29 Mohammed Bin Rashid Al Maktoum, "Our Ambitions for the Middle East," *Wall Street Journal*, 12 January 2008, p. A9.

30 Michele R. Gamburd, "Advocating for Sri Lankan Migrant Workers," *Critical Asian Studies* 41, no. 1 (2009): p. 69.

31 Karen Leonard, "South Asian Women in the Gulf: Families and Futures Reconfigured," in *Trans-status Subjects: Gender in the Globalization of South and Southeast Asia*, ed. Sonita Sarker and Esha Niyogi De (Durham, NC: Duke University Press, 2002), pp. 215–16. Cited from S. Suleri, "Women Skin Deep: Feminism and the Postcolonial Condition," *Critical Inquiry* 18, no. 4 (1992): p. 766; and S. Ardener, *Women and Space: Ground Rules and Social Maps* (Oxford: Berg, 1981), p. 12.

32 J. E. Peterson, "What Makes the Gulf States Endure?" in *Iran, Iraq and the Arab Gulf States*, ed. Joseph A. Kechichian (New York: Palgrave, 2001).

33 Under the Sharia law that is applied in the UAE, even if the father of the child is proved to be Emirati, he must recognize the child as his for citizenship to be granted. This again serves to create another barrier to obtaining citizenship. In a case where a foreign domestic worker was raped and became pregnant, and DNA tests proved that the father was the Emirati employer, the child was not granted citizenship as the father refused to recognize him as his child.

34 Onn Winckler, "The Immigration Policy of the Gulf Cooperation Council (GCC) States," *Middle Eastern Studies* 33, no. 3 (1997): pp. 484–5.

35 Longva, "Keeping Migrant Workers in Check," p. 21.

36 Stephen Castles, "Migration Settlement, Transnational Communities and State Strategies in the Asia Pacific Region," in *Migration in the Asia Pacific: Population, Settlement and Citizenship Issues*, ed. Robyn Iredale, Charles Hawksley and Stephen Castles (Cheltenham: Edward Elgar, 2003), p. 11.

37 Dubai Statistics Center, *Statistical Yearbook Emirate of Dubai* (Dubai: Dubai Statistics Center, 2006), p. 23.

38 Ten Guide, "United Arab Emirates [UAE] Visa Requirements." http://guide.theemiratesnetwork.com/living/visa.php. 9 December 2008. Other countries such as Singapore that are also highly dependent on migrant low-wage labour practise similar forms of discrimination.

39 "No Minimum Wage for Construction Workers," *Dubai Chronicle*, 29 June 2008. http://www.dubaichronicle.com/?p=219. 30 June 2008.

40 Pierrette Hondagneu-Sotelo, "Regulating the Unregulated? Domestic Workers' Social Networks," *Social Problem* 41, no. 1 (1994): p. 53.

41 A. Pecoud and P. de Gutcheneire, "Migration without Borders: An Investigation into the Free Movement of People" in *Global Migration Perspectives*, no. 27 (Geneva: GCIM 2005); see also D. A. Martin, "The Authority and Responsibility of States," in *Migration and International Legal Norms*, ed. T. A. Aleinikoff and V. Chetail (The Hague: TMC Asser Press, 2003), pp. 31–46, cited in Jean Grugel and Nicola Piper, *Critical Perspectives on Global Governance: Rights and Regulation in Governing Regimes* (London: Routledge, 2007), p. 35.

42 With the current global economic slowdown hitting Dubai hard, many low-wage labourers have had their visas cancelled as construction on many large-scale projects has been halted and have

been forced to leave before their contract was stipulated to end. This means many of them have returned to their home countries without repaying debts or making any substantial savings.

43 Anne McNevin, "From City to Citizen in Los Angeles: A Place-Based Approach to Emerging Citizen-Subjectivities," in *International Conference on Migration, Citizenship and Intercultural Relations* (Melbourne: Deakin University, 2009), p. 11.

44 "There is [...] international acceptance of the terms, 'irregular migration' and 'migrant workers in irregular status' in place of 'illegal migration' and 'illegal migrant workers.' The former terms do not criminalise migrants and are also more comprehensive in capturing different dimensions of irregularity." Piyasiri Wickramasekara, "Globalization, International Labour Migration and the Rights of Migrant Workers," *Third World Quarterly* 29, no. 7 (2008): 1248.

45 "Over 83,000 Residency Violators Last Year in Dubai," *Dubai Chronicle*, 18 Feb 2008. http://www.dubaichronicle.com/2008/02/over-83000-residency-violators-last.html. 18 February 2008.

46 Nicola Piper, "The Management of Migration: An Issue of Controlling or Protecting? Normative and Institutional Developments and Their Relevance to Asia," Asia Research Institute Working Paper Series, no. 69 (2006): p. 7.

47 Wickramasekara, "Globalization," p. 1253.

48 "DNRD to Implement New Visa Rules from July 29," *Dubai Chronicle*, 24 July 2008. http://www.dubaichronicle.com/?p=664. 25 July 2008

49 Wickramasekara, "Globalization," p. 1254.

50 Wickramasekara, "Globalization," p. 1253.

51 Nicola Piper, "Economic Migration and the Transnationalisation of the Rights of Foreign Workers: A Concept Note," Asia Research Institute Working Paper Series, no. 58 (2006): p. 7.

52 Gamburd (2008) mentions how more Sri Lankan low wage migrants are choosing to work in Italy given opportunities for family reunification and permanent settlement, which are impossible in the Gulf. This was also the reason why some of my informants saw Dubai merely as a stepping stone towards eventual migration to Singapore, North America or Europe.

53 Walton-Roberts, "Globalization," pp. 56–7.

54 Wickramasekara, "Globalization," p. 1247.

55 S. Krishna Kumar, "Migration Policy Reforms in India: Some Reflections," in *Governance and Labour Migration: India Migration Report 2010*, edited by Irudaya S. Rajan (New Delhi: Routledge, 2010), pp. 243–50.

56 There are regulations regarding the amount that authorized agents in India can charge potential migrants, but again, regulation is problematic. 44 per cent of potential migrants did not know who their sponsors were prior to migration, 16 per cent were preparing to emigrate without employment contracts and among those who did sign contracts, and only 37 per cent were aware of what the contracts stated. For details of this research see S. I. Rajan et al., "Looking beyond the Emigration Act 1983: Revisiting the Recruitment Practices in India," in *Governance and Labour Migration: India Migration Report 2010*, edited by S. I. Rajan (New Delhi: Routledge, 2010), pp. 251–87.

57 Selvaraj Velayutham and Amanda Wise, "Co-ethnic Exploitation and Indian Temporary Skilled Migrants in Australia," paper presented at the workshop on "The Globally Mobile Skilled Labour Force: Policy Challenges and Economic Opportunities" (Faculty of Business and Economics, Macquarie University, Sydney, 2009).

58 Marina de Regt, "High in the Hierarchy, Rich in Diversity: Asian Domestic Workers, Their Networks, and Employers' Preferences in Yemen," *Critical Asian Studies* 40, no. 4 (2008): p. 598.

59 Meena Janardhan, "Worker Friendly Laws Make a Difference," Inter Press Service News Agency, 11 January 2010.

60 Piper, "The Management of Migration," p. 21.

61 Piper, "The Management of Migration," p. 21.

62 Gamburd, "Advocating for Sri Lankan Migrant Workers," p. 74.

63 Gamburd, "Advocating for Sri Lankan Migrant Workers," p. 67.

64 Grugel and Piper, *Critical Perspectives on Global Governance*, p. 36.
65 Gamburd, "Advocating for Sri Lankan Migrant Workers."
66 Grugel and Piper, *Critical Perspectives on Global Governance*, p. 61.
67 Piper, "Economic Migration," p. 4.
68 They include the Migration of Employment Convention of 1949 (ILO Convention no. 97), the Migrant Workers (Supplementary Provisions) Convention of 1975 (ILO Convention no. 143) and the International Convention on the Protection of the Rights of All Migrant Workers and the Members of their Families, adopted by the UN General Assembly in 1990 (MWC). ILO Convention no. 97 (which came into force on 22 January 1952) has been ratified by 42 member states, while ILO Convention no. 143 (which came into force in 1978) has been ratified by only 18 member states. The MWC has so far only been signed by 19 member states and therefore has not yet come into force (20 ratifications are required).
69 Martin Ruhs, "Temporary Foreign Worker Programmes: Policies, Adverse Consequences, and the Need to Make Them Work," Center for Comparative Immigration Studies Working Paper, no. 56 (2002).
70 Grugel and Piper, *Critical Perspectives on Global Governance*, p. 21.
71 The *diya* payable to the family of the deceased is AED200,000 (approx. USD54,458 as of September 2014) for any male resident of the UAE and AED100,000 (approx. USD27,229 as of September 2014) for any female resident. These are substantially large sums of money which low-wage migrants would be unable to come up with.
72 Piper, "Economic Migration."
73 Wickramasekara, "Globalization," p. 1258.
74 Grugel and Piper, *Critical Perspectives on Global Governance*, p. 17.
75 Caroline Osella and Filippo Osella, "Once upon a Time in the West? Stories of Migration and Modernity from Kerala, South India," *Journal of the Royal Anthropological Institute* 12 (2006): 569–88.
76 Piper, "Economic Migration," p. 5.
77 Kate Meagher, "Culture, Agency and Power: Theoretical Reflections on Informal Economic Networks and Political Process," DIIS Working Paper 2009: 27 (Copenhagen: DIIS, 2009), p. 24.

References

Al Maktoum, M. B. R. "Our Ambitions for the Middle East." *Wall Street Journal*, 12 January 2008, p. A9.

Castles, S. "Migration Settlement, Transnational Communities and State Strategies in the Asia Pacific Region." In *Migration in the Asia Pacific: Population, Settlement and Citizenship Issues*, edited by Charles R. H. Iredale and Stephen Castles. Cheltenham: Edward Elgar, 2003, pp. 3–26.

Chishti, M. "The Rise in Remittances to India: A Closer Look." *Migration Information Source*. 1 February 2007. http://www.migrationinformation.org/Feature/display.cfm?id=577. 1 December 2008.

Datta, K., C. McIlwaine, J. Herbert, Y. Evans, J. May and J. Wills. "Men on the Move: Narratives of Migration and Work among Low-Paid Migrant Men in London." *Social & Cultural Geography* 10, no. 8 (2009): 853–73.

de Regt, M. "High in the Hierarchy, Rich in Diversity: Asian Domestic Workers, Their Networks, and Employers' Preferences in Yemen." *Critical Asian Studies* 40, no. 4 (2008): 587–608.

Dubai Chronicle. "DNRD to Implement New Visa Rules from July 29." 24 July 2008. http://www.dubaichronicle.com/?p=664. 25 July 2008.

______. "Dubai Non-oil Trade Up by 54% in H1." 7 September 2008. http://www.dubaichronicle.com/?p=1296&print=1. 8 September 2008.

______. "No Minimum Wage for Construction Workers." 29 June 2008. http://www.dubaichronicle.com/?p=219. 30 June 2008.

______. "Over 83,000 Residency Violators Last Year in Dubai." 18 February 2008. http://www.dubaichronicle.com/2008/02/over-83000-residency-violators-last.html. 18 February 2008.

Dubai Statistics Center. *Statistical Yearbook Emirate of Dubai*. Dubai: Dubai Statistics Center, 2006.

Elsheshtawy, Y. "Redrawing Boundaries: Dubai, an Emerging Global City." In *Planning Middle Eastern Cities: An Urban Kaleidoscope in a Globalizing World*, edited by Y. Elsheshtawy, pp. 167–99. London: Routledge, 2004.

Gamburd, M. R. "Advocating for Sri Lankan Migrant Workers." *Critical Asian Studies* 41, no. 1 (2009): 61–88.

Gardner, A. M. "Strategic Transnationalism: The Indian Diasporic Elite in Contemporary Bahrain." *City & Society* 20, no. 1 (2008): 54–78.

Grugel, J. and N. Piper. *Critical Perspectives on Global Governance: Rights and Regulation in Governing Regimes*. London: Routledge, 2007.

Hondagneu-Sotelo, P. "Regulating the Unregulated? Domestic Workers' Social Networks." *Social Problems* 41, no. 1 (1994): 50–64.

Indian Council of World Affairs (ICWA). *Report of the High-Level Committee on the Indian Diaspora*. New Delhi: ICWA, 2001.

Janardhan, M. "Worker Friendly Laws Make a Difference." Inter Press Service News Agency, 11 January 2010. http://ipsnews.net/news.asp?idnews=36133. 29 February 2012.

Khadria, B. "Actors and Models of Indian Diaspora in International Relations: From Social Parasites to Economic Boon?" Asia Research Institute Working Paper Series, no. 85. 2007.

Khalaf, S. and S. Alkobaisi. "Migrants' Strategies of Coping and Patterns of Accommodation in the Oil-Rich Gulf Societies: Evidence from the UAE." *British Journal of Middle Eastern Studies* 26, no. 2 (1999): 271–98.

Krishna Kumar, S. "Migration Policy Reforms in India: Some Reflections." In *Governance and Labour Migration: India Migration Report 2010*, edited by I. S. Rajan, pp. 243–50. New Delhi: Routledge, 2010.

Lal, B. et al. *The Encyclopedia of the Indian Diaspora*. Singapore: Editions Didier Millet, 2006.

Leonard, K. "South Asian Women in the Gulf: Families and Futures Reconfigured." In *Trans-status Subjects: Gender in the Globalization of South and Southeast Asia*, edited by S. Sarker and E. N. De, pp. 213–31. Durham, NC: Duke University Press, 2002.

Lessinger, J. "Indian Immigrants in the United States: The Emergence of a Transnational Population." In *Culture and Economy in the Indian Diaspora*, edited by B. Parekh, S. Gurharpal and S. Vertovec, pp. 165–82. London: Routledge, 2003.

______. "Non-resident Indian Investment and India's Drive for Industrial Modernization." In *Anthropology and the Global Factory: Studies of the New Industrialization in the Late Twentieth Century*, edited by Frances A. Rothstein and Michael L. Blim, pp. 62–82. London: Bergin & Garvey, 1992.

Longva, A. N. "Keeping Migrant Workers in Check: The Kafala System in the Gulf." *Middle East Report* 211 (Summer 1999): 20–22.

______. *Walls Built on Sand: Migration and Exclusion in Kuwait*. Boulder, CO: Westview Press, 1997.

Louer, L. "The Political Impact of Labor Migration in Bahrain." *City & Society* 20, no. 1 (2008): 32–53.

Marsden, M. "Lords of a Dubai Labour Camp: Pakistani Migrants in the Gulf." *IIAS Newsletter* 49 (2008): 5–6.

McNevin, A. "From City to Citizen in Los Angeles: A Place-Based Approach to Emerging Citizen-Subjectivities." *International Conference on Migration, Citizenship and Intercultural Relations*, pp. 1–28. Melbourne: Deakin University, 2009.

Meagher, K. "Culture, Agency and Power: Theoretical Reflections on Informal Economic Networks and Political Process." DIIS working paper 2009: 27. Copenhagen: DIIS, 2009.

Osella, C. and F. Osella. "Once upon a Time in the West? Stories of Migration and Modernity from Kerala, South India." *Journal of the Royal Anthropological Institute* 12 (2006): 569–88.

Osella, F. and C. Osella. "From Transience to Immanence: Consumption, Life-Cycle and Social Mobility in Kerala, South India." *Modern Asian Studies* 33, no. 4 (1999): 989–1020.

______. "Migration, Money and Masculinity in Kerala." *Journal of the Royal Anthropological Institute* 6, no. 1 (2000): 117–33.

Osella, F. and K. Gardner, eds. *Migration, Modernity and Social Transformation in South Asia*. Contributions to Indian Sociology, Occasional Studies, vol. 11. New Delhi: Sage, 2004.

Pallikadavath, S. and C. Wilson. "A Paradox within a Paradox: Scheduled Caste Fertility in Kerala." *Economic and Political Weekly*, 9 July 2005, pp. 3085–93.

Percot, M. and S. I. Rajan. "Female Emigration from India: Case Study of Nurses." *Economic and Political Weekly*, 27 January 2007, pp. 318–25.

Peterson, J. E. "What Makes the Gulf States Endure?" In *Iran, Iraq and the Arab Gulf States*, edited by J. A. Kechichian, 452–60. New York: Palgrave, 2001.

Piper, N. "Economic Migration and the Transnationalisation of the Rights of Foreign Workers: A Concept Note." Asia Research Institute Working Paper Series, no. 58. Singapore: ARI, 2006.

______. "The Management of Migration: An Issue of Controlling or Protecting? Normative and Institutional Developments and Their Relevance to Asia." Asia Research Institute Working Paper Series, no. 69. Singapore, 2006.

Pushpangadan, K. "Remittances, Consumption and Economic Growth in Kerala: 1980–2000." Centre for Development Studies Working Paper, no. 343. Trivandrum, 2003.

Rajan, S. I., V. J. Varghese and M. S. Jayakumar. "Looking beyond the Emigration Act 1983: Revisiting the Recruitment Practices in India." In *Governance and Labour Migration: India Migration Report 2010*, edited by I. S. Rajan, pp. 251–87. New Delhi: Routledge, 2010.

Ratha, D., S. Mohapatra and A. Silwal. *Migration and Development Brief*. Washington, DC: World Bank, 2009.

UAE Yearbook 2005. Abu Dhabi: Ministry of Information and Culture, 2005.

Van der Veer, P. "Virtual India: Indian IT Labour and the Nation-State." In *Sovereign Bodies: Citizens, Migrants, and States in the Postcolonial World*, edited by T. B. H. F. Stepputat, pp. 276–90. Princeton, NJ: Princeton University Press, 2005.

Velayutham, S. and A. Wise. "Co-ethnic Exploitation and Indian Temporary-Skilled Migrants in Australia." Paper presented at the workshop on "The Globally Mobile Skilled Labour Force: Policy Challenges and Economic Opportunities." Faculty of Business and Economics, Macquarie University, Sydney, 2009.

Vora, N. "Producing Diasporas and Globalization: Indian Middle-Class Migrants in Dubai." *Anthropological Quarterly* 81, no. 2 (2008): 377–406.

Walton-Roberts, M. "Globalization, National Autonomy and Non-resident Indians." *Contemporary South Asia* 13, no. 1 (2004): 53–69.

Wickramasekara, P. "Globalization, International Labour Migration and the Rights of Migrant Workers." *Third World Quarterly* 29, no. 7 (2008): 1247–64.

Winckler, O. "The Immigration Policy of the Gulf Cooperation Council (GCC) States." *Middle Eastern Studies* 33, no. 3 (1997): 480–93.

Zachariah, K. C., E. T. Mathew and S. I. Rajan. "Impact of Migration on Kerala's Economy and Society." Centre for Development Studies Working Paper, no. 297. Trivandrum, 1999.

______. "Socio-economic and Demographic Consequences of Migration in Kerala." Centre for Development Studies Working Paper, no. 303. Trivandrum, 2000.

Zachariah, K. C., G. P. R. Nair and S. I. Rajan. "Return Emigrants in Kerala: Rehabilitation Problems and Development Potential." Centre for Development Studies Working Paper, no. 319. Trivandrum, 2001.

Zachariah, K. C., B. A. Prakash and S. I. Rajan. "Gulf Migration Study: Employment, Wages and Working Conditions of Kerala Emigrants in the United Arab Emirates." Centre for Development Studies Working Paper, no. 326. Trivandrum, 2002.

______. "The Impact of Immigration Policy on Indian Contract Migrants: The Case of United Arab Emirates." *International Migration* 41, no. 4 (2003): 161–72.

Zachariah, K. C. and S. I. Rajan. "Gulf Revisited: Economic Consequences of Emigration from Kerala: Emigration and Unemployment." Centre for Development Studies working paper, no. 363. Trivandrum, 2004.

Postscript

SHIFTING WORLDS AND CHANGING IDENTITIES: THE RESHAPING OF THE CHINESE-INDIAN COMMUNITIES IN INDIA AFTER THE 1962 "SINO-INDIAN INCIDENT"

Kwai Yun Li

When I was an adolescent and later a rebellious teenager growing up in the Chinatown of Calcutta, I was very aware of the 1962 "Sino-Indian Incident." It hung over the Chinese community like a dark shadow. I knew that because of this shadow my mother decided to send me to study English instead of Chinese. I knew that because of this shadow my friends and relatives left the once-cosy Calcutta Chinatown for foreign countries, and I knew that one day, when I graduated from school, I would also leave India.

I settled in Toronto, Canada, where over two thousand Chinese-Indians had immigrated. Like the majority of the immigrants, settling into a job became my priority. I studied and worked and the shadow of the Incident faded somewhat. But it lurked in my peripheral vision, never fading and never solidifying, like an itch that I could not reach to scratch.

The opportunity to scratch the itch that was the 1962 Sino-Indian Incident appeared: I needed a topic for my MA thesis. I decided to write about it. A friend invited me to the annual meeting of the *Association of India Deoli Chinese Internees* (AIDCI) in Toronto. Four Chinese-Indians who were interned at Deoli during the Incident organized the meeting, which was attended by former Deoli detainees now living in Canada and the United States. I attended the meeting and recruited four detainees for my thesis, which I titled *Deoli Camp: An Oral History of Chinese Indians from 1962 to 1966.*[1] I have used the research and excerpts from my thesis and my book *The Palm Leaf Fan*[2] as the basis of this paper.

Ming, one of the participants, was picked up and interned in Deoli Detention Camp in December 1962. Her parents owned a restaurant in Digboi and had boarded her with a Chinese family in Shillong, where she went to a girl's day school. Ming met up with her parents when she arrived in Deoli. The family was later released in the summer of 1966, four years after they were interned. I have selected Ming's narratives for this paper. Her narratives give us a glimpse of life in the detention camp.

For a snapshot of the experience of those Chinese who were not interned in the Sino-Indian Incident, I have used excerpts from "Rally at Ochterlony Monument," a story from my book *The Palm Leaf Fan*, where the confused Chinese tried to survive by rallying against Mao, signing petitions to show support of the Indian government, practicing kung fu and praying to the Dalai Lama and Buddha.

I have also used oral history and narrative research methods, which allow me to highlight individual life experiences and perceptions, explore the cultural and social changes, and look at their struggle for meaning in the aftermath of the Incident. In my paper, I hope to illuminate the day-to-day life of average Chinese-Indians through the lenses of the two narratives.

In a statement to the Indian government, the Chinese government stated, "The Sino-Indian boundary question is a question left over by history."[3] British India and China had disputes over their boundaries and struggled over the Tibet issue for more than a hundred years. When India gained its independence, the disputes intensified. On 21 October 1962, the Chinese People's Liberation Army (PLA) advanced into the two disputed territories: Aksai Chin in the west, and North East Frontier Agency in the east. Aksai Chin, a high-altitude desert the size of Switzerland, with no permanent settlement and little rainfall, is rich in mineral resources. The Chinese government's Xinjiang–Tibet Highway, completed in 1958, runs 127 miles through Aksai Chin. The North East Frontier Agency stretched along the foothills of the Himalayas, carpeted with tea plantations and tea factories.

The PLA's advance was swift. By early November, they had advanced well into the disputed territories. On 21 November, China declared a unilateral ceasefire and withdrew behind its disputed line of control on the eastern and western fronts. China and India filed this month-long border war under "incident." As of 2010, the two countries have not settled their border "incident."

After the humiliating defeat, the Indian government published various reports that depicted the Chinese as the enemy, threatening India's independence and sovereignty. The publications also touted examples of Indians willing to fight for their country. By extension, the Chinese living in India became the enemy. Indians took up arms against Chinese residents in India: they ostracized, harassed or attacked them, and boycotted, vandalized or ransacked Chinese-owned properties.

The Indian government closed pro-Mao Chinese language schools, newspapers and organizations. They enacted anti-Chinese laws: laws to deport Chinese who "threatened" Indian national security, laws to ban Chinese from government jobs, laws that required Chinese residents to report to the Indian authorities for "registration" and residency permits, and laws that corralled the Chinese in the cities or towns they lived in.

The Indian government detained over two thousand Chinese residents. The soldiers "evacuated" Chinese from towns, schools and tea factories on its northeastern borders. In cities like Calcutta (now Kolkata), the government arrested those Chinese whom they regarded as communist sympathizers. These detainees were temporarily housed in the local jails, and, in Makum, the soldiers locked the "evacuated" Chinese in a cowshed. In December of 1962, these "evacuated" Chinese were put on trains under guard and sent to an internment camp in Deoli, Rajasthan.

Most of the detained Chinese were second- or third-generation Indian-born, their parents or grandparents having immigrated to India in the late 1800s or early 1900s, travelling on boats that stopped in Calcutta. Some moved to high-altitude towns and worked in tea factories, tea plantations, restaurants and shoe shops; the majority settled in Calcutta. The Chinese prospered in India. By the 1950s, there were over thirty-five thousand Chinese living in Calcutta, many of whom owned carpentry factories, shoe shops, restaurants, hairdressing salons and tanneries. In 2008, Paul Chung, president of the Indian-Chinese Association in Kolkata, estimated the number at five thousand.

My parents immigrated to Calcutta in the 1920s and settled in Calcutta Chinatown. My father worked in a shoe shop, and, when he died in 1956, he left three shoe shops to my brothers. Like the majority of the Chinese immigrants in India, my parents dreamed of retiring back to China to rebuild the family home in their ancestral village.

Ming's grandparents immigrated to Calcutta in the late 1800s. They did well, and sent their school-age sons and later their grandsons to China to study. They returned to India after graduating from the Chinese schools. Many of the Chinese parents in India sent their children, usually the sons, to China for education, so that they would grow up Chinese. My father sent his two eldest daughters there when they were 5 and 7 years old respectively. My eldest brother was born a year later. For those Chinese who could not afford to send their children to China for education, they sent them to one of the Chinese language schools in India.

Most of the Chinese in India regarded themselves as Chinese, even those who were born in India. But hybridization had slowly coloured the second and third generations, like my ten cousins, eight siblings and me. Instead of the *sanko* (mountain yodelling) that the Chinese elders howled out in Chinese celebrations, I preferred to belt out Bollywood songs. Instead of crushed peanuts rolled up in wafer-thin pork slices, I preferred channa and aloo curry wrapped in rotis. I enjoyed Diwali and Durga puja as much as I enjoyed the Moon Festival and Chinese New Year. The hybridization would have continued slowly, but the 1962 Sino-Indian Incident sped up the changes. The Incident forced the Chinese in India to choose either to return to China or stay in India. Many chose to go to China. Ming's family chose to stay. So did mine. Life in India changed for the Chinese during and after the Incident. The Chinese no longer dreamed of "returning" to China, they dreamed of going to the gold mountains over the ocean. They sent their children to English language schools, so that one day they and their children could escape from under the shadow of the Incident.

In Calcutta, the number of students in the Chinese language schools dwindled, mainly because of the dwindling Chinese population, but also because Chinese parents sent their children to English language schools instead. In Makum, the Chinese language school was closed when all the Chinese residents were "evacuated" to Deoli Detention Camp. The school never reopened.

Ming's Narrative

Ming was nine years old in 1962. Her parents boarded her with a family friend in Shillong, where she attended an English language school.

> When the "1962 Sino-Indian Incident" started, the Assamese shunned us. They taunted me and all the Chinese, like pulling the corners of their eyes upwards and shouted, "Cheena, Cheena, Chin, Chin." Sometimes they threw stones and yelled at us to go home. I had to change my route going to school. I went through the back alleys, and walking really fast. Most of my Indian friends became my tormentors overnight.

Ming was picked up at five in the morning with the family she boarded with. The Indian government "evacuated" the Chinese residents in Shillong to the local jail and then herded them onto a train to Deoli, Rajasthan. Ming remembers that the Chinese on the train were tense and uneasy. At each station when the train stopped for the soldiers to cook their meals, the Chinese stayed in their compartment and kept the shutters closed. Very often the Indians threw stones at the Chinese, shouting at them to go home. Ming's parents found her halfway through the journey. They were in the last compartment, with the Chinese from Digboi and Makum, and Ming was in the middle, with the Chinese from Shillong.

> We only stopped once a day to get our meal. Fortunately for us, in our car, the two soldiers guarding us were very nice. At each station, they bought samosas, and fed the little kids. I always got one samosa, and sometimes I got two.
>
> We reached Deoli in the late afternoon, about a week after the Indian Army put us on the train. The army guys herded us onto lorries and buses, and dropped us at the gate of the camp. I waited for my parents. It [*sic*] was so much confusion, and fear.
>
> When our parents finally got off [the] lorry, the army people processed us. I went with my mother to the women's side. A woman guard led us to the tent, and told us to remove all our clothes. Everyone was strip-searched, even the kids. They confiscated my mother's money and jewellery, but they supposedly made a record of what we owned.
>
> I walked into the concentration camp with only the clothes I had brought with me.
>
> My family shared the barracks with four or five other families. I think we were all rather big families. There were six of us – my parents, my three brothers and me. My parents set up our space in one corner of the barracks, other families at the other corners, and more families along the middle of the barracks. Each family had a cot for each person. You know the cots where you have jute ropes woven loosely together on bamboo frames? Yep, those were the beds we slept on. We piled blankets on the cots to sleep on, for the jute ropes were rather rough and they scratched the skin. We had no privacy. We could see everyone. So each family kept to itself.

There were quarrels, someone took more space than they should, or someone stepped on someone's belongings. We all sort[ed] it out amongst ourselves.

There were a lot of military guys walking up and down, guarding the compound and the barracks. Seven-foot-high barbed-wire fences surrounded our wing. A gate connected our wing to the next wing. Soldiers guarded the gate. A roll of barbed wire sprawled on top of the fence, to discourage anyone thinking of climbing over it. Just like a prison camp. It was a prison camp.

We didn't get food on the first day. The next day, the army sent in people to cook for us, three times a day. The cooks threw potatoes and other vegetables into a pot and added curry spices, and we got something like a bhaji. They didn't even wash the vegetables or the potatoes.

Three times a day, we lined up with our pots and pans, like you see in the war movies or movies about prisons or like the World Vision documentaries of disaster areas – all the people with pots and pans, lining up to get food.

We sat around, nothing to do, and lots to complain about. The grown-ups complained about the food, they complained about the camp, and they complained more about the food.

The grown-ups in each wing had a meeting. They discussed the food, mainly. Then the Chinese selected a representative in each wing to talk to the camp commander. My dad represented Wing E. The Chinese selected men who spoke English. The representatives asked the commander to let the inmates do their own cooking. "Just bring us the raw food," they said, "and let us cook for ourselves." The commander agreed.

So every morning the representative from each wing went to the canteen outside the camp to pick up the day's food supply. They couldn't leave the camp without a guard escort. So every morning, my dad went to the gate. The guard would open the gate, and a soldier would go with my dad to the canteen.

Each wing set up a schedule, a schedule where everyone in the wing took turns to cook.

The grown-ups gathered bricks left over from the construction of the barracks, stacked the bricks and mortared them with wet mud and built a stove in the compound, a huge wood-burning stove.

The girls, kids like me, helped out in the morning making parathas. The teenaged boys took turns stirring the food. We had to cook in a huge big wok, and it needed muscle power.

We ran into a major problem – knives. When we first entered the internment camp, the army people looked through everything we brought, and they confiscated anything that looked like a knife or scissors; they took away our butter knives, our pen knives and anything that looked sharp. They even strip-searched us in case we hide [*sic*] knives under our clothes. So there we were, with a big piece of mutton, a bag of potatoes and baskets of vegetables, and we didn't have anything to cut them up with. One of the inmates taught the men to take down the metal shelves in the barracks, and sharpen the pieces. He used to work with metals in Darjeeling. So for first couple of days, everyone – well, almost everyone – was happy.

There were, again, a lot of complaints – complaints that some people got more than their share, complaints that they got less than their share, complaints that some lazy Chinese were not taking their turns in cooking, complaints that food tasted too bland and complaints that the food tasted too spicy. The complaints got so bad that the grown-ups decided to split up the raw food and let each family do its own cooking.

The inmates needed one home-made knife for every family. The men surrounded the person who was sharpening the metal by the cooking fire, and some men loitered near the gate, as lookouts. They talked loudly and generally made a lot of noise to cover the scraping noise of metal on stones. When a guard wandered by, the lookouts would sing songs, usually in awful voices, to alert the bracket-sharpening crew. But, you know what? The guards knew what we were doing and they didn't do anything. So we made knives openly after that.

The grown-ups also found another job for the teenage boys: cutting up the firewood. The camp commander gave us huge chunks of firewood, which needed breaking up. The boys edged a sharpened metal into a crack in the wood, lifted the wood up, and threw it down, with the metal end hitting the ground, driving it into the wood and splitting it.

Shortly after we reached Deoli, the Chinese government sent a lot of stuff to Deoli, essential stuff for each family to use. They (the Chinese government) heard that we, all the families, barely took anything when we were evacuated. Supposedly each family had lots of different things. When the stuff came, the camp commander asked all representatives from each wing to help him to distribute the stuff. We were very excited, excited because someone in China cared, and excited because we were quite short of things. The commander and the guards picked over the things, and gave a small package to each family: tooth brush, tooth paste and face towels. My dad was one of the representatives of the wing. He was really disappointed.

The Chinese government also sent blank application forms to Deoli, applications for inmates to go to China. The camp commander passed around the forms. When the Chinese applied, the Indian government took them by train to the boats sent by the Chinese government especially to pick them up. I think there were three boats in total.

The military people started to build more barracks outside the compound. The soldiers said that it was to house the Chinese to be evacuated from Calcutta. But they just stopped. One day the soldiers worked day and night, hammering and sawing, keeping us awake, and then they just stopped, with the buildings half finished. At that time we didn't know why. Later we found out that the Chinese soldiers had retreated.

Life in the camp became more or less routine. The grown-ups set up classes, and asked the older kids to teach the younger ones. We had classes in English, Math and Hindi. My dad wrote to my aunt in Calcutta and asked her to send books. My second brother was one of the "teachers." My mother was a teacher in Calcutta. She sent for Chinese textbooks and we had Chinese lessons.

Although the winter was warm in the camp – you only needed a cardigan – the air around was dry, very dry; our heels cracked and bled and so we went to the clinic for Vaseline. The nurse smeared Vaseline onto a piece of paper. We took it back to the barracks and applied it to the sore or bleeding spots.

Everyone in the camp was given a stipend. I think it was Rs 3 a month. We bought things from the store inside the camp, things like material to make clothes, and also knives for preparing our food. I guess the guards trusted us by then.

My family bought live chickens from the camp store, and we had this egg-laying hen; without fail, she lay [*sic*] an egg with a double yoke, every week! My dad loved this hen. So we have [*sic*] eggs once a week, double yoke.

After two years in the camp, the commander started to release some of the families. I watched as my friends left with their parents. But my family's name stayed off the "release list." I watched the camp gradually empty.

For four years, I played in the camp, and, occasionally, I asked my parents when we could go home. They didn't know. The International Red Cross came to the camp. They brought things for the inmates. I tasted canned chicken soup for the first time. I asked one of them when we would be released. They didn't know. The Indian Prime Minister, Shastri, visited the camp. I remember other children and I posed with him for pictures. I asked Shastri when we can go home, he said he will talk to his cabinet when he got back to Delhi. They all left, I and my parents and brothers and other Chinese remained.

By the 4th year of internment, there wasn't [*sic*] that many Chinese left in the camp – a few families from the hill stations, and some Chinese from Tangra, Calcutta.

We were released in July or August of 1966, almost the last batch to leave Deoli. My dad wanted to take his favourite hen, the hen that lay the double yoke eggs with us, but the soldiers said, "No, no chicken, no pets." My dad refused to use the hen for our last evening meal. So he gave the hen to one of the Chinese who didn't have their names on the "release list." I think they were the Hakka from Tangra.

The military people dropped us outside our old address in Digboi. We didn't know where to go, as the restaurant and the house were taken over by someone else. Luckily the landlord saw us and he was able to give us a place to stay in his housing complex. The landlord took us to the *godown* [warehouse] where our stuff was kept. My dad found that most of the stuff had been picked over. All the good stuff was gone. The soldiers, when they came in 1962 and arrested my parents, confiscated all the money and we never got it back.

We stayed around Digboi for two or three months, then we left for Calcutta. My father didn't want to start a business and then lose it all over again. So we left for Calcutta, two or three months after we returned to Digboi.

Ming's father died a year after his release from Deoli. Ming, in spite of losing four school years in Deoli, managed to catch up and graduated with a Senior Cambridge certificate. She emigrated to Toronto in 1974.

My Narrative

Before the 1962 Sino-Indian Incident, I was very sure of my "Chinese-ness," a Chinese-ness that firmly connected me to Moi-Yan. This connection was made up of memories, customs and religious beliefs of Moi-Yan brought to India by my parents and my relatives. Like all the second- and third-generation Chinese in India, I knew that my Chinese-ness differed from the Chinese-ness of our parents. I had Indian friends, I liked speaking Hindi and I liked playing with my Indian friends.

When the Incident hit Calcutta Chinatown, everything changed. I had to constantly scan around for hostile faces when I went out and I had to walk fast when I heard the chant, "Cheena, Cheena, chin, chin." The teachers in my Chinese language school advised the students to travel in groups. The Chinese in Calcutta lived in fear of the midnight knock on the door, the usual time for the soldiers to come and "evacuate" families to Deoli. Here's an excerpt from my story, "The Rally at the Ochterlony Monument."

The story started on a hot and wet monsoon afternoon, when the teachers and students of Calcutta's three Chinese language schools showed up at a rally in support of India against China. After three hours of standing knee-deep in muddy water, we all went home.

> Mother was having her afternoon nap when I got home. She woke and wrinkled her nose. "Go and bathe first. Did you swim home?"
>
> Mother had tea and pastries ready when I had finished my bath. She pushed the food at me, "Here, eat, eat. You will feel better with some food in your stomach. How was Mr Wang's speech?"
>
> I bit into the steamed pork dumpling. "He talked for half an hour, standing on the dry platform. We stood in the rain for two hours, listening to the speeches."
>
> Mother shook her head, "You don't need to go for rallies. I signed the petitions. I signed three petitions."
>
> "What did the petitions say?" I asked.
>
> Mother shrugged, "I don't know. Mr Lee said we are supporting the Dalai Lama, or one of the lamas."
>
> "Mother! You can't sign the same petition three times."
>
> "No. I did not sign the same petition three times. Mr Lee, Mr Liu and Mr Chen wrote my name, I just put a cross beside my name." Mother did not read or write.
>
> "Besides," Mother wagged her fingers at me, "if the Indian police see my name more than once, they will know that we are not communists and we support Dalai Lama, and the police will not take us and lock us away in some horrible place."
>
> Later that evening, Fu practised martial arts with the Lai and Lim brothers on our third-floor terrace. Fu rushed at Chen and screamed "Yaaaaa!" Chen raised his left forearm over his head, punched with his right fist and screamed "Haaaa!" Jade and I watched. We told the boys that their yelling needed to be louder.
>
> The Chinese boys in my apartment also carried knives when they went out. Mother took Fu's knife away from him. Fu objected. Mother told him, "You run if the Indians come after you. You should practise running, not fighting."

That night, mother opened our packs. She examined the clothing inside. When the Indian police had started to intern the Chinese three months ago, mother made a pack for each of us. In my pack, I had two changes of clothing, three sweaters, a small blanket, a metal mug, plate and spoon, a small package of rice, two pairs of socks and one pair of shoes. We slept with our packs beside us, money pouches sewn into our pyjamas, and our shoes and socks by the bed. The police usually came in the middle of the night and did not allow the family to pack. Every Chinese in Calcutta had a pack.

"Now, remember. If we are separated, you find someone you know in the group. If you do not know the people in your group, always stick close to a woman. Always hang on to your packs. Scream and cry if someone tries to take your packs from you." Mother repacked the packs and we settled down to sleep.

Fu and I went through this ritual with mother once every three days.

Mother switched on the night light. The picture of the Dalai Lama sat behind the light. Like many of the Chinese, mother believed that the supporters of the Dalai Lama would not be put into concentration camps. She bought prayer beads with tiny pictures of the Dalai Lama on each bead. When Mother had to go out, she wore the beads around her right wrist like a charm bracelet.

The two excerpts show the different challenges faced by the Chinese residents in India in the aftermath of the Sino-Indian Incident. According to Ming and the three internees I spoke to, they were more or less left alone inside the wire fence in Deoli Detention Camp. The camp commander usually agreed to requests made by the representatives of the inmates, such as the cooking of food by the Chinese themselves. The inmates had elected leaders. They devised tools to improve the life in the camp, such as the sharpening of metals to cut up the food. They grew vegetables and kept chickens and they formed friendships that rivalled the bonds with their siblings. But the inmates felt adrift, their lives on hold. They mourned the friends and relatives who were deported or voluntarily went to China. They wondered about their future. Would the Indian government, on a whim, send them to China? Or would the Indian government ignore them and leave them in limbo, in a circle of barbed wire? When the Chinese were released from Deoli, they returned to homes occupied by strangers, their properties looted and their businesses auctioned off. The Chinese borrowed from relatives and friends and started again. Most students who were "evacuated" from the boarding schools and interned in Deoli never went back to school. These young Chinese went to work, either in other restaurants or shops, or helped the family to start their businesses afresh.

The mainstream Indians, whipped up by the nationalistic rhetoric of the Indian government, ostracized the Chinese residents. In Calcutta, the Chinese shops and properties were looted or vandalized and the residents were threatened or beaten. The anti-Chinese laws stripped the Indian-born Chinese of their citizenship, banned Chinese from government jobs, mandated Chinese residents from travelling outside their city or town of residence and required Chinese residents to report to the Indian authorities for residency permits. The Chinese needed to apply for a permit if they wished to travel outside their permitted residency area. Often the Indian authorities refused to issue these permits. All the Chinese in Calcutta waited for and dreaded the midnight or early morning knock on the door, when they would be arrested by Indian soldiers and interned in Deoli Detention Camp. Like the Chinese interned in Deoli, the "quit India" deportation order hung over the Chinese in Calcutta.

The Chinese in India emigrated and created a life overseas, leaving the shadow of the 1962 Sino-Indian Incident behind. Or so I thought.

In a cafe in Scarborough, a suburb of Toronto, I sat and chatted with three Chinese-Indians. They were interned in Deoli Detention Camp during the Incident and they had emigrated to Canada after their release from Deoli. We sat, sipping our coffee and chatting.

The three Chinese-Indian Canadians told me about Deoli. They told me how the Chinese huddled around the fire and sharpened pieces of metal. They told me how the teenagers sneaked out of the barracks after curfew to visit their friends and they told me how they used to make fun of the soldiers who guarded them.

Suddenly, their laughter died. One of them whispered, "Do you think they are listening?" His eyes darted towards a table beside ours.

At the next table, two South Asian men in navy blue uniforms sat with their coffee and bagels; their uniforms looked vaguely like a policeman's. White round badges on their shoulders read "Security."

We stared at the security guards. They looked back, startled. One of them paused with the bagel half way to his mouth.

We looked away. They must have been on their lunch break from the office building near the cafe.

The shadow of the 1962 Sino-Indian Incident had followed us from India to a cafe in Scarborough, Canada, and will probably stay with us forever, a part of our life that we cannot forget.

Notes

1 K. Y. Li, *Deoli Camp: An Oral History of Chinese Indians from 1962 to 1966* (MA thesis, University of Toronto, 2011). https://tspace.library.utoronto.ca/bitstream/1807/29477/3/Li_Kwai_Y_20116_MA_thesis.pdf. 12 November 2014.

2 K. Y. Li, *The Palm Leaf Fan* (Toronto: TSAR Publications, 2006).

3 "The Sino-Indian Boundary Question: Statement of the Government of the People's Republic of China," Marxists Internet Archive (2005). https://www.marxists.org/subject/india/sino-india-boundary-question/ch01.htm. 12 November 2014.

LIST OF CONTRIBUTORS

Sunil Amrith is a reader in modern Asian history at Birkbeck College, University of London. Amrith is the author of *Crossing the Bay of Bengal: The Furies of Nature and the Fortunes of Migrants* (Cambridge, MA: Harvard University Press, 2013), and *Migration and Diaspora in Modern Asia* (Cambridge: Cambridge University Press, 2011).

Jayati Bhattacharya is a lecturer in the South Asian studies programme at the National University of Singapore. Bhattacharya's research interests lie in business history, Indian trade diaspora, connected histories, South–Southeast Asian relations and comparative diasporas. Her current research focuses on India–Singapore relations and connectivities in the Bay of Bengal region. Her recent publications include *Beyond the Myth: Indian Business Communities in Singapore* (Singapore: ISEAS, 2011) and a co-edited volume with Oliver Pye, *The Palm Oil Controversy in Southeast Asia: A Transnational Perspective* (Singapore: ISEAS, 2012).

Jayani Bonnerjee is a cultural geographer, interested in postcolonial urbanism in South Asia and critical geographies of diaspora. She completed her PhD (geography) from Queen Mary, University of London, focusing on issues of identity and belonging for Calcutta's Chinese and Anglo-Indian communities. She is currently postdoctoral fellow in urban studies at the Centre de Sciences Humaines (CSH), New Delhi.

Sugata Bose is Gardiner professor of history at Harvard University. Bose's books include *His Majesty's Opponent: Subhas Chandra Bose and India's Struggle against Empire* (Cambridge, MA: Belknap Press of Harvard University Press; New Delhi: Allen Lane, 2011) and *A Hundred Horizons: The Indian Ocean in the Age of Global Empire* (Cambridge, MA: Harvard University Press, 2006). Bose has served as director of graduate studies in history at Harvard and as the founding director of Harvard's South Asia Institute. He is chair of the Presidency Mentor Group advising on the rejuvenation of Presidency University, Calcutta, and member of the Nalanda Governing Board. He is a Lok Sabha member (member of parliament) representing Jadavpur, Bengal.

Stephanie Chung Po-yin is a professor in the Department of History, Hong Kong Baptist University. Professor Chung received her PhD from Oxford University and taught at the Hong Kong Academy of Performing Arts. Her research focuses on social and economic history, business history, history of business laws and customs, and migration and enterprises in South China, Southeast Asia and the Middle East.

Renaud Egreteau is a former research assistant professor at the Hong Kong Institute for the Humanities and Social Sciences (incorporating the Centre of Asian Studies), University of Hong Kong (2009–13). Dr Egreteau is the author of *Wooing the Generals: India's New Burma Policy* (New Delhi: Authorspress, 2003) and co-author with Larry Jagan of *Soldiers and Diplomacy in Burma: Understanding the Foreign Policies of the Burmese Praetorian State* (Singapore: NUS Press, 2013).

Edmund Terence Gomez is a professor of political economy at the Faculty of Economics and Administration, University of Malaya. Professor Gomez has also held appointments at the University of Leeds (UK) and Murdoch University (Australia) and served as visiting professor at Kobe University, Japan, and at the School of Political Science, University of Michigan, Ann Arbor. The author of numerous publications on topics such as Malaysia's political economy and Chinese business in Malaysia, one of his most recent works is *Affirmative Action, Ethnicity and Conflict* (London: Routledge, 2013).

Hamashita Takeshi is a professor and dean of Sun Yat-sen University (Guangzhou). Takeshi Hamashita has worked on overseas Chinese history, Ryukyu history, Chinese economic history and regional history of East Asia at Tokyo University, Kyoto University and Ryukoku University. He has been a visiting scholar at Cornell University, Hong Kong University, National University of Singapore, Chengchi University (Taiwan) and several others. He is the author of numerous publications, one of the most recent being *China, East Asia and Global Economy* (London: Routledge, 2011).

Jia Haitao is professor of political science and international relations, serving currently as director of the Institute for Chindian Studies at Jinan University, Guangzhou, China. Jia's PhD thesis was on Confucianist political thought and ancient Chinese political systems. He has been to India as visiting residence scholar and visiting professor, doing research and teaching classes on China. Professor Jia is the author of many articles, essays and books in Chinese. He is the co-author of the monograph *A Comparative Study between the Indian Diaspora and the Chinese Diaspora in Terms of Their International Influences* (Jinan: Shangdong People's Publishing House, 2007).

Laavanya Kathiravelu is assistant professor in the Division of Sociology at Nanyang Technological University (NTU), Singapore. Kathiravelu's research interests lie at the intersections of urban studies and migration, with a focus on global cities and south–south mobilities. Her forthcoming monograph *Migrant Dubai: Building a Global City* will be published by Palgrave Macmillian.

Coonoor Kripalani is a honorary institute fellow at the Hong Kong Institute for the Humanities and Social Sciences (incorporating the Centre of Asian Studies), University of Hong Kong, and board member of the Asian Civilizations Museum, Singapore. Kripalani is the author of numerous scholarly articles on popular Hindi film and a succinct biography, *Mahatma Gandhi: Apostle of Non-violence* (New Delhi: Rupa, 2003). At present she is writing on radio broadcasting (AIR) in India. Kripalani also creates bilingual (Hindi/English) books for children aged 2 to 6. Her latest book, on yoga for children, is published by Scholastic India (2013).

Gauri Krishnan is director of the Indian Heritage Centre, as well as an art historian, museum specialist and exponent of Bharata Natyam. Dr Krishnan is the founding curator of the South Asian collection from its inception in 1993 and developed the South Asian galleries at the Asian Civilisations Museum (ACM), Singapore. She has authored and edited many books on Indian architecture, sculpture, textile, dance and modern art. Her most recent book is *The Power of the Female: Devangana Sculptures on Indian Temple Architecture* (New Delhi: DK Printworld, 2014).

Kwai Yun Li is a writer, accountant and researcher who graduated from the University of Toronto in 2011. Her MA thesis is on the ethnic Chinese living in India who were interned in the aftermath of the 1962 Sino-Indian War. Li is now working on the oral history of Chinese Indian Canadians.

Leo Suryadinata is a visiting senior fellow at the Institute of Southeast Asian Studies, Singapore, and professor (adj.) at the S. Rajaratnam School of International Studies, Nanyang Technological University, Singapore. Dr Suryadinata is the author of over fifty books and monographs and numerous articles on China's relations with ASEAN and the Chinese in Southeast Asia.

Tan Chee Beng is a former professor at the Department of Anthropology, Chinese University of Hong Kong. Professor Tan's research and publications have concentrated on the original ethnic communities of Malaysia, as well as overseas Chinese, in matters relating to religion, cuisine and identity, particularly the Peranakan culture, in Southeast Asia. His publications include *Chinese Overseas: Comparative Cultural Issues* (Hong Kong: Hong Kong University Press, 2004) and *Chinese Food and Foodways in Southeast Asia and Beyond,* edited by Tan Chee-Beng (Singapore: NUS Press, 2011).

Madhavi Thampi is an honorary fellow of the Institute of Chinese Studies, New Delhi, and editor of its journal *China Report.* Dr Thampi recently retired from Delhi University, where she taught Chinese history. Her publications include *Indians in China, 1800–1949* (New Delhi: Manohar, 2005), and *China and the Making of Bombay,* co-authored with Shalini Saksena (Mumbai: K. R. Cama Oriental Institute, 2009). She is also the editor of the volume *India and China in the Colonial World* (New Delhi: Social Science Press, 2005, 2010).

Zhang Xing is a lecturer at Peking University, China, and visiting research fellow at Humboldt-Universität zu Berlin, Germany. She received her PhD in South Asian studies. Her research focuses on Bengali literature and culture as well as the Chinese community in India. She is the author of *Preserving Cultural Identity through Education: The Schools of the Chinese Community in Calcutta, India* (Singapore: ISEAS, 2010).

INDEX

varsha